Artistic Truth

Aesthetics, Discourse, and Imaginative Disclosure

It is unfashionable to talk about artistic truth. Yet the issues traditionally addressed under that term have not disappeared. Indeed, questions concerning the role of the artist in society, the relationship between art and knowledge, and the validity of cultural interpretation have intensified. Lambert Zuidervaart challenges current intellectual fashions. He proposes a new critical hermeneutics of artistic truth that engages with both analytic and continental philosophies and illuminates the contemporary cultural scene.

People turn to the arts as a way of finding orientation in their lives, communities, and institutions. But philosophers, hamstrung by their own theories of truth, have been unsuccessful in accounting for this common feature in our lives. This book portrays artistic truth as a process of imaginative disclosure in which expectations of authenticity, significance, and integrity prevail. Understood in this way, truth becomes central to the aesthetic and social value of the arts.

Lambert Zuidervaart is Professor of Philosophy at the Institute for Christian Studies, Toronto, and an Associate Member of the Graduate Faculty in the Department of Philosophy at the University of Toronto.

Artistic Truth

Aesthetics, Discourse, and Imaginative Disclosure

LAMBERT ZUIDERVAART

Institute for Christian Studies, Toronto

CAMBRIDGE
UNIVERSITY PRESS

PUBLISHED BY THE PRESS SYNDICATE OF THE UNIVERSITY OF CAMBRIDGE
The Pitt Building, Trumpington Street, Cambridge, United Kingdom

CAMBRIDGE UNIVERSITY PRESS
The Edinburgh Building, Cambridge CB2 2RU, UK
40 West 20th Street, New York, NY 10011-4211, USA
477 Williamstown Road, Port Melbourne, VIC 3207, Australia
Ruiz de Alarcón 13, 28014 Madrid, Spain
Dock House, The Waterfront, Cape Town 8001, South Africa

http://www.cambridge.org

First published 2004

Printed in the United States of America

Typeface ITC New Baskerville 10/12 pt.   *System* LATEX 2$_\varepsilon$ [TB]

A catalog record for this book is available from the British Library.

Library of Congress Cataloging in Publication data

Zuidervaart, Lambert.
  Artistic truth : aesthetics, discourse, and imaginative disclosure /
Lambert Zuidervaart.
    p. cm.
  Includes bibliographical references and index.
  ISBN 0-521-83903-3
    1. Truth (Aesthetics)   I. Title.
BH301.T77Z85   2004
111'.85 – dc22

2004040679

ISBN 0 521 83903 3 hardback

For Cal, Henk, and Nick

Contents

Preface	*page* ix	
List of Abbreviations	xiii	

	Introduction: Critical Hermeneutics	1
	1.1 Locations	2
	1.2 Directions	7
	1.3 Border Crossings	11

PART I. HERMENEUTICAL MATRIX

1	Beardsley's Denial	17
	1.1 Meaning and Metaphor	19
	1.2 Contested Theories	24
	1.3 Literary Predications	29

2	Reciprocations	34
	2.1 Existential Affirmation	35
	2.2 Postmetaphysical Deconstruction	46
	2.3 Toward Reconstruction	51

3	Kant Revisited	55
	3.1 Aesthetic Validity	56
	3.2 Cultural Orientation	65
	3.3 Art Talk	68

PART II. CONSTRUCTIVE CLEARINGS

4	Truth as Disclosure	77
	4.1 Heidegger's Disclosedness	79
	4.2 Assertion and Interpretation	84
	4.3 Correspondence and Disclosure	90

5 Imaginative Disclosure   101
   5.1 Heidegger's Anti-Aesthetics   102
   5.2 Art and Vocation   109
   5.3 Cogency and Truth   113

6 Artistic Truth   118
   6.1 Critical Aesthetic Theory   119
   6.2 Authenticity, Significance, Integrity   127
   6.3 Art Talk and Artistic Truth   134

                  PART III. LINGUISTIC TURNS

7 Logical Positivist Dispute   143
   7.1 Emotivism versus Propositionism   145
   7.2 Propositional Acts   151
   7.3 Meaning and Integrity   157

8 Goodman's Nominalism   162
   8.1 Art as Symbol System   163
   8.2 Truth without Truth Bearers   171
   8.3 Appropriateness and Significance   175

9 Wolterstorff's Realism   182
   9.1 Fictive World Projection   183
   9.2 Propositions without Import   191
   9.3 Actuality and Authenticity   196

10 Aesthetic Transformations   203
    10.1 Traces of Truth   204
    10.2 Footprints in the Sand   213

Notes   219
Bibliography   259
Index   271

Preface

The preliminary sketch of this book arose from two studies that had recently come to completion. The first, published as *Adorno's Aesthetic Theory*, raised questions about Theodor W. Adorno's conception of artistic truth. But it also defended Adorno from criticisms on precisely the same topic. As the Adorno study drew to a close, I participated in a second study, an interdisciplinary research project on mass-mediated culture. Published as the collaboratively written book *Dancing in the Dark*, edited by Roy Anker, that project convinced me of something I already knew from my work on Adorno: philosophical aesthetics, as traditionally understood and practiced, is outdated with respect to hotly contested cultural issues. To address such issues, it needs to be reconceived, in conversation with social theory, with newer fields of inquiry such as communications and cultural studies, and with emerging discourses on public art and cultural policy. So I set myself the ambitious challenge of reconceptualizing philosophical aesthetics in a single volume to be titled "Cultural Politics and Artistic Truth."

While working my way into relevant literature in several different areas, I discovered that two volumes would be required. The first, which you are reading, examines the aesthetic, linguistic, and epistemological underpinnings of contemporary art. It does so in conversation with several twentieth-century philosophers on the topic of truth in art. Although nonphilosophers might find these conversations abstruse, their intent in this book is to help illuminate the current cultural scene. The second volume, which is still being written, will address political, economic, and broadly cultural issues. It will develop a social philosophy designed to accommodate newer forms of public art as well as older artistic practices either denigrated or ignored by modernist aesthetic theories. Reconceptualizing the field as "art-in-public," I shall propose a new understanding of art's societal roles and recommend new approaches to cultural policy. The two volumes remain closely linked, even though they can and will be read separately.

I have had the good fortune to be in hospitable settings for this work. In the 1990s I served as the board president and chief volunteer fund raiser for the Urban Institute for Contemporary Arts (UICA) in Grand Rapids. UICA is the largest multidisciplinary center for contemporary art in the state of Michigan. Daily interactions with dancers, film makers, musicians, visual artists, and writers, together with practical immersion in the challenges facing arts organizations, have thoroughly shaped my philosophical reflections. I am grateful for this opportunity to be a "public intellectual" within a local microcosm of the North American cultural scene. Among the hundreds of volunteers, staff, and board members with whom I worked, let me single out a few for special mention: Marjorie Kuipers, UICA's executive director at the time; Gail Philbin, the program manager; Hank Meijer and Kate Pew Wolters, honorary cochairs of a major capital campaign; Julie Christianson Stivers, the immediate past president of UICA's board and my capital campaign cochair; and Daryl Fischer, the board vice president and my frequent discussion partner. Of the hundreds of West Michigan artists for whom UICA provides a cultural nexus, let me mention several whose work and conversations have animated my thoughts: Jay Constantine, Linda Nemec Foster, Dana Freeman, Darlene Kaczmarczk, James Karsina, Steve Nelson, Deb Rockman, Steve Schousen, Paul Wittenbraker, and Diane Zeeuw. I have also learned much from an informal discussion group for civic leaders organized by City Commissioner George Heartwell, who has since become mayor of Grand Rapids. These cultural workers demonstrate the commitment to dialogue and creative experience that marks contemporary art at its best. To all of them, and to the many others I have not named, I simply say, Thank you.

The academic settings for this project have been equally hospitable. Calvin College, where I taught for seventeen years, stands out among liberal arts colleges for its promotion of faculty scholarship. I am grateful for excellent services provided by the Hekman Library and the Information Technology Center, as well as for generous research funding provided by the college and its Alumni Association. My writing also received significant grants from the German Academic Exchange Service (DAAD) and the National Endowment for the Humanities (NEH), an independent federal agency in the United States. Without such support I could not have completed this book. My former colleagues at Calvin College, both in the Department of Philosophy and in an interdisciplinary reading group on continental philosophy, proved to be stimulating discussion partners. Again, I cannot mention everyone, but let me name a few. In philosophy, Ruth Groenhout, Lee Hardy, John Hare, and David Hoekema provided constant encouragement for the project as a whole and insightful comments on specific chapters. I received the same from colleagues in other disciplines: Simona Goi, Clarence Joldersma, Will Katerberg, and Henry Luttikhuizen, with whom I have published two books whose topics intersect this project. I also want to thank

Donna Kruithof for her secretarial help, and Victoria Zapata for the research assistance she provided one summer as a McGregor Fellow.

I left Calvin College in 2002 to take up a position at the Institute for Christian Studies (ICS), a graduate school for interdisciplinary philosophy in Toronto. My colleagues at ICS have welcomed me into their intellectual community and cheered on the completion of this book. I especially want to thank Adrienne Dengerink Chaplin, James Olthuis, and Bob Sweetman for their attentiveness to my ideas and their remarks on parts of the manuscript. I am also grateful for the research assistance Matt Klaassen has provided.

Because the book has been so long in the making, with many excerpts presented as conference papers, it is impossible to list all the scholars whose comments have prompted new insight or whose collegiality has sustained my work. But let me mention many: Jay Bernstein, James Bohman, Deborah Cook, Maeve Cooke, Michael Nyhof-DeMoor, Alessandro Ferrara, Stefan Forrester, Victor Haines, Tom Huhn, Martin Jay, Bert Kögler, Ron Kuipers, Stephen Lake, Thomas McCarthy, L. Ryan Musgrave, Ira Newman, Heinz Paetzold, David Rasmussen, Karla Schultz, Yvonne Sherratt, Robert Stecker, James Swindall, Marcus Verhaegh, Merold Westphal, and Eddie Zemach. The early stages of writing benefited from a highly productive research visit to the Freie Universität Berlin in 1994. There I presented the first draft of Chapter 4 in an evening lecture series organized by Christoph Menke and Ruth Sonderegger. I appreciate their interest and that of Axel Honneth and Albrecht Wellmer, the cosponsors for my visit. A more recent research visit, this time to Frankfurt in 2001, and equally productive, was cosponsored by Axel Honneth and Rolf Tiedemann. I am also indebted to James Schmidt at Boston University, whose NEH Summer Seminar on *Dialectic of Enlightenment* came at a crucial time when my intellectual energies were flagging.

As a result of such widespread encouragement, earlier versions of several chapters and sections appear as journal articles and essays. Details for the journal articles, in *Philosophy & Social Criticism*, can be found in the bibliography. Parts of the Introduction and Chapters 3 and 6 come from the essay "Artistic Truth, Linguistically Turned: Variations on a Theme from Adorno, Habermas, and Hart," in *Philosophy as Responsibility*, edited by Ronald A. Kuipers and Janet Catherina Wesselius (Lanham, Md.: University Press of America, 2002), pp. 129–49. An earlier version of Chapter 4 appears as "If I Had a Hammer: Truth in Heidegger's *Being and Time*," in *A Hermeneutics of Charity*, edited by James K. A. Smith and Henry Venema (Grand Rapids, Mich.: Brazos Press [a division of Baker Book House], 2004). I am grateful to the editors and publishers for permission to include these materials here. I am also appreciative of the astute criticisms given by two anonymous readers for Cambridge University Press. They prompted significant revisions that, I trust, have made this a better book.

One of the most important members of UICA during my tenure there, both as a volunteer and as an artist, was Joyce A. Recker. She is also my companion for life. I thank Joyce for providing both lively inspiration and untiring support. As I write this I cast a reassuring glance at the beautiful golden lab who joined our household shortly before this project began – reassuring as much to me as to her. It is not common, I suppose, for philosophers to thank their canine companions, but Rosa Luxemburg Parks has been a source of sanity and delight for more than thirteen years. And the very human friendship of Ron Otten, who lived with us in 1991 and who has been our household's mutual soul mate for even longer, is a gift that exceeds description.

The first sketch for "Cultural Politics and Artistic Truth" emerged in 1991 from graduate seminars I led at ICS as a sabbatical replacement for Calvin Seerveld. Little did I know then that the project would mushroom into two volumes. Nor did I know that, a few months before completing the final draft of the first volume, I would become Hendrik Hart's successor in systematic philosophy at ICS. With their broad European training, both Cal and Henk have taught me over the years to think outside rigid disciplinary boxes without giving up the rigor of philosophy at its best. So has my former colleague at Calvin College, Nicholas Wolterstorff, a leading analytic philosopher in the intellectual tradition to which the four of us belong. Cal, Henk, and Nick are generous and gifted mentors. Over the many years required for this book to take flight, they were the eagles whose wings carry their young. All three are emeritus professors now. I can think of no more fitting tribute to their presence in my life and work, and in that of my contemporaries, than to dedicate this volume to them.

Abbreviations

AT Theodor W. Adorno, *Aesthetic Theory*, trans., ed., and introd. Robert Hullot-Kentor (Minneapolis: University of Minnesota Press, 1997).

ÄT Theodor W. Adorno, *Ästhetische Theorie* (1970), *Gesammelte Schriften* 7, ed. Gretel Adorno and Rolf Tiedemann, 2d ed. (Frankfurt am Main: Suhrkamp, 1972).

CJ Immanuel Kant, *Critique of the Power of Judgment*, ed. Paul Guyer, trans. Paul Guyer and Eric Matthews (Cambridge: Cambridge University Press, 2000).

OW Martin Heidegger, "The Origin of the Work of Art" (1935–36), in *Off the Beaten Track*, ed. and trans. Julian Young and Kenneth Haynes (Cambridge: Cambridge University Press, 2002), pp. 1–56.

SZ Martin Heidegger, *Sein und Zeit* (1927), 15th ed. (Tübingen: Max Niemeyer, 1979).

TM Hans-Georg Gadamer, *Truth and Method*, trans. Joel Weinsheimer and Donald G. Marshall, 2d rev. ed. (New York: Crossroad, 1989).

WM Hans-Georg Gadamer, *Wahrheit und Methode: Grundzüge einer philosophischen Hermeneutik* (1960), 4th ed. (Tübingen: J. C. B. Mohr [Paul Siebeck], 1975).

UK Martin Heidegger, "Der Ursprung des Kunstwerkes," in *Holzwege* (Frankfurt am Main: Vittorio Klostermann, 1950), pp. 7–68.

Artistic Truth

Aesthetics, Discourse, and Imaginative Disclosure

Introduction

Critical Hermeneutics

The question, famed of old, by which logicians were supposed to be driven
into a corner, ... is the question: What is truth?
Immanuel Kant[1]

The idea of artistic truth has fallen on hard times. It has received few
sustained visits in Anglo-American philosophy since midcentury analyses
by John Hospers (1946) and Monroe Beardsley (1958). Even continental
philosophers after Martin Heidegger and Theodor W. Adorno have come
to doubt its viability. The topic is complex and contentious, and the most
important contributions come from thinkers whose work resists paraphrase.
One must think twice before entering labyrinthine ruins where contemporary philosophers fear to tread.

Yet the issues traditionally addressed under the label of "artistic truth"
have not disappeared. If anything, they have intensified: the role of artists
in society, relations between art and knowledge, and questions about validity
in cultural interpretations. What has changed is the paradigm with which
philosophers work. Whereas philosophers used to sort out such issues in
terms of a mediation between epistemic subject and epistemic object and
whatever transcends this mediation, now they emphasize interpretation,
discourse, and historicity. To revisit the idea of artistic truth is to test the
potential and limitations of a postmetaphysical paradigm in contemporary
philosophy.[2]

The shift in philosophical paradigm finds a counterpart in the movement
from modern to postmodern arts. As I have indicated elsewhere, this artistic movement involves three changes in emphasis: from the autonomy of
art to the social constructedness of the arts; from the primacy of form to
the primacy of context; and from an orientation toward the future to an
embrace of contemporary contingency.[3] These developments dramatically
reconfigure the field onto which the idea of artistic truth must map. They
also intensify the issues that artistic truth theories traditionally addressed.

1

Unless one rejects such developments in the arts, or finds little of worth in them, one's theory of artistic truth must take them into account.[4]

These two cultural conditions, the one philosophical and the other artistic, provide the broad context in which "artistic truth" is to be reconsidered. After some remarks on the history and significance of the topic, let me indicate the sources for my own account of artistic truth, sketch the argument of this book, and comment on its scope and methods.

1.1 LOCATIONS

The Western philosophical debate about truth in art goes back to Plato and Aristotle. Whereas Plato's *Republic*, on a nonironical reading, denies the representational arts of his day any capacity to carry truth, Aristotle's *Poetics* suggests that Greek tragedy (and, by extension, other "imitative arts") can provide true insight into the sorts of events and characters that could occur under certain conditions. The difference between Plato and his most famous student turns on their contrasting accounts of the nature and location of universals, and on corresponding differences in their theories of knowledge and representation.

The Plato-Aristotle debate in its many versions lasted until the nineteenth century, when new theories of art as expression transformed the ways in which truth is attributed to art. Now the most forceful advocates of "artistic truth" would link it with creativity, imagination, and the expression of that which exceeds the grasp of ordinary or scientific understanding. One glimpses this new tendency in Immanuel Kant's account of artistic "genius" as an imaginative capacity for expressing "aesthetic ideas." Yet Kant would have rejected romantic claims that art's imaginative character makes it a "higher" source of truth than are science and bourgeois morality – a higher source alongside philosophy and religion, in G. W. F. Hegel's account of "absolute spirit."

The debate shifts once more with the so-called linguistic turn in twentieth-century philosophy.[5] Although many traces remain of both pre-Kantian accounts of representation and post-Kantian emphases on expression, a philosophy whose head is linguistically turned cannot easily posit direct connections either between (representational) art and reality or between (expressive) art and the inner self. Increasingly, the questions whether art can carry truth, and whether this capacity or its lack is crucial to art, get posed in one of two ways: (1) Can arts-related language (commentary, criticism, historiography, and the like) be true or false? (2) Are the arts themselves languages, such that, depending on one's theory of language, the arts lack or possess truth capacities in the way that languages do?[6] Because of the turn toward language, the traditional idea of truth's being "in" art, whether representationally or expressively, seems increasingly outdated or difficult to sustain.

Two responses to the linguistic turn characterize much of twentieth-century aesthetics. Continental philosophers such as Theodor W. Adorno claim that the ability to challenge ordinary language gives art a unique capacity to carry truth. Analytic philosophers such as Monroe Beardsley, by contrast, employ conceptions of language that render art an unlikely vehicle of truth. As a result, the topic of artistic truth hovers between aesthetic conceptions of artistic truth that oppose traditional theories of knowledge, on the one hand, and epistemological conceptions of propositional truth that underestimate art's cognitive capacities, on the other. Yet contemporary philosophy contains resources for a more robust conception of artistic truth, as this book will show.

If the debate over truth in art, in its shifting guises, were merely a philosopher's concern, others might find it interesting but unimportant. This is particularly so of the way the debate has proceeded since philosophy became institutionalized as an academic profession and began to doubt its own social relevance. Yet I believe the topic has societal importance at a time when mass media, entertainment industries, and new computer technologies have become driving forces in an increasingly globalized consumer capitalist economy. A deep ambivalence pervades contemporary Western societies concerning the role of visual imagery, literature, and public performances in human life. Many people regard these as "mere entertainment" providing diversion for consumers and profits for producers and investors. Others, however, worry about the pedagogical, political, or moral impact of the arts, holding these at times to unyielding standards that the critics do not meet in their own lives. Neither side seems to grasp what enables the arts to provide either the "entertainment" or the "instruction" that people find satisfying or troubling, as the case may be. Nevertheless, everyone turns to visual imagery, literature, and performing arts to gain orientation and to confirm or disconfirm orientations already found. Gaining orientation is essential to the acquaintance, recognition, understanding, and know-how that belong to "knowledge" in a broad sense. To that extent, it is not esoteric to regard the arts as ways of acquiring and testing knowledge or to consider specific works or events or experiences of art to be more or less truthful. The challenge for philosophers is to give an account of artistic truth that illuminates the contemporary cultural scene. Such an account should provide theoretical insight of use to those who develop public policies, educational strategies, and personal or group decisions in connection with the arts.

Let me illustrate the search for orientation in music, a field many philosophers have found highly resistant to a theory of artistic truth. Writing in the *New York Times* about the fifteenth annual Mahler Festival in Boulder, Colorado, Stephen Kinzer explains the attraction of Gustav Mahler's music:

Mahler's music is deeply complex and almost unbearably emotional. Its great themes are despair in the face of tragedy, followed by redemption and determination to live on. That message perplexed his contemporaries. . . . Many of them were far removed from the depths of human torment and lived in societies where death was often idealized as something ethereal and even beautiful.

Today, after the 20th century's world wars and mass slaughters, Mahler's music touches many more souls than it did when it was written. Its difficulty also attracts ambitious musicians, and 90 or more arrive here at their own expense each year to play it.[7]

So both the "complexity" of Mahler's music and its "great themes" of despair and redemption help explain its attraction today.

Kinzer's article documents this assessment in detail, quoting both musicians and audience members, both seasoned professionals and eager students. For example, Richard Oldberg, a professional horn player and the festival's music director, says Mahler "deals with the most profound questions of life." Calling Mahler's compositions "music for our time," Oldberg observes that "the events of Sept. 11 make him more contemporary than ever. Mahler is the great prophet of the idea that life involves great pain and suffering, but also that after it all, there is resurrection and triumphant affirmation." In a more personal vein, twenty-one-year-old student Ana Mahanovic says that Mahler's music has had "an enormous influence on my life. It has such a connection to the great questions of who we are, why we're here and where we're going. It's given me a real emotional focus, and also a focus to my studies. I want to devote myself to this music."[8]

There was a time, and perhaps there still is, when professional philosophers disdained talk like this of "great themes" and "great questions" in music, of how, by "dealing with" these themes or "having such a connection" to these questions, certain music can foster social and personal orientations. These philosophers would declare such talk "merely metaphorical," as if the claims made could not be meant "literally" or be regarded as true. The time has come, it seems to me, for philosophy not to be so dismissive. If philosophers have learned anything from the linguistic turn, it should be to pay close attention to ordinary language in daily usage. As Kinzel's newspaper account illustrates, people do regularly claim that music helps them find orientation or reorientation, that this comes by way of what music says, and that in some related sense such music is true. A contemporary account of artistic truth should shed light on such language usage and on the experiences to which it belongs.

Unfortunately, standard general theories of truth often prove deficient in this regard. I do not have the space to review them here.[9] The easiest way to indicate their inadequacy is to observe that they restrict their attention to linguistic and conceptual bearers of truth. Richard Kirkham lists the following as candidates for the sorts of things that Anglo-American philosophers have considered capable of being true or false: "beliefs, propositions, judgments, assertions, statements, theories, remarks, ideas, acts of thought, utterances, sentence tokens, sentence types, sentences (unspecified), and speech acts." Although Kirkham urges tolerance about which candidates to admit, arguing that "there is no sort of entity that cannot in principle bear truth values," he does not actually expand the field beyond linguistic and conceptual entities.[10] But few philosophers after Kant regard linguistic and conceptual truth bearers as central to the arts. Hence, so long as general theories of truth restrict the class of truth bearers in these ways, it will be difficult to construct a theory of truth in art.

Difficult, but not impossible. I can think, for example, of two ways to regard propositions as vehicles of artistic truth.[11] One way is to say that works of art simply *are* propositions or that artworks can be true or false only insofar as they function as objects of logical discrimination, in both production and reception. Reminiscent of early Wittgenstein's description of propositions as pictures, this first approach says nothing about the unique manner in which art "carries" truth or falsehood. Another way to locate artistic truth in propositions is to say art *embodies* propositions in a variety of phenomena and media. On this approach artistic truth would exist independently of its embodiment, even though certain propositions could be unique to art, in the sense that they cannot be expressed or communicated except by way of art.[12] The disadvantage to this second approach is that it reifies a logical function into a thing in itself, as if propositions are independent and eternal universals simply waiting to be instantiated. Not only is this a questionable view of propositions, as this book argues, but also it ignores the social, historical, and political character of artistic truth.

Although some other version may be possible, and although I have not given a detailed account of the two versions mentioned, I think the propositional view of artistic truth is beyond redemption. If there is truth in art, it will have to be located in something other than propositions. The same applies to the other conceptual and linguistic contenders – judgments, sentences, utterances, assertions, and the like. For what distinguishes much of art, as it has developed historically in various societies and under various political conditions, is its tendency to favor the nonconceptual, nonlinguistic, and nonpropositional. In fact, partly because Western societies have privileged science and technology but have failed to find meaning in instrumental rationality, much of art has become antipropositional. To expect its truth to be propositional would misread recent history. A better approach is that recommended by Adorno: to try to understand such art's unintelligibility. This book argues against a propositional view of truth bearers and in favor of an account of artistic truth as nonpropositional.

Philosophically, however, a dogmatically antipropositional approach also will not do. This can be observed from one antipropositional approach to truth bearers that might seem compatible with a theory of artistic truth but actually undermines the entire project. Some philosophers have used speech-act theory to propound a deflationary thesis to the effect that "is true" is not a genuine predicate. Consequently, "there are no such properties as truth and falsity," and "nothing can bear truth values."[13] The deflationary thesis has one potentially salutary effect, namely, to break a fixation on conceptual and linguistic entities as privileged bearers of truth. But this potential is purchased at the price of rendering theories of truth superfluous, and that would apply to a theory of artistic truth as well. The deflationary thesis is a parallel in the analytic tradition to a questioning of the very idea of truth within some of French poststructuralism.

Although the characterization of truth bearers forms only part of an adequate theory, it is decisive for the question whether truth can be meaningfully attributed to art. That is why I find Adorno's idea of truth content (*Wahrheitsgehalt*) so instructive.[14] Adorno's idea allows one to attribute a nonpropositional import to art phenomena that is true or false but is neither representational along either Platonic or Aristotelian lines nor expressive in the manner proposed by romantic theories. Once that fundamental point is granted, one can address the other questions of truth theory – roughly, what truth is, what it means, and what it does.[15]

Another prominent feature to standard theories of truth lies in their criterion of truth. Many are correspondence theories. Correspondence theories of truth hold that there are truth bearers and that a truth bearer is true if and only if it corresponds to a state of affairs that obtains. They differ concerning the class of truth bearers (e.g., beliefs, propositions, sentences, or statements), the nature of states of affairs (whether they are facts, and whether they are mind-independent, as realists hold), and the type of correspondence required (congruence [e.g., Bertrand Russell] or correlation [e.g., J. L. Austin]).[16] In addition, most correspondence theories are propositionally inflected, even though many propositionally inflected theories of truth are not correspondence theories. "Propositionally inflected" theories (my term) regard propositions as the sole or the primary bearers of truth. The historical roots to such theories, and to the conflicts among them, lie in the metaphysics of Plato and Aristotle, with whom the debate about truth in art began.

Propositionally inflected correspondence theories of truth have dominated Anglo-American arguments concerning "artistic truth," both for and against. Among philosophers whose theories I discuss at some length, T. M. Greene, Monroe Beardsley, and Nicholas Wolterstorff all employ propositionally inflected correspondence theories of truth. Their "opponents" – I. A. Richards, Albert Hofstadter, and Nelson Goodman, respectively – either demote propositions as truth bearers or dismiss the criterion of correspondence or both.[17] Holding a correspondence theory does not preclude giving an account of artistic truth. Both Greene and Hofstadter, for example, give such accounts within the general framework of a correspondence theory. Yet, by insisting on correlation or congruence with states of affairs that obtain, correspondence theories miss the intrinsically interpretive character of art making, art experience, and art phenomena. Such theories usually lead to the conclusion that, to be true, art phenomena must be true independently of their being interpreted as true. This conclusion cannot be right, however, if, as Joseph Margolis has argued and as I hold, art itself is interpretive through and through.[18] A nonpropositional and noncorrespondence theory of artistic truth is required, which I shall attempt to provide. Although it needs to incorporate insights from traditional representational and expressive accounts, this alternative theory will take seriously both the linguistic turn in philosophy and the hermeneutic character of the arts. Now let me mention some sources to my alternative and outline the book's argument.

1.2 DIRECTIONS

This book describes artistic truth as a multidimensional process of imaginative disclosure. The primary sources for this description lie in Adorno's idea of artistic "truth content," already mentioned, and in Martin Heidegger's general conception of truth as "disclosedness." Attentiveness to truth's hermeneutic character helps make Heidegger's conception fruitful for a theory of artistic truth. Heidegger holds that even assertions and propositions are results and means of interpretation. The key to their truth, and to any truth, resides not in correspondence to states of affairs but in the hermeneutic openness of the interpreter. Correlatively, truth is not primarily the property of certain "truth bearers" such as assertions and propositions. Rather it is a process in which assertions and propositions, like artworks and speech acts, get their bearings. Although Chapters 4 and 5 point out problems in Heidegger's conception, it offers a way to think about truth that does justice to the interpretive character of the arts.

In addition to Adorno and Heidegger, another source to my account lies in Searlian speech-act theory, as modified and extended by Jürgen Habermas into a theory of communicative action. On the one hand, John Searle's theory of speech acts enables one to recognize and reconceptualize the limited but important role of assertions and propositions in the pursuit of truth. On the other hand, Habermas's tripartite differentiation of validity claims into propositional truth, normative legitimacy, and expressive sincerity suggests a model for distinguishing among three dimensions of artistic truth and linking these with arts-related language. Chapter 6 pursues this suggestion in detail.

I use "art" and "the arts" to include not only the traditional fine arts but also newer forms of mass-mediated or site-specific art. The labels also include folk art and so-called popular art. My most comprehensive term for the objects and occurrences people experience as art is "art phenomena." Within the category of art phenomena I distinguish "art products" from "art events." A piece of music or a novel would be an art product, whereas a recital or a public literary reading would be an art event. Western philosophers have mostly concentrated on art products rather than art events, to the impoverishment of our theories of art. Western philosophy of art since Kant has also concentrated on what I take to be a subcategory of art products, namely, artworks. On my own account, artworks are art products that have been institutionally constituted to "stand on their own." The means of such constituting are many. I think, for example, of the writing and publishing of musical scores, coupled with the training of professional musicians, the availability of dedicated sites for music performance and enjoyment (e.g., concert and recital halls), the rise of specialized music organizations (e.g., symphony orchestras and concert choirs), and the development of technological modes of music dissemination (recordings, broadcasting, and the like). The development of educated listeners, together with a philosophical notion of artistic autonomy, also help constitute certain products of music as musical works of art.[19]

Distinguishing between artworks and other art products helps sort out various dimensions of artistic truth. In particular, the truth of artistic import – what Adorno calls "truth content" – has prominence in artworks but not in other art products, some of which have little import. Unlike Adorno, I do not take the relative absence of artistic import to spell a complete lack of artistic truth or to signal artistic falsity. On the three-dimensional model constructed in Chapter 6, rock concerts and lullabies can also be found true in certain respects.

My account of artistic truth unfolds in three stages: exploration (Chapters 1–3), articulation (Chapters 4–6), and confirmation (Chapters 7–9). The conclusion (Chapter 10) recapitulates this account and indicates its societal implications. I begin in Chapter 1 with the challenge posed by Monroe Beardsley's highly influential denial that artworks can be true. His position marks a watershed in Anglo-American aesthetics. It collects the unresolved issues in logical positivist debates and channels them into a resolution that permeates most of analytic aesthetics. Beardsley denies artistic truth in order to promote the arts as autonomous fields of aesthetic experience that is intrinsically worthwhile. But his scientism, empiricism, and inconsistently behaviorist theory of language undermine his efforts to promote art's intrinsic value, casting doubts on his denial of artistic truth.

Chapter 2 considers two alternatives to Beardsley's approach, both of them within continental philosophy. Albert Hofstadter affirms existentially what Beardsley metacritically denies. For Hofstadter, there is artistic truth, and it is not propositional. Unfortunately Hofstadter provides no art-internal ways to distinguish between truth and falsity. Herman Rapaport, by contrast, pronounces a plague on both metacritical and existential houses. Not only does he dismiss any effort to theorize truth as correspondence but also he challenges all attempts to tie artistic truth to distinctively human existence. Yet he heaps such grand postmetaphysical expectations on the artwork that modernist autonomism à la Beardsley and Hofstadter collapses. What is required now, I argue, is an account of artistic truth that abandons a fixation on autonomous artworks and recognizes the sociohistorical situatedness of both art and aesthetics. Beyond metacritical denial, existential affirmation, and postmetaphysical deconstruction, we need a critical hermeneutic reconstruction of artistic truth.

Chapter 3 completes my explorations in this direction. It revisits Kant's aesthetics, from which contemporary philosophical stances toward the idea of artistic truth derive.[20] My reconstructive reading of Kant derives the aesthetic dimension from three polarities in modern Western societies: between play and work, between entertainment and instruction, and between expression and communication. From these polarities I develop a notion of the aesthetic as the intersubjective exploration, interpretation, and presentation of aesthetic signs. My general term for such intersubjective processes is "imagination." Then I describe aesthetic validity as a horizon of imaginative cogency. I argue that aesthetic processes, so construed, are crucial to cultural pathfinding, and that aesthetic validity claims in art talk contribute to this pursuit. Aesthetic validity, cultural orientation, and art talk constitute the hermeneutical matrix from which questions of artistic truth emerge.

With these explorations as background, I articulate my own account of artistic truth in Chapters 4–6. Chapter 4 examines the general conception of truth proposed by Heidegger's *Being and Time.* The chapter aims to fashion an alternative conception that frees Heidegger's insights from a reactionary garb. I propose to conceive of truth as the life-giving disclosure of society. This process is marked by fidelity to historically contested principles such as solidarity and justice. It is a process to which a differentiated array of cultural practices and products can contribute in distinct and indispensable ways. Linguistic claims and logical propositions belong to such an array, but so do the practices and products of art. The pursuit of assertoric correctness or "propositional truth" is one important but limited way in which life-giving disclosure can occur. This pursuit goes astray when it either does not support or does not receive support from the pursuit of other principles such as solidarity or justice.

Chapter 5 carries my critical dialogue with Heidegger into a discussion of his essay "The Origin of the Work of Art." The chapter aims to retrieve a conception of artistic truth as imaginative disclosure for which questions of aesthetic validity remain crucial. Within art, I argue, truth as disclosure must always be related, but not restricted, to imaginative cogency, which is important in nonartistic cognition and conduct as well. Imaginative cogency is not identical with disclosure in art. It is a principle of aesthetic validity to which any disclosive art practices must appeal, as must evaluative judgments about disclosure in art.

Chapter 6 works out the details of my idea of artistic truth as imaginative disclosure. First I review Habermasian responses to Adorno's idea of artistic truth content or import (*Wahrheitsgehalt*). Then I propose an approach that combines insight from both sides. I consider artistic truth to be internal to art phenomena, as Adorno claims, yet differentiated into three dimensions, in a manner reminiscent of Habermas's theory of validity. I identify these three dimensions using the terms "authenticity," "significance," and "integrity." These dimensions intersect in their needing to measure up to a principle of aesthetic validity: all three occur within the horizon of imaginative cogency. They also intersect in supporting pursuits of cultural orientation and in opening our personal and social worlds to ones we do not currently inhabit. By connecting artistic truth with world relations, I am able to show how art conversation makes the truth dimensions of art available for art discourse.

Chapters 7–9 seek confirmation for my account by testing it with regard to Anglo-American debates. The first debate, discussed in Chapter 7, occurs between emotivists and propositionists during the heyday of logical positivism. Whereas I. A. Richards thinks the arts epitomize an "emotive language" that has no cognitive function, Theodore Meyer Greene presents art as a cognitive enterprise to be evaluated according to the truth or falsity of artworks' propositional content. I demonstrate problems and potentials on both sides of this debate, neither of which provides an adequate account of artistic integrity.

In contrast to the epistemological character of the logical positivist dispute, the next debate is primarily ontological. Chapters 8 and 9 examine two opposed ontologies within analytic aesthetics concerning art's cognitive functions. Nelson Goodman proposes a nominalist and conventionalist theory of art as a symbol system. Nicholas Wolterstorff offers a realist and intentionalist theory of art as a field of action. They disagree on two crucial topics, namely, whether propositions are the locus of truth, and whether correspondence governs art's cognitive functions. I argue that Goodman liberates truth from its propositional cage but at the expense of art's significance. Wolterstorff emphasizes art's significance, but, in restricting truth proper to asserted propositions, he ignores artistic authenticity.

My assessment of Anglo-American debates shows that, although emotivists, propositionists, nominalists, and realists all draw attention to various aspects of artistic truth, none of them proposes a sufficiently comprehensive approach. Emotivists and nominalists do not account for the artwork's integrity. Propositionists and realists provide such an account but misconstrue art's hermeneutic character. Of the theories considered, Wolterstorff's realist theory comes closest to giving an adequate account of significance, but it neglects authenticity.

I propose instead to regard authenticity, significance, and integrity as intersecting dimensions of artistic truth, with the expectation of integrity being more prominent for artworks than for other art phenomena. What all three dimensions involve is best characterized as "truth with respect to" rather than either "truth-about" or "truth-to." People in modern Western societies expect art products and art events to be true with respect to the artist's experience or vision (i.e., authentic), with respect to a public's need for worthwhile cultural presentations (i.e., significant), and with respect to an artwork's own internal demands (i.e., integral). We expect art phenomena to be imaginatively disclosive in these regards. As Chapter 10 indicates, this multidimensional expectation is intrinsic to art's aesthetic worth and societal importance.

My account of artistic truth is a general account, in the sense that if it holds for any of the arts, it should hold for all of them. It is not a general theory of truth, however, even though it both employs elements of such a theory and has implications for its subsequent elaboration. Although Heidegger and Adorno, put into conversation with one another and with, say, Searle and Habermas, offer significant clues to how such a general theory of truth should be articulated, this book marks only the first steps. One hopes these steps move in a fruitful direction.[21]

1.3 BORDER CROSSINGS

Many new forms of public art are projects of "creative border crossing."[22] Perhaps a similar phrase can summarize the scope and methods of this book. Although not collaborative and interventionist, it resembles such art projects in its crossing disciplinary boundaries and promoting dialogue across cultural traditions. The boundaries in question lie primarily among the philosophical subdisciplines of aesthetics, epistemology, ontology, and philosophy of discourse.[23] Implicitly, however, topics in social philosophy and related subdisciplines also enter my discussion.[24] Both the topic of this book and the state of contemporary philosophy encourage such cross-disciplinary roaming. Let me comment on each in turn.

To propose an account of artistic truth, one must make claims about both art and truth. Post-Kantian philosophy increasingly assigns questions about art to the field of aesthetics. Insofar as aesthetic considerations prevail in art as a differentiated cultural domain, this division of labor has some justification. If one thinks that art is multidimensional, however, and that the aesthetic occurs across contemporary life and society, then a rigid division makes little sense. If in addition to an aesthetic dimension art has technological, economic, political, and ethical dimensions (to mention some), then discussions of nonaesthetic matters should also inform one's philosophy of art and one's account of artistic truth. Moreover, even granting that special connections hold between artistic truth and aesthetic processes, someone who finds the aesthetic throughout life and society will want to pay attention to nonartistic matters when proposing an account of artistic truth. So restricting one's considerations to what professional aestheticians prefer to discuss would truncate one's account. Indeed, even standard debates about artistic truth among specialists in aesthetics either make or assume claims about much more than art and the aesthetic dimension.

A similar logic applies when emphasis falls on "truth." To philosophize about truth in art, one needs to make or assume claims about truth in general, one of the oldest and most controversial topics in all of Western philosophy. Historically, this topic was always central to what became subdisciplines of logic, epistemology, and ontology. But it was also connected to questions of right living and the good society. With the linguistic turn in twentieth-century philosophy, the topic of truth became central to hermeneutics, philosophy of language, and philosophy of science as well. Not surprisingly, then, specialized debates about artistic truth raise or imply claims in epistemology or ontology or philosophy of discourse or even social philosophy that go well beyond the purview of aesthetics proper. Both "art" and "truth" are such that the topic of artistic truth demands the trespassing of subdisciplinary boundaries.

Correlatively, a deliberately cross-disciplinary approach invites criticisms from many subdisciplinary directions. Although this is not an altogether welcome prospect – at least it is a challenging one – I take consolation from the fact that contemporary philosophy is in a similarly unruly condition. Or perhaps I should say that the contemporary philosophers whose work I find most provocative either transgress philosophical subdivisions or navigate nimbly among them: Jacques Derrida, Julia Kristeva, Martha Nussbaum, Hilary Putnam, Richard Rorty, and Charles Taylor, to name a few. In giving up philosophy's claims to ground other disciplines and to be the chief arbiter of culture,[25] contemporary philosophers have found new freedom of movement within their own discipline. The worry, of course, is that, while blithely skipping across subdisciplinary spaces, we have little to say beyond our professional confines, or that no one outside philosophy's gilded halls will listen, or that we are whistling in the dark.

The other border crossings in this book occur among philosophical traditions and schools. The summary already given shows that my account of artistic truth interacts with both "continental" and "analytic" philosophy. It also constructs a critical dialogue among schools of philosophy within each tradition that have been openly antagonistic in the past: Heideggerian thinking and Critical Theory within continental philosophy, and nominalism and realism within analytic philosophy.

Some of this stems from my own training and experience. Having been steeped in the writings of Adorno and the Frankfurt School, I have absorbed Adorno's aversion to both "positivism" and "the jargon of authenticity." Although I remain unconvinced by his harsh rejections of Karl Popper's philosophy of science and Heidegger's ontology of existence, the utopian notes in Adorno's social philosophy, which have unexpected resonances in Heideggerian philosophy, offer a crucial counterpoint to the sober restraint in Habermasian Critical Theory, which adds precision to Adorno's critique of both Popper and Heidegger. At the same time, doing philosophy in North America teaches one to interact with analytically trained colleagues, many of whom have a remarkable ability to unravel conceptual tangles. Someone with primarily continental training can learn from them the importance of bringing careful analyses of arguments to the close reading of texts.

Another source to the emphasis on critical dialogue in this book is the fact that its author did not enter philosophy under the tutelage of the philosophical schools already mentioned. He became a philosopher within the "Amsterdam School" of "reformational philosophy."[26] Such schooling teaches one to look for both insights and oversights in major philosophers' writings, regardless of the traditions or schools to which they belong. Moreover, the work of Herman Dooyeweerd, D. H. Th. Vollenhoven, and their successors provides instructive alternatives to the dialectic between Heidegger and Adorno or between Goodman and Wolterstorff. One does not need to be a "school philosopher" to recognize the dialogical potential opened by being trained in a different school of thought.

My emphasis on critical dialogue reflects a conviction that good philosophy requires appreciating when another philosophy is good and approaching other philosophies in that spirit. Confronted with a distinction between light music and serious, Johannes Brahms said the only distinction he found crucial lay between good music and bad. I hold a similar position about philosophy. But this does not imply the naive assumption that standards of goodness in philosophy remain constant across philosophical traditions and schools. Some philosophers regard Heidegger's writings as "gobbledygook." Others find Goodman's to be "incredibly thin." They do so not simply out of intolerance or ignorance, but because they employ different standards from those to which Heidegger or Goodman subscribed.

The challenge for a continentally trained philosopher writing in an Anglophone context is not to let such tradition-specific standards become an overriding norm for how one does philosophy. Wherever possible one needs to relativize such standards, for the sake of the subject matter and the audience one addresses. This need to relativize helps explain the book's choice of texts to be discussed and the manner of its discussion. Philosophers familiar with the continental tradition will note the lack of attention to central figures in European philosophy of art, other than Heidegger: G. W. F. Hegel, Friedrich Nietzsche, Hans-Georg Gadamer, Jacques Derrida, and Julia Kristeva. Even Theodor W. Adorno, to whom my account owes much, receives only a cursory treatment. Their relative absence from the discussion does not signal a lack of appreciation for their insights. But it does indicate a hermeneutical judgment about what one can reasonably hope to cover and still remain intelligible to analytic colleagues. It also reflects my conclusion that Martin Heidegger is the single most influential philosopher in twentieth-century European philosophy and that his influence continues today.

Conversely, analytic philosophers will be struck by the amount of attention this book devotes to historically dated Anglo-American figures such as

I. A. Richards, T. M. Greene, and perhaps even Monroe Beardsley. Post-analytic philosophers may wonder why the book says so little about Anglo-American thinkers such as R. G. Collingwood, John Dewey, and Susanne K. Langer, whose positions comport fairly well with my own. This odd coupling derives from a historiographic judgment that the figures selected, and the positions they defend, are highly representative of the mainstream in Anglo-American aesthetics as it has developed since the 1920s. It also stems from the conclusion that to make my alternative account plausible, the book must address the most cogent articulations of propositionally inflected correspondence theory in Anglo-American aesthetics.

To this effort the book brings two methodological assumptions. The first methodological assumption is this. If a philosopher has written at some length on a topic one wishes to consider, then one should try to understand that philosopher's texts from within. Only through a close reading should one discover the contributions and limitations of that philosopher's position. My other methodological assumption is that significant light will shine on a position when one considers another position, worked out in sufficient detail, that opposes the position being interpreted. By constructing a dialogue, even where a dialogue did not exist prior to the interpretation, one can achieve a more nuanced understanding of both positions and a stronger articulation of one's own position, whether this agrees in sum or in part with either position, or whether it forms an alternative to both.

Those assumptions generate the methods this book employs. It develops an alternative account of artistic truth by constructing dialogues with and between various opposing positions. The book tries to provide enough commentary on the texts discussed to assure and demonstrate close readings. It aims to elicit the contributions and limitations of each position by considering another in opposition to it. And where my own account provides an alternative to the positions discussed, the book endeavors to show how the alternative makes up for the deficiencies I identify. The book's methods are dialectical with a dialogical twist. In that sense, both the account and the manner of its articulation seek to exemplify a critical hermeneutic approach.[27] This approach requires repeated migrations across both subdisciplinary and orientational boundaries. Like the cultural scene it aims to disclose, it calls for creative border crossings.

PART I

HERMENEUTICAL MATRIX

1

Beardsley's Denial

Paintings and musical compositions are not, and do not give, knowledge about reality.

Monroe Beardsley[1]

Three mutually incompatible stances toward the idea of artistic truth characterize recent philosophy in Anglophone countries: sober rejection, enthusiastic affirmation, and deep skepticism. Rejection has been the majority opinion. Historically it stems from a combination of scientism and aesthetic modernism for which Monroe Beardsley's *Aesthetics* is emblematic. The enthusiasts, a tiny minority among professional philosophers, tend to combine an antipositivist conception of knowledge with a high view of art. The skeptics, informed by postpositivism in analytic philosophy of science and by postmodernism in continental aesthetics, question the ontological premises on which both rejection and affirmation rely.

This array of positions is far from transparent, however, and the philosophers who hold them rarely engage in sustained debates. Nor do the "final vocabularies" of each position readily translate into those of the others. My first task, then, is to consider a representative formulation of each position and to place it in conversation with the other two. For this conversation I have selected books from different decades by Beardsley (1958), Albert Hofstadter (1965), and Herman Rapaport (1997). After discussing them in Chapters 1 and 2, I turn to a common source for all three positions, namely, the aesthetics of Immanuel Kant. Chapter 3 revisits Kant to discover how a more viable idea of artistic truth would need to be reconstructed, once rejection, affirmation, and skepticism all prove insufficient. Once I have proposed such an idea in Chapters 4–6, I shall show how it stands with respect to Anglo-American debates that precede and succeed Beardsley's denial.

Anyone who proposes a contemporary theory of truth in art must address Beardsley's *Aesthetics*, possibly the most influential book in postwar

Anglo-American aesthetics. Beardsley's book turns the central claims of literary New Criticism into a philosophically rigorous argument for the uniqueness and importance of the arts and literature. His argument includes a strong case against the idea of artistic truth. Empiricist in its epistemology, and inclined to see natural science as the stronghold of knowledge and truth, his book epitomizes the "objectivism" that, according to Joseph Margolis, dominated analytic aesthetics and led to its "eclipse."[2]

After the eclipse, however, Beardsley's book looks more deeply schizophrenic than it did during pre-Rorty days of analytic innocence. On the one hand, he brusquely denies that truth can properly be ascribed to artworks or to elements within them.[3] On the other hand, "meaning" and "truth" remain core values for his philosophy, and these topics are central to his book's anti-intentionalist and antirelativist aesthetics. So Beardsley's denial of "artistic truth" does not come easily. Indeed, the resolute language concluding his chapter on the topic suggests suppressed self-doubt, as if wistfulness hides behind stoic acceptance of the inevitable: "It seems that we must draw this chapter to a somewhat negative conclusion.... Paintings and musical compositions are not, and do not give, knowledge about reality, whether nature or supernature, whether in propositions, by revelation, or for intuition. Nor is this to be regretted, on any just estimate of the arts themselves or of the plural values of life. For knowledge is not the only thing the possession of which can dignify and justify the place of the arts in the life of [humanity]" (p. 391). Beardsley does not tell us here how he would rank the importance of cognitive capacities relative to, say, the ability to evoke aesthetic experience.

Only much later does the book argue that aesthetic experience itself is so valuable that surrendering art's cognitive capacities would not be too great a loss. Yet this argument is remarkably tentative and incomplete. The final chapter, titled "The Arts in the Life of Man," begins boldly: "Certainly anyone who contends that the arts deserve a high place among the goods of culture and the ends of education must back up this contention with evidence that the experiences they afford are, in some important way, good for us." One paragraph later, however, Beardsley admits that "it is just at this point ... that the available evidence is most scarce." He then prepares his reader for the disappointments to follow, saying "a great deal of thinking ... remains to be done" (pp. 557–8).

Beardsley's denial of artistic truth embodies an unresolved tension between a high view of art and a high view of knowledge. The schizoid character of his position stems from an uneasy marriage between modernist aesthetics, with its valorizing of autonomous works of art, and empiricistic scientism, with its inductivist and hypotheticodeductive paradigm for legitimate knowledge. Beardsley tries to keep both parents happy by turning philosophy of art into metacriticism – into the philosophy of art criticism. But this violates exactly those impulses of modern and contemporary art which flout empiricist epistemology or resist academic explanation. The result is an aesthetics of denial, one that, to parody Kant, limits art to make room for science and thereby limits science as well.

The denial begins long before Beardsley's chapter on "Artistic Truth" (chap. 8), in a consideration of language and literature titled "The Literary Work" (chap. 3). I summarize parts of that chapter before I review his argument concerning artistic truth and then his account of literary predications (chap. 9). The reason for discussing three chapters rather than one is that his argument concerning artistic truth relies heavily on claims about language that receive more elaborate treatment in the chapters on literature. More specifically, my discussion has three stages: the distinction between literal and metaphorical language in Beardsley's literary theory (section 1.1), his refutation of theories that ascribe truth to nonliterary artworks (section 1.2), and his argument that literature contains true and false predications but does not assert them (section 1.3). At each stage I raise questions about both the details and the framework of Beardsley's position. Then the next chapter puts Beardsley's metacriticism into discussion with two continental alternatives. Elaborating my own response to his denial of artistic truth takes up the rest of this book. So the current chapter does not pretend to give a complete criticism of Beardsley's position. Nor does it consider refinements from within subsequent analytic philosophy that could have alleviated some puzzles in his theory of language. I am primarily interested here in unearthing epistemological and ontological underpinnings. My aim is to begin to problematize the empiricist epistemology and the propositionally inflected correspondence theory of truth that his denial of artistic truth assumes.

1.1 MEANING AND METAPHOR[4]

In chapter 3 Beardsley proposes a theory of "the literary work" as "a discourse in which an important part of the meaning is implicit" (p. 126) in order to argue for a "logic of explication" prescribing how literary works should be read. This argument requires both a general account of linguistic meaning and a specific account of the "implicit meaning" in literature. Whereas the account of linguistic meaning relies on Beardsley's concept of "cognitive purport," his account of "implicit meaning" depends on his concept of "connotation." A fundamental assumption in both accounts stems from behavioral psychology. For Beardsley, a linguistic expression is "a piece of voluntary human behavior" whose "import," like the import of other such behaviors, is its "tendency to affect perceivers in some fairly definite way" (p. 116). Linguistic expressions have import for people who are behaviorally conditioned to respond. The type of import depends on what the expression tends to cause in the hearer (or reader, presumably). An expression has *emotive import* when it tends "to evoke certain feelings or emotions in the hearer." It has *cognitive import* when it tends "to cause certain beliefs about the speaker," about the speaker's beliefs, feelings, or other characteristics. Within cognitive import, Beardsley distinguishes further among "cognitive purport" (conveying information about the speaker's beliefs), "emotive purport" (conveying information about the speaker's feelings), and "general purport" (conveying information about the speaker's "other characteristics" – nationality, class, religion, etc.).

Linguistic "meaning" in the strict sense is cognitive purport, he says. It is a linguistic expression's capacity to affect the hearer's beliefs about the speaker's beliefs. For example, the meaning of the utterance "It's growing dark" is its "tendency to make *B* think that *A* believes it is growing dark." Although Beardsley does not want to equate meaning with reference, he does think a sentence's capacity "to formulate beliefs" explains its capacity to refer "truly or falsely, to something going on in the world outside the speaker's mind" (and not merely to convey the speaker's belief): "[T]o understand the sentence is to know what beliefs it *could* formulate. And this is the same as knowing what it would be like to believe it ourselves: what we would expect to see if we looked out the window" (p. 117).[5] Sentences are the primary vehicles of linguistic meaning, he says. Words have meaning derivatively, through the role they play in sentences.

Beardsley is not altogether consistent on the question of word meaning, however. Earlier in the chapter he says descriptions of a literary work can have two topics: the "world of the work" (e.g., the characters, actions, and settings in a novel) and the work as a "discourse" (as "a verbal design" or "an intelligible string of words," p. 115).[6] In that context he portrays words as "meaningful sounds" that can be the "elements" of such discourse. One wonders retrospectively why he posits words as the elements of literature and describes them as "meaningful sounds," when, on his theory of linguistic meaning, words are not intrinsically meaningful but derive their meaning from sentences or linguistic expressions.

The answer may have to do with his reception of the theory of language in Charles Stevenson's ethics.[7] For Stevenson the primary unit of linguistic meaning is the word or the "sign"[8] rather than the sentence, which Beardsley usually makes the primary unit. To explain the relative constancy of a sign's meaning, Stevenson describes meaning as a "dispositional property," as the tendency under various conditions for a certain stimulus to cause a certain response. Signs have both "emotive meaning" (what Beardsley discusses as emotive import and emotive purport) and "descriptive meaning" (roughly, Beardsley's cognitive purport and general purport). Emotive meaning is a sign's disposition to cause certain feelings or attitudes in the hearer or to be used to express these in the speaker. This disposition arises from "an elaborate process of conditioning, of long duration."[9] A sign's descriptive meaning also involves prior conditioning. In addition, however, descriptive meaning follows linguistic rules: "The 'descriptive meaning' of a sign is its disposition to affect cognition, provided that the disposition is caused by an elaborate process of conditioning that has attended the sign's use in communication, and provided that the disposition is rendered fixed, at least to a considerable degree, by linguistic rules."[10] Beardsley employs the same fundamental distinction between emotive and descriptive, with modifications. Although he rejects Stevenson's notion of "independent emotive meaning,"[11] Beardsley sometimes follows Stevenson in making words rather than sentences the primary units of linguistic meaning.

This lack of clarity about word meaning plays into Beardsley's account of "implicit meaning" in literature. He gives a "semantic definition" of the literary work as "a discourse in which an important part of the meaning is implicit" (p. 126). The notion of implicit meaning draws on two distinctions, one involving sentences and the other involving words: between the primary and secondary meaning of a sentence, and between what a word designates and what it connotes. The first distinction derives from comparing declarative sentences (e.g., "The window is shut") with imperative sentences (e.g., "Please shut the window"). Declarative sentences are statements, he says. They state beliefs that can be true or false. Imperative sentences do not *state* beliefs. They may *suggest* beliefs, however, showing indirectly that the speaker has a belief. Only a declarative sentence can do both – "state one thing and suggest another" – both of which may be true or false (p. 123). Whereas the primary meaning of a sentence is the beliefs it states, the secondary meaning is the beliefs it suggests. As secondary meaning, the suggestion is "part of the full meaning of the sentence, but its presence is not felt to be as central or as basic as the primary meaning, on which it nevertheless depends. . . . It is usually less emphatic, less obtrusive, less definitely and precisely fixed than the primary meaning, but it may be no less important, even from a practical point of view" (p. 123).

Thus Beardsley recognizes that there is more to linguistic meaning than stated beliefs. But his distinction between primary and secondary meaning compounds his unclarity concerning word meaning by giving an unduly restrictive account of sentence meaning. From a speech-act perspective, he seems to deny primary meaning to all illocutionary acts that do not assert or state – commands, requests, questions, warnings, promises, and the like. This would imply that the vast majority of linguistic expressions in ordinary usage have no primary meaning. Moreover, if "what a sentence suggests . . . is what we can infer . . . beyond what it states" (p. 123), and if most linguistic expressions do not state beliefs (since most illocutionary acts are not assertions or statements), then it is hard to see how they can have secondary meaning either. This casts doubt on the claim that stated beliefs are the primary meaning of sentences. It also raises the question whether most linguistic expressions have any meaning at all, in Beardsley's sense of sentence meaning.

The other distinction underlying Beardsley's notion of implicit meaning is that "between the standard, or central, meaning of a word and its marginal or accompanying meanings." The standard meaning is what a word such as "sea" designates (e.g., being a large body of salt water). Its marginal meaning is what it connotes (e.g., being dangerous, endlessly changeable, etc.): "What a word connotes, then, are the characteristics that it does not designate but that belong ... to many of the things it denotes. This is the word's range of connotation. But what it connotes in a particular context – its contextual connotation – is always a selection from its total range" (p. 125).

Here again Beardsley ignores his earlier qualification that words only derive their meaning from sentences, and he seems to equate word meaning with reference. He writes as if the meaning of words stems directly from their corresponding to certain objective properties or "characteristics" rather than from their ability to appear in sentences that, according to Beardsley, can affect the hearer's beliefs about the speaker's beliefs. It remains a mystery, however, why, for any specific word, certain characteristics are central designata and others are substandard marginalia. Even more surprisingly, a few pages later he completely nullifies his earlier qualification, claiming that the "regional meaning" of sentences is "a unique function of the meanings of the constituent words plus their grammatical relations." That is why, he says, one should have no difficulty understanding the sentence "The crocodile is on the piano" (p. 131). But if this is so, then sentence meaning would not be primarily linked to how an expression affects the hearer's beliefs about the speaker's beliefs but rather to how words hook up with "real-world" objects. Ambivalence concerning "words," prompted perhaps by Charles Stevenson's assigning meaning to signs as such, takes a toll on Beardsley's notion of implicit meaning.

Be that as it may, when Beardsley defines literature as "discourse with important implicit meaning" (p. 127), he is saying that in literature, more than in other types of discourse, much of the meaning is secondary and marginal, occurring by way of suggestion (e.g., through the use of rhetorical and compositional devices) and connotation (e.g., through the use of metaphor). Literary discourse "contains deep levels of meaning that are only hinted at through connotation and suggestion." It displays "a kind of semantical *thickness* when compared with mathematical and technical discourse." Because of this thickness, this "air of being more than it seems," literary discourse often requires the "explication" of its meaning (p. 129).[12] Beardsley argues, against relativist theories, that such explication is not arbitrary or person-specific, both because, as "objective parts" of the meanings that words have within "a certain speech-community," connotations are "a function" of the words' designations (pp. 132–3), and because there is a reliable "method" or "logic" for explicating poems and the like (pp. 133–47).[13] In these ways, despite the confusions and possible inconsistencies I have noted, Beardsley can generate an account of literary meaning that takes seriously its allusive character.

Here his theory of metaphor plays a crucial role, even as it helps illuminate his accounts of language and truth. On Beardsley's "Controversion Theory," metaphors belong to the genus of "self-controverting discourse." What characterizes all such discourse is logical absurdity at the level of primary meaning or designation. Not all of it is absurd at the level of secondary meaning or connotation, however. Rather, for example, "it is the logical absurdity of statements in poems that gives them meaning on the secondary level" (p. 138). The key to metaphor, and to poetry, where metaphor dominates, is that the self-controversion is "significant."

More specifically, metaphors usually involve significant self-contradiction due to "self-contradictory attribution," Beardsley says. By "attribution" he means any linguistic expression containing at least two words, one (the "subject of the attribution") denoting and characterizing a class, and the other (the "modifier") modifying the characterization. In the phrase "large dogs" or the sentence "The dogs are large," for example, "dogs" would be the subject and "large" would be the modifier. Beardsley describes self-contradictory attribution and significant self-contradiction as follows: "A *self-contradictory attribution* is one in which the modifier designates some characteristic incompatible with the characteristics designated by the subject – 'four-legged biped,' 'Circles are square.' A bare self-contradiction is just that; but when the modifier connotes some characteristic that can be meaningfully attributed to the subject, the reader jumps over the evident self-contradiction and construes it indirectly, on the principle that the writer knows he is contradicting himself and wouldn't utter anything at all unless he had something sensible in mind. Then the expression becomes a *significant self-contradiction*" (pp. 140–1). In most cases of metaphor the significant self-contradictory attribution is indirect. This occurs, for example, when one calls a man a "fox" or calls streets "metaphysical." But metaphors can also arise when an attribution is obviously false and the conditions for using a word correctly are misapplied in a way that has significant connotations. Beardsley's example is "a saying among theatrical people that 'Outside Broadway, everything is Bridgeport.'" He summarizes: "[A] metaphor is a significant attribution that is either indirectly self-contradictory or obviously false in its context, and in which the modifier connotes characteristics that can be attributed, truly or falsely, to the subject" (p. 142).

Because Beardsley thinks connotations are never fully knowable in advance (unlike designations, presumably), he says metaphors have creative capacity: they often let us "discover new connotations of the words when we see how they behave as modifiers in metaphorical attributions" (p. 143). This creative capacity does not preclude nonrelativist explications, however, because of two principles for explicating metaphors and poems. The "Principle of Congruence" requires that the modifier's connotations fit the subject, and the "Principle of Plenitude" requires that "[a]ll the connotations that can be found to fit . . . be attributed to the poem: it means all it *can* mean, so to speak" (p. 144). These two principles constitute the "logic of explication." Accordingly, proper explications of poetry will be "fully open and alive to all its semantical richness, however subtle or recondite" (p. 147).

From all of this, then, the following account of linguistic meaning emerges. Linguistic expressions have meaning, according to Beardsley, insofar as they tend to affect the hearer's (or reader's) beliefs about the speaker's (or writer's) beliefs. Such meaning has two levels, explicit and implicit. Explicitly, beliefs are stated or objective characteristics are designated. Implicitly, beliefs are suggested or objective characteristics are connoted. Implicit meaning prevails in literature. Indeed, poetry and metaphor are modes of (literary) discourse in which implicit meaning gains its significance via the logical absurdity of the explicit meaning. This account assumes, but does not really explain, a relation between meaning and reference. Similarly, it employs a notion of logical absurdity without explaining what would make the primary meaning of a linguistic expression logically absurd. Both topics – reference and logical absurdity – presuppose theories of knowledge and truth that surface later, in chapters 8 ("Artistic Truth") and 9 ("Literature and Knowledge").

Before turning to those chapters, let me summarize my worries about Beardsley's theory of language. His theory lacks clarity about the source of word meaning, about the relation between linguistic meaning and reference, and about the ability of nonconstative speech acts to be meaningful in a straightforward way. Underlying these unclarities is a behavioral account of linguistic meaning that is inadequate for the work Beardsley wants his linguistic theory to do. Because his account of "implicit meaning" and his recommended "logic of explication" presuppose a problematic account of linguistic meaning, I have serious doubts about Beardsley's attempt to distinguish "literary" from "nonliterary" language. Closely related doubts arise from similar moves to distinguish (aesthetically qualified) artworks from (linguistically meaningful) statements and their vehicles. This latter distinction sustains his case against theories of artistic truth, as we shall see.

1.2 CONTESTED THEORIES

Chapter 8 addresses the question whether paintings and musical compositions can be true or false and concludes that they cannot. A similar question concerning literary works is reserved for chapter 9.[14] Chapter 8 begins by distinguishing between linguistic meaning and truth: "The [declarative] sentence has not merely a meaning; it also has the characteristic of being either true or false, and consequently believable or disbelievable. In virtue of having this characteristic, it can record and communicate knowledge. In other words, it has a *cognitive function*" (p. 367). By implication, Beardsley also distinguishes "recording and communicating knowledge" from "conveying information about the speaker's (or writer's) beliefs," since the latter is the core of linguistic meaning in his account. Potential slippage becomes apparent, however, from his regarding linguistic meaning as cognitive purport, itself a species of cognitive import. In fact, the key question for distinguishing truth from linguistic meaning within Beardsley's framework – namely, the difference between knowledge and belief – does not come up until later, and then only in passing.

Instead, he proposes three "ground rules" for discussing artistic truth (p. 368). (1) Truth is connected with knowledge, and other familiar senses of "true" such as "loyal, sincere, or genuine" are "irrelevant." (2) Truth is not a psychological state. (3) Truth involves something's "correspondence" to ontologically unspecified reality.[15] Thanks to the unexplained notions of "knowledge" and "correspondence," these rules already preclude applying "true" to anything nonlinguistic (other than, perhaps, to beliefs, on Beardsley's conception of beliefs). Playing by his own rules, Beardsley then considers and rejects three theories of artistic truth: the Proposition Theory (e.g., T. M. Greene), the Revelation Theory (e.g., G. W. F. Hegel), and the Intuitionist Theory (e.g., Benedetto Croce).

Beardsley rejects the Proposition Theory by arguing that propositions ("anything that is either true or false," p. 369) cannot exist "apart from linguistic vehicles" (p. 372). Because paintings and musical compositions are nonlinguistic, they can neither be nor contain propositions. Nor do they display the two-part structure of "index" and "characterizer" (i.e., subject and predicate) that enables sentences to be or to contain propositions. At most, a representational painting can be "true *to*" (but not "true *of*, or true *about*") the subject it portrays, in the sense that the painting depicts characteristics the subject really has.[16] So a painting could *show* "the President as sheeplike," but it could not *state* "that the President is sheeplike" (p. 375). Musical compositions, however, are not even capable of such similarity to something external to them.

On Beardsley's reading, the other two theories do not claim that the artwork is a "bearer of knowledge," a role he restricts to certain linguistic expressions. They claim instead that the artwork is "related to our knowledge in some direct and intimate way" (p. 379). Beardsley does not explain why he needs to refute such theories. After all, on his construal, they are not arguing that artworks or elements within them can be true or false. Perhaps he worries that, by claiming the artwork's direct and intimate relation to knowledge, such theories lift the flap to a different epistemological tent from the one his ground rules have staked out. Certainly his interpretive frame is inadequate for Hegel, who places artworks among the supreme "bearers of knowledge." To acknowledge the inadequacy, however, would require much more expansive notions of knowledge, truth, and art than Beardsley's ground rules permit.

Beardsley portrays Revelation Theory as claiming that paintings and musical compositions reveal "the nature of reality" in ways that are "illuminating," "enlightening," or "instructive." Ignoring the many lexical meanings and synonyms of "reveal," yet appealing to "common speech," Beardsley idiosyncratically restricts its meaning to both suggesting "a new hypothesis" and providing "fairly strong and direct evidence for that hypothesis" (p. 379).[17] Some paintings, he admits, may suggest hypotheses about reality in general, but music cannot, and neither paintings nor musical compositions can confirm (i.e., give evidence for) such hypotheses. At best they can be "symptoms of personality or culture" (p. 380). The arts cannot be fully revelatory in Beardsley's sense of the term "reveal." Indeed, his comments about the 1956 movie *Baby Doll* indicate a further restriction in his usage of "reveal": he only considers factual hypotheses, ones that can be formulated as "that" clauses. *Baby Doll*, he writes, "may *suggest* the hypothesis that retarded Southern girls are frequently kept in unconsummated wedlock." But since the movie "does not present a single authenticated case history (being fiction)," it does not *confirm* this hypothesis. If he had recognized hermeneutic hypotheses involving "what" clauses, Beardsley might have seen that *Baby Doll* suggests a hypothesis about what it would be like to be a disadvantaged southern girl, and the movie confirms the hypothesis by presenting a powerful filmic "case study." His restricted notion of revelation prevents him from considering such hermeneutic "hypothesis-suggestion-and-confirmation" (p. 380) as no less conducive to knowledge acquisition and knowledge legitimation than a sociological study or historical report on conditions in the American South.

Nevertheless, he does consider a range of ways in which Revelation Theories might themselves claim that nonliterary artworks reveal what reality is like. Beardsley discusses several varieties to "the Universalist version" of Revelation Theory (pp. 381–7). They all assume a distinction, he says, between particulars ("individual persons, places, and things that are named by singular terms") and universals ("repeatable qualities or relations that can appear in various particulars"). Universalist Revelation Theories claim that by disclosing universals an artwork calls attention to universals and acquaints us with them.[18] Beardsley's refutation of each variety of universalist Revelation Theory follows the same pattern. First he grants that paintings and musical compositions can present universals and call attention to them. Then he denies that doing this can constitute knowledge or contribute to it without the use of propositions, a capacity he has already withheld from nonliterary arts.

Beardsley's first argument for this denial is especially instructive, because it "reveals" his own epistemology. The argument rejects Bertrand Russell's well-known distinction between "knowledge by acquaintance" and "knowledge by description."[19] So-called knowledge by acquaintance is not knowledge, says Beardsley, but simply acquaintance, and acquaintance is all the

nonliterary arts can provide. Listening to the music's cheerfulness or contemplating the painting's somberness, "we are *getting* something, to be sure,"
but what we get is simply "raw material" for knowledge, not knowledge itself:
"[I]t does not become knowledge, in the strict sense, until there is inference,
until the data are combined and connected by reasoning." So universalist
Revelation Theory is wrong to claim either that art's acquainting us with
universals is knowledge or that this acquainting "is very important before
it is turned to account by the mind and confronted with more general and
more remote hypotheses" (p. 383). Clearly Beardsley's paradigm for knowledge proper is the empirical sciences, as construed through the lenses of an
empiricist epistemology.[20]

Even with this paradigm in place, however, it is not obvious that he has
successfully countered the primary claim of universalist Revelation Theory
as he construes it. Perhaps he has shown that, on an empiricist conception
of knowledge, nonliterary artworks are not "bearers of knowledge." But
he has not demonstrated that they are not "related to our knowledge in
some direct and intimate way" (p. 379). Because Beardsley himself grants
that the universal qualities presented by nonliterary artworks "may become
the data for future knowings" (p. 383), and because his own epistemology
claims that empirical knowledge depends heavily on appropriate data, he
owes his readers an account of whether and in which respects artistically
generated data are important for empirical knowledge. This he does not
offer or attempt. Even if propositions are required that nonliterary artworks
cannot provide, this does not preclude such propositions being available,
say, in art critical or philosophical discourse. Why could not the requisite
"revelation" occur via the sort of reciprocation between art and theory that
Adorno makes central to the notion of artistic truth content (*Wahrheitsgehalt*)
or that, in a different way, Arthur Danto makes central to art itself?[21]

The third theory of artistic truth, in addition to Proposition Theory and
Revelation Theory, Beardsley labels "Intuitionist Theory." He portrays this
as a theory of knowledge at odds with both rationalism (e.g., Descartes) and
his own empiricism. His description of the latter is worth quoting in full:
"Empiricism is the theory that all knowledge consists of propositions that
we are justified in believing because of their connection with experience,
the data of sensation and introspection. According to this theory, all true
propositions except tautological ones are either generalizations induced
from experience or hypotheses confirmed by experience because they explain why our experience is what it is" (p. 387). The Intuitionist Theory,
by contrast, postulates "a unique faculty of insight that is independent of
both sense experience and the rational intellect. It delivers knowledge to
us in nonconceptual form, as immediate conviction; there is no inference,
or reasoning, so it cannot go wrong" (p. 388). On Beardsley's description,
the intuitionist account entails "direct communion with the object" and
"ineffable" intuitive knowledge that only artworks can convey. What they

convey is insight into individual objects in all their uniqueness and indivisible wholeness. Indeed, only the nonliterary arts, and not the sciences, provide knowledge of reality; not even attempts to talk about artworks can put into words what we have learned from them.

Beardsley acknowledges that his refuting such a theory would be difficult, since its conception of knowledge runs completely contrary to his own epistemology. Yet he quickly pulls the following objections from an empiricist bag of tricks: (1) What *evidence* can intuitionists give that their art experiences have given them new knowledge? (2) Can intuitionists provide any *examples* of knowledge, supposedly gained by intuition, that empiricists would also accept as knowledge and could not explain in an empiricist fashion? (3) What *criterion* of truth can intuitionists provide, failing which their theory of knowledge would be "fatally incomplete" (p. 390)?

All three objections attempt to make intuitionism accountable to empiricist standards. This becomes apparent from Beardsley's final salvo. One must distinguish, he says, between having an experience, whether intuitive or not, and acquiring knowledge by means of experience: "[T]he jump from having the experience to believing something about the object *is* a jump, and involves an act of inference. This inference has to be justified, and by the rules of reasoning. Therefore there is no such thing as *self*-authenticating, or intrinsically justified, intuitive knowledge" (pp. 390–1). By "knowledge" in this context Beardsley means, at a minimum, the justified believing of something about the object experienced. I say "at a minimum" because this would not count as knowledge on a more full-blown empiricist account. It would have to be not only justified (or warranted) but also *true*, and not just a believing but a *belief*.[22] Beardsley holds that something believed intuitively, without inferential justification, is "not yet knowledge, but a hypothesis to be investigated": genuine knowledge "is something more than intuitive conviction" (p. 391). Nor can paintings and musical compositions convey the "intuitive knowledge" that artists supposedly have, since the artworks would have to mediate the knowledge. Being mediated, such knowledge could not be direct and therefore could not be intuitive.[23]

In general, Beardsley's argument against theories of artistic truth goes like this. To be true or false, a nonliterary artwork (or elements within it) must either contain propositions, or suggest and confirm hypotheses about reality, or directly contribute to knowledge about reality, or convey nonpropositional "knowledge" about reality. Because knowledge must be both propositional and inferential, and because nonliterary artworks are neither propositional nor inferential, no nonliterary artwork can be true or false. No such artwork can have propositional content that either corresponds or fails to correspond to reality. Given Beardsley's uninformative definition of propositions as "anything that is either true or false" (p. 369), the argument threatens to become circular: what is propositional must be true or false, and what is true or false must be propositional. Moreover, Beardsley mostly assumes that knowledge must be propositional and inferential, and he simply posits that truth consists in some sort of correspondence with reality. As his idiosyncratic stipulation of "reveal" and his hasty response to intuitionism show, his approach is inhospitable to all nonempiricist epistemologies. Someone who resists his conclusions but does not challenge his framework is nearly forced by his argument to revert to the Proposition Theory he refutes at the outset. For his entire argument against other theories of artistic truth depends upon a propositionally inflected correspondence theory of truth, conjoined with an empiricist theory of knowledge.[24] Yet Beardsley himself must entertain the Proposition Theory for literary works, since they clearly contain the linguistic "vehicles" for propositions.

1.3 LITERARY PREDICATIONS

Because literary works employ language, literature poses additional challenges for Beardsley's anticognitivist metacriticism: "To make out a case for saying that a painting is true, or that music gives us knowledge, we must find some way in which they can do, without words, what words naturally and essentially can do. But in poems and stories we are already in the realm of language, of indicative moods and declarative sentences. And . . . there is not one word in poetry or fiction that does not, or could not, appear in some other discourse in which it would clearly be used to tell us something about the world" (p. 400). Not surprisingly, given the arguments of previous chapters, chapter 9 ("Literature and Knowledge") culminates in a contest between empiricism and intuitionism in which empiricist epistemology carries the day. It does so by admitting literature's cognitive capacities but restricting their importance, for the sake of aesthetic autonomy (what Beardsley calls "literary value"): "Of course literary works cannot be understood apart from their language; of course they have social roots and fruits; . . . of course the themes and theses of literary works are taken from, or contributed to, the whole life of [humankind]. But what makes literature literature, in part, must be some withdrawal from the world about it, an unusual degree of self-containedness and self-sufficiency that makes it capable of being contemplated with satisfaction in itself. And the secret of this detachment seems to lie in its capacity to play with . . . all the vast array of human experiences, including beliefs, without that personal allegiance and behavioral commitment to them that constitutes assertion in the fullest sense" (pp. 436–7). Such simultaneous admitting and restricting of literature's cognitive capacities requires a sophisticated argument. I discuss here only those parts of the argument which complete Beardsley's position on truth in art.

This position limits the occurrence of truth and falsity in literature to predications within literary works. Beardsley describes predications as follows: "Each distinguishable respect in which a discourse or part of a discourse may be said to be true or false I shall call a *predication* in that discourse.... A predication is statable in a 'that' clause, though it may not be so stated in the discourse" (p. 404). Unfortunately, like Beardsley's earlier definition of propositions, this description is circular: what can be said to be true or false in a discourse is a predication, and a predication is what can be said to be true or false in a discourse. The description is also ontologically vague. Beardsley introduces "predication" to avoid talking about propositions "as nonlinguistic entities, abstractions of some kind" (p. 404). Yet it is unclear whether "predication" actually avoids the same fate – unclear, because he says so little about the ontological status of predications. He obviously wants to keep them linked to suitable linguistic expressions. As we shall see, however, once he introduces the notion of nonasserted and implicit predications, the link to linguistic expressions becomes tenuous at best.

Beardsley says that predications in literature occur in (or in connection with) two sorts of sentences: reports, in which a story's situation, objects, and events are narrated; and reflections, "in which the narrator generalizes in some way, or reflects upon the situation" (p. 409). Both reports and reflections can be either explicit or implicit. Most literary reports involve "fictional sentences," defined as "sentences that contain references to fictitious persons, places, or things" (p. 410). To that extent, reports are not predications: "[F]ictional sentences do not really make predications, because their capacity for doing so assumes the existence of something that does not exist" (p. 413).[25] Explicit reflections such as the morals stated within Aesop's fables, by contrast, are not fictional. They can be predications. The difficult question is whether implicit reflections can be predications and thus either true or false. Beardsley's convoluted response (pp. 415–19) seems to be this: implicit reflections can be predications – understood as "either predications purportedly believed by the [dramatic] speaker or the ironically suggested contradictories of purported beliefs" (p. 416) – but it is extremely difficult to determine the content and weight of such predications.

The admission of predications into literary works, whether as nonfictive reports or as explicit and implicit reflections, does not settle the question of literature's cognitive capacities, however, since the distinction between fiction and nonfiction applies to literature as a whole. At this macrolevel Beardsley proposes a Nonassertion Theory of fiction. It builds on "a distinction between *uttering* a sentence and *asserting* it" (p. 420), the difference between, say, my quoting someone else's statement that the weather is miserable and my own claiming that the weather is miserable. Literature, being fiction, is like a quotation: "But a fiction, in the literary sense, is a discourse in which the Report-sentences are not asserted. They may still be true or false – except those which refer to nonexistent things – but the writer is not claiming that they are true; he indicates in some way that he neither believes them nor expects us to believe them" (pp. 420–1). At the level of literary reports, then, sentences in literature will be either unasserted predications or unasserted nonpredications.

But what about reflective predications? Beardsley argues that the "pragmatic context" of literary production rules against considering reflective predications to be asserted by the author (or, presumably, by anyone else, although Beardsley does not consider other possibilities for who could be making the assertion): "Does the act of writing a novel and publishing it, if the novel contains an implicit thesis, constitute a sufficient pragmatic context of the utterance to make it an assertion?... it seems best to say that it does not.... Thus even the Reflective predications of a literary work are unasserted; they are part of the story... or part of the act" (p. 422). Implicit in this account is a strong distinction between genres, such that when a publisher makes available a piece of nonfiction, say, Beardsley's *Aesthetics*, the predications within it are asserted, whereas when the same publisher publishes a piece of fiction, say, James Joyce's *Ulysses*, the predications within it are not asserted. Beardsley does not reflect on the peculiarities and historical novelty of this genre distinction, nor does he deal with genre-bending examples such as historical fiction. His Nonassertion Theory allows a literary work to contain true or false ideas that a reader can reasonably accept or reject. But no one outside of the work has asserted these ideas within the work, he says, and therefore the work is not a means of communicating ideas or beliefs to the reader. Nor is the literary work a source for the reader's beliefs, although understanding and enjoying the work presupposes certain beliefs on the reader's part (pp. 423–9).

Although not asserted, then, literary predications can be true or false and can be believed or disbelieved. Hence they can serve as potentially important hypotheses "worth testing on their own account" (p. 429). But the evidence for and against them cannot come from literary works themselves. The "cognitive value" of literature is merely heuristic – valuable, to be sure, but not fully cognitive: "The literary work does not... give us the evidence, and without the evidence the hypothesis can hardly be called knowledge; still, in scientific inquiry the hard thing is often not the testing of a hypothesis once we think of it, but the thinking of an original and fruitful hypothesis in the first place. Therefore literature may have immense cognitive value even if it merely suggests new hypotheses about human nature or society or the world, and even if only a few of these hypotheses turn out to be verifiable, perhaps after some analysis and refinement" (pp. 429–30). On Beardsley's epistemology, such literary hypotheses, if true, would be empirically true, and to count as empirically true they would need to be confirmed. Confirmation of an empirical hypothesis occurs "by deducing consequences from it with the help of general laws already known, and testing these consequences by observation" (p. 430).

The complication with literary hypotheses is that the most important ones "exist in literature only implicitly" and therefore cannot be subjected to straightforward inference in which their meaning does not change. The only way to confirm them, especially metaphorical ones, is to translate literary predications into "literal statements that are equivalent to the metaphor" (p. 431) and then to test the literal statements. Unlike intuitionists, who deny that literary cognitive content can be "literally paraphrased," Beardsley regards such paraphrasing as possible in principle, albeit "usually impossible in practice" (pp. 435–6). So he does not deny the cognitive value of literature, even though he makes that value dependent on extraliterary operations. Hence he can eat his empiricist cake and have it too. He can grant literary works a truth potential because of their linguistic character but make the confirmation of literary predications so unlikely that empirical science remains the paradigm of knowledge, and literature's greatest worth lies outside its truncated cognitive capacities.

No doubt intuitionists and adherents of Revelation Theory would regard Beardsley's minor concessions on literary truth like scraps from the master's table. Perhaps their objection could go like this: why would anyone bother with the considerable effort required to paraphrase and empirically confirm literary predications if these have not been asserted and if their truth and falsity has only a loose connection to literary value? So far as I can tell, Beardsley has no satisfactory answer to this question. In fact, I think his underlying theories of value and truth preclude a satisfactory answer. On Beardsley's "instrumentalist theory" of "aesthetic value," the worth of aesthetic objects depends on their capacity to produce aesthetic experiences of a certain magnitude. Aesthetic experiences have different magnitudes, according to their degree of unity, intensity, and complexity. The value of aesthetic objects, including works of literature, is their capacity to generate aesthetic experience (i.e., intense, coherent, and self-contained perceptual attention) "of a fairly great magnitude" (pp. 527–30). Accordingly, he rests the entire weight of literary interpretation, both its motivation and its outcome, on the aesthetic experience literary works make possible. The true value of literature is not the truth of literature but the work's "literary value."[26]

Now we are in a position to extract the general theory of truth that sustains Beardsley's denial of artistic truth and his devaluing of literary truth. Nowhere does Beardsley state his general truth theory in so many words. It is somewhat implicit, like the predications he finds important in literary works. Yet one can piece it together from the summaries already given for his denial of artistic truth and his account of literary predications. On Beardsley's conception, truth proper consists in the correspondence between linguistically formulated (or formulatable) beliefs and empirically perceived (or perceptible) facts. The criteria of truth are the rules of first-order logic and the principles of empirical science. Words, in their capacity to designate features (characteristics, properties) of the real world, are the basic units through which such correspondence occurs, and declarative sentences, in their primary meaning as statements of belief, are the main vehicles of truth. What makes declarative statements capable of carrying truth is both their syntax (the grammar of subject and predicate), which allows them to be or convey predications (or "propositions," a term Beardsley questions but nonetheless uses), and their pragmatics (their being asserted and assertible). Declarative sentences that share this syntax but lack the pragmatics of assertion can be true or false, but only in a derivative and incomplete sense. So too, the connotations of words and the secondary meaning of sentences can be truth-related, but only by virtue of their dependence on designations and statements, not in and of themselves. Moreover, supposed modes of expression or communication that do not employ language as their primary medium cannot be vehicles of truth, even though true and false statements can be made *about* paintings, musical compositions, and the like. The only modes that can have a full-blown "cognitive capacity" are ones in which declarative and sentential statements can be made. In other words, Beardsley conceives of truth as linguistically stated (or statable), logically consistent (or potentially consistent), and empirically confirmed (or confirmable) beliefs or predications about features of the real world.[27] His is a type of propositionally inflected correspondence theory in which "beliefs" and "predications" play the role that other correspondence theories assign to "propositions."[28]

Contemporary attempts to formulate a theory of artistic truth will need to employ an alternative to the general theory of truth supporting Beardsley's approach. I have not tried to hide my reservations about Beardsley's denial of artistic truth. Internally, it suffers from the inconsistencies and unclarities I have pointed out along the way. Externally, it sometimes misconstrues the claims of rival theories. Yet my reservations are tempered by the fact that Beardsley works out his conception in admirable detail, and he genuinely engages the claims of rival theories. Given the prevalence of scientism in Anglo-American philosophy during Beardsley's lifetime, he can be credited with a thorough attempt to find an equally legitimate place and role for the arts in modern culture while retaining science as the paradigm of knowledge. A contemporary and alternative account of artistic truth would need not only to surpass the limitations of empiricistic scientism but also to show how the cognitive functions of the arts are constitutive to their societal importance and aesthetic worth.

2

Reciprocations

The true being that becomes an object of love for us in art is finally the true
being of the human spirit itself.

Albert Hofstadter[1]

The difference between truth and untruth...cannot be reduced to...
vouching for the Being...of people and things.

Herman Rapaport[2]

The European schools of thought that analytic philosophers love to hate
are antiscientistic.[3] The love-hate relation is reciprocal. This is so of exis-
tentialism, the best-known school of continental philosophy in Beardsley's
day. It is also so of deconstruction, perhaps the most prominent continental counterpart to contemporary analytic and postanalytic philosophy. But
such stylized polarizations overlook continuities between the apparent opponents and fail to recognize how one side serves to correct the other. A
contemporary attempt to theorize artistic truth cannot afford to be short-
sighted in these ways. Instead it should foster a dialogue between the analytic
and continental schools, both of which have come to recognize the limitations of empiricistic scientism. To surpass those limitations with regard to
artistic truth requires an alternative to the propositionally inflected correspondence theory of truth that sustains Beardsley's metacritical denial.

Continental philosophy has something to offer in that regard. Initial
clues to an alternative come from two directions, both of which oppose
the restriction of truth bearers to propositions or their equivalents. One
is Albert Hofstadter's more expansive version of correspondence theory,
which incorporates elements from what Beardsley labels Revelation Theory and Intuitionist Theory into an existential affirmation of artistic truth
(section 2.1). The other is Herman Rapaport's deconstruction of the ontology that underlies both Hofstadter's affirmation and Beardsley's denial –
a postmetaphysical effort whose general theory of truth appears to be both

antipropositional and anticorrespondence (section 2.2). I summarize each of their approaches, in order to compare them with Beardsley's approach and with one another. In this way I hope to bring out more forcefully how an adequate theory of artistic truth must surpass empiricistic scientism (section 2.3). Here "surpass" is a rough equivalent for the German term *aufheben*, familiar to dialectical thinkers since Hegel. Surpassing scientistic empiricism is not the same as rejecting it outright or simply leaving it behind. My critical hermeneutics assumes that thinkers like Beardsley had important insights; that these can serve to correct problematic claims in another approach; and that they need to be reframed as a result of having undergone dialogical correction themselves.

2.1 EXISTENTIAL AFFIRMATION

Albert Hofstadter's book *Truth and Art* distinguishes three comprehensive forms of truth: theoretical truth (the truth of statement), practical truth (truth of things), and spiritual truth (truth of spirit). Because all three are forms of adequation between intellect and thing, Hofstadter claims to employ "the traditional formula for truth" as correspondence: *adaequatio intellectus et rei* (p. 91). The differences among these three forms of truth stem from the direction of adequation. Theoretical truth involves the adequation of intellect to thing; practical truth involves the adequation of thing to intellect; and spiritual truth, which incorporates and synthesizes the first two forms, involves a mutual conformity between thing and intellect. The truth of art, like the truth of religion, ethics, and philosophy, is spiritual rather than simply theoretical or practical.

Theory, Practice, Spirit

As in much twentieth-century philosophy, the key to Hofstadter's conception of truth lies in his theory of language. He introduces this theory after criticizing three philosophies of art. Ernst Cassirer's "expression theory" radically subjectivizes the phenomenon of art, Hofstadter claims (p. 15). Jacques Maritain's "joint revelation theory" does not recognize the genuine creativity of imaginative vision, "in which *more is arrived at than is possessed to begin with and in which the point is to arrive at this more*" (p. 35). And Benedetto Croce's equation of expression with intuition, although it correctly identifies art as the primary way in which human imagination "first comes into being and remains in being" (p. 49), fails to recognize the qualitative difference between genuine art and everyday aesthetic activity. To acknowledge this difference, and to surpass the expression and joint revelation theories, we must understand art as a language "in which meaning is associated in an essential way with a special medium" (p. 51). Science and religion are also languages in this sense.

Already here we find an instructive contrast with Beardsley's approach. Whereas Beardsley criticizes what he calls Revelation Theory and Intuitionist Theory for failing to demonstrate how artworks can contain or contribute to propositional and inferential knowledge, Hofstadter criticizes the same theories for failing to recognize the element of creative imagination that characterizes art as a human language. By calling art a language, Hofstadter is not saying art provides "primary meanings" and "designations" of the sort Beardsley privileges. Rather he is suggesting a hermeneutical and nonbehavioral account of language.

On Hofstadter's account, language is fundamentally meaningful articulation: "[A]ll language, whether in science, practical life, or spiritual life, has the same generic character of meaning. Namely, all language articulates human being. Differences that separate language into the languages of science, practice, and spirit, are due to the different ends toward which they are directed. Each such end is related to an ideal of truth" (p. 52). Articulation, then, not expression or revelation, and certainly not designation, is the central function of language. Articulation of what? Articulation "of human being," says Hofstadter, articulation of what it means to be human. Just as we normally perceive nonhuman entities as having meaning, so we normally hear utterances or read inscriptions as articulations of human pain, desire, and the like: "[W]e hear them *as* utterances of human beings, and consequently we hear, as their specifically linguistic meaning, the special kind of entity that belongs to man" (p. 71). The function of language "consists in opening for linguistic imagination a segment of human being as a meaning. . . . Language is the medium, the pathway, and the mode of operation of the imagination by which we become aware of human existence – the existential imagination" (p. 73). And since articulation, unlike expression and revelation, does not presuppose established content or ready-made forms, the function of language is fundamentally creative: "Articulation is the process by which a living formative impulse works itself out. It is creation . . . out of that relative nothing which the existent . . . is before it has attained to the status of being. In speech, man articulates his being out of the relative nothingness which he is as mere existent (or nonexistent)" (pp. 85–6).

Rather than modify this approach to accommodate logical positivist or analytic concerns, Hofstadter follows Heidegger in deriving propositions, sentences, and statements from an existential account of linguistic meaning. Statement (*Aussage*, in Heidegger's account) has a fundamentally "existence-disclosing character," Hofstadter argues (p. 73). It has two semantical functions, namely, referring and predicating.[4] In referring, a statement picks out and exhibits an entity as an entity. In predicating, a statement selects and sets forth an attribute and thereby determines the exhibited entity. Together these two functions serve both the "presentation of objectivity" and the "manifestation of subjectivity," such that the statement "gives us the two [i.e., objectivity and subjectivity] in their unity" (p. 81). And, as oral utterance, the statement makes all of this audible. It is as much an audible articulation of human existence as is the cry of pain: "[L]ike the cry of pain in its general linguistic function, even the statement form, apparently so distant from the selfhood of the self, also makes a totality of human being accessible to the linguistic imagination by way of the saying of it" (p. 82). Hence existential articulation characterizes statements just as much as it characterizes other forms of linguistic utterance, and the asserting of propositions, which Beardsley considers primary in language usage, is itself a mode of existential articulation.

"Truth of statement" is the first of three comprehensive modes of linguistic validity in Hofstadter's account. As the adequation of intellect to thing, such "theoretical" truth consists of an identity between the entity intended by the statement and the entity as it is: "We might therefore say that statement, as such, articulates a human aiming at what-is. This aiming is an attempt at . . . the uncovering of what-is. If the effort succeeds, so that the intended entity is selfsame with the real entity, the statement is true. It uncovers the entity . . ." (p. 97). Assertion is the concrete linguistic form in which people pursue this ideal of theoretical truth (pp. 98–101).[5]

The second comprehensive mode is practical truth or the "truth of things." Here the ideal is the adequation of thing to intellect, in accordance with human will. Such "practical truth" consists of an agreement between an entity as it is and a concept of what that entity ought to be. The thing is true "if it conforms" to this concept, this standard, and false "if it fails to conform" (p. 105). Performatives, imperatives, and valuations are the concrete linguistic forms in which people pursue such conformity.[6] Although we can distinguish between teleological standards (ends, goods, and values) and deontological standards (rules, laws, and obligations), all of them derive their force from a human will to govern existence, whether as groups or as individuals.

But this introduces a limitation within practical truth, one that complements a limitation within theoretical truth. Whereas the pursuit of theoretical truth restricts the self's comportment toward an entity, requiring the self to be (or become) "identical in intention with the existent" (p. 104), the pursuit of practical truth subjects us to a self-imposed "ought-to-govern" that can never be grounded in practical life itself (pp. 120–5). The scope of human governance cannot be derived from the will to govern. Hence, "the limitation of practical life consists precisely in its inherent lack of limitation. . . . Something else must give it a limit and provide it with measure" (p. 127).

What limits and thereby liberates practical life lies in the third and most comprehensive mode of linguistic validity: the truth of spirit. Spirit, Hofstadter writes, "is subjectivity in search of the truth of its being" (p. 174). It is a mode of human existence that encompasses understanding and will within itself. As spirit, human beings "exist in such a way as to comprehend both uncovering and governing, both understanding and will, in the unity of a new truth" (pp. 128–9). The truth of spirit transforms the adequation of intellect to thing (i.e., theoretical truth) and the adequation of thing to intellect (i.e., practical truth) into a mutual adequation between intellect and thing where the thing's concept (what it is and ought to be) and the self's concept of the thing are identical (pp. 130–1). For this to occur, the self must be a person that recognizes the "thing" as another person. In such an interpersonal relation of mutual recognition, "governance by violence" gives way to "governance by consent," and the understanding of "brute facts" and "mere means" gives way to respect for the "cogency" of another person's will and understanding (pp. 132–5). This leads Hofstadter to identify "the field in which spiritual truth is most authentically at home" as "that of personal interrelationships, namely the ethical and, eventually and ultimately, the religious." Like Hegel, however, he regards art and the aesthetic dimension as "the first form in which spiritual truth exhibits itself, namely the form of its immediacy or the form of imaginative presentation" (p. 136).

Hence the truth of spirit is not simply the truth of our statements with regard to entities or the truth of entities with regard to our practical purposes. Rather, in Hegelian terms, it is the truth of entities in and for themselves. Spiritual truth occurs "objectively" when an entity's intention and its realized existence are identical. To be objectively true in this sense, the entity "must be one whose being . . . is a realization of its *own* intention and whose *own* intention uncovers itself eventually as what it is" (p. 140). Spiritual truth occurs "subjectively" when such an entity shows itself to us "as being what we ourselves intend as understanding of truth, and . . . what we ourselves intend as willing of truth" (p. 142). Hofstadter calls the objective side "truth of being" and the subjective side "truth of recognition" (p. 153). This, then, is the general conception of spiritual truth governing his account of artistic truth. Clearly it is a more expansive conception than the empiricist strictures under which Beardsley denies that nonliterary artworks can be true.

Truth in Art

Hofstadter introduces his account of artistic truth by discussing the aesthetics of nature. This discussion is, for the most part, speculative and uninformative. Yet it introduces two concepts – cogency and seizure – that have relevance for our topic. It is specifically in the aesthetic recognition of natural beauty, he suggests, that the limitation of practical life first shatters. This happens because a reciprocal movement sets in between the cogency of the (naturally beautiful) object and a seizure that occurs to the (aesthetically attentive) self: "In this phenomenon the beautiful thing exhibits a real and effective power, the power it has of persuading the self of the thing's own truth" (p. 159). In such aesthetic experience "we identify our practical intention with that of the object, . . . because of the persuasive power of cogency of the object itself. . . . Aesthetic experience is living in the grip of the valid object" (p. 160). Cogency, then, is the "authoritative weight" and "effective binding power" that marks genuinely beautiful objects. Cogency is to aesthetic experience (and, more broadly, to spiritual existence) what "evidence" is to cognition and what "normativity" (my term) is to practical life: all three are figures of validity that combine authority and power (pp. 161–2).[7] And the seizure we experience aesthetically occurs in an act of self-giving love (p. 165).[8]

This account of nonartistic aesthetic experience provides the basis for Hofstadter's discussion of artistic truth. The final chapter, titled "The Spiritual Truth of Art" (pp. 171–212), begins by emphasizing the importance of spiritual truth. Spiritual truth is the highest destiny of human existence, Hofstadter suggests: "[I]n the life of the human spirit a tiny fragment of being has open to itself the possibility of meaningfulness and truth of being. . . . [Human] dignity consists in [our] being the entity whose existence is a task the only solution of which . . . is truth of spiritual being" (p. 173). Accordingly, both theory and practice must "be brought into the unity of truth of our own . . . being of spirit, on pain of the neglect and consequent destruction of our humanity" (p. 174). Such unification, in turn, is made possible by the "spiritual element in will" that enables us to love the truth of being, which itself "seizes will by its cogency and persuades it to cling to it" (p. 175). In this love lies the key to personhood, as distinct from mere selfhood or subjectivity. People exist as persons, Hofstadter claims, only insofar as they have "opened" themselves "to love." One "finds the truth of [one's] own being ultimately only in discovering, in love, the truth of being that lies beyond [one]" (p. 176).

What does this have to do with art? Hofstadter applies the notion of spiritual truth to art in three respects: truth in the artwork (pp. 178–83), truth in artistic interpretation and creation (pp. 183–99), and artistic truth in relation to other forms of spiritual truth (pp. 209–12).[9]

Truth in Artwork Hofstadter insists that the artwork is not so much true about or true to something else as it is true in and of itself. In this way he avoids the choice posed by empiricists such as Beardsley and Hospers who deny that "knowledge by acquaintance" can be genuine knowledge. We can put his point like this: the artwork manifests the truth of being by being true in its very own being. This does not mean that the artwork lacks import or neither expresses nor represents. Rather, it means that the artwork brings external import into itself. What the artwork expresses or represents is internal to itself. The artwork is an aesthetic symbol, according to Hofstadter. As aesthetic, it provides a way to seek the truth of being. As symbol, it articulates this search for (and discovery of) truth of being, especially truth of spiritual being. Unlike the articulation that occurs in statements and practical utterances, however, the aesthetic symbol – the artwork – "*is*, as such, the entity that it intends" (p. 179).

For example, the meaning or import of the horse of Selene sculpted by Phidias "contains two essential components, the beautiful horse and the human admiration of it." The first component does not represent an actual horse but, as an image, brings "whatever is of import in a horse outside" into the artwork itself (pp. 180–1). Similarly, the human admiration of that image does not express the artist's or spectator's or a surrounding culture's attitude but, as an articulation, brings "admiring love" into the artwork itself (pp. 181–2). Summarizing, Hofstadter writes: "The only pointing . . . in the work lies within it. The admiration articulated in it points to or intends the image presented in it, and the image presented in it fulfills that intention. The meaning of the work as a whole is a certain *fulfilled intention* (the core of all truth), a certain love in the presence of its beloved" (p. 182). Presenting the image and articulating the admiration, and thereby containing these within its own import, the artwork "intends as work" exactly "what it itself is." Hence there is no need "to look beyond the work to something outside it to understand what it means and is" (p. 183). Perhaps we can say that, on Hofstadter's account, the artwork's truth is strictly internal and nonreferential. His account is almost exactly the opposite of what propositionally inflected correspondence theories say concerning the general notion of truth. For such theories, nonreferential import that is not about something outside itself cannot be true or false, both because it cannot be propositional and because it cannot correspond to something else.

Interpretation and Creation   Such internalism shapes Hofstadter's account of "the beholder's interpretation" and the artist's "creation" of the artwork. Both activities have their truth. Aesthetic "beholding" is a spiritual form of understanding, and artistic "creating" is a spiritual exercise of the will. Whereas the first elevates the truth of statement into the truth of interpretative projection, the second elevates the truth of things into the truth of loving formation. Spiritual concern for true being – love in the grip of a cogent object – is what beholding and creating have in common.

Beholding, says Hofstadter, goes beyond our aesthetic experience of nature in grasping the meaning of an aesthetic symbol. The beholder of the artwork must "grasp the aesthetic experience of which the work is the articulation" and, to do this, must "project an interpretation of the work" (p. 184). This "interpretative project" is "*a projected concern* which . . . intends to coincide with the concern articulated in the work." Although the work's meaning is sufficiently "indefinite" to allow various interpretations, beholding aims at "actual participation in the work," at an identity between the beholder's concern and the concern articulated in the work (p. 185). Such an identity is the truth of aesthetic beholding, in which the truth of statement is surpassed. Aesthetic beholders of an artwork can "enter into the truth of the *spiritual* being that has been articulated in the work and thus participate in such truth on [their] own account" (p. 186).

What permits such participation, in turn, is the truth of artistic creation. The artist's aim is "to form a symbol whose meaning is a form of concern in the aesthetic dimension." The creative process is not guided by an ordinary concept that can serve as an explicit standard, but by an "aesthetic idea" (Kant) whose conceptually inexhaustible meaning combines "a certain concern" with "a specific imaginative form" (p. 187). In the resulting artwork, says Hofstadter, "the spiritualized will articulates itself in a definite form" (p. 189). And because the will is at work, an "essential *rightness* . . . characterizes a successful work of art" (p. 189). A successful artwork has a "clear, complete, and necessary" form, in accordance with the artist's aesthetic idea (p. 192). Such a work can be said to be true, for it follows "a living will's demand for the truth of its own being" (p. 193).[10]

As the focal point for both aesthetic beholding and artistic creation, then, the artwork "is a fragmentary articulation of something that can never be fully articulated, but that lies at the ground of our being and demands utterance. It is the primal thrust of the will-to-be toward its own truth" (p. 190). "The love of true being . . . lies at the heart of all aesthetic-artistic construction." The idea of the artwork is "the total complex volition" that spirit channels into "a love for true being." This love "will be satisfied only when it finds the rightness and necessity of true being in its object." Ultimately, the artwork's truth is its being "true to the truth of the spiritualized will's being. . . . In so far as it is aesthetic, the work of art *is* the spiritualized will as true, in the particular form of meaning in a symbol that is what it symbolizes; it is itself an instance of love in the form of an ontological symbol" (pp. 198–9).

Spiritual Truth Like Hegel, Hofstadter gives art special status as a site of "spiritual truth" but situates it at a lower level than religion. Compared with natural beauty, art contains the "higher ranges" of the love of true being, because art directs our love toward "the true being of the human spirit itself." Art is "a form of human existence" that, in its very being, lets us solve "the problem of existing" (p. 209). Compared with the full range of what human existence requires, however, "the truth of art is a limited truth." It can only be "a symbolical medium" that articulates truth in "a purposely isolated section of the world." Phidias's imaged horse "bears a great burden of truth" but "it is, after all, an imaged horse," and human beings need more: they need, for the truth of their own being, "the living reality of another who really exists" (p. 210).[11] Yet art can articulate the "forms of concern" that such a search for ultimate recognition can take: admiration, grief, gladness, "carefree unconcern," or "piercing despair," for example. So art can reveal the "possibilities of human existence" and "the shapes of love of true being" (p. 211). But art cannot make them actual. For that we must move "into the sphere of ethics and religion," where "the problem of human existence" is not limited to a symbolical universe; here, on the contrary, we face our responsibility for what we do "with the whole of what *is*" (p. 212).

Dialectical Corrections

Despite many obvious differences between Hofstadter's and Beardsley's approaches to the topic of artistic truth, they have at least three things in common. First, they subscribe to a correspondence theory of truth. Second, they derive their accounts of artistic truth from a philosophy of language. Third, they insist on the autonomy of the artwork and anchor this autonomy in the artwork's aesthetic dimension. The differences between their approaches stem in large part from differences concerning the nature and significance of correspondence, of language, and of the aesthetic dimension. Furthermore, it is precisely in these respects that Hofstadter's existential affirmation of artistic truth provides important corrections to Beardsley's metacritical denial.

In Beardsley's vocabulary, Hofstadter's account of artistic truth is a version of Revelation Theory that bears traces of an intuitionist epistemology. The account depends on a comprehensive notion of correspondence and an equally expansive definition of language. Whereas Beardsley compresses truth-making correspondence to that between asserted beliefs and empirical facts, Hofstadter decompresses it to include all adequations between cultural endeavors and the "objects" of cultivation, including the self and other persons. This allows Hofstadter both to recognize the legitimate and worthwhile role of science in the pursuit of truth and to resist turning science into the paradigm of knowledge. As we saw earlier, Beardsley understands language as the behavioral medium in which people convey information about their feelings, beliefs, and other characteristics. He regards the formulation of beliefs about external "reality" as the most important linguistic function. Hofstadter, by contrast, portrays language as the way in which what it means to be human gets articulated, with the creative work of imagination being central to this process. This allows Hofstadter to do greater justice than Beardsley can to the multidimensional character of language in all its syntactic, semantic, and pragmatic complexity. It also enables Hofstadter to avoid the causal stimulus-response model that bedevils Beardsley's theory of language, as well as the concomitant reduction of illocutionary meaning to perlocutionary effects. On Hofstadter's theory language is more fully intersubjective and dialogical than it is on Beardsley's.

These fundamental differences concerning correspondence and language frame a central divergence about truth bearers. For Beardsley, assertible beliefs or predications carried by declarative sentences are the only bearers of truth, in the strict sense. Hofstadter does not deny that sentences and statements, by virtue of their referential and predicative functions, can "carry" truth, although he might prefer simply to say that they can *be* true or false. But he anchors this truth capacity in their being means of articulating human existence. In this way he ranges sentences and statements along-side a virtual plethora of truth bearers. In principle, any result of cultural endeavor could "carry" truth or be true or false, whether theoretically, practically, or spiritually. No doubt more chaste epistemologists like Beardsley would shudder at such profligacy. Yet Hofstadter's approach has a double virtue. First, it returns reference and predication from the thin world of epistemological theory to the thick world of human culture. Second, it does not have such a restricted notion of how people use sentences in ordinary language that it defines nonscientific truth out of existence.

Accordingly, whereas Beardsley finds artworks mostly incapable of truth or falsity because they do not contain linguistic predications, Hofstadter finds all artworks capable of being true just by virtue of being themselves. Initially this equating of being true with truly being seems counterintuitive. Beardsley might dismiss it as sheer nonsense. Yet it gains some plausibility when one recalls that the truth Hofstadter has in mind is "spiritual": it is intrinsically personal and intersubjective. Such artistic truth cannot be forced into a one-model-fits-all theory according to which only certain functions of certain linguistic products have any true purchase on a "reality" that has already been assumed to be extramental, impersonal, and "objective." Insofar as art is a range of cultural practices and patterns of interaction in which people participate, a "correspondence" between people might be more crucial for artistic truth than one between facts and beliefs or predications. There is a danger, of course, that Hofstadter's intersubjective "correspondence" will float into clouds of ethical platitudes. Perhaps that is why he introduces the notion of cogency: the cogency of a person's life, and the cogency of an object embodying human life.[12] Moreover, he posits a reciprocation between an artwork's import and the projected concerns of both artist and spectator.

This suggests that the truth of an artwork is both stable and dynamic, both intrinsic to the artwork and open to creative interpretation, as Hans-Georg Gadamer also argues. For Hofstadter, creative interpretation, not fictive perception,[13] is central to both the making and appropriating of art. Whereas Beardsley carefully distinguishes among descriptive, interpretative, and evaluative statements,[14] Hofstadter would consider all of them intrinsically hermeneutic. He would say that all talk about art "paraphrases," but not in Beardsley's sense: Hofstadter's theory of language does not permit a clean distinction between prosaic paraphrase and fictive predication, for example, or between literal and metaphorical language. Indeed, if language itself is an imaginative articulation of human existence, as Hofstadter insists, then "connotation" and "metaphor," not "designation" and "literal meaning," will be constitutive for all language usage, including the making of "descriptive," "interpretative," and "evaluative" remarks about artworks.

Although Hofstadter does not say this "in so many words," it is a clear implication of his theory of language.

The differences between these two approaches to artistic truth could hardly be more stark and comprehensive. Not surprisingly, then, without Beardsley's having addressed this specific version of Revelation Theory, his denial of artistic truth calls attention to problematic aspects of Hofstadter's affirmation. These involve three issues on which Beardsley has strong positions: criteria for truth, the "objectivity" of the artwork, and the accessibility of truth. Without embracing Beardsley's empiricism and scientism, one can rearticulate his critique of Revelation Theory to show the limits to Hofstadter's approach.

In the first place, Hofstadter's generous construal of "correspondence" makes it nearly impossible to identify criteria for theoretical, practical, and spiritual truth. For example, even if one grants that theoretical truth consists of an identity between the constatively intended entity and the entity as it is, one needs clues about what marks such an identity. Otherwise the notion of "identity" will be so unlimited that either all statements and assertions or no statements and assertions can be said to achieve it. Hofstadter's formulation leaves open the prospect that either all statements are true or they are all false. This would make theoretical truth in any careful sense either insignificant (if theoretical falsity were impossible) or unachievable (if all statements were false).

So too, when Hofstadter characterizes artistic truth as the artwork's being true to its very own being, he sidesteps the question as to what distinguishes a "true" artwork from one that is not true. We can assume that for Hofstadter an artwork's truth has to do with the quality or character of its "import." His notion of artistic import is so vague, however, as to be unusable for generating criteria of artistic truth. The notion is vague in three respects. First, it does not explain how "whatever is of import" in the world outside the work becomes import within the work itself. Second, it fails to address the universality and particularity of art-internal import. Third, it establishes no guidelines for appropriate and inappropriate interpretations of such import.

The discussion of Hofstadter's favorite example – Phidias's horse of Selene – illustrates the problems I have in mind. He says this sculpture's import articulates "whatever is of import in a horse outside," wedded to an "admiring love" of that image (pp. 180–2). Surely this account lacks precision. A few paragraphs earlier he had said this sculpture is "a representation of the ontical truth of the horse." Which horse, one might ask: the sculpted horse, some particular horse, or the horse as a class or kind? Hofstadter doesn't say. He does say that this ontical truth of the horse "transcends any merely animal beauty." It is "of the sort that the Greek mind found in the world as a cosmos" and "that simply manifests itself in one proper degree in the peculiar form of the horse" (p. 179). Is the ontical truth in question not horse-specific, then, but simply an emanation of the One Truth? (I find more than a trace of Plotinus in Hofstadter's account of spiritual truth.) Yet Hofstadter claims that we understand this sculpture "only when we grasp the beauty of the represented horse as a specific mode of beauty" (p. 179). In what, specifically, does that beauty consist? The only quality hinted at in this paragraph is the horse's "nobility." But which horse is the "noble animal" in which "the Greek mind" discerned "truth of being": the sculpted horse, or (certain) living horses as a class? From Hofstadter's compressed language, one simply cannot tell. Nor can one tell much about the source and quality of the "admiring love" supposedly wedded to the image of the horse. Since Hofstadter rules out the artist's, the spectator's, and the surrounding culture's attitudes, the love in question seems to be a generic human love. But if this sculpture's import came down to generically human love of (a) the sculpted horse or (b) some particular horse or (c) the class of all horses, why would this particular sculpture be needed to articulate this "truth"? And how could any particular sculpture "of" any horse be anything other than true?

These critical questions need not lead to Beardsley's argument that, absent the use of propositions or predications, nonliterary artworks can only call attention to universals (such as the horse's [which horse's?] dignity) and cannot be true or false with respect to those universals. Yet my questions do indicate the fundamentally correct intuition within Beardsley's argument: to be capable of truth, artworks (or their import) must also be capable of falsity, and there must be art-internal ways to distinguish between artistic truth and falsity. Such ways Hofstadter does not provide. Nor is it apparent how he could.

A second set of concerns, closely connected to the issue of alethic criteria, pertains to the "objectivity" of the artwork. I do not support Beardsley's and Hofstadter's fixation on the autonomous work of art. Yet I share Beardsley's intuition that, to tie artistic truth to (the import of) the artwork itself, one's theory needs to elaborate the artwork's independence from the processes of its creation and appropriation, not to mention from the sociohistorical conditions that inform such processes. Certainly elaborating this independence is Beardsley's strength, as well as the fatal armor that traps his metacriticism into an unremittingly anticognitivist stance. Hofstadter has nothing to match Beardsley's "objectivism" concerning the artwork as such. Although Hofstadter uses the concepts of "being" and "cogency" to argue for the artwork's independence and internal validity, his arguments turn the artwork into an inherently incomplete conduit of the search for overarching spiritual truth. Ultimately, what makes the artwork true is not its particular being but its participation in "the true being of the human spirit itself" (p. 209). Nor does the specifically formal or aesthetic cogency of a particular artwork matter nearly as much as the "truth of being" as a whole that (through the artwork) "seizes will by its cogency and persuades it to cling to it" (p. 175).

To put the point crassly, artworks matter on Hofstadter's theory only insofar as they are midwives to personhood, not because of intrinsic and unique worth they themselves might have. Or, to put it paradoxically, the true being by virtue of which artworks can be true is not what they are but what they are not.

Hence Hofstadter both denigrates art relative to ethics and religion and renders artistic truth inaccessible. I suggested earlier that he corrects Beardsley's scientism, yet does not deny science's role in the pursuit of truth. Thanks in part to Hofstadter's affirming artistic truth, he has more success than Beardsley does in recognizing art's significance in human culture. Unfortunately these contributions rely on a hierarchical ordering of cultural endeavors. Hofstadter's ordering is more complex than Beardsley's bipolarity – science on top and everything else beneath – yet it renders artistic truth both insufficient and inaccessible. For Hofstadter, true revelation lies in ethics and religion, where symbolical mediation drops away and persons meet persons. Indeed, there they meet "the whole of what *is*" (p. 212), not in an artistic glass darkly, but ethically and religiously face-to-face. It is precisely this exaggerated double bind, this mystifying denigration of art, this rendering art oh-so-special-but-never-quite-enough, this making artistic truth both insufficient and inaccessible, that Beardsley, the straight-shooting, sober-minded empiricist, so efficiently unravels. Better to deny artistic truth altogether, he seems to say, than to sanctify art as the vestibule to ethics and religion (or to speculative philosophy, if one is of Hegelian persuasion).

But what if neither metacritical denial nor existential affirmation is sufficient? What if Beardsley's and Hofstadter's approaches share underlying assumptions concerning correspondence, language, and autonomy that are themselves problematic? Then the mutual corrections I have staged between them would also need to be reexamined. A Derridean deconstruction of our topic will show why further scrutiny is required.

2.2 POSTMETAPHYSICAL DECONSTRUCTION

Although Herman Rapaport's book never mentions Beardsley or Hofstadter, *Is There Truth in Art?* can be read as dismantling both of their theories. On the one hand, Rapaport dismisses any attempt to theorize truth as an epistemic or ontological correspondence. On the other hand, he challenges all attempts to tie artistic truth to distinctively human existence. Imagining his own work as "a reprise" of Jacques Derrida's *The Truth in Painting*,[15] Rapaport tries to unsettle both the denial and the affirmation that there is truth in art. But the denial he disturbs follows from continental poststructuralism, rather than from analytic metacriticism, and the affirmation is one that prevails in the Western metaphysical tradition prior to Nietzsche: "[M]y purpose here is to inquire into how the question of truth in art needs to be thought from the hither side of its having been deconstructed and discredited. . . . [T]he .

truth in art persists in the wake of its demise because it is neither an entity or content that has been put into the work nor a transcendental universalizing concept or ground that exists outside the work as a guarantor of its authenticity as art" (p. ix). Rapaport shares Derrida's suspicion of both substantial truth bearers (such as artworks or their "truth content") and universal criteria of truth (such as correspondence or coherence). Indeed, he wishes to undo the entire metaphysical framework surrounding such notions of truth. His method is less one of philosophical argument against other theories than of philosophically informed commentaries on particular artworks. He offers "a thick description of truth from a postmetaphysical orientation" (p. x).

Rather than reconstruct Rapaport's commentaries, which are instructive in their own right, let me summarize the theoretical gist of his approach to the question of truth in art. This is an amalgam of insights and claims from Heidegger, Derrida, and Emmanuel Lévinas, an antitheory having premises and arguments but few firm conclusions. Two such premises justify the book's emphasis on commentary: first, that "the question of truth in art ought to be considered 'site specific' – dependent on the particular work in which truth is disclosed," and, second, that the "philosophical implications" of particular "cultural works" are "at least as important" as those of the philosophies from which Rapaport takes his bearings (p. x). These two premises already suggest a philosophical conception of artistic truth, it seems to me. According to that conception, truth can be "disclosed," can be disclosed in (and only in?) particular artworks, and can be disclosed in such a way that major philosophical implications follow (concerning the question of truth itself?). But there is no human agency for this process of disclosure, as we shall see, and therefore also neither a structural location nor a set of criteria according to which the disclosure of truth (or truth as disclosure) can be distinguished from nondisclosure (or untruth). That, at least, I take to be the theoretical gist of Rapaport's approach, as I now seek to show from his first chapter.

Metaphysical Crossroads

Chapter 1 begins by reviewing the Western metaphysical tradition surrounding the question of truth in art (pp. 1–11). Rapaport identifies two polarities in this tradition, each of which art has been thought to mediate: the "ontological" difference between beings and Being, and the "existential" difference between the human and the inhuman. Located at the intersection of these two polarities, art was assigned the task of aligning human existence with cosmic order. In such alignment truth was thought to consist. Art helped verify that beings, and especially human beings, are grounded in Being, in cosmic order. Citing Erwin Panofsky, Rapaport claims that Western metaphysics gave art the task of manifesting "the Idea – *the inspired thoughtful*

form given to matter by the artist" (p. 2). The differences between, say, Aristotle
and Plotinus, or between medieval and Renaissance conceptions, are differences in emphasis but not in paradigm. Although Aristotle emphasizes art's
ability to provide insight into human excellence, and Plotinus its ability to
convey divine truth, both place art at the crossroads between beings and
Being and between the human and the inhuman (whether divine, subhu-
man, or not fully human). Similarly, the medievals, inspired by the doctrine
of incarnation, may have married Aristotle with Plotinus, and Renaissance
figures, newly fascinated with human perspective, may have challenged this
marriage, but art's truth function still connected human existence with cosmic order. All of this began to change in the eighteenth and nineteenth
centuries, as art became a field of social and cultural critique. Only in the
twentieth century, however, did certain artists and philosophers thoroughly
challenge the ontological-existential paradigm for asking about truth in art.

Friedrich Nietzsche is "the most significant precursor of a postmetaphysical consideration of art and truth," according to Rapaport (p. 11). We have
art, says Nietzsche, not to live the truth, not to align human existence with
cosmic order, but to avoid dying of the truth – to avoid both the destructive
demands of metaphysical order and our own perversity, which metaphysics
papers over: "Art [for Nietzsche] takes the place of a truth we cannot acknowledge because of truth's overpowering and humiliating irrefutability.
It is because the truth *is* true that we cannot face it" (p. 14). Yet, as Nietzsche
himself recognizes, this gives art a new truth function, namely, to expose
the truth about truth, also about the truth art itself was supposed to convey
within a metaphysical frame. This "displacement of one truth by another"
is a type of "restitution," which Rapaport takes in a Derridean direction
(pp. 11–13).[16]

Whereas Nietzsche permits "the metaphysical persistence of art *as* art,"
Heidegger opposes this through "an understanding of art that comes *prior*
to the advent of the Idea" (p. 15), prior to the ontological differentiation
between beings and Being, prior to the existential differentiation between
the human and the inhuman.[17] What Heidegger seeks is "a truth that pre-
cedes the formalization of the ontological difference between beings and
Being which metaphysics constructs so that [this difference] can be bridged"
(p. 17). The advent of such preontological truth would signal "an a priori
destruction of truth as the metaphysical ligature between beings and Being" (p. 16). It would release art from the task of mediating ontological and
existential differences. Instead art could be a site for the occurrence of "a
more originary difference that came prior to its metaphysical formalization"
and that "Heidegger's considerations of truth ... attempt to name or describe" (p. 17). Together with Derrida's notion of *la différance* and Levinas's
emphasis on "the otherwise than Being," Heidegger's excavation of "a
more originary difference" gives Rapaport a way to regard truth in art as
"otherwise-than-human" (pp. 16–19). Such truth would precede or exceed

the ontological and existential differences that traditionally have defined the "human" import of art. Indeed, Rapaport's subsequent commentaries aim to argue "that the otherwise-than-human is especially crucial to a consideration of truth from various postmetaphysical perspectives and that its ethical and political consequences are vexing and unpredictable in ways that elude a strictly ideological scripting of ideas" (p. 19).

Originary Difference

For Heidegger, the more originary difference – the truth before metaphysical truth – is an event or process of *Seinsvergessenheit*. Rapaport explains this as "the forgetting or oblivion of Being" in "an appropriative event (*Ereignis*) wherein the relation between beings and Being is disappropriated (*Enteignis*)" (p. 15). He traces the emergence of this more originary difference in three stages: Heidegger's dismantling of the ontological difference between beings and Being (pp. 19–26), his deconstruction of the existential difference between the human and the inhuman (pp. 26–9), and his postmetaphysical restitution of these differences "as a destabilizing interplay between concealment and unconcealment" (pp. 29–35; quotation from p. 34).

Ontological Difference   Rapaport finds the key to Heidegger's postmetaphysical conception of truth in a contrast Heidegger draws between *veritas* and *aletheia* in the 1942–3 seminar on *Parmenides*.[18] The Roman notion of *veritas* turns truth into a hard-and-fast distinction between what is the case and what is not. This distinction necessarily serves the domination of one over an other. It is subject-centered and imperialistic. Against *veritas*, Heidegger presents the Greek term *aletheia*. *Aletheia* indicates "an attunement to beings that depends on the freedom of Dasein to be 'open' and not bound by . . . rigid directedness, such as the command of an imperium" (p. 22). *Aletheia* is an event of dis-closure, of an entity's simultaneous emergence and withdrawal, such that "the difference between truth and untruth . . . is fluctuating as an eventfulness or happening that cannot be reduced to . . . vouching for the Being (spirit, beauty, goodness, truth) of people and things (beings, entities)" (p. 24). This explodes the mimetic notion of art according to which an artwork's truth lies in "the correspondence or bridging of beings to Being" (p. 25). By comparison, as we have seen, Beardsley's denial of artistic truth rests on the expectation that, to be true, the artwork would need to achieve such correspondence, as a correspondence between fact and proposition. And Hofstadter's affirmation of artistic truth is even more explicit in its reliance on the idea of a correspondence between a being and true being.

Existential Difference   According to Rapaport, Heidegger deconstructs the existential difference by redefining freedom as letting beings be the beings they are. In *Being and Time* Heidegger describes Dasein as the being which, unlike other creatures, cares for the truth. In his subsequent writings on freedom and truth during the early 1930s, however,[19] Heidegger points toward something "more originary or primordial" that goes "*beyond* the existential difference between the human and the nonhuman" (p. 27). This primordial freedom is the essence of truth as *aletheia*. It is concealed when human beings "come into their own as beings who are said to possess freedom," but also unconcealed, in that very process, as that which gives human beings the opportunity to understand "Being as dis-closure" (p. 28). This seems to imply that the primordial freedom to let beings be is not distinctive of humankind, and certainly not subservient to human needs and concerns. Yet such freedom does let "Dasein be the being that it is, namely, a being that can err or go astray" (p. 29).[20]

It should be obvious that neither Beardsley nor Hofstadter would follow Rapaport's Heidegger down these *Holzwege*.[21] Not Beardsley, because of his emphasis on empirical science as the peculiarly human enterprise that allows us to "get things right." And not Hofstadter, because of the importance he attaches to the ethical and religious dimensions in which human beings become most truly human. Neither Beardsley nor Hofstadter tries to go behind or around or beyond the "existential difference" between human and nonhuman.

Postmetaphysical Restitution   Following such dismantlings of metaphysical differences, Rapaport sees their postmetaphysical "restitution" in Heidegger's *Beiträge zur Philosophie*, and he traces this restitution in "The Origin of the Work of Art." Heidegger's restitution takes the form of equating truth and Being, thereby restoring "the very metaphysical jointure . . . so characteristic of a metaphysical understanding of truth and being, namely, their interchangeability." Yet their interchangeability rests on or in the abyss (*Abgrund*, literally "not-ground"). In the abyss occur both "that very concealment which is so essential to the disclosure of truth" and that vanishing of Being which is "the very precondition" for the emergence of Being (p. 30). Hence Heidegger's restitution "is constituted as a hyphenated interplay of grounding/ungrounding within the word *Abgrund* that deconstructs metaphysics as such" (p. 31). This reading allows Rapaport to frame Heidegger's in/famous description of van Gogh's painting of(?) (a peasant woman's?) shoes as a subtle disowning of that same description's admittedly Nazist surface grammar. Because of the peasant woman's absence from the painting, and the shoes' withdrawal from their equipmental character, says Rapaport, the shoes are disclosed in van Gogh's painting "in their 'truthfulness,' their temporal eventfulness as a destabilizing interplay between concealment and unconcealment, emergence and withdrawal, ground and not-ground." The shoes "appear as the truthful breaking open of beings in their diversity and alterity" (p. 34).

Generalizing, and thereby reintroducing his own position concerning truth in art, Rapaport concludes his reading of Heidegger as follows:

> Because art is temporal, it disrupts the closure in which Being would house it . . . and opens . . . a withdrawal, renunciation, or refusal of Being that comes to pass in the disclosure of *Ab-grund* as Openness. That the human with all its motivations, purposes, and designs conceals or prohibits the disclosure of art in its grounded/ungrounded relation to being and truth is just as crucial to Heidegger as the recognition that essential for the truth in art to appear is the trait or trace of the human that ought to be thought of as otherwise-than-human because the trait is postmetaphysical and posthuman. It is here that Heidegger enables us to rethink traditional understandings of how the existential and the ontological come into a truthful relation. (p. 35)

Rapaport interprets Derrida and Lévinas as providing variations on this theme of art's opening a withdrawal of Being and bearing a trace of the posthuman.[22] Common to all three, and to Rapaport's own conception of truth in art, is the attempt not only to undo the ontological and existential differences but also to "restitute" these in a postmetaphysical way.

Here again we confront a space that both Beardsley and Hofstadter would refuse to enter: Beardsley, because the "destabilizing interplay between concealment and unconcealment" would let all that is inferentially and empirically solid melt into air; and Hofstadter, because "diversity and alterity" not linked to interpersonal recognition would shatter the love of being that he finds central to all truth. Heidegger's purported restitution of truth in the abyss lies on the far side of what Beardsley and Hofstadter can seriously consider.

2.3 TOWARD RECONSTRUCTION

Rapaport's deconstruction makes obvious both the metaphysical burden of traditional conceptions and the cultural implications of attempts to shed that burden. His book suggests that correspondence theory, which is common to both Beardsley's denial and Hofstadter's affirmation of artistic truth, has much more than epistemological significance. If Rapaport's story is to be believed, then philosophical efforts to identify specific truth bearers and to articulate universal criteria of truth are also attempts to circumscribe (truly) human existence and to align it (and perhaps all creation) with cosmic order. At this metalevel it matters little whether a philosophy identifies the truth bearers as assertible predications (Beardsley) or existential artworks (Hofstadter), whether it restricts the criteria to logical consistency and empirical accuracy (Beardsley) or expands them to encompass all theoretical, practical, and spiritual adequation (Hofstadter). Both sides assume that there are truth bearers and universal criteria, and that truth is the aligning of human existence with cosmic order. These underlying assumptions are what deconstruction exposes and questions: not only the "existence" of truth bearers and universal criteria, not even only the need for alignment, but also and especially the ideas of properly human existence and cosmic order. Whether one can propose a theory of truth, and a theory of artistic truth, without employing such ideas, in however modified a form and fashion, remains an open question.

Rapaport's postmetaphysical deconstruction also uncovers the limits to the theories of language we have considered, even though he does not give his own theory. Both Beardsley and Hofstadter regard language as a primary link between human existence and cosmic order. They do not use this terminology, of course. For Beardsley, language provides the main means to link beliefs with facts about the "real world." For Hofstadter, language articulates human existence in such a way that humans can seek fulfillment in true being. If one pressed Beardsley about the importance of linking beliefs with facts, however, or asked Hofstadter about the importance of humans seeking spiritual fulfillment, an intersection between ontological difference and existential difference would quickly appear. Language, not simply art, has received the Western metaphysical task of proper alignment. The effect of this continues even in antimetaphysical theories of language, such as Beardsley's, that deny art's truth capacity.

The limitation common to Beardsley's and Hofstadter's theories of language is a function of that metaphysical task. In their concern with how language facilitates cosmic ("real world" or "spiritual") alignment, both authors ignore or marginalize the role of language in intersubjective understanding. Neither one has made the turn from a philosophy of consciousness to a philosophy of communication, from an epistemic model of subject and object to a critical-hermeneutic model of subject and subject,[23] although Hofstadter comes closer than Beardsley does. Rapaport also remains locked into the same epistemic model, however, despite challenging its metaphysical underpinnings. Perhaps we should say that he "restitutes" this model, on the far side of deconstructing it, when he makes the question of truth in art depend on particular works of art. Now the object (a very peculiar object, to be sure) gains the initiative that posthumans forfeit in their no-longer-innocent forgetfulness of Being.

Ironically enough, Rapaport helps correct a modernist emphasis on the artwork's autonomy (shared, as we have seen, by Beardsley and Hofstadter) by heaping such grand postmetaphysical expectations on the artwork that autonomism collapses under its own weight. For Beardsley, the autonomy of the artwork secures both the work's inestimable aesthetic value and its cognitive insignificance. For Hofstadter, such autonomy allows the work to be true and thereby to contribute significantly to spiritual fulfillment. Rapaport challenges the metaphysical underpinnings to these constructions of autonomy. Yet he helps himself to the very same notion of autonomy to let art lead in challenging metaphysics. Rapaport thereby inadvertently demonstrates the problems surrounding modernist autonomism, whether it be aestheticist or existentialist in tone. He also lets slip why one cannot simply continue with the autonomist construction once its metaphysical support has collapsed under philosophical and artistic hammering. In other words, it is not simply "truth" or "art" that needs to be questioned. How can Rapaport or anyone else assume that, by virtue of the supposed autonomy of individual artworks, either truth or art can be "in" the other?

In reframing the question of truth in art, then, Rapaport does not so much dismantle the metaphysical tradition as shift its weight. Whereas Western metaphysics loaded art with the salvific vocation of mediating universal order and human particularities, Rapaport's postmetaphysics charges art with the transgressive hyperbole of deranging purported order in the direction of "posthuman" dedifferentiation. As a result, art becomes a line of tension between the primordial occurrence (*Ereignis*) that has no name and many "site-specific" occurrences (artworks) whose sole truth function is to nominate ever and again the occurrence that has no name. This "posthuman" charge carries more than a trace of the prehuman, otherwise known as myth.

Three problems in Rapaport's account have special relevance for my own conception of truth in art. In the first place, there is little evidence – certainly no argument – that whatever Rapaport means by "truth" has much to do with either more traditional or more recent theories of truth. One can grant that both traditional theories such as Plato's or Aristotle's and modernist theories such as Beardsley's and Hofstadter's share a problematic metaphysical frame. But this would not tell us whether (nevertheless) such theories offer valid insights that are worth reframing. Nor would simply deconstructing the metaphysical frame necessarily result in a more viable conception of truth. Specifically, it need not result in a conception of artistic truth that is recognizably about truth and not about some other topic altogether. So one challenge suggested by Rapaport's book is to show how one's conception of truth in art relates to other theories and to more comprehensive theories of truth. For this, art criticism and commentary do not suffice. In Adorno's words, they must be philosophically "honed."[24]

A second problem arises from the unexamined assumption that particular artworks are the only appropriate locus for artistic truth talk. Why should truth be linked to artworks rather than, say, to art events or art practices or language usage about art? Sharing the metaphysically framed thing-fixation of most post-Renaissance philosophy, Rapaport simply assumes that artworks – themselves modern cultural phenomena – are *the* location for considering the question of truth in art and for expecting a disclosure of truth. This, despite his Derridean suspicion of substantial truth bearers and definite intellectual content. So, for example, he simply follows Heidegger in thinking that truth happens within van Gogh's finished painting rather than in the processes from which the painting arises and to which it contributes. Once this all-too-common reification of art becomes apparent, an alternative conception of artistic truth must explain the relationship between artworks and how art works. The key to this, it seems to me, is an account of aesthetic validity that neither ignores the hermeneutic character of aesthetic experience nor reduces validity to the validity claims that arise in strictly linguistic practices.

A third problem pertains to the "social ontology of art," as I have labeled it elsewhere.[25] Rapaport's critique of "the metaphysics of art" is too metaphysical. Despite his emphasis on occurrence and temporality, he shows little concern for the specific sociohistorical shape that the arts and philosophies of art have acquired in different societal formations. He does not ask, for example, whether different art phenomena take on different truth functions at different times. Nor does he have any notion of the historical unfolding of artistic truth content. It is especially telling that, despite his emphasis on particular artworks, he does not ask how the particularity of various works is historically constituted. Nor does he ask why, historically, art could be considered a mediator between universal and particular, or why, historically, art can now be considered a site of antimetaphysical transgression. Hence Rapaport's account leaves open a third challenge: to situate one's conception of artistic truth within a sociohistorical understanding of art itself.

So Rapaport inadvertently provides a clearing for three open questions: the relation between truth "in general" and truth in art; the intersection of language, art, and aesthetic validity; and the sociohistorical situatedness of art and aesthetics. Neither Beardsley's metacritical denial of artistic truth nor Hofstadter's existential affirmation provides adequate answers; Rapaport's postmetaphysical deconstruction does not let the questions arise. My next chapter examines connections among language, art, and aesthetic validity. Subsequent chapters map the relation between truth and artistic truth. Throughout I refer to sociohistorical themes. My proposed alternative attempts to go beyond metacritical denial, beyond existential affirmation, and beyond postmetaphysical deconstruction, in the direction of a critical hermeneutic reconstruction.

3

Kant Revisited

The beautiful is the symbol of the morally good, and...only in this
respect...does it please with a claim to the assent of everyone else.
Immanuel Kant[1]

To examine connections among language, art, and aesthetic validity, one
must revisit Kant: the roots to contemporary debates about artistic truth lie
in Kant's aesthetics. Kant recognizes that validity encompasses more than
propositional truth. He considers validity to be multidimensional. In distinguishing aesthetic validity ("beauty") from epistemic validity ("truth")
and moral validity ("goodness" or "rightness"), however, Kant gives an ambiguous account. On the one hand, he demarcates an unusual zone of
experience and activity where imaginative cognition and creative conduct
can occur. He emphasizes an irreducible dimension of valid aesthetic judgment and, by extension, of aesthetic experience and aesthetic objects. And
he defines the fine arts with reference to this dimension, as those areas of
production and reception in which "aesthetic ideas" and "taste" prevail. On
the other hand, Kant's descriptions of this zone untether it from his usual
anchors of validity, namely, intellectual concepts and rational ideas. Hence
aesthetic experience and activity, as aesthetic, are neither theoretical nor
practical and are not fully constituted in a Kantian sense. His account of
the subjective universality and exemplary necessity of taste judgments reflects this untethering, as does his account of the beautiful as purposiveness
without purpose. To be sure, Kant's subsequent descriptions of (aesthetic)
reflective judgment as a "common sense" and of beauty as "the symbol of
the morally good" try to establish ties from the aesthetic to the epistemic
and the moral. Yet his demarcation of the aesthetic does not allow him fully
to secure the aesthetic dimension as one in which valid experience and activity occur. Many followers of Kant, Monroe Beardsley among them, do not
expect to find truth or goodness in aesthetic matters, or in those arts where

aesthetic considerations prevail. How to anchor aesthetic validity remains obscure.

When Hegel, criticizing Kant, reintroduces truth and goodness into art's vocation, he simultaneously cuts art loose from ordinary aesthetic experience and activity (i.e., the realm of natural beauty, in Kant's account), and he makes art subservient to philosophical interpretation. For the most part, recent philosophers in the English-speaking world have followed Kant rather than Hegel, even when they focus on art rather than on natural beauty or on other aesthetic phenomena. They approach art as primarily aesthetic. By contrast, twentieth-century German philosophers such as Gadamer[2] and Adorno[3] prefer Hegel's emphasis on artistic truth to Kant's emphasis on aesthetic judgment. Not surprisingly, they also make art seem esoteric. One challenge facing a nonesoteric account of artistic truth, then, is to establish a notion of aesthetic validity that neither collapses it into either epistemic or moral validity nor renders it irrelevant or impotent with respect to ordinary cognition and conduct. The challenge is to retain a Kantian emphasis on the irreducibility of the aesthetic while giving an account of aesthetic validity that connects it with artistic truth.[4]

My response to this challenge requires three steps. First I propose a critical-hermeneutic conception of aesthetic processes and aesthetic validity (section 3.1). Second, to show the relevance of aesthetic experience and activity for questions of truth and goodness, I explore the relation between aesthetic validity and what I label "cultural orientation" (section 3.2). Third, given the role of language in the raising of validity claims, I examine how the arts, where questions of aesthetic validity become prominent, enter into ordinary conversation and discourse (section 3.3). Aesthetic validity, cultural orientation, and what I label "art talk" circumscribe the hermeneutical matrix from which questions of artistic truth emerge.

3.1 AESTHETIC VALIDITY

Despite the prevalence of "anti-aesthetic" theories and artworks since the 1960s, it is a fact of contemporary life in North America and Europe that society and culture have an irreducible aesthetic dimension. This dimension's differentiation and institutionalization are historical achievements, for better and for worse. A permanent reversal or subversion of such processes would require that the societal formation as a whole be transformed. Hence, as Adorno indicates, a critique of "the aesthetic" that does not simultaneously criticize the political and economic systems framing the aesthetic would miss its target, because this lies too far away. So too, attempts to describe the aesthetic dimension that do not situate it in a larger societal formation would attribute features to objects as such that actually are functions of a complex sociohistorical process. Since one cannot do everything at once, however, I restrict myself to giving a partial phenomenology of the aesthetic dimension, with an important caveat: I do not attempt an eidetic intuition aimed at some ahistorical essence. Rather, I provide a brief dialectical reconstruction of certain sociohistorical patterns that have become prominent in Western societies since the eighteenth century.

Aesthetic Signs

Three polarities prevail in the aesthetic dimension of modern Western societies and cultures. All three can be found in Kant's account of fine art. The fact that they surface there does not mean that they are peculiar to the arts as such, however. All three are versions of the dialectic between nature and freedom that pervades Kant's entire *Critique of Judgment*. They help constitute the aesthetic dimension as a whole, and not simply those arts in which the aesthetic dimension becomes prominent. The polarities in question occur between play and work, between entertainment and instruction, and between expression and communication. In each case Kant tries to "split the difference," as it were, arguing that the fine arts are more like play than like work but are not merely play; that they serve neither entertainment nor instruction but a delightful cultivation of the mind; and that they must express aesthetic ideas with a view toward communicability. I propose that these three polarities are constitutive for the aesthetic dimension in modern Western societies: its content emerges from tensions between play and work, between entertainment and instruction, and between expression and communication. If it were constituted as a recognizable zone of experience and activity in a different societal formation, the aesthetic dimension would have a different framework and hence a significantly different meaning. Let me comment on each polarity.

"Play" has been a central concept of aesthetics since Kant and Schiller, reemerging in the twentieth century as the purported origin of all culture and as a semisacred alternative to the grim secularity of technocapitalist society.[5] Gadamer tries to wrest "play" from "the subjective meaning that it has in Kant and Schiller" (*TM* 101, *WM* 97), making it an ontological concept from which to derive the structure of artistic truth. Adorno, by contrast, criticizes regressive elements in play and reactionary tendencies in theoretical celebrations of play, preferring to define art as a negation of play rather than its mere continuation (*AT* 317–19, *ÄT* 469–72). In both cases, however, an underlying tension between play and work remains in effect. The aesthetic (and, by extension, art) gets defined as a zone where serious play sublimates purposeful activity or where an illusory freedom from function provides a necessary critique of praxis.

What such theories have in common, and what makes up the positive content to the play-work dialectic, is an emphasis on exploration. It is less the prevalence of play or a liberation from work that marks the aesthetic than the opportunity or setting to explore, where an exploration's goal emerges from the process of exploring and usually is not predetermined. The process of exploration is just as important to meaningful work as it is to lively play – as the problems caused by its absence in Taylorized industry and hypercommercialized sport attest. Similarly, open-ended inquiry helps sustain substantial scholarship just as much as hypothetical role playing provides impetus for Kohlbergian postconventional morality.[6] It is understandable that exploration gets framed by a play-work dialectic in a technocapitalist society. Yet this framing, both in theory and in social reality, risks turning exploration into what Adorno calls a *Naturschutzpark,* a nature preserve where people go for relief, only to leave everything outside as it is. The same thing occurs when art becomes *the* bastion of exploration, as if the rest of life can do without it. A better alternative, it seems to me, is to identify those elements of exploration which are indispensable across the board and to promote their flourishing within dominant institutions. This cannot be done without a critique of such institutions and of the societal formation to which they belong.

Essential to such a critique would be to reexamine the dialectic between entertainment and instruction that also frames the aesthetic dimension. On Kant's analysis of taste judgments, purely aesthetic experience serves neither to entertain nor to instruct. The definitive feature of taste judgments is their resting upon a feeling of delight or "favor" (*Gunst*) that arises in disinterested reflection upon an object of perception (*CJ* §§1–5, pp. 89–96; V: 203–11). This rules out sensory gratification and instrumental or moral achievement as primary goals for aesthetic experience. His subsequent description of fine art as promoting a delightful cultivation of the mind simply continues this delicate balancing act (*CJ* §§43–5, pp. 182–6; V: 303–7). His description distinguishes fine art from "agreeable arts," whose primary purpose is entertainment,[7] from craft, which has primarily instrumental ends, and, implicitly, from religious and political art, whose ends might not be strictly instrumental but closer, perhaps, to what Kant defines as moral goodness.

Yet Kant also sees aesthetic experience and fine art as potential propaedeutics to the moral life. Morality is not their aim, but it could be one of their benefits under appropriate conditions. His contorted depiction of beauty as the symbol of the morally good indicates the importance he attaches to the nonentertaining and noninstructing "cultivation of the mind" wrought by aesthetic experience and fine art (*CJ* §59, pp. 225–8; V: 351–4). Gadamer and Adorno continue this Kantian focus, through Hegelian lenses, in their appeals to *Erfahrung* and *Bildung.* The difference between them lies in their contrasting appraisals of how such formation should occur under contemporary conditions. Whereas Gadamer embraces the continuity of a classical humanist tradition, Adorno endorses modern art's critique of culture-industrial *Halbbildung.*

If aesthetic practices serve neither to entertain nor to instruct, and if they are not identical with mass-mediated "infotainment," which often neither amuses nor informs, how should aesthetic "cultivation" or "formation" be understood? Perhaps as a training in creative interpretation. This suggestion does not lie so far afield from Kant as it might first seem.[8] Once one strips mentalist trappings from his account of reflective judgment, one can see "taste judging" as a process of interpreting signs before, alongside, or against their established usages and significations. The same "object" that in other contexts functions as a conventional signal or symbol acquires or displays multiple layers of possible meaning in an aesthetic context. Kant would say that the object in such a context gives occasion for imagination and understanding to engage in freely harmonious play. On my own critical hermeneutic approach, it would be preferable to say that aesthetic practices let the meaning of the sign become an open question, or that they let the openness of meaning be constitutive for the sign. It is not so much the case that meaning in such contexts is endlessly deferred (Derrida) as meaning is multiply referred beyond the sign's established usages and significations.[9]

To forestall misunderstandings, let me introduce three qualifications. First, such creative interpretation is not monological, on the Kantian model of a judging subject and a perceived object. Rather it is dialogical, involving communities and practices of interpretation within which different interpreters interact. Second, creative interpretation is not unbounded. There are limits to the possible meanings that can "make sense" for any particular sign, even though the limits often are discovered in the process of interpretation. Third, creative interpretation itself calls upon preunderstandings and vocabularies that are intrinsic to aesthetic practices as these have developed in sociohistorical settings.

If my proposal is on the right track, then framing the aesthetic within a dialectic of entertainment and instruction is both understandable and inadequate. Understandable, because the creativity in aesthetic practices makes them intrinsically "entertaining," and the interpretation they involve can be "instructive." Yet inadequate, both because creative interpretation exceeds the confines of conventional entertainment and instruction and because these conventions themselves need the expansion and disruptions that occur under the impetus of creative interpretation. Hence, as I have argued with respect to exploration, so too creative interpretation should not be safely cordoned off in a special zone outside ordinary cognition and conduct. Rather it should be recognized and promoted within the ordinary as an indispensable ingredient for human flourishing under contemporary conditions.

The third polarity occurs between expression and communication. Kant articulates this as a tension between genius and taste in which "genius," as an uncommon gift for fashioning and expressing "aesthetic ideas," must give way to taste, as a "common sense" that makes such feeling-laden and creative intuitions publicly accessible or "universally communicable" (*CJ* §49, p. 195; V: 317). More specifically, Kant concludes that taste, not genius, is "the

primary thing to which one must look in the judging of art as beautiful art,"
since the richness and originality of (aesthetic) ideas "is not as necessary for
the sake of beauty as is the suitability of the imagination in its freedom to
the lawfulness of the understanding" (*CJ* §50, p. 197; V: 319).[10] If forced
to choose, Adorno would come down on the side of genius and Gadamer
on the side of taste, even though Adorno rejects Kant's subject-centered
notion of expression, and Gadamer criticizes Kant for denying taste "any
significance as knowledge" and for failing to define taste "positively by what
grounds commonality and creates community" (*TM* 43, *WM* 40–1).

What both authors retain from Kant, by way of Hegel, is the notion of
aesthetic presentation (*Darstellung*).[11] Presentation, I would suggest, makes
up the positive content to the aesthetic-framing dialectic of expression and
communication, where "expression" concerns what an agent presents to others, and "communication" pertains to what others interpret the presenting
agent to have "said." Although modern aesthetic practices have an expressive side, such that contemporary explorations and creative interpretations
cannot avoid asking who or what some object or product or event expresses,
the aesthetic sign cannot be reduced to a mere expression. Similarly, modern aesthetic practices have a communicative side, such that people engaged
in aesthetic experience and activity cannot help wondering about the public
significance of an aesthetic sign. Yet aesthetic signs cannot be reduced to
mere means of communication. Instead aesthetic signs are presentations.
They make multiple nuances of meaning available in ways that either exceed or precede both idiosyncratic expressions of intent and conventional
communications of content. What aesthetic signs present can be called their
purport. Although media of imagination play a special role in the formation
of aesthetic signs, the purport of aesthetic signs need not be equated with
Kant's "aesthetic ideas."[12]

Yet Kant's conception of "aesthetic ideas" does provide hints in the direction I propose, as Rudolf Makkreel has shown. Kant makes discovering and
expressing aesthetic ideas central to the fine artist's work.[13] Even our finding
nonartistic objects beautiful involves taking them as expressions of aesthetic
ideas.[14] Aesthetic ideas are themselves presentations, regardless of whether
fine artists present them in works of art. As perceptually based intuitions
whose meaning exceeds the grasp of ordinary language and concepts, they
can suggest rational ideas and "present rational ideas to sense." They "add
to our interpretation of experience by suggesting significant affinities even
when direct conceptual connections are lacking."[15] Read in this way, Kant
assigns to imagination, in conjunction with reflective judgment, an ability to
present "the meaning of something" in a preconceptual and prelinguistic
way. Whereas the schemata of imagination directly present conceptual categories, making them perceptually applicable, aesthetic ideas, as symbolic
presentations, "are indirect modes of expressing certain [rational] ideas
that cannot be directly articulated by means of concepts." They provide

"a nonreferential type of meaning" and "allow us to arrive at a reflective interpretation of things that surpass nature."[16]

If one substitutes "aesthetic practices" for Kant's "imagination," "aesthetic signs" for "aesthetic ideas," and "purport" for "rational ideas," one comes close to the notion of presentation I wish to propose. When "objects" function as aesthetic signs, they are already caught up in intersubjective processes of exploration and creative interpretation. These processes allow them to be meaningful in ways that are not so much inexplicable as ever in need of explication. Such explication presupposes that aesthetic signs are about something other than themselves, and that such "aboutness" is both sharable and shared by various interpreters. A "reading" of aesthetic signs, while exploratory and creative, is neither private nor arbitrary, even when what is read lacks the apparent settledness of lexical meanings or the apparent definiteness of asserted propositions. It is so, of course, that aesthetic signs have an important propensity to unsettle language and disturb thought. Yet this is only possible because they are not private and are not arbitrary. Aesthetic signs – that is, "objects" in their functions as aesthetic signs – present nuances of meaning on which the vividness of language and the acuity of thought depend, as does the attunement of conduct to complexities and uncertainties in concrete situations.

As was the case with exploration and creative interpretation, my account refuses to restrict the occurrence of presentation to art, proposing instead that presentation is a constitutive function within ordinary cognition and conduct. This also pertains to modern perceptions of "nature," which Adorno makes thematic in ways that neither Hegel nor Gadamer would allow. Despite, and amid, the advancing exploitation of creatures and habitats for technological and commercial ends, they retain their capacity to astonish, to shock, and to confuse and, in that capacity, to function as aesthetic signs. A sensitivity for such features might not indicate moral proclivities, as Kant thought, but it does suggest an openness for what Adorno calls "the nonidentical" and for alternative interpretations of such creatures' importance.

From my partial reconstruction of three modern polarities, exploration, creative interpretation, and presentation emerge as central to the aesthetic dimension in contemporary Western society. These are not peculiar to art, for they occur in many areas of culture, even when neither recognized nor encouraged. They are best understood as intersubjective processes rather than as the capacities or contents of a subjective consciousness facing either independent or subjectively constituted objects. Although "objects" enter such processes – or, better, various creatures, events, and products enter such processes as "objects" – they do so as aesthetic signs. That is to say, the "objects" of exploration, creative interpretation, and presentation simply are creatures, events, and products in their capacities to sustain discovery, to call forth reflective readings, and to acquire nuances of meaning in intersubjective contexts. While such capacities would remain dormant if people did not together engage in the relevant experiences and activities, it would be a mistake, and a reversion to the subject-object paradigm of so much modern philosophy, to think that aesthetic experiences and activities simply assign, impute, or create the objects' capacities. Moreover, when aesthetic practices concern the agents or results of exploration and the like, aesthetic initiative often resides in the "objects" themselves. Either, in the case of some animals and all humans, these "objects" are able to engage in aesthetic experiences and activities; or, in the case of cultural events and products, access to their "objective" aesthetic capacities requires an acknowledgement of their having arisen, in part, from prior intersubjective processes of exploration, creative interpretation, and presentation.

Imaginative Cogency

Given this account of "the aesthetic," what sense can be made of the notion of aesthetic validity – for example, Kant's notion that taste judgments raise a claim to subjective universality and exemplary necessity? One cannot simply assume that all intersubjective processes raise claims to validity. When people wordlessly share a certain mood (what Heidegger thematizes in his discussion of "attunement"), they typically raise no such claim. Absent any reference to an epistemic or moral end that the mood "should" or "should not" serve, people would find it odd or insulting to be told that the feeling they share is somehow incorrect or inappropriate. Is there a plausible sense in which intersubjective exploration, interpretation, and presentation can have more or less merit and can give rise to intrinsic validity claims?

Not only do I wish to answer yes, but also I hold that neglecting aesthetic validity impoverishes both philosophical theories of validity and ordinary aesthetic practices. Initially I plan to develop this answer without reference to art, where most philosophers who acknowledge aesthetic validity tend to locate it.[17] To simplify the discussion, I henceforth use "imagination" and its derivatives as a shorthand for the processes I have identified as central to the aesthetic. "Imagination" should be understood as referring to intersubjective processes rather than to a mental capacity, and as involving aesthetic signs rather than mental contents. I summarize the notion of aesthetic validity with the term "imaginative cogency." Let me explain.

At first it sounds paradoxical to say of aesthetic experiences and activities that they can have more or less merit or can give rise to validity claims. Is it not definitive of imaginative processes in contemporary settings that they are exploratory, allusive, and transgressive? Do they not, in that sense, defy any expectation of validity? And does not such defiance lend them weight as a site of opposition to prevailing norms and institutions?

On second thought, however, it is precisely these features of imagination that prompt the question about validity. This becomes apparent when one reverses the rhetoric of the previous paragraph. Can a site of opposition be genuinely oppositional (and not simply anarchic or reactionary) if it lacks boundaries and direction? Can expectations of validity be defied by something that cannot claim any validity for itself? Can exploration, allusion, and transgression occur if the processes in question are completely unlimited? Is not the concept of complete lack of limitation itself thoroughly paradoxical?

As a matter of fact, the vocabulary people use to talk about aesthetic processes and signs is loaded with evaluative terms. These go beyond simple labels for private preferences (like-dislike) or for consumerist attitudes (interesting-boring). We say, for example, that certain jokes "pack a punch," while others "fall flat." One metaphor is "trite" or "forced," while another is "original" or "convincing." One story is "profound," another "mere fluff." Some decorations are "attractive," others are "tawdry." Some public celebrations are "tedious," others are "exciting." Some landscapes are "gorgeous," and others are "ugly." And we find much more agreement in these assessments on specific occasions than the myth of individual "taste" would lead one to expect. Indeed, conflict in the usage of such terms is no more an argument against the notion of aesthetic validity than differences about facts or values are arguments against the notions of epistemic or moral validity.

These examples suggest that discrimination and assessment are intrinsic to aesthetic experiences and activities. The examples need not suggest, however, that the standards to which such experiences and activities appeal are universally binding, either in the sense that they obtain regardless of social, cultural, or historical setting, or in the sense that they are obligatory for every human being. In Kantian language, the implicit standards do not have either epistemic or moral validity. Within the Kantian framework, which anchors validity in concepts of understanding and ideas of reason, this apparent absence of epistemic or moral validity gives rise to the so-called antinomy of taste (*CJ*§56, pp. 214–15; V: 338–9). The antinomy is a conflict between two incompatible claims, each of which is equally well founded: (1) There is no rational basis for aesthetic evaluations; otherwise we could prove which of two conflicting evaluations is correct. (2) There is a rational basis for aesthetic evaluations; otherwise we would not argue about them when they differ.

If, however, one does not anchor the validity of all standards in human rationality as described by Kant, and if one detaches the question of a "rational basis" from the question of "aesthetic standards," then this antinomy need not arise. In keeping with the etymological roots of "standard" in the old French *estandard*, aesthetic standards can be regarded as "rallying points" around which people congregate in order to recall, project, contest, and attain identity-constituting commitments. Aesthetic standards are more or less widely shared expectations concerning the outcomes of aesthetic processes in which people engage. As such, aesthetic standards (and perhaps other standards as well) will not be universally binding in a Kantian sense.[18] Each one can be contested, moved, or replaced. Yet the very process of contesting a standard requires that people appeal to some notion of validity. Hence it makes sense for people to argue about conflicting aesthetic evaluations even if they cannot point to some "rational principle" on the basis of which the conflict could potentially be settled. Arguments about conflicting aesthetic evaluations primarily appeal to shared expectations concerning intersubjective processes,[19] not to a universal principle of abstract reason. What gives rise to the apparent antinomy of taste is too narrow a conception of what counts as validity, one that ties validity too closely to a restricted notion of rationality.

Indeed, within the context of modern aesthetic processes, it is possible to articulate a general idea of aesthetic validity that is less vague and less mentalist than the Kantian notion of taste as a "common sense" pointing toward a "supersensible substrate" connecting nature and freedom. The idea I want to postulate is that of imaginative cogency. Although this idea recalls Hofstadter's notion of the "cogency" of the aesthetic object,[20] I do not attribute imaginative cogency directly to the object as such. Rather I regard it as a horizon of aesthetic validity within which an intersubjective process unfolds, a horizon that encompasses the "objects" of this process in their function as aesthetic signs. Imaginative cogency is not a "property" of the objects as such. Returning to my previous examples, one can say that, from an aesthetic vantage point, what distinguishes a pungent joke from a flaccid one is that the successful telling of a joke weaves its story together well, builds up to its punch line, and then delivers this with a surprising consistency and flair. A trite metaphor lacks the innovative connections that would characterize an original one, and a superficial story lacks the depth of insight provided by one that is profound. Poorly "orchestrated" public celebrations lack the dramatic pacing, ceremonial setting, and vigorous interactions that would make them less tedious. And so on.

In such cases what makes for a greater degree of aesthetic validity is the complexity, depth, and intensity with which the imaginative process unfolds. Or, to say this more carefully, when evaluating the relative aesthetic merits of modern cultural events and products, people employ implicit standards of complexity, depth, and intensity, and the horizon of such standards is something like imaginative cogency. Not surprisingly, given the reciprocation between theory and practice in modern Western cultures, these standards resemble the marks of aesthetic merit identified by aestheticians since the eighteenth century: Nicholas Wolterstorff's unity, internal richness, and "fittingness-intensity," for example,[21] or integrality, articulation, intensity, and depth in Adorno's *Aesthetic Theory* (*AT* 186–92, *ÄT* 277–87).[22]

Two qualifications are required here, however. First, such standards cannot be abstracted from the imaginative character of the processes in question without losing much of their content. Such loss would occur, for example, if one regarded aesthetic standards as mere analogues of the consistency, coherence, and explanatory power scholars might expect in the context of empirical investigations and theoretical arguments. The "cogency" to which people appeal when they expect complexity, depth, and intensity in aesthetic processes is a cogency of exploration, creative interpretation, and presentation, all of which are inherently open-ended, although neither directionless nor infinite. Second, imaginative cogency is a horizon rather than merely a rule or principle.[23] It can be approximated in a theoretical description but cannot be pinned down in an axiomatic statement. Although this might appear problematic for theorists who wish to secure categorical clarity, it might also suggest the limits of inquiry, not only with respect to aesthetic processes but also with respect to epistemic and moral processes where theoretical success has seemed more likely in the past.

3.2 CULTURAL ORIENTATION

All of this becomes relevant for a theory of artistic truth when one recognizes, with Habermas, that art has become an expert culture in which aesthetic validity claims can be thematized. Unfortunately this development in Western societies has brought with it three tendencies, both in theory and in practice, that isolate such expert thematization, to the impoverishment of both art and culture, and to the detriment of artistic truth. First, the pursuit of aesthetic merit gets channeled overwhelmingly into the artworld, in compensation, as it were, for the ongoing exploitation of everyday life and environments for nonaesthetic purposes. Second, nonaesthetic concerns become marginal within the artworld itself, so that the relevance of art for science or politics or morality becomes opaque. Then, as a final step in art's self-involvement, aesthetic merit becomes a questionable goal within art itself, giving rise to an anti-aesthetic expert culture where the last resistance to "business as usual" threatens to disappear, albeit with a transgressive gesture. Hence contemporary Western societies face either the much-heralded "death of art" or art's much less heralded rebirth. Because my theory of artistic truth aims to contribute to art's rebirth, I refuse to restrict the pursuit of aesthetic merit to the artworld, to make nonaesthetic concerns marginal to art, or to embrace the deaestheticization of either art or culture.

"Cultural orientation" is a crucial concept in this regard. Although the concept carries echoes of Kant's "cultivation of the mind" and "symbol of the morally good,"[24] it is closer to Hegel's conception of art as a sensuous appearance of the (culturally embedded and culturally unfolding) idea. Following Hegel, I do not restrict the process of cultural orientation to art itself, although, following Adorno's critique of Hegel, I also do not retain Hegel's construction of a progressively self-actualizing absolute spirit. Cultural pluralism and historical contingency are unavoidable features of contemporary society. Any theory of cultural orientation should take these features into account.

By "culture" I mean the entire network of practices, products, and institutions through which traditions are shaped and transmitted, social solidarities are generated and contested, and personal identities are molded and embraced. It is similar in some respects to Habermas's conception of "the lifeworld." I do not locate art outside of culture. Rather, art is a part of culture in a complex society, as are language, education, organized religion, and the network's many other nodes. "Cultural orientation" refers to how individuals, communities, and organizations find their direction both within and by way of culture. As Gadamer has suggested, such cultural pathfinding is never pure or neutral. It is always already underway, drawing upon cultural resources that are historically effective to a greater or lesser extent. Accordingly, cultural orientation unavoidably involves both disorientation and reorientation.

Contrary to the tendency since Kant to divorce the aesthetic from the cultural, I wish to argue that aesthetic processes are intrinsic to processes of cultural orientation and have a special role to play in this regard. This is not to deny that epistemic and moral processes also play special roles, but to claim that their roles are not sufficient by themselves and that the aesthetic provides part of what the epistemic and the moral lack. Epistemic processes typically appeal to standards of empirical accuracy and logical consistency, giving rise to claims to epistemic correctness. Moral processes typically appeal to standards of obligation and appropriateness, giving rise to claims to normative legitimacy. In any given situation, however, a proposed course of action can be deemed both correct and right, "all things considered," and yet be found "unimaginative." Conversely, another proposed course of action can be considered highly imaginative but either epistemically ill-founded or wrong in some moral or ethical regard. Whereas Beardsley tries to keep the aesthetic and the epistemic in watertight compartments, and Hofstadter lets the aesthetic flow into the ethical without remainder, I argue for both the necessary interdependence and the irreducible plurality of these three dimensions in modern Western societies.

My suggestion is that aesthetic failure is no less problematic than epistemic or moral failure, even though people may find it more difficult to specify in advance what would make for aesthetic "success" in a given situation. The reason why aesthetic failure is problematic has to do with the role of imaginative processes in cultural orientation. "Finding one's way," whether as an individual, community, or organization, is a multidimensional, complex, and unending task in contemporary societies. The time is long past when widely shared "worldviews" or dominant political or religious institutions, such as the nation-state or the church, mosque, or synagogue, provided comprehensive road maps that most people follow.[25] This does not mean, however, that the need for orientation has disappeared or that no other institutions have stepped into the breech. If anything, the burdens of "finding one's way" have increased, as each individual, community, and organization must repeatedly uncover anew where it should be headed and why. At the same time, technocapitalism has had the cumulative effect of prescribing direction while undermining a sense of worthwhile alternatives. Technological and economic imperatives have become dominant in culture.

Although such dominance does not eliminate the burdens of finding one's way, it does increase the difficulty of recognizing this task's multi-dimensionality and complexity and of pursuing orientation with sufficient nuance and vigor. It is precisely here that imaginative processes become crucial. In order not to pursue whatever is technologically feasible just because it is technologically feasible, people need to explore alternatives without a predetermined goal. In order not simply to do whatever the marketplace seems to dictate, communities and organizations need to engage in creative interpretation that is open to multiple nuances of meaning. In order not to be seen either as frivolous time-wasting or as a salvific escape, such exploration and interpretation must have their own worth, and this worth must be tied to the worth of the presentations to which the interpreters attend. To pursue exploration and creative interpretation as ways of gaining (re)orientation, participants must discriminate between better and worse aesthetic processes and must raise claims to aesthetic validity.

This does not mean that aesthetic processes suffice for purposes of cultural orientation in the face of technocapitalist pressures. The exploration of alternative courses of action, for example, usually does not, by itself, provide an adequate basis for communal or organizational decisions. Other factors must enter the mix, such as a relatively accurate understanding of the situation and a practical weighing of what is right and appropriate, not to mention the omnipresent questions of technical feasibility and economic viability. Yet sufficient emphasis on exploration can bring to the fore considerations that are easily suppressed, such as how participants might feel in relation to a proposed course of action. It can also remind participants of hopes and needs that exceed the established vocabularies of decision making – the plight of people who would not be immediately affected by the decision, for example, or aspirations for a good society that no single group or decision can realize. In this sense, although not entirely on their own, aesthetic processes can help retain the social-critical and social-utopian potentials that Adorno mistakenly limited to negative tendencies within art and philosophy.[26]

It is useful in this connection to distinguish some tracks in the pursuit of aesthetic validity as a way of cultural orientation. Along one track, aesthetic validity claims get raised with respect to the anticipated outcome of an aesthetic process. Along another track, aesthetic validity claims arise with respect to the process itself. Imagine, for example, a nonprofit organization that wishes to turn a run-down warehouse into a community center. Much of the planning and decision making will focus on "the final product" and how to achieve it. In an organization attuned to aesthetic considerations, one topic of discussion will be how the building can be redesigned to elicit those elements of exploration and creative interpretation that would make it an aesthetically rich environment for the organization and the people it serves. Another part of the discussion will be more reflexive, pertaining to the process of planning and decision making itself. Is this process structured to support imaginative participation? Is it carried out in a way that elicits open-ended dialogue about what the building should be like and how it will function in its urban environment? Aesthetic validity claims would rise along both tracks, as claims about not only the aesthetic merits of the envisioned building but also the aesthetic merits of the envisioning itself. Later, when the organization has completed its renovation project, a new track will arise: is the building actually an aesthetically rich environment for its users, and does it need further improvements in that regard? Traditional aesthetics has restricted its attention to the third track and restricted this track to the aesthetic merits of finished artworks. By expanding the notion of aesthetic validity beyond finished products of the artistic sort, I hope to have shown more clearly the importance of aesthetic validity for cultural orientation. Nevertheless, art remains an indispensable site for aesthetically laden pursuits of cultural orientation. To see why this is so, we must consider next how the arts enter into ordinary conversation and discourse.

3.3 ART TALK

Once Kant had described aesthetic ideas as creative intuitions that exceed the grasp of ordinary thought, the relation between art and language became a contested topic in Western aesthetics. It is common knowledge, and a basis for much of analytic aesthetics, that language usage pervades experiences of art. Viewers, listeners, and readers talk about art, write and read about it, watch videos and television programs about art, read reviews, listen to their acquaintances talk about art, and so forth. Let me introduce the term "art talk" as a way of summarizing all these sorts of language usage. When art talk occurs as a relatively unproblematic use of language to reach an understanding, it can be called "art conversation." When it enters a more "reflective" mode where implicit validity claims become an explicit topic of discussion, art talk can be called "art discourse."[27] In everyday art talk people regularly and almost imperceptibly slide between conversation and discourse. There are many possible topics (depending on the artistic medium, the background and experience of the participants, and the setting and occasion), and many different dimensions to art can provide points of entry: technical, economic, political, and ethical, among others. Like language usage in most other contexts, art conversation tends not to thematize the validity claims implicit in speech acts, but it does make dimensions of validity available for art discourse.

TABLE 3.1. *Habermas's Correlations of Validity Claims, Language Functions, and Speech Acts*

Validity Claims	Universal Pragmatic Language Functions	Types of Speech Acts
Propositional truth	Representing a world	Constative
Normative legitimacy	Establishing interpersonal relations	Regulative
Sincerity	Expressing personal experience	Expressive

This initial description of art talk derives from Habermas's theory of communicative action. Habermas's theory suggests that three dimensions of validity have special significance in what I call conversation and discourse.[28] He identifies three validity claims for which every speaker is accountable when she or he uses language to reach an understanding: truth (*Wahrheit*), normative legitimacy or rightness (*Richtigkeit*), and sincerity or truthfulness (*Wahrhaftigkeit*). As is illustrated in Table 3.1, the three validity claims correspond to three universal pragmatic functions of language: to represent something in the world, to establish interpersonal relations, and to express the speaker's experience, respectively. These functions can be derived by considering the three types of illocutionary force that, according to Habermas, speech acts can have: constative (assert, inform, etc.), regulative (promise, request, etc.), and expressive (wish, avow, etc.).

Habermas regards propositional truth as the primary validity claim that we attach to constative speech acts. He says that language users raise a claim to truth whenever they make utterances as a way of asserting, informing, describing, and the like. In ordinary conversation this claim often accompanies language use without calling attention to itself. Truth becomes an issue, however, when an asserted proposition is called into question. At this point it becomes apparent that the speaker has raised a truth claim when asserting the proposition. The only way to "redeem" this truth claim is to engage in discourse. Habermas distinguishes "discourse" (*Diskurs*) from communicative action (*Handlung*). In communicative action we silently presuppose and accept the validity claims implicit in our utterances. In discourse, by contrast, we engage in argumentation, thematizing validity claims that have become problematic and investigating their legitimation (*Berechtigung*). In discourse we do not exchange "informations" as we might in an ordinary conversation about the weather, but rather we exchange arguments that serve to ground or refute validity claims that have been problematized. For the most part, "facts" become a topic in discourse, not in conversation.[29]

Habermas tends to view aesthetic validity claims as expressive rather than constative or regulative. In other words, when people call something beautiful or publicly judge the quality of a musical performance or literary work,

they are primarily[30] expressing their own experience and raising a claim to
be sincere or truthful in that expression. Such a claim can, of course, be
challenged by any conversation partner. The sorting out of such challenges
would characterize aesthetic discourse. Habermas also tends to regard art
and art criticism as a differentiated value sphere in which expressive validity
claims can be thematized. Science-technology and law-morality, by contrast,
are differentiated value spheres for the thematizing of constative and regulative validity claims, respectively.

Here my own departure from Habermas begins, despite my indebtedness
to his theory of communicative action in many other respects. Like Martin
Seel, I find it implausible to regard aesthetic validity claims as primarily
expressive.[31] My earlier account of aesthetic validity as imaginative cogency
points rather in a hermeneutic direction. That direction includes a notion
of artistic truth that neither restricts the general concept of truth to propositional truth à la Habermas nor limits art's validity to aesthetic validity à la
Seel. Yet I do agree with Habermas that the raising of validity claims occurs in
intersubjective linguistic practices, just as I agree with Seel that nonexpres-
sive but aesthetic validity claims are among those raised in this way. Art talk
is not the only arena in which aesthetic validity claims arise, however, nor
are aesthetic validity claims the only ones that commonly and legitimately
arise in art talk. What distinguishes art talk in modern Western societies
is not the occurrence of aesthetic validity claims but the precedence these
have there, whether explicitly or implicitly, over the other types of claims
made in art talk. Aesthetic validity claims have precedence because of the
way the artworld has developed as an institutionalized setting for promoting
aesthetic processes and adjudicating aesthetic validity claims.

Recent moralizing and transgressive art conversations, and the discourses
they generate, provide interesting test cases for my conception. Let's suppose
that a prominent elected official (Mayor Rudolph W. Giuliani, for example)
denounces an exhibition at a publicly funded art museum (the Brooklyn
Museum in New York City, for example), calling the art offensive, immoral,
and sacrilegious. And let's say the museum's director and trustees, the exhibition's sponsors, and some prominent art critics defend the exhibition as
a well-curated provocation about which mature citizens should make their
own judgments. Aesthetic considerations would appear to play little role on
either side, except insofar as the phrase "well-curated" implies them. If we
probed such talk further, however, and arranged for the participants to explain their pronouncements – arrangements obviously difficult to achieve
in mass-mediated public disputes of this sort – we would find that certain
aesthetic prejudgments actually play a crucial role. The mayor, for example, thinks that publicly funded art should be primarily "aesthetic" but in a
conventional way, such that exploration, creative interpretation, and presentation do not "get out of hand." The exhibition's advocates, by contrast, take
disrupting aesthetic conventions and pushing the imaginative "envelope" to

be marks of "aesthetic" authenticity and badges of artistic courage. When prompted to say what makes art "immoral" and why it should not be "immoral," moral critics return to the primacy of the aesthetic in art, just as do advocates of transgressive art, when encouraged to say what makes specific products or events "transgressive" and why these should be "transgressive." In the midst of such anti-aesthetic controversies the key players could decide, of course, that imaginative processes are not crucial to art and that questions of aesthetic validity are not worth discussing. Then, conceivably, the artworld might collapse or turn into its opposite. But until that occurs, the raising of aesthetic validity claims will be unavoidable and central to contemporary art talk. In addition, the raising of aesthetic validity claims in other contexts will receive considerable impetus and content from the way these claims arise in art talk.

On my account of art talk, then, when aesthetic validity claims arise in conversations about art, and when they are thematized in art discourse, this does not occur in separation from pursuits of cultural orientation. (That distinguishes my approach from a tendency toward aestheticism in much of post-Kantian philosophy of art.) Neither, however, does cultural orientation supplant aesthetic validity claims. (This, in turn, distinguishes my approach from a tendency toward anti-aestheticism on the part of both moralizing and transgressive art critics.)[32] Rather, the implicit appeal to aesthetic standards such as complexity, depth, and intensity, as it occurs in conversations about art, is part of a search for cultural orientation. This is so in two respects. First, talking about art with a view to aesthetic merits is indispensable to finding one's way within art itself. Such talk helps individuals, communities, and organizations understand art within their culture and reach decisions about how to use it and what to learn from it. Second, aesthetically focused art conversations serve the finding of one's way in aesthetic matters outside of art. It helps people direct their attention to imaginative processes, and it gives them vocabularies and syntax for making ordinary aesthetic judgments. Moreover, in both respects a conversational raising of aesthetic validity claims about art can follow the tracks I distinguished earlier, and can strengthen people's movements along those tracks both within and outside art: (1) envisioning an aesthetic outcome, (2) participating in an envisioning process, and (3) evaluating a finished event or product. The first and second of these tracks are especially important in the interactive procedures characteristic of new genre public art, which I have discussed elsewhere.[33]

In contexts of cultural pluralism and conflict, however, the appeal to aesthetic standards seldom remains implicit. When people have different understandings of the same art phenomena or reach contrary decisions about their worth, aesthetic validity claims will rise to the surface and become topics for discourse. This can take a number of foci. The discussion can focus on the *meaning* of aesthetic validity claims (e.g., What do you mean when you say this novel is profound?), on the *status* of these claims (e.g., Calling this photograph prurient is aesthetically irrelevant, isn't it?), on their *motivation* (e.g., When you say that was a great dance performance, you're just expressing your own personal bias, aren't you?), or on their *justification* (e.g., Why do you think a musical composition should be original?). Discourses that never move beyond issues of status and motivation tend to be less illuminating with respect to the art phenomenon under discussion, since they easily evade questions about a product's or event's aesthetic merits. This does not mean that such issues have no legitimate role to play in art discourse, however: the status of a claim indicates whether it properly belongs to the original conversation, and a claim's motivation suggests whether discourse about it is worth pursuing. Accordingly, when it comes to art discourse, I do not accept Habermas's restriction of discourse to argumentation aimed at legitimation. Nor do I share Seel's view that claims to validity get raised and justified by maintaining and confirming theoretical assertions. Certainly argumentation in the strict sense and theoretical assertions properly so called can play a role in art discourse. Yet it would be inaccurate to say that art discourse as a whole is a process of argumentation or theorization, and inappropriately restrictive to say that it should be such a process. Kant already recognized this when he spelled out the apparent antinomy of taste.

One additional point about art discourse needs to be made. Art discourse also belongs to the search for cultural orientation, and this makes aesthetic processes doubly reflexive. Earlier I said that exploration, creative interpretation, and presentation provide important ways in which individuals, communities, and organizations find their direction both within and by way of culture. Because the artworld has developed as an institutionalized setting for promoting aesthetic processes, art is a crucial site for the aesthetically laden pursuit of cultural orientation. That in itself gives art a certain reflexivity, making it a place where aesthetic processes can themselves be explored, interpreted, and presented. As a constituent of art's institutionalization, art talk makes such reflexivity palpable by serving simultaneously to help find one's way in art and to help find one's way in aesthetic matters outside art. Double reflexivity occurs when discourse about aesthetic validity claims, as raised in art conversation, points such talk toward the horizon of aesthetic standards. That happens, for example, when participants in an art talk say the talk itself is unimaginative. Saying this raises a different claim from the claim that this talk or some aspect of it is inaccurate or inappropriate. It has the effect of raising the stakes of art talk to an unsurpassable limit, similar to the effect of calling a theoretical debate illogical or a practical discussion illegitimate. Yet this metaclaim occurs fairly frequently within art talk, under various guises, and it contributes to double reflexivity.

The question of truth in art evinces the double reflexivity of aesthetic processes. The question arises from within art itself, at the conjunction of concerns about art talk, cultural orientation, and aesthetic validity. The prominence of aesthetic validity claims in art talk makes one wonder about the significance of such claims relative to epistemic and moral validity claims, both within art and outside it. The pursuit of cultural orientation by way of art, and by way of aesthetic processes outside art, raises questions about the authenticity of our learning through this pursuit. The processes of exploration, creative interpretation, and presentation pose puzzles about the import and integrity of artworks as aesthetic signs. As we shall see in subsequent chapters, the question of truth in art pertains to the significance, authenticity, and integrity of processes, events, and products to which people in Western societies assign special aesthetic merit.

PART II

CONSTRUCTIVE CLEARINGS

4

Truth as Disclosure

Assertion is not the primary "locus" of truth, but ... is based ... in the *disclosedness* of Dasein.

Martin Heidegger[1]

By considering a metacritical denial, an existential affirmation, and a postmetaphysical deconstruction, the first part of this book has demonstrated a need to reconstruct the idea of artistic truth. It has also explored the hermeneutical matrix from which this need arises, namely, the intersection in art between cultural orientation and aesthetic validity, as these become thematic in art talk. The question of artistic truth arises because people in modern Western societies experience art phenomena as aesthetic signs whose meaning can support searches for personal, cultural, and institutional orientation. It also arises because validity claims about such meaning regularly occur in our talking about art. Whereas metacritical denial and postmetaphysical deconstruction throw doubt on the validity of such claims, existential affirmation tends to embrace artistic import without worrying sufficiently about its distinctive validity. My challenge now is to fashion an idea of artistic truth that both addresses questions of validity and distinguishes artistic truth from the logical validity of propositions. It must be an idea that does not employ a propositionally inflected correspondence theory of truth, yet does not entail an antipropositional stance.

My response to this challenge has three stages. First Chapter 4 develops a general conception of truth as life-giving disclosure. According to this conception, propositional truth is one legitimate mode of such disclosure, but it is not the mode to which all other modes of truth should be either subordinated or reduced. This chapter sketches a general truth theory that is neither propositionally inflected nor a version of correspondence theory. It does so in critical dialogue with Martin Heidegger's conception of truth. The next chapter unfolds the implications of this general theory for the more specific idea of artistic truth. It describes artistic truth as "imaginative disclosure" for which questions of aesthetic validity remain crucial. Then Chapter 6 works out the details, navigating between Adorno's "esoteric" conception of artistic truth content and Habermasian emphases on public communication. It articulates three dimensions to the idea of artistic truth – authenticity, significance, and integrity – and it shows how they intersect dimensions of validity in ordinary language. The result is an internally differentiated idea that neither reduces artistic truth to propositional truth nor makes the two mutually incompatible. This idea gives credence to the element of "aboutness" that correspondence theories emphasize, but without turning the artwork into a representation or copy of something outside it. For, like all other aesthetic signs, artworks are intrinsically hermeneutical, involving exploration, presentation, and creative interpretation.

The conception of truth proposed by Martin Heidegger's *Being and Time* is both provocative and problematic. On the one hand, Heidegger provides a way to reconnect technical accounts of truth within logic, epistemology, and philosophy of language with the cultural practices and social institutions from which such accounts take distance. He does so by developing an ontological alternative to a pervasive "logical prejudice" in Western philosophy.[2] On the other hand, Heidegger takes such a dim view of "everydayness" and public communication that attaining truth becomes the inexplicable privilege of "authentic" existence. This privileging of authentic existence ensnares his conception in the self-referential incoherence of theorizing what, according to his own theory, cannot be theorized.[3] The promise and the problems of Heidegger's proposal are meshed. To redeem its potential, one must criticize its inherent flaws and ideological functions.

I hope to show that *Being and Time* has important insights to offer a critical hermeneutic theory of truth, more than could be acknowledged by Theodor W. Adorno, whose critique of Heidegger shapes my own interpretation. My aim is to begin to fashion an alternative general conception of truth that frees Heidegger's insights from what I consider to be a reactionary garb. As will become apparent, my alternative is to conceive truth as a process of life-giving disclosure, marked by human fidelity, to which a differentiated array of cultural practices and products can contribute in distinct and indispensable ways. Linguistic claims and logical propositions belong to such an array, but so do the practices and products of art. Let me first summarize Heidegger's argument for conceiving truth as disclosedness (section 4.1). Then I consider his claims that assertion or statement (*Aussage*) is a derivative mode of interpretation (section 4.2) and that Dasein's disclosedness is the primary locus of truth (section 4.3). I argue that assertion is indeed a mode of interpretation, but it is not derivative. I also argue that the larger truth of assertion does stem from its role in life-giving disclosure, even though, contra Heidegger, the disclosedness of human existence is not the primary locus of truth.

4.1 HEIDEGGER'S DISCLOSEDNESS

Section 44, titled "Dasein, Disclosedness, and Truth" (*SZ* 212–30), gives the central presentation of Heidegger's conception of truth in *Being and Time*. This section simultaneously concludes the book's first division, titled "The Preparatory Fundamental Analysis of Dasein," and the sixth chapter in this division, titled "Care as the Being of Dasein." It not only summarizes and deepens Heidegger's analysis of "being-in-the-world" as the "basic state of Dasein" but also marks a transition to interpreting this state as thoroughly temporal in Division Two (titled "Dasein and Temporality"). In this doubly laden context, Heidegger argues that the primary locus of truth is not propositions or assertions or discursive claims. Rather, the primary locus is the disclosedness of that being (Dasein) which, among other activities, understands and formulates and discusses assertions. While making this argument, Heidegger transforms the correspondence theory of truth, traditionally formulated as the *adaequatio intellectus et rei*, into a conception of "disclosedness" (*Erschlossenheit*) and "discoveredness" (*Entdecktheit*).

Heidegger aims to ask about the meaning of Being. He approaches this question by analyzing and interpreting Dasein (i.e., human being) as that entity for whom Being is a question. He distinguishes Dasein from entities such as tools that are "at hand" or "handy" (*zuhanden*) as well as from entities such as scientifically defined properties that are "objectively present" (*vorhanden*). He also analyzes the three directions taken by Dasein's "being-in-the-world" (*In-der-Welt-sein*): "being together with the world," "being-with" others, and "being-one's-self." In more traditional language, which Heidegger carefully avoids, he distinguishes three types of relations – subject-object, subject-subject, and subject–self relations – only to argue that they form a unitary structure founded in Dasein's "being-in." Their unity becomes apparent from the terms he uses to summarize Dasein's orientation in the first two types of relations: taking care (*Besorgen*) of that which is handy, and concern (*Fürsorge*) toward fellow human beings. Both orientations rest in a more fundamental care (*Sorge*). Moreover, Dasein's dealings are guided by circumspection (*Umsicht*) toward the handy and by considerateness (*Rücksicht*) and tolerance (*Nachsicht*) toward others. These guides are made possible by the sight (*Sicht*) that characterizes Dasein's being-in per se. Such sight is what Heidegger calls understanding (*Verstehen*). Together with attunement (*Befindlichkeit*) and talk (*Rede*), understanding is one of three "equiprimordial" modes or structures (*existentialia*) of Dasein's being-in (*SZ* 161).[4]

Two fundamental points affect everything Heidegger writes about understanding and talk. First, both understanding and talk are modes of Dasein's disclosedness. Second, since Dasein's disclosedness follows the orientation of care, and since temporality (*Zeitlichkeit*) is "the ontological meaning of care" (section 65), temporality characterizes both understanding and talk (section 68). Let me briefly elaborate each point.

The first point pertains to the essential openness that characterizes Dasein. Unlike other entities, Dasein not only occupies a field of relationships but also holds itself open in these relationships. For Dasein, that which is at hand resides in a significant totality of relevance (*Bewandtnis*), even when Dasein experiences or analyzes what is at hand, in abstraction from its relevance, as something merely objectively present. So too, Dasein's selfhood is always constituted by coexistence with others for whom what is at hand has significance, even when we regularly experience ourselves as indifferent members of a mass public (as *das Man* or "the they"). In other words, human beings are essentially open to their world and fellow human beings: the world lies open to human dealings and, even amid inauthenticity and indifference, human beings remain open to themselves and one another. In Heidegger's own words, Dasein (literally "there-being") "bears in its ownmost being the character of not being closed. The expression 'there' means this essential disclosedness. Through disclosedness, this being (Dasein) is 'there' for itself together with the Dasein of the world. . . . By its very nature, Dasein brings its there along with it. . . . *Dasein is its [disclosedness]*" (*SZ* 132–3).

The second point pertains to the kind of temporality that underlies understanding and talk, respectively, and unites them in the structure of care.[5] Heidegger arrives at the theme of temporality by examining "anticipatory resoluteness" as the authentic and most primordial truth of Dasein (*SZ* 297). He claims that understanding, which always projects Dasein's potentiality-of-being (*Seinkönnen*), is essentially futural, even when understanding is inauthentic. In contrast to understanding, talk, which articulates the disclosedness constituted by understanding and attunement, does not have an essential temporalization, whether future, past, or present. "Factically," however, the "making-present" that characterizes inauthentic understanding has "a *privileged* constitutive function" in ordinary talk (*SZ* 349). Crucial in this context is the claim that both Dasein's disclosedness and its "basic existentiell possibilities" of "authenticity and inauthenticity" are "founded in temporality" in the manner described (*SZ* 350). By extension, the futural character of understanding, and the anticipatory resoluteness of authentic understanding, provide preconditions for the disclosure of other entities.

Reconstructed primarily from sections 31–34 and 44, Heidegger's argument against propositionally inflected correspondence theories of truth, and for his own conception of truth as disclosedness, involves accounts of understanding, assertion, and talk. Dasein understands itself, others, and its world, he says, by projecting its own potentials and possibilities from within its own factual context. Understanding is characterized by projective thrownness or thrown projection. Through projection, understanding (*Verstehen*) lets entities be encountered in their discoveredness (*Entdecktheit*) by Dasein in its disclosedness (*Erschlossenheit*). Such an encounter is developed in interpretation (*Auslegung*) as a working out (*Ausarbeitung*) of projected possibilities. When directed at understanding the world, as distinct from oneself or others, interpretation works out the purposes for which something exists by elaborating its embeddedness in a purposive whole. It always does so on the basis of a prior understanding, and often in a pre-predicative manner. More specifically, Heidegger argues that such "circumspect interpretation" rests on the three projective involvements that understanding has with the world: fore-having, fore-sight, and fore-conception (*Vorhabe, Vorsicht,* and *Vorgriff*), which could also be translated as pre-possession, pre-view, and pre-conception. An interpretation is never a neutral gathering of bare facts. According to Heidegger, there is a circle in all interpretation, even in so simple an act as finding the right hammer for a particular task. "Every interpretation which is to contribute some understanding must already have understood what is to be interpreted" (*SZ* 152). That is the ontological basis for a familiar hermeneutical circle in the interpretation of texts.

Heidegger's account of projective understanding and its interpretive elaboration forms the basis for his approach to propositional truth. His approach treats assertion or statement (*Aussage*) as a derivative mode of interpretation (*Auslegung*), which itself is an outworking (*Ausbildung*) of understanding.[6] Assertion is derivative because of the abstraction it requires from the holistic context in which interpretation ordinarily occurs. Assertion points out or indicates an entity in abstraction from its purposive involvements. Through such "pointing out" (*Aufzeigen*), assertion "determines" (*bestimmt*) something (predication – *Prädikation*) and communicates this indication and predication to others (communication – *Mitteilung*). At the same time, unlike ordinary circumspect interpretation, which approaches a hammer, for example, as something serviceable within a context of relevance, assertion forces the hermeneutical "as" back to "the uniform level of what is merely objectively present. . . . This levelling down of the primordial 'as' of circumspect interpretation to the as of the determination of objective presence is the specialty of the [assertion]" (*SZ* 158). So assertion involves a transition from handiness to objective presence or, in non-Heideggerian terms, from pragmatic usefulness to propositional identity.

A similar concern about the transition from handiness to objective presence marks Heidegger's account of talk (*Rede*) as a second equiprimordial mode of Dasein's disclosedness. Talk makes possible the communication of shared attunements and common understandings, he claims. It gets expressed in language (*Sprache*), and it articulates meaning.[7] For Heidegger it is crucial that whatever is intelligible has already been articulated (*gegliedert*), even prior to being interpreted and asserted: "[Talk] is the articulation [*Artikulation*] of intelligibility. Thus it already lies at the basis of interpretation and statement [*Aussage*]" (*SZ* 161). Likewise, the making of assertions is only one of the many ways in which we communicate in talk. Assertoric communication is a special case of a more comprehensive "articulation of being-with-one-another understandingly" (*SZ* 162). But such articulation of what we have in common usually occurs in inauthentic ways. In a mass society, where Dasein is thrown "into the publicness [*Öffentlichkeit*] of the they" (*SZ* 167), talk ordinarily occurs as idle talk (*Gerede*), which closes off our being-in-the-world and covers over the "innerworldly beings" (*SZ* 169) to which we are nevertheless related. So too, understanding ordinarily occurs as a restless, distracted, and uprooted curiosity (*Neugier*) that makes it impossible to decide "what is disclosed in a genuine understanding, and what is not" (*SZ* 173). Such idle talk, curiosity, and ambiguity manifest the "falling prey" (*Verfallen*) to public existence that characterizes Dasein in its inauthentic mode of being-in-the-world.[8]

These accounts of understanding, assertion, and talk provide the impetus to Heidegger's critique of modern epistemology and of the premodern metaphysics from which it arose. The modern conception of truth treats assertion (*die Aussage*) or judgment (*das Urteil*) as the locus of truth, he claims. The modern conception also defines truth as the judgment's agreement (*Übereinstimmung*) with its object (*Gegenstand*). Heidegger then gives a novel account of what such agreement comes to. Contrary to Descartes or Kant, Heidegger argues that the agreement between a judgment and an object does not mean that mental representations (*Vorstellungen*) get compared among themselves or in relation to the so-called real thing. Rather it means the asserted entity "shows itself *as [that] very same thing.*" The truth of an assertion is a being-true (*Wahrsein*), in the sense of the assertion's discovering the asserted entity as it is in itself (*SZ* 218).[9] An assertion's being-true is its capacity to discover, its to-be-discovering (*Entdeckend-sein*). This capacity, in turn, depends ontologically upon Dasein's basic state of being-in-the-world (*SZ* 219).[10] The truth of assertion reaches back via interpretation "to the disclosedness of understanding" (*SZ* 223). More specifically, just as discovering (*Entdecken*) and the discoveredness (*Entdecktheit*) of entities are grounded in the world's disclosedness (*Erschlossenheit*), so the assertion's capacity to discover (*Entdeckend-sein*) is grounded in Dasein's disclosedness (*Erschlossenheit*), without which the world would not be disclosed.

Along this rather circuitous route, then, we return to the central point of Heidegger's analytic of Dasein, namely, that in all relationships, and in every mode of their being, human beings are essentially open. That essential openness is also the key to Heidegger's general conception of truth. For "only with the disclosedness of Dasein is the *most primordial* phenomenon of truth attained.... In that Dasein essentially *is* its disclosedness, and, as disclosed, discloses and discovers, it is essentially 'true.' Dasein *is 'in the truth'*" (*SZ* 220–1). This existential condition, if you will, is what Heidegger finds missing both in modern notions of correspondence between judgment and object, or between proposition and fact, such as Beardsley assumes, and in premodern notions of an adequation between intellect and thing, such as Hofstadter revives. These notions miss the open-ended connections that sustain both sides within a larger whole and that make any "correspondence" possible. They also miss the complexity and risk that truth involves. For, according to Heidegger, Dasein's disclosedness is both authentic (i.e., governed by Dasein's "ownmost potentiality-of-being," *SZ* 221) and inauthentic (i.e., governed by "public interpretedness," *SZ* 222). Hence Dasein is equiprimordially not only in the truth but also in untruth. Yet inauthenticity and being in untruth are made possible by disclosedness and discoveredness; truth must be wrested from the inauthenticity of Dasein and the concealment (*Verborgenheit*) of entities.

To summarize: Heidegger thinks that propositionally inflected correspondence theories cover up the ontological foundations from which any agreement between assertion and object derives (*SZ* 223–6). Contrary to such theories, "[Assertion] is not the primary 'locus' of truth," but is itself grounded in the primary locus of truth, namely, in Dasein's disclosedness. Dasein's disclosedness is "the ontological condition of the possibility that [assertions] can be true or false (discovering or covering over)" (*SZ* 226). Moreover, because disclosedness is essential to Dasein's being, "*all truth is relative to the being of Dasein*" (*SZ* 227). This does not mean that truth is left to subjective discretion or is constituted by a transcendental subject. Rather it means that without Dasein's disclosedness there would be neither authenticity nor inauthenticity, neither discovering nor covering over, neither discoveredness nor concealment, and neither true assertions nor false ones.[11] Truth is relative to Dasein's *being*, not to Dasein's will or to its consciousness. In this way Heidegger thinks he has found a way beyond either absolutism or skepticism with regard to truth. Neither the dogmatic claim that there are eternal truths nor general skepticism about truth has an adequate ontological basis, he says. Both positions overlook the reciprocal and foundational relationship between truth and Dasein: just as truth belongs to the core of Dasein's being, so Dasein exists for the sake of truth. Moreover, such reciprocity extends to Being, toward whose understanding Dasein, in its disclosedness, is predisposed. "'There is' [*Es gibt*] Being – not beings – only insofar as truth is. And truth *is* only because and as long as Dasein is. Being and truth 'are' equiprimordially" (*SZ* 230).

Some readers have accused Heidegger of "subjectivizing" truth, in the sense of reducing it to a condition or quality of human existence: after all, he does claim that all truth is relative to Dasein's being. Yet this accusation ignores his explicit opposition to subjectivism and his marked preference for substantives such as disclosedness and discoveredness over verbs such as disclose and discover. That leads other readers to claim that Heidegger turns truth into a state of Being, one for which Dasein's being-in-the-world is crucial but perhaps not decisive. Accordingly, the fatal flaw in Heidegger's conception, one that deepens in his later writings, might lie in his both dehumanizing and structuralizing a dynamic process of disclosure. It seems to me that neither the first nor the second reading by itself does justice to the scope of Heidegger's project and to an unavoidable tension in his own conception of truth. There is a sense in which Heidegger both subjectivizes and dehumanizes truth. To derive an adequate alternative, one must wrestle with both tendencies in their dialectical tension.[12] I develop this "foreconception" by criticizing Heidegger's accounts of assertion (section 4.2) and disclosedness (section 4.3). The criticisms serve to articulate my own general conception of truth as one that, like Heidegger's, is neither propositionally inflected nor a correspondence theory.

4.2 ASSERTION AND INTERPRETATION

Heidegger lays out the derivative character of assertion in order to deconstruct the ontological foundations of propositionally inflected correspondence theories of truth. In the process, he makes a number of claims that, when taken together, diminish the role of assertions in the pursuit of truth and belittle their significance. Although such may not have been the clear intent of his formulations, arguably it has been their dominant effect. It has led to readings such as Rapaport's that exaggerate *anti*propositional tendencies in Heidegger's conception of truth and go beyond the *non*propositional emphasis that I endorse. Let me first sketch two examples of how Heidegger can be read to this effect, and how alternative readings could counter what may not have been his clear intent. Then I analyze the claim that assertion is a derivative mode of interpretation.

Heidegger points out that the making of assertions – "*Aussagen machen*" – is only one of many practices within talk (alongside commanding, wishing, interceding, etc., *SZ* 161–2), and that self-expression, hearing, and keeping silent are constitutive for talk (*SZ* 162–5). Here he can be read as saying that the making of assertions is not nearly as important as traditional philosophy and linguistics have claimed, and that other practices and "existential possibilities" are more important to ordinary language than is the making of assertions. But on a different and, I think, preferable interpretation, the main point about asserting would be that it normally occurs in connection with these other practices and as a way to actualize such existential possibilities. It is precisely because of such embeddedness, and because of the role of assertions in pursuing intersubjective understanding, that the making and discussing of assertions become crucial to public "talk" and deserve the special attention of philosophers and linguists, no matter how misguided previous accounts may have been. The task, then, would not simply be to free grammar from logic, as Heidegger puts it (*SZ* 165), but also to liberate logic from its reification of the practice of making assertions.

Similarly, when Heidegger argues that the agreement of assertion and object derives from the disclosedness of Dasein and the discoveredness of entities, he embeds a thinner epistemological correspondence between subjective product and independent object in a thicker ontological harmony between the state of Dasein and the state of other entities. Described by Heidegger as a relation commonly understood as merely "objectively present" (*SZ* 224), the thinner correspondence comes to appear less important for truth than the thicker harmony. This despite the fact that Heidegger's account of the thicker harmony seems to remain within the modern correspondence theory's subject-object paradigm, to which he explicitly objects. On a different and more fruitful reading, however, the crucial "agreement" would not be between the assertion and the object. It would occur instead among those who make assertions about the object, as well as between the process of making assertions and recognized principles for intersubjective conversation. Such an alternative, with its emphasis on the search for intersubjective "agreement" in accordance with recognized principles, can be extracted from Heidegger's account of "being-in-the-world" as including "being-with" others. Yet his critique of correspondence theories and his locating of truth in Dasein's disclosedness make little of intersubjective relations. In fact, his initial orientation to circumspect interpretation of the handy, combined with his disparaging view of the public sphere, makes it difficult to extract this alternative without violence.

What, more specifically, needs to be said about the purported derivativeness of assertion or statement (*die Aussage*)? To examine this topic, let me introduce a distinction and make a related comment. In the first place, the intelligibility of Heidegger's claims depends on a distinction between the making of assertions as a cultural *practice* and the availability of assertions as cultural *accomplishments*. Heidegger tends to elide this distinction. I mark it by using "asserting" and "assertion" as technical terms, respectively, for the practice and the accomplishment at issue. In the second place, the derivation of asserting and assertion from (the practices and accomplishments of) interpretation does not entail that the asserted (*das Ausgesagte*) simply acquires a definite character when asserted. Rather, the asserted can already array itself (or offer itself) in definable ways, and this array can impinge on interpretation, even when interpretation is nonassertoric. Although such arraying and impinging do not by themselves give the asserted a definite character, neither does the asserted's becoming definable simply depend on its being asserted.[13] The reasons for making this comment will emerge from my more detailed discussion of the purported derivation of *die Aussage* from interpretation (*Auslegung*). Let me turn first to Heidegger's account of what I have distinguished as asserting and assertion, before I examine his account of the asserted.

Asserting and Assertion

Heidegger distinguishes three significations of the term assertion (*die Aussage*): pointing out (*Aufzeigung*), predication (*Prädikation*), and communication (*Mitteilung*). Of these, pointing out, which lets an entity be seen from itself (*SZ* 154), is the primary signification. Heidegger considers predication to be founded in pointing out, which is broader, and he describes communication as an extension of pointing out and predication. The primacy he assigns to "pointing out" becomes apparent from his unifying definition of assertion as "*a pointing out which communicates and defines*" (*mitteilend bestimmende Aufzeigung*) (*SZ* 156). He does not define assertion as predication that points out and communicates or as communication that points out and predicates. So too, he does not describe assertion as a mode of talk but as a mode of interpretation.

Heidegger's account of interpretation has a prior orientation to the purposive conduct of craftspersons and the users of tools. This orientation shapes the contrast Heidegger draws between the categorical statement "the hammer is heavy," understood by logicians to mean "this thing, the hammer, has the property of heaviness," and related formulations common to ordinary talk: "'Initially' there are no such statements in heedful circumspection. But it does have its specific ways of interpretation which . . . may take some such form as 'the hammer is too heavy' or, even better, 'too heavy, the other hammer!' The primordial act of interpretation lies not in a theoretical sentence, but in circumspectly and heedfully putting away or changing the inappropriate tool 'without wasting words'" (*SZ* 157). Given this prior orientation to purposive conduct, Heidegger analyzes assertion primarily as a practice rather than an accomplishment, and one that is originally purposive, although tending toward abstraction: "The [assertion's] pointing out is accomplished on the basis of what is already disclosed in understanding, or what is circumspectly discovered. The [assertion] is not an unattached kind of behavior which could of itself primarily disclose beings in general, but always already maintains itself on the basis of being-in-the-world" (*SZ* 156). By emphasizing the practice of asserting and its ontological roots in Dasein, Heidegger creates the impression that assertions as such, as accomplishments, are cut off from the totality of human involvements with the world, and that theoretical assertions are the farthest removed.

Unfortunately, Heidegger's approach presupposes a problematic hierarchy of originality according to which the accomplishment derives from the practice, and a more explicit and more definite practice derives from ones less explicit and less definite. Only such a hierarchy can explain why predication should be considered "narrower" than pointing out (rather than, for example, more precise and inclusive), or why asserting "x is y" should be thought to arise via modification from circumspect interpretation (rather than simply constituting one type of purposive conduct, perhaps, or shaping or even giving rise to circumspect interpretation). While I acknowledge, with Heidegger, that, once accomplished, an assertion can be discussed and analyzed in its own right and in abstraction from the occasion and circumstances for making the assertion, this fact in itself does not warrant the view that accomplished assertions are cut off from other human involvements with the world.

In addition, the force of "pointing out" depends on its connections with predication and communication. I see no reason to think that a pre-predicative and noncommunicative pointing out would have any intrinsic connection with asserting and assertions. Consider, for example, Heidegger, alone in his shop, simply pointing his finger at a hammer while thinking "The hammer is too heavy." He might be pointing something out, but he would not be asserting anything, nor would any assertion become available as an accomplishment. Far from being founded in pointing out, predication is that which allows any pointing out to become assertoric. Insofar as assert-ing is an illocutionary act that requires an interpretable utterance in a public language, a private thought not communicated to anyone else, no matter how "pointed," would be neither predicative nor assertoric. What allows the entity to be "seen from itself" is not the pointing out as such, but rather the predication by way of which something can be taken as something dis-tinct from something else.[14] Furthermore, predication as a practice cannot get off the ground in the absence of predications as accomplishments: not only does the practice simply consist of formulating and discussing predica-tions but also such formulation and discussion necessarily refer to previously accomplished predications.

My criticisms have implications for two corollaries to Heidegger's posi-tion that assertion is a derivative mode of interpretation. The first corollary is that assertion has the same thrown projection that characterizes under-standing as a mode of Dasein: "Like interpretation in general, the [assertion] necessarily has its existential foundations in fore-having, fore-sight, and fore-conception" (*SZ* 157). Looked at from one direction, this characterization of assertion is unobjectionable: to the extent that it is an interpretive prac-tice, the making of assertions draws on a hermeneutical fore-structure. This hermeneutical account of asserting contains an important insight, and it distinguishes Heidegger's epistemology from the empiricism of Monroe Beardsley. Looked at from another direction, however, Heidegger's charac-terization detaches assertions as such from their conversational texture and demotes their predicative status. He does not emphasize sufficiently that the hermeneutical fore-structure on which asserting draws is itself shaped in part by the predications already available in conversation and language. Nor is such predicative pre-shaping of the hermeneutical fore-structure a mark of falling prey. It is, one could say, ontologically unavoidable, even for "authentic" existence. Yet Heidegger is right to resist the tendency for accomplished assertions, when singled out for discussion in contexts of ar-gument or theory, to float free from their hermeneutical matrix. He is also correct to counter any privileging of accomplished assertions in the forma-tion of that matrix.

The second corollary is that, according to Heidegger, assertion charac-teristically turns the "existential-hermeneutical as" of circumspect interpre-tation into an "apophantical as." Heidegger describes this transition as the leveling down of "the primordial 'as'" (*SZ* 158). The term "leveling down" (*Nivellierung*) captures the gist of Heidegger's account. He does not call the transition from the hermeneutical to the apophantic a "heightening" or an "enriching" or a "making more precise." He says that under the impact of assertions the "as" of circumspect interpretation gets "cut off" (*abgeschnitten*) and "forced back" (*zurückgedrängt*), that it "dwindles" (*sinkt herab*) (*SZ* 158). Such strong language presupposes that the fullness of pre-predicative interpretation is somehow paradigmatic for all interpretive practices, and that the apophantic "as" peculiar to assertion is primarily a modification of the hermeneutical "as." If instead, as I have suggested, one anchors the making of assertions in conversation and ordinary language, and if one ties the possibility of asserting to the availability of predications, then the transition from interpretation to assertion need not involve a leveling or dwindling. The transition would be not so much a modification as a movement from one level to another, not a leveling but a leap. Accordingly, the "leveling" would lie not in the transition from *hermeneuein* to *apophansis* but in Heidegger's account of the transition. In fact, this is where I think the leveling lies.

The Asserted

Heidegger's leveling undermines his account of what gets asserted (*das Ausgesagte*). Although his account promises to break with epistemic subjectivism and the representational theory of knowledge that has dominated modern philosophy, it also introduces ambiguities that take a toll on his conception of truth.

Heidegger rightly insists in various places that what is asserted is not a "representation" (*Vorstellung*), neither a mental object nor a state of consciousness (*SZ* 62, 154, 217–18). At the same time, the asserted is not the "content" or "meaning" of an accomplished assertion (*SZ* 155–6). Much less is the asserted a free-floating proposition that "exists" independently of assertoric practices and accomplishments (*SZ* 159–60). Rather, what is asserted, he argues, is the entity itself in a certain mode of its givenness. For example, when one says "The hammer is too heavy," what is asserted – and in this is allowed to "be seen from itself" or "discovered for sight" – is the hammer itself, a "being in the mode of its being at hand" (*SZ* 154). The hammer is put forward (*ausgesagt*) and is explicitly determined as being "too heavy" for some purpose. And in uttering this assertion, one is sharing with others the hammer as so "seen" with such a definite character: "As something communicated, what is spoken [*das Ausgesagte*] can be 'shared' by the others with the speaker [*mit dem Aussagenden*] even when they themselves do not have the beings pointed out and defined in a palpable and visible range. What is spoken [*das Ausgesagte*] can be 'passed along' in further retelling.... But at the same time what is pointed out can become veiled again in this further retelling, although the knowledge and cognition growing in such hearsay always means beings themselves and does not 'affirm' a 'valid meaning' passed around" (*SZ* 155).

In elaborating this analysis, Heidegger is of two minds. On the one hand, he wants to say that the asserter does not constitute or create the asserted in its specific character as asserted, but rather lets the entity stand out as it is in itself in a certain mode of its givenness. The hammer simply is too heavy or too light or too large for some purpose, and the asserter simply points the hammer out (or lets it be seen) in this regard. On the other hand, because Heidegger insists on the derivativeness of assertion, he also wants to claim that, as predication and communication, assertion does something to the asserted: predication "narrows" (*Verengung*) the asserted, "determines it" (*bestimmt*), and makes it "*explicitly* manifest" (ausdrücklich *offenbar zu machen*); and communication shares the asserted with others (*teilt . . mit dem Anderen*) (*SZ* 154–5). In principle, assertion turns something at hand, such as the hammer, into something objectively present (or lets it turn into such) and veils its handiness (or lets this become veiled): "Something *at hand with which* we have to do or perform something, turns into something 'about which' the [assertion] that points it out is made. . . . Within this discovering of objective presence which covers over handiness, what is encountered as objectively present is determined in its being objectively present in such and such a way. Now the access is first available for something like *qualities*" (*SZ* 158).[15] Heidegger seems to claim both that the asserted entity simply presents itself and that asserting affects the asserted.[16]

Heidegger's account of the asserted argues correctly that the accomplished assertion is about an entity (or a range of entities) in a certain mode of its givenness. This "aboutness" is not a third thing in addition to the assertion and the entity; indeed, it is not a thing at all. Rather, "aboutness" simply indicates the mutual mediation of the assertoric practice and that toward which one can engage in this practice.[17] Moreover, Heidegger rightly suggests that the entity asserted allows itself to be asserted and even, in a sense, calls forth the assertion.

To indicate the entity's "givenness" for assertoric practice, let me introduce "predicative availability" as a technical term.[18] The term suggests that, among the many ways in which entities are available (Heidegger: at hand) for human practices, they also offer themselves to us in a way that lets us make assertions about them. We do not impose such availability upon them, nor does our assertoric practice alone create their identity, even though asserting can help shape their identity, for better or worse. At the same time, the predicative availability of entities is only one of the many ways in which they can engage us. It is also one way in which many entities, lacking predicative capacities and practices of their own, cannot engage one another: nails are not predicatively available for hammers, and a hammer cannot engage other hammers in their predicative availability.

Heidegger's account of predicative availability goes astray when he tries to ground the asserted in the discovered. This attempt leads him to claim both that the asserted entity is predicatively and nonpredicatively available and that, when asserted, the entity's nonpredicative availability becomes veiled or, as it were, undiscovered. Two problems come to the fore. In the first place, predicative availability comes to be seen as a distorting or an opposing of nonpredicative availability, rather than simply another mode of availability that can support nonpredicative modes and can receive support from them. By contrast, I would argue that, rather than covering up the hammer's nonpredicative availability for hammering, for example, the hammer's availability for being predicated as "too heavy" makes its nonpredicative availability more broadly and precisely accessible. In the second place, Heidegger assigns assertoric practice a constitutive or constructive force that belies its limited "space" in the range of human practices. Heidegger sometimes suggests that asserting determines (*bestimmt*) the asserted and that the true assertion discovers the entity. It would be better, I think, to say that asserting discovers not the entity as such but the entity in its predicative availability. Hence, in my own terms, asserting is an interpretive practice, as Heidegger suggests, but it is not derivative from other interpretive practices, nor is it possible without reference to already accomplished assertions. So, too, the asserted is available in many nonpredicative ways, as Heidegger's account of handiness indicates, but its predicative availability neither opposes nor occludes the asserted entity's multifaceted and nonpredicative availability. My alternative formulation has a direct bearing on Heidegger's conception of truth as Dasein's disclosedness, the topic of the next section.

4.3 CORRESPONDENCE AND DISCLOSURE

When he analyzes the derivative character of assertion in section 33, Heidegger has in view the position, advanced in section 44, that Dasein's disclosedness, not assertion, is the primary locus of truth. To establish this position, the three subsections of section 44 (a) explore the ontological foundations of traditional correspondence theories that regard truth as the agreement of assertion and object (*SZ* 214–19), (b) demonstrate the derivative character of such theories (*SZ* 219–26), and (c) analyze the kind of Being that truth as disclosedness possesses (*SZ* 226–30). Without rehearsing every step in Heidegger's extended argument, I follow his outline to discuss (1) the connection between truth and the correctness of accomplished assertions, and (2) the connection between assertoric agreement and Dasein's disclosedness. Several clues for my critical reading of section 44 come from the work of Ernst Tugendhat.[19]

Correctness and Truth

In harmony with my own criticisms of Heidegger's account of the asserted, Tugendhat argues that the first subsection of section 44 slides through three different formulations of the truth of an assertion, implicitly taking distance from Husserl's theory of truth, to arrive, without sufficient argumentation, at Heidegger's own characteristic idea of truth.[20] In moving from Husserl's static conception of the assertoric act as a mode of intentionality to a more dynamic conception of assertion as a mode of disclosedness, Heidegger capitalizes on an unexamined ambiguity in the concept of "uncovering" or "discovering" (*Entdecken*): "In the first instance, [discovering] stands for pointing out (*apophainesthai*) in general. In this sense every assertion – the false as well as the true – can be said to [discover]. Nevertheless, Heidegger [also] employs the word in a narrow and pregnant sense according to which a false assertion would be a covering up rather than [a discovering]. In this case ... the truth lies in [being-discovering] [*Entdeckendsein*]; however, what does [discovering] now mean if it no longer signifies pointing out [*Aufzeigen*] in general? How is *aletheia* to be differentiated from *apophansis*?"[21] Tugendhat replies that Heidegger gives no answer, for he "fails to expressly differentiate ... between the broad and the narrow meaning of [discovering]."[22]

Against Heidegger, Tugendhat insists that the truth or falsity of an assertion cannot lie merely in its discovering or covering up an entity, but must lie more specifically in how such discovering or covering up takes place. Just as the true assertion discovers the entity *as the entity is in itself*, so the false assertion "[covers up] [*verdeckt*] the entity as it is in itself, and it does this in that it [discovers] it in another way than the way it is in itself."[23] Although Heidegger is right to ground the truth of assertions as correctness (*Richtigkeit*) in the truth of entities as discoveredness or (in the term he later prefers) unconcealment (*Unverborgenheit*), he simply bypasses Husserl's insight that the truth of entities is not their givenness as such but rather their self-givenness, a "superior mode of givenness."[24] As a pointing out that aims at truth, assertion tries to measure the entity's givenness against that entity's self-givenness. Hence, Tugendhat argues, assertion must be directed not simply by the entity as it shows itself but by the entity as it manifests itself *in itself*: "Self-sameness is the critical measure of unconcealedness [*des Entbergens*]. Only if this second meaning of being-directed is recognized in its autonomy can it profitably be clarified with the help of the first; so that one can say that the false assertion covers up the entity and that only the true assertion genuinely unconceals [*entbirgt*] the entity – that is, as it is in itself."[25] According to Tugendhat, it is only because Heidegger first ignores the distinction between givenness and self-givenness, and then equates truth with discovering as *apophansis*, that he can subsequently regard untruth as an aspect of truth, rather than as something opposed to truth.

To provide terminological markers for Tugendhat's criticisms, I distinguish between the "correctness" of an accomplished assertion and the "predicative self-disclosure" of the asserted entity in its predicative availability. By "predicative self-disclosure" I mean a process whereby an entity, in its predicative availability, offers or manifests itself in relevant accord with nonpredicative aspects of its availability.[26] I agree with Heidegger (using my own terminology) that both assertoric correctness and predicative self-disclosure are grounded in a more comprehensive mediation of disclosive practices and systatic availability.[27] But I also agree with Tugendhat that, to connect this mediation with the concept of truth, one must have a way to distinguish between true and untrue "discoverings," "unconcealments," and the like.

At the same time, I want to avoid Tugendhat's tendency to anchor the distinction between true and untrue in the "self-givenness" of the asserted entity. Although an accomplished assertion about an entity does aim to discover the entity as that entity manifests itself "in itself," not all accomplished assertions are about entities, nor is such discovering sufficient for the assertion to be correct, nor does an entity's manifesting itself occur in isolation from other entities. Accomplished assertions can be about processes or actions rather than about entities (e.g., "To err is human"); the correctness of accomplished assertions depends in part on how they are formulated and used, and not merely on how they "accord" with what is asserted; and the entity's manifesting itself occurs in relationship to other entities, including those entities (i.e., human beings) to whom the entity is manifesting itself. Moreover, many of the entities about which we make assertions have a historical character that precludes their having a permanently fixed identity. The Husserlian notions of self-givenness and "evidence" have a static quality that belies the dynamics uncovered, albeit only partially, by Heidegger's notion of discoveredness. To avoid the static connotations of "self-givenness," I have adopted the term "predicative self-disclosure."

All that having been said, an account is still required for the predicative self-disclosure of asserted entities and the correctness of accomplished assertions. Earlier I introduced the term "predicative availability" to refer to the fact that entities (and not only entities) offer themselves to us in ways that let us make assertions about them. I also said that asserting something discovers the entity in its predicative availability. Now it can be added that, when correct, an accomplished assertion discovers the entity in its predicative availability in a manner that accords with other relevant ways in which the asserted entity is available. Imagine, for example, that a carpenter says "too heavy, give me the other one" in a certain context. If correct, her (implicit) assertion "The hammer is too heavy" discovers the hammer as something of which relative heaviness can be predicated. It discovers this in a way that accords with the (un)suitability of the hammer for the task at hand.

Accordingly, asserting can go wrong in two ways: (1) by failing to discover the entity in its predicative availability and (2) by discovering this in a manner that fails to accord with other relevant ways in which the entity is available. The first way usually results in assertions that are "false" in the sense of being misleading or misplaced (e.g., claiming "The hammer is too heavy" when the tool in question offers itself for predication not as a hammer but as a pipe wrench). The second way usually results in assertions that are "false" in the sense of being inaccurate (e.g., claiming "The hammer is too heavy" when the hammer in question is very well suited for the task and for the carpenter in question).

Those are not the only ways in which asserting can go wrong. For example, the asserter can misspeak or can respond inappropriately to a question or can deliberately lie. In addition, the "fore-structure" of a speech community can be such that false assertions are routinely made about an entire range of entities. Hence, looked at from the side of assertoric practice, the measure of assertoric truth cannot be a single criterion such as the traditional "correspondence with the object" or the Heideggerian "discovering the entity [(just as it is) in itself]." Rather the measure must be a complex of considerations that may not be specifiable as necessary and sufficient conditions.

Satisfying this complex depends in part on the entity's predicative self-disclosure. In the usage proposed here, "predicative self-disclosure" refers specifically to the asserted entity in its predicative availability. This usage acknowledges that entities disclose themselves when they are neither asserted nor predicatively available. In fact, if entities did not disclose themselves in nonpredicative ways for nonassertoric practices, most of them would be incapable of predicative self-disclosure. This is an indispensable insight to be retained from Heidegger's account of handiness. But my usage of "predicative self-disclosure" also notes that entities do disclose themselves when they are asserted and are predicatively available.

The predicative self-disclosure of an asserted entity lies in its offering itself for predicative practice reliably and in accordance with other ways in which the entity is available. The self-disclosing entity offers itself not simply "just as that entity is in itself," as Tugendhat claims, but rather just as that entity is available to us in some other respect. When the hammer discloses itself as something about which one can accurately claim "The hammer is too heavy," it offers itself just as that hammer is available for a particular task of carpentry, say, for setting nails. As is the case with asserting, an entity's predicative self-disclosure can misfire in a couple of ways: (1) either the entity can withdraw from the assertoric field, in which case it becomes or remains predicatively unintelligible (although most likely available in other ways), or (2) the entity can offer itself for predicative practice but not just as it is available in some relevant way, in which case the entity becomes predicatively confusing. In the first case, we might find ourselves "unable to say anything," in the sense of being unable to make an assertion about the entity. In the second instance, we might find ourselves "not knowing quite what to say," in the sense of finding our assertions about the entity repeatedly "off the mark." Although neither of these misfirings may be prevalent in our dealings with hammers and the like, they occur frequently in our dealings with one another.

My account of assertoric correctness and predicative self-disclosure has the advantage of differentiating *aletheia* from *apophansis* without either resorting to a static notion of self-givenness, à la Tugendhat, or turning incorrectness and predicative hiddenness into aspects of truth, à la Heidegger. At the same time, this account serves to strengthen the Heideggerian intuition that assertoric correctness or propositional validity, although an aspect of truth, is neither the sole or primary locus of truth nor the key to a comprehensive conception of truth. Clues to a more comprehensive conception of truth occur when Heidegger grounds the "agreement of assertion and object" in Dasein's disclosedness.

Agreement and Disclosedness

Midway through section 44, Heidegger tries to show how the purported agreement of assertion and object derives from Dasein's disclosedness, and thereby to transform traditional conceptions of truth as correspondence. To do this he traces a path from ordinary language to what could be called theoretical metalanguage. His account goes roughly as follows (*SZ* 223–6).[28] Dasein expresses itself in talk, Heidegger says, as a being whose relationship to entities always involves discovering entities. Although the practice of asserting is only one mode of such self-expression, it allows Dasein not only to express its capacity to discover entities but also to express itself *about* discovered entities and to communicate how these are discovered. Indeed, an accomplished assertion has an "aboutness" in which (*in ihrem Worüber*) the assertion preserves the discoveredness of the entity asserted. Once expressed by Dasein, the accomplished assertion itself becomes something at hand and further discussable. The entity's discoveredness also becomes handy. Yet the accomplished assertion, which preserves discoveredness, continues to sustain a relation to the asserted entity.

Here, however, the original connection between Dasein's ability to discover (*Entdeckendsein*) and the discovered entity begins to go underground. Heidegger claims that subsequent discussion of the accomplished assertion exempts Dasein from discovering entities in an original way, even though in such discussion Dasein does enter a relationship to those entities whose discoveredness the assertion preserves. In such discussion at one remove, which is common in public talk, the assertion's handiness gets covered up. Correlatively with this covering of the assertion's handiness, the discoveredness of the asserted entity becomes an objectively present conformity between the accomplished assertion and the asserted entity. Hence the original connections among Dasein, entities, and assertion get reduced to an objectively present agreement between an objectively present assertion and an objectively present object. One could say the original connections become that correspondence between proposition and fact which propositionally inflected correspondence theories regard as the very essence of truth. "Truth as disclosedness and as a being toward discovered beings – a being that itself discovers – has become truth as the agreement between innerworldly things objectively present" (*SZ* 225). Truth as disclosedness – the most fundamental condition of human existence – has become a mere agreement between assertion and object. Moreover, this objectively present agreement seems primary and not derivative because Dasein ordinarily understands itself in terms of what it encounters as objectively present. Traditional metaphysics and modern epistemology simply strengthen such an understanding.

By reconsidering "correspondence" or "agreement" along these lines, one can learn from Heidegger why propositionally inflected correspondence theories such as Beardsley's have enough plausibility to make the idea of artistic truth seem implausible. One can also see why Heidegger thinks his own conception of truth as disclosedness is ontologically preferable. Yet Heidegger's highly instructive explanation for both the plausibility and the inadequacy of correspondence theories employs a questionable premise at the outset. Let me elaborate.

Earlier I questioned two corollaries to Heidegger's claim that assertion is a derivative mode of interpretation: that assertion has the same thrown projection as understanding has, and that assertion "levels" the existential-hermeneutical "as" into an apophantical "as." Heidegger's derivation of agreement from disclosedness brings to light a third and equally questionable corollary. The third corollary is that the sharing and discussing of accomplished assertions spares Dasein a direct encounter with entities themselves in "'original' experience" and thereby helps turn accomplished assertions into objectively present things (*SZ* 224). Deep in the "fore-structure" of Heidegger's phenomenology lies the image of authentic existence as having direct dealings with equipment and with that which equipment makes available – the image of homo faber as the attentive craftsperson who can get on with his or her work "without wasting words." The image suggests that the more indirect and mediated our dealings become, the more we drift from authentic understanding, interpretation, and talk. Once one abandons this image, already ideologically loaded in the 1920s, one becomes dubious about the entire notion that public talk spares us a direct encounter. There are two reasons for this: first, no experience of entities is direct and original, and, second, public talk mediates even the most "original" experience. Heidegger's account of assertion remains caught in the dream of eidetic intuition, despite his shifting Husserlian phenomenology from the realm of theoretically perceived noemata to the realm of circumspectly interpreted entities.[29]

The dream of a direct encounter clouds Heidegger's account of the connection between agreement and disclosedness. His account begins with the

assumption that Dasein's original self-expression and orientation and discovering are such that the entities discovered are truly discovered and that
their discoveredness itself is true. Hence Dasein's disclosedness can itself be
described as truth. But, as Tugendhat points out, to describe disclosedness as
truth is to preclude asking how Dasein's disclosedness can be truly disclosive
and how it can be false. Even if the agreement between assertion and object
is derivative from a more primordial truth, that from which such agreement
derives must be such that it can itself be distinguished from untruth. As it
stands, Heidegger's account of the connection between agreement and disclosedness could just as readily be given for the lack of agreement between
assertion and object. And that leads Tugendhat to accuse Heidegger of abandoning the idea of critical consciousness: "If truth means unconcealedness
as Heidegger understands the word, then everything depends on the fact
that an understanding of the world actually opens up, not that we scrutinize
it [such understanding] critically."[30]

Yet Tugendhat's alternative also will not do, since it seems intent on
deriving any broader conception of truth from an account of assertoric
correctness.[31] There is something fundamentally right, it seems to me, about
Heidegger's refusal to reduce truth to the correctness of assertions or the
discoveredness of entities. He is correct not to exclude the ontological stance
of those beings for whom truth itself, like Being, is a question and can never
not be a question. Heidegger has successfully removed this question from
the realms of Platonic perfection and Cartesian certainty. He has relocated it
in those regions of human striving and disillusionment where getting things
right often involves also getting them wrong, and where genuine discoveries
seldom occur without difficult self-sacrifice.

So we appear to have arrived at an impasse: we can neither derive correspondence from disclosedness nor make propositional validity the key to a
general conception of truth. Escaping this impasse is crucial for elaborating an idea of artistic truth that withstands metacritical denial yet retains
the question of validity that an existential affirmation of artistic truth occludes. For this, postmetaphysical skepticism will not suffice. Ways must be
found to link assertoric correctness with a more comprehensive conception
of truth without either reducing truth to correctness or simply absorbing
correctness into truth. Both Tugendhat's emphasis on critical consciousness and Heidegger's emphasis on existential disclosedness must undergo
dialectical correction. Nothing less would satisfy the demands of a critical
hermeneutics.

Life-Giving Disclosure

One way out of the impasse is to recognize principles according to which human self-expression, orientation, and discovering can be more or less true.
Just as "correctness" indicates such a principle for the practice of asserting,

so parallel principles obtain for other ranges of human practice, such as resourcefulness in the production and use of goods and services or solidarity in the development of human communities or justice in the governance of social institutions. It would make no sense, of course, to equate adherence to such principles with the achievement of assertoric "truth." Yet there may be a more comprehensive sense of truth according to which "being in the truth" requires fidelity to that which people hold in common and which holds them in common. That which holds them in common are principles of the sort already mentioned. That which people hold in common may or may not be in line with such principles. Yet their holding something in common requires appeals or gestures toward such principles, even when the appeal is self-serving or the gesture is ideologically distorted. Moreover, for the principles to hold people in common, people must themselves hold something in common. Correlatively, infidelity to the commonly holding/held amounts to "being in untruth." From this description it appears that Dasein's "disclosedness" is itself a site of public struggle over principles for human existence. Whether the commonly holding/held sustains and promotes life is always implicitly at issue.

A second, complementary way out of the impasse is to replace the notion of disclosedness, as an ontological state of essential openness, with the notion of life-giving disclosure, as a historical process of opening up society. By "life-giving" I mean a process in which human beings and other creatures come to flourish, and not just some human beings or certain creatures, but all of them in their interconnections. Clearly this is, in Adorno's terms, an "emphatic idea," or, in Hegel's terms, a speculative concept. It must go beyond any specific societal formation, even though what counts as "flourishing" always derives its content from specific circumstances and experiences. Hence, for example, to envision a society in which no one is poor and the environment is not polluted would let the idea of life-giving disclosure acquire content, through negation, from contemporary society, where poverty and pollution persist. Given such content, the idea of life-giving disclosure would point toward cultural practices and social institutions that promote greater equity in the ownership and distribution of economic resources. It would also point toward societal arrangements that do not turn creaturely habitats into mere resources for myopic exploitation.

Here John Dewey's aesthetics helps fill a gap left by Heidegger's ontology. Among Heidegger's philosophical contemporaries, John Dewey had the keenest sense of the holistic societal context in which both art and science find their purposes. This allowed Dewey to resist the separation of art and science that came to characterize analytic philosophy, including Beardsley's metacriticism,[32] and that set up an antipropositional turn in postmetaphysical deconstruction. Although Dewey preferred to speak of art's role in society as aesthetically enriching experience and did not explicitly link the arts with the unfolding of truth, he always tied "experience" to the social pursuit of human interests and the communal satisfaction of human needs. Consequently he also assigned the arts a role in transformative social critique.

Writing during the Great Depression in North America and the *Nazi Zeit* in Germany, Dewey posits a direct link between artistic flourishing and the democratic transformation of society as a whole: "The values that lead to production and intelligent enjoyment of art have to be incorporated into the system of social relationships. . . . [A]rt itself is not secure under modern conditions until the mass of men and women who do the useful work of the world have the opportunity to be free in conducting the processes of production and are richly endowed in capacity for enjoying the fruits of collective work."[33] Dewey's reason for so interlinking art and political economy lies in those imaginative processes that, according to my own account, give rise to questions about artistic truth. It lies in the ability of imagination to elicit "the possibilities that are interwoven within the texture of the actual. The first stirrings of dissatisfaction and the first intimations of a better future are always found in works of art."[34] Dewey says such processes allow the arts to provide social criticism "not directly, but by disclosure, through imaginative vision addressed to imaginative experience (not to set judgment) of possibilities that contrast with actual conditions."[35] To quote the poetry with which Dewey ends *Art as Experience*, such "imaginative disclosure," as I shall call it, lets art "tell a truth/Obliquely, do the deed [that] shall breed the thought."[36] In my own terminology, artistic truth belongs to a larger process of life-giving disclosure.

Despite resonances with my own conception, however, Dewey's pragmatism makes freedom rather than fidelity the watermark of life-giving disclosure. His emphasis on both individual and collective freedom supports a tendency in modern societies to make everything subserve the satisfaction of human needs. It also turns principles for evaluating such needs and their satisfaction into instruments to be measured by their consequences. Heidegger's notion of disclosedness, by contrast, rightly resists such privileging of human needs. Accordingly, in transforming Heidegger's notion into one of life-giving disclosure, I emphasize fidelity to principles that people hold in common and that hold them in common. But I do not wish to anchor these principles in an unchanging and universal "human nature." I see them as shared reference points that have emerged historically through clashes between societies and within them.[37]

Fidelity to the commonly holding/held and life-giving disclosure are indissoluble correlates. Just as the telos of such fidelity is to promote a process in which human beings and other creatures come to flourish, so life-giving disclosure depends in part upon the degree to which cultural practices, social institutions, and entire societal formations align themselves with principles such as solidarity and justice. As life-giving disclosure, truth occurs in part by way of people being true – pursuing fidelity – in the various dimensions of their social existence. But only in part, since such disclosure also occurs both beyond and despite our principles and alignments. As will become apparent in the next chapter, there is always more to truth than our "being in the truth," whether in our theoretical assertions or in our political engagements.

My emphasis on fidelity to the commonly holding/held recalls an etymological link between "truth" and "troth" that Heidegger had discovered before he wrote *Sein und Zeit*. Although one does not want to make etymology do the work of philosophical argument, it is at least noteworthy that "truth" derives from the Old English word "treowth" – "fidelity" – which is also a source of the word "troth." Moreover, "true" is commonly used to mean steadfast, loyal, honest, or just, and one archaic meaning of "truth" is fidelity.[38] If one regards the more comprehensive sense of truth as a process of life-giving disclosure marked by fidelity to the commonly holding and commonly held, then one can see the pursuit of assertoric correctness as one important but limited way in which truth occurs. Similarly, the failure or refusal to pursue assertoric correctness can be regarded as contrary to truth, not only in the sense of leading to assertoric "falsehood" but also in the sense of undermining other ways in which fidelity to the commonly holding/held is to be practiced. For the persistent avoidance or rejection of assertoric correctness would render unlikely or impossible the pursuit of resourcefulness, solidarity, and justice. In that way, propositional validity is indispensable to life-giving disclosure, even though truth in this latter and more comprehensive sense exceeds assertoric correctness, just as it exceeds artistic truth.

Such an approach has several advantages over the account given by Heidegger. In the first place, a more comprehensive conception of truth need not preclude distinguishing truth from untruth. Rather, it can make available a number of respects in which to draw such a distinction. Second, there is no need to see the discussion of accomplished assertions as more remote from primordial truth, since such discussion is simply one of several ways in which the pursuit of truth occurs. Third, truth does not turn into a state of Dasein's being. It can be seen as a dynamic, multifaceted, and fragile calling in which everyone always has a stake and to which no one can avoid making a reply. Fourth, the agreement between assertion and object, which itself is only one component of assertoric "truth," would no longer direct our understanding of what truth is like, not even in the inverted Heideggerian sense that comes from trying to show how such agreement derives from disclosedness. The relation of epistemic subject to epistemic object that strongly colors Heidegger's account of disclosedness would no longer be the point of departure for a general conception of truth.

At the same time, the proposed conception respects Heidegger's insistence on the temporal character of truth. The principles already mentioned are not timeless absolutes but rather historical horizons. They are historically learned, achieved, contested, reformulated, and ignored, and their pursuit occurs amid social struggle. Moreover, the description of these principles as "commonly held" does not mean that they are always and everywhere recognized, or that they provide the heavy artillery of common sense. Rather, it means that when people in modern societies find themselves pushed to the extremes of their self-understanding and their shared talk, they cannot avoid a struggle over these very principles. And contemporary struggles over resourcefulness, solidarity, and justice cannot but rely on efforts to make correct and corrigible assertions in ongoing public debates.

This is why I have criticized Heidegger for underestimating the role of predication in assertion, and for portraying predicative availability as a distorting of nonpredicative availability. Heidegger is right to try to ground the correctness of assertions in a more comprehensive mediation of disclosive practices and systatic availability. For this attempt to succeed, however, assertoric correctness must be seen as one of several principles in accordance with which the disclosure of culture, society, and human life can be more or less true. Contra Heidegger, what helps distinguish true disclosure from false is not the authenticity with which human beings face the possibility of their own death. Rather it is their life-promoting and life-sustaining fidelity to principles that they hold in common and that hold them in common.

I have said that questions of artistic truth arise at the intersection of aesthetic validity, cultural orientation, and art talk. Now I can add that these questions arise here because of the role art plays in letting people sort out what the correlation of fidelity and life-giving disclosure requires. Within the arts, such sorting out does not usually rely very heavily on our making and discussing assertions. Recognition of this negative fact about art is the correct intuition shared by Beardsley, Hofstadter, and Rapaport, despite their mutually incompatible responses to the idea of artistic truth. The challenge, then, is to account for this fact while neither divorcing art from the pursuit of truth nor reducing the general conception of truth to one which only the arts can enact. A closely related challenge is to show that propositional validity, although not the key to artistic truth, is also not irrelevant to it. Artistic truth will need to be seen as part of a process of life-giving disclosure in which fidelity to principles occurs. It will need to be regarded as itself a process in which the principle of aesthetic validity gives guidance. It will need to be characterized as a process of imaginative disclosure.

5

Imaginative Disclosure

> The artwork opens up ... the [B]eing of beings. ... Art is the setting-itself-to-work of truth.
>
> Martin Heidegger[1]

The concern to combine social critique and hermeneutical openness, announced in the previous chapter, stems in part from dissatisfaction with a *Kommunikationsverweigerung* (refusal to communicate) between two schools of continental philosophy.[2] Both the general question of truth and the more specific question of artistic truth have been central points of contention between Heideggerian thinking and Critical Theory. Whereas Martin Heidegger orients his conception of truth toward the unveiling of Being in beings, Jürgen Habermas regards truth as a dimension of validity in "communicative action" that comes to the fore when propositions are asserted and tested. Heidegger insists that the "truth" of assertions and propositions derives from a more original and comprehensive event of truth. Habermas, by contrast, resists expanding the notion of truth beyond one dimension of intersubjective validity, even though he considers the other dimensions analogous to truth. And, while not denying the disclosive functions of ordinary language – its ability to open new perspectives on world, self, and interpersonal relations – he does not make disclosure central to language in the way that Heidegger and Hans-Georg Gadamer do.[3]

These differences become especially evident in their conceptions of art. Habermas seems to be of two minds concerning art. On the one hand, he regards art as an expert culture in which aesthetic validity claims can be thematized. On the other hand, he retains from Adorno, and perhaps indirectly from Heidegger, a view of autonomous art as uniquely disclosive of "the extraordinary" that Habermas thinks philosophy can no longer claim for itself: "In the wake of metaphysics, philosophy surrenders its extraordinary status. Explosive experiences of the extraordinary have migrated into an art that has become autonomous."[4] These two emphases – aesthetic validity and disclosure of the extraordinary – do not go together easily. Their dissonance in Habermas's conception of art signals a larger tension between validity and disclosure in contemporary Critical Theory.

In an interesting way, and from an opposite direction, a similar dissonance runs through Heidegger's "anti-aesthetic"[5] thinking. Whereas Habermas usually emphasizes validity at the expense of disclosure, Heidegger tends to emphasize disclosure at the expense of validity. To play with Gadamer's title, Heidegger's philosophy of art lets truth (disclosure) trump method (validity). Or so I should like to suggest, using Heidegger's essay "The Origin of the Work of Art" as my point of departure.

Several considerations compel me to comment on this essay. First, it is one of the most far-ranging and concentrated discussions of artistic truth in twentieth-century philosophy. Second, it is among the few writings by Heidegger that, having been widely anthologized and discussed in Anglophone countries, is familiar to both analytic and continental aestheticians. Third, it forms a common point of reference for the two continental accounts of artistic truth with which I have already taken issue, namely Hofstadter's and Rapaport's. Fourth, and perhaps most important, the essay sharpens both the insights and the problems that I have already identified in Heidegger's general conception of truth. If my alternative conception is to prove fruitful for the topic of artistic truth, I need to demonstrate that through a critical reading of his most important treatment of this topic. More specifically, I need to show how my emphasis on fidelity to principles does not undermine the nonpropositional character of artistic truth. I must indicate how to combine validity and disclosure in an idea of artistic truth.

I do not intend to give a thorough interpretation of Heidegger's essay, something others have provided.[6] Instead let me select three topics that are relevant in the current context: the nonpropositional[7] character of artistic truth (section 5.1), the relation between validity and disclosure in art (section 5.2), and connections between aesthetic validity and artistic truth (section 5.3). My aim is to retrieve a conception of artistic truth as imaginative disclosure for which questions of aesthetic validity remain crucial.

5.1 HEIDEGGER'S ANTI-AESTHETICS

Heidegger's essay characterizes art as "the setting-itself-to-work of truth" (*das Sich-ins-Werk-Setzen der Wahrheit*, OW 19, UK 28). This characterization provides a way into three questions that occupy much of his essay. (1) What must be the character of this "setting" in order for it to connect the artwork and truth? (2) What must be the character of the artwork in order for it to serve the self-setting of truth? (3) What must be the character of truth in order for it to set itself to work in art? Let me take up this last question, whose answer sheds light on the other two.

Truth must have at least three characteristics in order to set itself to work in the manner Heidegger describes. First, truth must be dynamic, not static, and temporal, not transcendent or transcendental. Second, truth must be original, not derivative, and autonomous, not heteronomous. Third, truth must be situated, not abstract, and available for articulation, not remote or inaccessible. Summarizing Heidegger in my own terms, then, to set, to set itself, and to set itself to work, truth must be processual, originary, and historical. Such truth need not be propositional, however, whether in the sense that it is a quality of assertions and propositions or in the sense that it requires assertions and propositions in order to become available. In fact, science, traditionally considered the best home for propositional validity, does not even enter Heidegger's list of historical ways in which truth takes place (*Wahrheitsgeschehens*).[8] Moreover, the ways by which truth's self-setting occurs are themselves nonpropositional.

Self-Setting Truth

Heidegger's account identifies two dimensions along which the process of self-setting occurs: (1) the dimension of creating (*Schaffen*) and preserving (*Bewahren*), which other philosophers might identify as the production and reception of art; and (2) the dimension of figure or configuration (*Gestalt*) and thrust (*Anstoss*), which other philosophers might discuss as the dialectic of form and content within the work of art.[9]

(1) Seen as a way in which truth sets itself to work, the creating of an artwork cannot be the mere crafting of an aesthetic object by an individual artist (OW 33–6, UK 46–9), any more than the preserving of an artwork can be merely private enjoyment, public appreciation, or scientific analysis. Rather, the creation of an artwork amounts to a receptive bringing forth of a unique entity such that truth can emerge within this entity (OW 37, UK 50–1). So too the preservation of an artwork amounts to an active standing within the truth by letting the work transport one out of ordinary relationships and activities. Hence both creating and preserving are ways of knowing that truth which happens by setting itself into work. Yet it is the self-setting truth, and not the creating or preserving as such, that turns the work into a site of truth, just as art is the origin of the work and of the work's creator and preserver, rather than the other way around (OW 36–7, 44; UK 49–51, 58–9).

(2) The second dimension along which truth's self-setting occurs is that of configuration (*Gestalt*) and thrust (*Anstoss*) within the artwork itself. The background to this dimension is the strife between earth and world, discussed midway through the essay in a section titled "The Work and Truth" (OW 19–33, UK 29–46). Using the example of a Greek temple, this section suggests that the work of art sets up (*aufstellen*) a world, in the sense that it opens up the most fundamental and prior historical paths along which

people live their lives, and it keeps these paths uncovered.[10] At the same time, the work of art sets forth (*herstellen*) the earth, in the sense of allowing that which shelters our world to stand forth in its inexhaustible variety and self-seclusion. The work of art has its character as a work (*das Werksein des Werkes*, OW 27, UK 38) in instigating an "essential strife" between the world it sets up and the earth it sets forth. Truth occurs amid this strife. "The world is the self-opening openness of the broad paths of simple and essential decisions in the destiny of a historical people. The earth is the unforced coming forth of the continually self-closing, and in that way, self-sheltering. World and earth are essentially different and yet never separated from one another. World is grounded on earth, and earth rises up through world.... The opposition of world and earth is strife.... In essential strife ... the opponents raise each other into the self-assertion [*Selbstbehauptung*] of their essences.... In setting up world and setting forth earth the work instigates this strife" (OW 26–7, UK 37–8).

Against this background, Heidegger subsequently describes the artwork's figure or configuration (*Gestalt*) as that which allows truth to establish itself (*sich einrichten*) as a world-earth striving (OW 37–9, UK 51–2). This self-establishment has a double character. On the one hand, the strife becomes an intimate rift (*Riss*) within the work, such that the opposition of worldly measure and earthly boundary acquires a shared outline (*Umriss*). On the other hand, because of the work's own earthiness (i.e., its stone, wood, colors, etc.), the strife-become-rift is set back into the earth. In non-Heideggerian terms, the structure of an artwork mediates a tension between sociocultural orientation and transhistorical preorientation, and it does so in such a way that this very tension, in this particular mediation, acquires extraordinary importance.

At the same time, the artwork foregrounds its own uniqueness as something created. Such foregrounding is what Heidegger calls the work's "thrust" (*Anstoss*) (OW 39–40, UK 53–4). The work thrusts its createdness on us and thus impresses upon us that truth has happened here and for the first time. This foregrounding explains the work's self-subsistence (*Insichruhens*), according to Heidegger. Again in non-Heideggerian terms, the artifactuality of the artwork is such that the work's unavoidable autonomy makes its truth content sociohistorically unique.

This combination of structural mediation (*Gestalt*) and artifactual autonomy (*Anstoss*) distinguishes artworks from other products. It allows them to challenge the familiar, to highlight the unfamiliar, and to carry preservers of art into the truth: "[F]or the more purely is the work itself transported into the openness of beings it itself opens up, then the more simply does it carry us into this openness and, at the same time, out of the realm of the usual. To submit to this displacement means: to transform all familiar relations to world and to earth, and henceforth to restrain all usual doing and prizing, knowing and looking, in order to dwell within the truth that is happening in the work" (OW 40, UK 54).

Summarizing, we can say that Heidegger conceives of artistic truth (i.e., the truth that sets itself to work and into work [*ins Werk*]) as a processual, originary, and historical occurrence of disclosure. It sets itself into work by way of art practices (i.e., creation and preservation) that are attuned to what this occurrence requires. It acquires overriding importance by way of the artwork's own mediatory structure (i.e., its configuration [*Gestalt*] of world-earth striving) and unique artifactuality (i.e., the work's "thrust" [*Anstoss*]).

Here questions about validity and disclosure begin to emerge. For in describing how truth can occur as disclosure in art, Heidegger indicates both what makes certain practices and products valid as art and what excludes others as not being up to the standards required by self-setting truth. His account of world-earth striving suggests that artistic truth involves an unusual mixture of validity and disclosure. To sift through this mixture, we must consider the overarching conception of truth that Heidegger proposes in this essay.

Unconcealment

The phrase "openness of beings" (*Offenheit des Seienden*, OW 40, UK 54) suggests the conception of truth around which the entire essay circles. A first approximation occurs in the section titled "The Thing and the Work" (OW 4–19, UK 10–28), in connection with Heidegger's much-disputed description of Vincent van Gogh's painting of (a peasant woman's?) shoes. Heidegger claims that the van Gogh painting "lets us know what the shoes, in truth, are" (OW 15, UK 24), in a double sense: it opens up the equipmental quality of equipment (i.e., its utility [*Dienlichkeit*] and reliability [*Verlässlichkeit*]), and it uncovers the strife of earth and world in which these shoes "stand." Just as in this painting the pair of shoes "steps forward into the unconcealment of its [B]eing [*die Unverborgenheit seines Seins*]," so in every work of art a being or entity (*ein Seiendes*) comes "to stand in the light of its [B]eing [*Sein*]" (OW 16, UK 25; cf. OW 32, UK 44).[11]

Accordingly, art is not simply the self-setting of truth but rather the setting-itself-*into-work* of the truth *of entities* (*das Sich-ins-Werk-Setzen der Wahrheit des Seienden*, OW 16, UK 25; my translation). In its own work-related way, art opens up the Being of beings (*Sein des Seienden*); or, approached from another direction, art opens up entities in their Being.[12] Yet it is neither an entity as such nor some particular truth that comes to fruition in the work of art, but rather the ever occurring event of truth as a whole as this takes place in ever new guises. To grasp this central thought, we must turn to the pages (OW 27–33, 36–7; UK 38–46, 49–50) where Heidegger both recapitulates and revises the account of truth given in *Being and Time*.[13]

Heidegger begins his recapitulation by describing truth as "the essence of what is true" (*das Wesen des Wahren*) and by identifying this essence as *aletheia* or the "unconcealment of beings" (*die Unverborgenheit des Seienden*) (OW 28, UK 39). The usual conception of truth as the agreement between proposition (*Satz*) and fact (*Sache*), or between assertion and object, misses the more original essence of truth, he says. As correctness (*Richtigkeit*), the truth of a proposition presupposes that the *Sache* shows itself to be such. For this self-showing to occur, the *Sache* must stand in the unconcealed, in the true. Or, in a phrasing Heidegger does not use, the *Sache* must stand unconcealedly. A "true" (i.e., correct) proposition conforms to the unconcealed (*sich nach dem Unverborgenen richtet*), whose essence is not correctness but unconcealment. Hence Heidegger holds that the correctness of propositions, and of knowledge in general, "stands and falls with truth as the unconcealment of beings" (OW 28, UK 40). Indeed, unconcealment itself determines that our knowledge must be oriented to (*nachgesetzt*) unconcealment. There could be no correct knowledge if the unconcealment of beings had not already placed us in that "illuminated realm" or lighted clearing (*jenes Gelichtete*) where all entities enter and withdraw (OW 29, UK 41).

The metaphor of the lighted clearing, already familiar from Heidegger's explication of Dasein in *Being and Time*, provides the *Leitgedanke* in his account of unconcealment. Although all entities, including human beings, stand in Being, there is much that we cannot master and know. Yet, prior to entities as a whole, and in their midst, there occurs an opening (*eine offene Stelle*), a clearing (*eine Lichtung*), that mysteriously encircles all that is (*alles Seiende*). Entities can be only if they step into this clearing and stand out within it, and human beings can find their way to other entities and to themselves only because the clearing provides a passage (OW 30, UK 41–2). For Heidegger, truth as unconcealment is the prismatic event that allows entities to shine forth, however dimly, in the clearing that encircles all that is.

The word "dimly" takes us into the most obscure passage of Heidegger's account. He writes: "Each being which we encounter and which encounters us maintains this strange opposition of presence in that at the same time it always holds itself back in a concealment [*Verbergung*]" (OW 30, UK 42). Here he has at least two claims in view. One is that entities can only be concealed if unconcealment is occurring. The second claim is that unconcealment cannot occur unless concealment is also occurring. This concealment takes two forms: refusal (*Versagen*), in which entities completely exceed our grasp, and obstructing (*Verstellen*), in which entities present themselves as other than they are. Whereas refusal can lead to human ignorance, obstructing makes possible our mistakes, misdeeds, and excesses (*uns vermessen*). Moreover, concealment "obstructs itself," in the sense that we cannot be certain in any particular case whether either refusal or obstructing is taking place. And that leads to a third and stronger claim, namely, that the unconcealment of entities occurs "only as this twofold concealment" (OW 30, UK 42).[14]

Heidegger's point is that refusal – the way in which entities remain within the shadows or retreat into them (or, more strongly, into the abyss)[15] – is not accidental or peripheral to the ongoing unconcealment of entities. Rather, entities could not emerge into the lighted clearing if they did not also stand beyond it. In this sense concealment as refusal provides the "continuing origin of all clearing" (OW 31, UK 43). Similarly, obstructing – the way in which entities hide behind other entities – is not accidental or peripheral to the ongoing unconcealment of entities. Rather, entities could not step out of their mutual hiddenness if they were not also hidden. Concealment as obstructing "metes out to all clearing the rigorous severity of error [*Beirrung*]" (OW 31, UK 43). Accordingly, truth is essentially a primal conflict between clearing and double concealment. It is in this conflict that the open center is won where entities can emerge (*hereinstehen*) and withdraw (*in sich selbst zurückstellen*).

Let us pause to consider what the proposed conception of truth as unconcealment comes to. Clearly Heidegger opposes not only the epistemological subject-object paradigm of modern conceptions such as Kant's but also the metaphysical form-matter paradigm of pre-modern conceptions such as Aristotle's. Heidegger seeks a conception that surpasses and recontextualizes both paradigms. In that sense his conception can be called hypermetaphysical. I think this conception runs the risk of eliminating distinctions between validity and disclosure worked out by previous philosophers. Admittedly, the *notion* of validity does not disappear altogether, for Heidegger continues to differentiate between unconcealment and concealment, and he provides a description of each. Yet it becomes difficult to find an *account* of validity within his differentiation. Unconcealment happens, he says, when entities stand in the lighted clearing, but this clearing simultaneously conceals entities. Further, although Heidegger points to distinctions between ignoring and learning, between mistaking and understanding, between misdeeds and right actions, he seems to assign the "responsibility" for these affairs not to the human beings who can learn, understand, and act aright but to the process of concealment, which is itself constitutive of truth. In place of modern philosophy's hubris, with its emphasis on moral autonomy and discursive rationality, Heidegger seems to propose the false modesty of hypermetaphysical philosophy, with its tendency to absolve human beings of social obligations and mutual corrections.[16]

Before elaborating my concern, however, I want to reclaim a Heideggerian insight that recent critical theorists seem to ignore, forget, or misconstrue. The insight is that there is more to validity than the intersubjective principles and validity claims that Habermas has done so much to elucidate. While one can hardly speak about this "more" without raising the suspicion of being "metaphysical," that by-now routinized criticism should not block exploration of Heidegger's insight. The "more" can be given various accounts, whether as historically acquired wisdom that has no precise historical origin, or as a proleptic vision of liberation that keeps breaking through the horizons of cultural practices and social institutions, or as a spiritual connection with the earth or the universe or the divine. It is a recognition of this "more" that unites the accounts of artistic truth given by both Heidegger and Adorno, despite their many differences. I suspect that no conception of artistic truth will be able to dispense with this dimension, which I consider simultaneously utopian and critical.

Heidegger posits the "more" by insisting that no principle such as the correctness of propositions is valid just by virtue of operating as a court for incessant appeals, both implicit and explicit, in human practices and institutions. There is something more to the principle of correctness, namely, in Heidegger's terms, the ongoing disclosure of Being in beings. In that sense, to make incorrect assertions is not simply to disappoint a mutually or even universally shared expectation. It is also, and profoundly, to ignore or resist or subvert a calling that comes to us from beyond ourselves and beyond the entities and people with which we have dealings. In that sense, the principle of propositional or assertoric correctness, like that of imaginative cogency, is a horizon within which we move that both propels us and moves with us.[17]

Hence disclosure and validity are not as easily separated as Habermas and other critical theorists suggest. The very holding of principles (in the double sense of their holding for us and our holding to them) is itself a disclosure of that which would hold us to them. Conceived as a process of life-giving disclosure marked by fidelity to that which people hold in common and which holds them in common, truth is also a process in which the holding/held principles or horizons point us beyond themselves and beyond ourselves. The pursuit of propositional validity, or of imaginative cogency, opens onto the question whether this pursuit is life-promoting and life-sustaining. Such disclosure cannot be reduced to or replaced by the "inner-worldly" disclosure discussed by critical theorists such as Martin Seel.[18] Whereas Seel's "inner-worldly" disclosure involves the creation of new forms of life and praxis, the disclosure that occurs via validity places in question both existing and not-yet-created practices and institutions. This placing in question is not a dismissal or doubt. Rather it is a calling that urges upon us the necessity and desirability of practices and institutions that are attuned to that which sustains validity. It urges upon us an orientation toward that which gives life. The calling does not absolve us of responsibility for our practices and institutions, but it does continually reorient our world. In that sense – one quite different from Seel's use of the phrase to describe art's special contribution – we can speak here of a "disclosure of world disclosure." Such second-order disclosure is not so much "otherworldly" as it is transworldly: it crosses our worlds, in the triple sense of spanning them, connecting them with worlds we do not inhabit, and placing all of them and each of them in question. Whether art has any special role to play in this regard remains to be seen.

5.2 ART AND VOCATION

Heidegger accounts for the relation between validity and disclosure in art by connecting truth's primal conflict between unconcealment and double concealment with the strife between world and earth. This striving occurs between the lighted clearing (*Lichtung*) of fundamental cultural paths and the self-secluding ground upon which any such path is followed.[19] Both sides of the world-earth strife belong to the open center that is won in the occurrence of truth. Indeed, the strife takes place "only insofar as truth happens as the ur-strife between clearing and concealment" (OW 32, UK 44). Because the work of art sets up a world and sets forth the earth, the artwork is one of the few essential ways in which this primal conflict occurs and "the disclosure [*Unverborgenheit*] of beings as a whole – truth – is won" (OW 32, UK 44). Truth happens in van Gogh's painting, for example, not in the sense that the shoes are accurately portrayed, or in the sense that their particular nature is made manifest, but rather in the more encompassing sense that, in the work's revelation of the shoes' equipmental character (*Zeugsein*), beings as a whole attain to unconcealment amid the world-earth strife. Heidegger insists that the more simply and essentially the shoes emerge in their essence (*in ihrem Wesen aufgehen*), "the more immediately and engagingly do all beings become, along with them, more in being [*wird mit ihnen alles Seiende seiender*]," and thereby "self-concealing [B]eing [*Sein*] becomes illuminated [*gelichtet*]" (OW 32, UK 44).

Indeed, under certain conditions truth requires artworks "in order to have its being as truth" (OW 33, UK 45). Heidegger explains that, as the openness of the open center, truth can "be" only to the extent that truth establishes itself (*sich selbst einrichtet*) in this open center. Such self-establishment can occur only insofar as there is some entity in the open center.[20] Truth does not exist in and by itself. It occurs only in connection with entities that can be in the opening cleared by the primal conflict (i.e., by truth), the very same opening in which this conflict establishes itself (OW 36–7, UK 49–50). Although the artwork might not provide the only avenue for truth so to establish itself, the artwork does provide an excellent opportunity for truth to be extant amid entities.[21] This opportunity is excellent because the establishment of truth in the artwork brings forth a completely new and unrepeatable entity, places it in the open center, and makes the placement in such a way that this unique entity "first clears the openness of the open into which it [the entity] comes forth" (OW 37, UK 50).

By virtue of its temporal uniqueness, then, the artwork allows truth to establish itself amid that which is and thus to loosen customary ties to both world and earth that ordinarily govern our dealings with entities, including

ourselves. As Heidegger puts it in his concluding argument that all art is
poetry (*Dichtung*) (OW 44–50, UK 59–65), art breaks open a place in whose
openness everything usual and customary becomes an unbeing (*wird zum
Unseienden*) and loses its capacity to measure Being (*Sein*) (OW 44–5, UK
59). This is one of the three modes in which art is a founding (*Stiftung*)
of truth, a mode Heidegger describes as "bestowing" (*Schenken*) – thrusting
down the familiar and thrusting up the unfamiliar (OW 47, UK 62).

The other two modes have less to do with defamiliarization and more to
do with reorientation. In the second mode, that of "grounding" (*Gründen*),
art opens up (*Eröffnung*) the earth as the self-secluding ground upon which a
historical people (*ein geschichtliches Volk*) rests. Art lets a people draw its world
up from the sustaining earth and expressly set its world upon this ground.
Although art defamiliarizes and does not simply accept the familiar and
traditional, art is not arbitrary, for it projects the withheld vocation of historical Dasein itself (*die vorenthaltene Bestimmung des geschichtlichen Daseins selbst*)
(OW 48, UK 63). The third mode, that of "beginning" (*Anfangen*), brings
together the defamiliarization of bestowing and the orientation of grounding in the notion of a grounding leap ahead (*Vorsprung*). The leap occurs in
reply to a demand from that which is as a whole (*das Seiende im Ganzen*) for a
"grounding in openness." Art can instigate (*Anstiftung*) "the strife of truth"
and thereby help "a new and essential world" to arise (OW 48, UK 63–4). At
such moments, which can take centuries to unfold, history begins anew as
a people is transported (*Entrückung*) "into its appointed task [*Aufgegebenes*]"
and enters (*Einrückung*) that people's "endowment" (*Mitgegebenes*) (OW 49,
UK 64).

Hence, in its three modes of founding truth, art is essentially historical:
art grounds the history of a people. In that sense the origin of the work of art
is art itself as an essential origin (*Ursprung*) – as "a distinctive way in which
truth comes into being [*seiend wird*], becomes, that is, historical" (OW 49, UK
65). The point of Heidegger's essay is to ask whether the German people (or
perhaps, more expansively, European culture) is at such a historical origin,
and whether contemporary art and its "creators" and "preservers" are up to
the task this would imply: "Are we, in our existence [*Dasein*], historically at
the origin? Or, do we, rather, in our relationship with art, appeal, merely, to
a cultured knowledge of the past?" (OW 50, UK 65)

This is not the place to examine the ideological functions of such questions in lectures first given in Nazi Germany not long before the Degenerate
Art show. Anyone familiar with the culture-political setting can hardly miss
the disturbing overtones of words like *Volk* and *Erde* and *Ursprung*. Instead
I wish to play out the Heideggerian composition of validity and disclosure
in art to which such overtones attach. Heidegger argues that art's vocation
is to stage the conflict between concealment and unconcealment and to do
this in a way that is unique, disturbing, (re)orienting, and historically significant. The origin of the work of art lies in this vocation; the vocation itself

requires the creation and preservation of unique works of art. Heidegger's concluding rhetorical questions suggest, however, as does the "Afterword" (OW 50–2, UK 66–8), that modern art (indeed, any art of the modern age) fails to live up to this vocation.[22]

Setting aside Heidegger's worry about the departure of "great art," let me pursue two questions. In what sense is it art's vocation to stage the conflict between concealment and unconcealment? In what sense do uniqueness, historical significance, and the capacity to disturb and to (re)orient indicate the validity of that staging?

Concealment and Unconcealment

Earlier I claimed that, although Heidegger's conception of truth blurs the distinction between validity and disclosure, it nonetheless opens validity to that which calls and questions us through claims and principles of validity. The primary sense in which art can stage the conflict of truth, then, is that art can hold claims and principles of validity open to that which calls and questions us through them. I would say that art's fulfilling this vocation depends on the sociohistorical formation to which it belongs. If, for example, capital, technology, and science have become "unquestionables" in Western society, then art's vocation in this sociohistorical formation may well be to put their dominance in question by urging something "more" for human life than efficiency, productivity, and empirical or theoretical "truth." Similarly, if the prevailing standards of human conduct in Western society are tailor-made to support these unquestionables in their unquestionability, then art's vocation may very well be to transgress the standards, with a view to their transformation. Both the urging of something "more" and the transgressing of prevalent standards would stage a conflict between concealment and unconcealment. Art can reorder how matters stand in a society, bringing to the fore considerations that had retreated, casting a shadow on what seems self-evident, and opening new spaces for both the appropriate and the inappropriate.

Is art alone in having this vocation? I would say, not at all. Depending on the societal formation, various cultural domains can stage the struggle of concealment and unconcealment: education, scholarship, or religion, for example. Art has been especially important in Western societies because its imaginative character is troublesome for the dominant "unquestionables," which until recently certain notions of progress and truth have ratified. Art hasn't "fit," and, paradoxically, that has made art a fitting site for thinking and doing otherwise. To understand this dynamic, it is crucial, like Heidegger, to refuse to reduce art to a safe and irrelevant domain of fiction, play, and aesthetic experience. Art can stage a conflict of truth in Western society precisely to the extent that its fiction is not fictitious, its playfulness is not ludicrous, and aesthetic experience is not merely aesthetic. Art can

stage a conflict among the standards currently in effect, the horizonal principles to which contemporary practices and institutions appeal, and what
the promoting and sustaining of life might require.

Artistic Validity

Heidegger appeals to "great art," and subtly laments its demise, as a way
to raise questions of artistic validity without reducing this to the aesthetic
or formal criteria of post-Kantian aesthetics. To claim ontologically that art
is "the setting-itself-to-work of truth" does not settle the question whether
all art accomplishes this vocation or whether some artworks fulfill it more
adequately than others. Hence Heidegger introduces his own criteria: the
uniqueness of the artwork, its ability to disturb customary ties to both world
and earth, its ability to let a community ground its world in the earth, and its
ability to let a community embrace a new world.[23] In other words, uniqueness, provocativeness, integrity, and originality are the marks of a valid work
of art, one that lives up to art's vocation to carry out the un/concealment
of entities.

It would be a mistake, however, to reduce these marks of validity to "aesthetic" qualities and to think that they obtain only within the field of artworks
as such. One of Heidegger's crucial points is that an artwork's temporal
uniqueness has to do with the new and unrepeatable manner in which it
carries out a tension between sociocultural orientation (world) and transhistorical preorientation (earth). An artwork's uniqueness, then, is not simply
its incomparability among other artworks but, more importantly, its peculiarity as an "instigating" of this sociohistorical tension. To do justice to
the artwork, one would need to attend to the world-earth striving as this
is configured in the work. Such attention would require some extra-artistic
acquaintance with the orientation and preorientation the work configures.
So, too, the provocativeness, integrity, and originality of the "truthing" work
of art are not simply aesthetic qualities to be judged within the field of other
artworks. There is an important sense, of course, in which some artworks
are judged more provocative, integral, or original than others on the basis
of aesthetic or formal qualities. An installation is provocative because of the
unexpected way in which it mixes media; a musical performance has great
integrity because it avoids mere showmanship and delves into the inner life
of a composition; a novel is praised for its originality because it convincingly
rewrites the "rules" of narrative voice. Heidegger suggests, however, that
the larger significance of such qualities in art has to do with their role in
disturbing, (re)orienting, and (re)establishing a community. To create, interpret, and evaluate artworks along Heideggerian lines would require some
familiarity with – indeed, some attachment to – a community's sociocultural
orientation and transhistorical preorientation. Aesthetic competence, as defined by the modern artworld, would not suffice.

Herein lies Heidegger's provocation: he upholds the autonomy of the work of art in order to reject the modern principle of artistic autonomy. His stance is provocative both because he does not acknowledge just how indebted he is to the modern principle of autonomy and because he mounts a frontal attack on how that principle has tied art's vocation to notions of aesthetic validity. For Heidegger, to be autonomous or self-subsistent, the artwork must have larger sociohistorical importance. It must instigate the striving of earth and world and must stage the conflict between clearing and double concealing. To be unique, provocative, integral, and original, the artwork must not be a mere product of aesthetic creativity ("genius") or a mere object of aesthetic judgment ("taste"). Hence the question whether great art remains – art that is valid according to the proposed criteria and that "truths" in the manner described – is also the plea for a community that such art could serve: do "we" hear the call of truth in art today?

5.3 COGENCY AND TRUTH

Precisely here, however, the concern about adequately distinguishing between validity and disclosure returns. On Heidegger's account of artistic validity, any community that is sufficiently "attuned" to the ongoing conflict between concealment and unconcealment would set the direction of art. In culture-political terms, artists, museums, orchestras, mass media, audiences, art critics, art scholars, and every other participant in the modern artworld would serve a community that itself is "in the truth." Ultimately the validity of the work of art rests in the historical destiny of a community.

Now we can see that the inadequacy of Heidegger's account surfaces in two mutually reinforcing fields, in art as disclosive and in truth as disclosure. It surfaces in the field of art because Heidegger's criteria of artistic validity are themselves modes of disclosure. Uniqueness, provocativeness, integrity, and originality, as Heidegger describes them, are simply the ways in which artworks open claims and principles of validity to that which calls and questions us through such claims and principles. This means that the validity of the work of art depends entirely on whether truth "sets itself to work" here, on this occasion, amid these creators and preservers of the work. The work has no independent validity, nor do interpretive or evaluative judgments about its validity. The only validity the work or such judgments can claim is to be disclosive of the self-setting truth that governs the historical destiny of a community.

Perhaps one could salvage Heidegger's account of validity and disclosure in art if he had worked out an adequate distinction between validity and disclosure in his overarching conception of truth. This, however, is not the case, despite my earlier attempt to reclaim his insight that validity is itself disclosive. In arguing that there is more to validity than intersubjective principles and validity claims, Heidegger suggests that there is nothing more to validity than the process of disclosure – the ongoing conflict of unconcealment and double concealment. In that sense, his accounts of art and truth mutually reinforce one another: both accounts absorb validity into disclosure.

To avoid this absorption, one would need to distinguish more clearly than Heidegger does between the necessity and the essentiality of concealment to unconcealment. One would also have to return to human beings the responsibility for concealment that Heidegger palms off on the process of disclosure. In addition, one must provide an account of disclosure in art that allows for a measure of aesthetic validity. Let me explain these three requirements.

Truth and Untruth

As I indicated before, when Heidegger says clearing is itself concealment, he claims that the unconcealment of entities occurs only as (double) concealment. This amounts to asserting that concealment is not simply necessary but essential to unconcealment: "Truth, in its essence, is un-truth" (OW 31, UK 43). Heidegger's assertion is highly problematic. Even though he cautions against interpreting his assertion to mean "that truth, fundamentally, is falsehood" or "is always its opposite as well" (OW 31, UK 43), he himself regards truth as the primal conflict between clearing and concealing. This turns truth into an ever occurrent event in which the validity of any insight or judgment or action or, for that matter, any artwork depends entirely on how the event plays out. Moreover, Heidegger's measure of whether an insight, judgment, action, or artwork is valid cannot be the degree to which it honors the unconcealment of entities but only the degree to which it lets the primal conflict between clearing and concealing show up.[24] It is difficult to see how this conception of truth can support criteria such as accuracy, correctness, appropriateness, sincerity, or "aesthetic validity." Heidegger's conception threatens to boil all of these criteria down to a notion of insightfulness, with the degree of insight measured by an ability to disclose the double nature of disclosure itself. The first step toward avoiding this reduction of validity to disclosure would be to abandon the claim that concealment is essential to unconcealment.

Human Responsibility

A second step would be to return responsibility for concealment to human beings. On Heidegger's conception of truth, there is no categorical or methodological guarantee of "getting things right," but there is also little epistemic or ethical responsibility for "getting things wrong." While I follow him in abandoning the search for guarantees, which modern philosophy since Descartes usually has located in subjectivity, I resist the apparent surrender of human responsibility. To say that the obstructing of entities "metes out to all clearing the rigorous severity of error" (OW 31, UK 43) is to project into the very structure of "reality" the misdirections of finite and fallible human thought and action. The facts that entities resist and exceed our grasp ("refusal") and that entities present themselves as other than they are ("obstructing") are humbling reminders of human finitude and fallibility. They are not the source of epistemic or ethical failures, however, no more than the unconcealment of entities is the source of epistemic or ethical accomplishments. Unless one is ready to give up the notion of failure (which Heidegger, with his talk of our making mistakes, going astray, and overreaching [OW 30, UK 42], clearly retains), one will need to find its source in precisely those entities – Dasein – which do not simply refuse and obstruct but ignore, misunderstand, err, and act badly. Similarly, unless one is ready to give up the notion of accomplishment, one will need to locate its source in human practices and institutions that do not simply receive the gift of unconcealment but sustain challenging pursuits of discovery, understanding, reorientation, and right conduct.

If responsibility for concealment and unconcealment returns to human beings, then disclosure cannot absorb validity. The two must be distinguished. To the extent that human beings are involved, one can always ask, concerning any instance of disclosure, in which respects the accompanying claim, whether implicit or explicit, is valid. As soon as this question occurs, it is subject to discussion and debate. Human responsibility with regard to disclosure cannot be recognized or attributed without raising and trying to redeem claims to validity. Making a discovery gives rise to the question whether the discovery is genuine or worthwhile. Reaching an understanding raises the question whether it is correct. Changing one's ways poses the question whether that change is the one required. Doing the right thing makes one wonder whether it is also appropriate. All such accomplishments may be instances of disclosure, but that in itself does not establish their validity.

At the same time, however – and this is the Heideggerian insight I wish to retain – questions of validity do not settle questions of disclosure. All the human practices and institutions in the world, no matter how well they support discovery, understanding, reorientation, and right conduct, cannot guarantee that what needs to be disclosed is disclosed. Yet, contrary to Heidegger's language, the struggle for direction at this fundamental level cannot occur as an anonymous conflict between the unconcealment and concealment of entities. In the middle of the struggle are those entities whose own unconcealment is at issue for them, beings for whom the struggle's ongoing outcome is a matter of life and death and who cannot avoid responsibility for pursuing validity – without guarantees.

Aesthetic Validity and Artistic Truth

If disclosure is a human responsibility for which distinct claims and principles of validity obtain, then a measure of aesthetic validity must enter the account of disclosure in art. Contrary to much of post-Kantian aesthetics, which construes the aesthetic dimension as a free zone where neither natural necessity nor epistemic or ethical responsibilities obtain, Heidegger portrays art as a field of conflict and striving where decisive questions of historical destiny go to work. Unfortunately, to bring about this provocative reversal in philosophical aesthetics, Heidegger absorbs artistic validity into disclosure and strips it of any specifically aesthetic validity. Yet his account opens up the possibility of relating disclosure to aesthetic validity in such a way that specifically aesthetic responsibilities obtain in art, and not only in art, and are neither divorced from nor identical with epistemic or ethical responsibilities.

One can derive the requisite notion of aesthetic validity from Heidegger's account of the uniqueness, provocativeness, integrity, and originality that mark a valid work of art. Although Heidegger regards these primarily as modes of disclosure, I see no reason not to consider them marks of aesthetic validity.[25] Furthermore, their province need not be restricted to works of art, because issues of aesthetic validity occur in a wide range of practices and institutions. To call these marks of aesthetic validity is to suggest both that other sorts of validity obtain in art, including epistemic and ethical validity, and that aesthetic validity is especially important for the occurrence of disclosure in art.

Immediately, however, two pitfalls appear. One is to reduce disclosure in artworks to their ability to "offer possibilities of understanding that are not now realized," such that "art is fictional because it deals with imaginatively conceived possibilities."[26] As J. M. Bernstein rightly points out, Heidegger's essay challenges precisely this post-Kantian fictionalization of art. The other pitfall is to deny the capacity of modern artworks to disclose a world and, as if in compensation, to give them the vocation of disclosing their own incapacity and thereby challenging the sway of science and technology.[27]

One way to avoid both pitfalls is to give a different account of aesthetic validity than either Kant or Heidegger provide. Whereas in Kant aesthetic validity amounts to lawfulness without (epistemic or ethical) law, in Heidegger it amounts to responsiveness without (human) responsibility. In contrast, I have proposed an account in which aesthetic validity is no less principled than epistemic validity and no less solicitous of human responsibility than ethical validity.[28] Just as questions of correctness guide cognition, and questions of rightness and appropriateness guide conduct, so questions of imaginative cogency guide aesthetic creation and preservation. The cogency must be imaginative, not in the sense that it is fictional, but in the sense that it obtains for the exploration, presentation, and creative interpretation of aesthetic signs. Being imaginative in this hermeneutical sense, questions of cogency cannot be settled by appeals to either assertoric correctness or ethical normativity. As cogency, however, it is also not arbitrary or irresponsible. It is a distinct sort of validity, without which cognition would lose persuasiveness and conduct would lose flexibility.

Even though cognition and conduct, with their validity correlates of correctness and normativity, belong to art just as much as they belong to science or law, aesthetic creation and preservation, with their validity correlate of imaginative cogency, are the leading edge of art in the modern world. To the extent that an anti-aesthetic account of art such as Heidegger's reconnects art with cognition and conduct, it corrects the marginalization of the aesthetic in post-Kantian philosophy. Yet, by avoiding the question of aesthetic validity, or by collapsing it into the question of disclosure, an anti-aesthetic account loses sight of art's vocation in the modern world. This vocation cannot be the nondifferentiated revelation Heidegger attributes to "great art." Rather it is the pursuit of imaginative cogency in a manner that discloses both the limits and the contributions of other practices and institutions of cognition and conduct.

Imaginative cogency is not identical with disclosure in art: it is a principle of aesthetic validity to which any disclosive creating and preserving in art must appeal, as must interpretive and evaluative judgments about artistic disclosure. When we say of artworks that they are unique or provocative or integral or original, we make discussable aesthetic validity claims. Such claims cannot be "settled" by raising cognitive or ethical claims, even though consideration of the cognitive and ethical dimensions of art can enrich the discussion. Nor can aesthetic validity claims be "settled" by considering technical matters, even though technique plays a constitutive role in the aesthetic "success" of an artwork. Aesthetic claims require an aesthetic response, one that encourages thinking and doing otherwise to prevail – otherwise than in many established practices and institutions of cognition and conduct. To work out the details of the correlation between disclosure and validity in the arts is the task of the next chapter.

6

Artistic Truth

All aesthetic questions terminate in those of the truth content of artworks.
                                       Theodor W. Adorno[1]

The aesthetic "validity"... that we attribute to a work [of art] refers to its singularly illuminating power... to disclose anew an apparently familiar reality.
                                       Jürgen Habermas[2]

Heidegger's eliding of disclosure and validity stems from his insisting on the
nonpropositional and disclosive character of truth. Habermas has precisely
the opposite intuition, namely, that truth properly so called is propositional,
and that other dimensions of validity are at most analogous to propositional
truth. Like Tugendhat, Habermas argues that one must distinguish sufficiently between validity and disclosure to have an adequate conception of
truth. That, too, is what the previous two chapters have argued, in their own
way, against Heidegger's hypermetaphysical anti-aesthetics. But a corollary
also holds: unless one traces detailed links between disclosure and validity,
one cannot have an adequate conception of artistic truth. That is what the
current chapter attempts, partly in response to Habermas's postmetaphysical account of validity.

The chapter begins with debates about artistic truth in contemporary
Critical Theory. The idea of artistic truth is a crossroad for third-generation
critical theorists. Few ideas were more crucial for Theodor W. Adorno's social philosophy, arguably the most important contribution to Critical Theory by the first generation.[3] Yet it finds little place in Jürgen Habermas's
theory of communicative action, the dominant paradigm among second-
generation critical theorists. The divergence of paths between "Adornians"
and "Habermasians" in the third generation runs directly through this idea.
A scholar who thinks both sides have important insights on the topic faces an
apparent dilemma. If one tries to retrieve Adorno's intuitions about artistic
truth, one faces the danger of becoming unintelligible to postmetaphysical

theorists. Alternatively, one can soldier on using Habermasian concepts and risk losing the critical-utopian thrust of Adorno's social philosophy.

Kant famously suggested in a very different context that concepts without intuitive content are empty, and intuitions without concepts are blind. Adorno would add, in a Hegelian critique of Kant, that neither intuitions nor concepts can be pure.[4] Accordingly, one might be able to mediate the apparently incompatible positions of Adorno and Habermas and, modifying both sides, to develop a fruitful account of artistic truth. That is what this chapter attempts, building upon the previous chapters. First I review Adorno's idea of artistic truth content (*Wahrheitsgehalt*) in light of Habermasian concerns about validity and disclosure. This gives further content to the previous chapter's notion of imaginative disclosure (section 6.1). Then I propose a three-dimensional conception of artistic truth (section 6.2). My conception tries to combine the best insights of Adorno and Habermas, but in a language that does not merely derive from either one. The final section (section 6.3) explores correlations between the three dimensions of imaginative disclosure and three validity dimensions in art talk and, more generally, in communicative action.

6.1 CRITICAL AESTHETIC THEORY

The divergence between Adorno and Habermas in matters aesthetic replicates a divergence in their general conceptions of truth. Whereas Adorno regards truth (*Wahrheit*) as an "emphatic idea" whose content exceeds propositional articulation in a "false" society, Habermas regards it as a dimension of propositional validity anchored in the structure of ordinary linguistic communication. Although Adorno does not dismiss questions of propositional validity, he does not make them decisive for truth. Instead, like Heidegger and Hegel, but in his own negative dialectical way, Adorno regards truth as a process of disclosure in which art plays an important role. Conversely, although Habermas does not dismiss questions of disclosure, especially as they pertain to how ordinary language opens up new perspectives on the world, interpersonal relations, and one's self, he makes such questions subservient to questions of propositional, normative, and expressive validity. Not surprisingly, links between validity and disclosure have become central concerns for third-generation critical theorists. The Adornians among them challenge Habermas's account of validity, and they return to Adorno's emphasis on "the nonidentical."[5] The Habermasians, by contrast, accept Habermas's account of validity, but they worry about his relative neglect of disclosure.

Validity and Disclosure

The worry about a neglect of disclosure takes Habermasian critical theorists in two different directions.[6] On the one hand, Martin Seel and James

Bohman, who insist on the propositional character of truth, portray disclosure as an enabling condition for propositional truth. Seel, for example, regards world disclosure as a change in already existing orientations "regarding the right and the true."[7] This change unsettles a linguistic community's relationship to its social and objective worlds. Bohman says that world disclosure occurs within the discursive testing of validity claims, such that the "radical critic" can help "change the relation of the hearer to the social world."[8] Neither Seel nor Bohman shares the weakened utopian impulse that second-generation critical theorists redirect from Adorno's truth aesthetics into the search for an "inner-worldly utopia."[9] Whereas Seel rejects Habermas's identifying the artwork's "singularly illuminating power" with the work's "aesthetic validity,"[10] Bohman questions whether artworks even have this disclosive power.

On the other hand, while accepting the propositional character of truth and distinguishing truth from disclosure, Nikolas Kompridis argues that world disclosure and validity-oriented action are interdependent. As a process of discovering meaning, and especially as a process of creating meaning,[11] world disclosure has "potential truth effects" that require validity-oriented reconstruction. This is especially important, he says, for the practices of "creative democracy."[12] And art has something special to offer in this regard. Hence Kompridis seems more attuned to Adorno's utopian impulse, which he does not limit to the artwork's "singularly illuminating power."

Neither approach, neither the validity-oriented emphasis of Seel and Bohman, nor Kompridis's meaning-creative account, provides an adequate basis for a theory of artistic truth. The reason is quite simple. In tying truth so firmly to propositions, whether by enthusiastic affirmation or by reluctant concession, third-generation critical theorists lose Heidegger's insight, which Adorno shares, into the nonpropositional and disclosive character of artistic truth. Moreover, because they turn disclosure into an inner-worldly process whose validity must be discursively secured, they do not ask whether, and in which respects, propositional truth itself derives from a process of disclosure that exceeds contemporary societal horizons.

These tendencies become particularly evident in the writings of Martin Seel, who has worked out a detailed conception of aesthetic validity. His essay on art, truth, and world disclosure[13] credits traditional "truth aesthetics" with correctly intuiting that a distinctive validity clings to artworks and to evaluations of their merits. Yet this validity is not a matter of truth, properly speaking, but one of aesthetic validity, he says. Whereas "truth" (*Wahrheit*) pertains primarily to the theoretical validity that attaches to assertions (*Aussagen*), and "appropriateness" (*Richtigkeit*) pertains primarily to the practical validity of actions or maxims, "aesthetic validity" (*ästhetische Geltung*) pertains primarily to the success of cultural modalities of perception.[14]

Aesthetic validity is distinct from both theoretical and practical validity. In each zone, however, claims to validity are made and tested by maintaining (*Behauptung*) and confirming (*Bewahrheitung*) assertions, whether these be theoretical, practical, or aesthetic.[15]

According to Seel, art's distinctive task resides in the "basic function of cultural perception."[16] Artworks are "*signs* of a specific view of the world" that "present human life-situations in their existential significance." They do this by making present (*Vergegenwärtigung*) (1) the significance of circumstances and events, (2) the construction of patterns and signs guiding human perception, and (3) the media and procedures supporting such significance (1) and construction (2). Most important, artworks do all of this by presenting (4) "the significance of artistic experience for human experience." Such a multifaceted and reflexive cultural perception is structurally constitutive for art and normatively central.[17] When artworks are aesthetically valid, they succeed in articulating cultural perception, and their articulative success is what art criticism should elucidate.[18]

In my view, Seel's efforts to define art's validity as aesthetic validity point to a deep source of tension, not only in his conception but also in much of Western aesthetics. A thoroughgoing conflict occurs between insisting on artistic autonomy, specified in terms of aesthetic criteria for works of art, and giving art an orienting role in society, a role Seel defines in terms of existential significance for modalities of cultural perception. Contra Heidegger, and contra Adorno too, Seel tries to resolve this tension by subsuming the second pole (disclosure) under the first (validity). Accordingly, all questions about the societal importance and social merit of art's disclosure get reduced to questions about extra-artistic "effects" (*Wirkungen*). Neither a social critique of art nor an artistic critique of society seems conceivable within Seel's framework. Artworks come to be considered successful just by virtue of articulating cultural perceptions, regardless of whether they endorse, question, or oppose those perceptions, and regardless of whether those perceptions deserve to be affirmed, challenged, or destroyed. He seems to have given up not only Adorno's utopian impulse but also the societal critique it sustained.[19]

Indeed, Seel's approach precludes any idea of artistic truth. By circumscribing the theoretical validity of assertions as the sole domain of truth, he surrenders this idea. On his account truth can pertain to the practical and aesthetic domains only to the extent that value assertions occur in these domains and become the topic of theoretical discussion. Hence we cannot properly speak about the truth of art as such, but only about the truth of certain assertions we make about art. Seel tries to forestall this consequence. His proposal does not preclude having claims to truth arise in nontheoretical ways, he says, for "the value of truth presupposes the truth of [practical and aesthetic] values."[20] Unfortunately the cleverness of Seel's formulation masks an equivocation: whereas "truth" in the first phrase just quoted means

theoretical validity, "truth" in the second phrase means nontheoretical validity, and nontheoretical validity cannot be truth, according to Seel's own
distinctions. His approach to artistic truth clearly privileges assertions, especially those which are empirically based. The phrase "artistic truth" becomes
an oxymoron.

Of course, this would not count as an internal criticism of Seel's position,
had he not set out to rescue "the correct intuition of all truth aesthetics"
that art has a distinctive validity.[21] This intuition, as elaborated in a complex
tradition stretching from Hegel and Nietzsche to Heidegger and Adorno,
is not simply that successful artworks are articulate and articulated – a commonplace of post-Kantian aesthetics. Rather the intuition is that something
like true insight or revelation or critique can come to the fore within art
itself, and that the emergence of such truth as disclosure is crucial to an
artwork's validity, including (but exceeding) what Seel identifies as an artwork's aesthetic validity. By reducing the intuition of "truth aesthetics" to
a notion of aesthetic and nonalethic validity, Seel has given up the most
provocative part of the tradition's intuition. And in this essay he does not
demonstrate why that part deserves to be given up.

Even if one granted Seel's restriction of truth to assertions, which for
obvious reasons I would not do, a problem would remain. For if one distinguishes aesthetic validity from truth, and restricts truth to the theoretical
domain, then a theory of connections between art and truth would require
an account of relationships between the articulateness of artworks and the
correctness of assertions about artworks. Such an account Seel does not
provide, not even in a subsequent essay that makes art's role in world disclosure dependent on the formulation of "interesting [propositional] truth
about the work of art."[22] Seel seems to assume that assertions about art are
relatively nonproblematic, that one faces no unique challenges when trying to formulate claims about an artwork that are both "interesting" and
correct. Yet such confidence is belied by the amount of ink spilled and computer memory used on precisely this topic since the 1950s. Distinguishing
aesthetic validity from assertoric or propositional truth does not solve traditional issues of "artistic truth." It simply moves them to a somewhat different
field.

Adorno's Truth Content

Theodor W. Adorno was keenly aware of both sorts of tension: between truth
and aesthetic validity, and between artistic and propositional truth. That is
why, compared with Seel's Habermasian revisions, Adorno's idea of artistic
truth content (*Wahrheitsgehalt*) remains a crucial resource for critical aesthetic theory. Adorno clears away all remnants of logical positivism when he
describes the truth content of artworks as neither factual nor propositional
yet perceptible and structural: "They have truth content and they do not

have it. Positive science and the philosophy derived from it do not attain it. It is neither the work's factual content nor its fragile and self-suspendable logicality.... What transcends the factual in the artwork, its spiritual content, cannot be pinned down to what is individually, sensually given but is, rather, constituted by way of this empirical givenness.... [A]rtworks transcend their factuality through their facture, through the consistency of their elaboration" (*AT* 128–9, *ÄT* 194–5).

Can Adorno give a fuller, more positive, and general characterization of truth in art? In one sense he cannot, since he insists that the truth content of each artwork is unique to it and cannot be cleanly extracted from it: "The truth content of artworks cannot be immediately identified. Just as it is known only mediately, it is mediated in itself" (*AT* 129, *ÄT* 195). Yet Adorno's discussion allows for a number of additional characterizations, such as these.[23]

1. Truth in art has historical, societal, and political dimensions. Truth content is not a metaphysical idea or essence, for it is bound to specific historical stages, societal formations, and political contexts.
2. Truth in art is not merely a human construct, even though it would not be available in art were it not for the production and reception of particular works in specific media.
3. Truth in art emerges from the interaction between artists' intentions and artistic materials. It is the materialization of the most advanced consciousness of contradictions within the horizon of possible reconciliation.
4. Truth in art requires both the successful mediation of content and form and the suspension of form on behalf of that which exceeds this mediation.
5. Truth in art is nonpropositional, yet it invites and needs critical interpretation.
6. Truth in art is never available in a directly nonillusory way: "Art has truth as the semblance of the illusionless" (*AT* 132, *ÄT* 199).

On Adorno's conception, then, truth in art is carried by sociohistorical meaning or import (*Gehalt*) that emerges from artistic production, depends on the mediation of content and form, resides in particular works, transcends them, and invites critical interpretation. Perhaps not every work has truth content (*Wahrheitsgehalt*), but every work having import (*Gehalt*) calls for judgments about the truth or falsity of its import. In a sense, then, truth in art has a double location. First, it is located in the truth content of autonomous works of art.[24] The concept of truth content suggests that truth is *in* artworks and not simply prompted or denoted by them. Second, truth is located in a reciprocation between critical interpretation and art phenomena, a reciprocation that occurs by way of the truth content of particular works.

The advantage to Adorno's approach is twofold. First, it refuses to divorce truth from the phenomena of art, insisting instead that truth is thoroughly mediated by the phenomena. Second, it resists the philosopher's temptation to read into art whatever truth the philosopher wishes to find there. But this advantage comes with a double disadvantage. Not only does Adorno privilege autonomous art, specifically autonomous artworks, as the site of truth in art, but also he privileges philosophy, specifically negative dialectical philosophy, as the most authoritative interpreter of artistic truth. Both tendencies make artistic truth esoteric.[25]

Admittedly it is difficult to give a philosophical account of artistic truth that does not fall into one of these two traps. Like Albrecht Wellmer, I have found Jürgen Habermas's theory of communicative action helpful in that regard. So have Seel and other third-generation critical theorists, who simply follow Habermas's lead in retaining propositions as bearers of truth and turning the claim to truth into an intersubjective validity claim. Habermas regards the claim to truth (*Wahrheit*) as one of three validity claims for which every speaker is accountable when she or he uses language to reach an understanding. The other two validity claims are normative legitimacy or rightness (*Richtigkeit*) and sincerity or truthfulness (*Wahrhaftigkeit*).[26] The three validity claims correspond, respectively, to language's universal pragmatic functions of representing something in the world, establishing interpersonal relations, and expressing personal experience. In using language, speakers refer to things in "objective," social, and personal worlds.[27]

Because Habermas grounds his theory of validity in a reconstruction of social theory and of ordinary language, his approach privileges neither autonomous artworks as the site of truth in art nor philosophy as the most authoritative interpreter of artistic truth. This provides a worthwhile correction to Adorno's truth aesthetics. Unfortunately, it comes at the expense of nearly eliminating art's capacity to carry truth. At best, in a modification borrowed from Wellmer, Habermas accords artworks a "truth potential" as a singular power "to disclose anew an apparently familiar reality" and thereby to address ordinary experience, in which the three validity domains intermesh.[28] The notion of "truth potential" implies that art is not entirely locked up in an autonomous sphere of aesthetic validity overseen by professional artists and expert critics, that art can directly stimulate transformed relations among ordinary selves or between them and the world. Nevertheless, given the distance Habermas himself has pointed out between ordinary experience and the expert culture of the artistic domain, his appeal to artistic truth potential is not grounded in a social-theoretical account of how this potential could be actualized. Unlike the critical and utopian roles art receives in Adorno's social philosophy, its disclosive power seems to float free from society in Habermas's theory of communicative action, in keeping with his tendency to underestimate the disclosive functions of ordinary language.[29] For Habermas, linguistic disclosure is a prestaging, as it were, of the communicative action in which validity claims are raised.[30] In fact, he considers the truth potential of artworks and the disclosive functions of language to be similar in precisely this regard.[31]

Given the insights and blind spots on both sides of the Adorno-Habermas divide, critical aesthetic theory needs to develop an idea of artistic truth that neither renders it esoteric, à la Adorno, nor reduces it to aesthetic validity, à la Seel. It must be an idea in which validity and disclosure are distinguished, as Habermas insists and as the previous chapter has argued, but disclosure does not float free from ordinary language, and art's critical and utopian roles in society do not disappear. It must be an idea in which validity and disclosure are intimately linked.

Critical Mediation

To meet this challenge, let me propose an approach to artistic truth that combines Adorno's insight into artistic "truth content" with Habermas's insight into the differentiated character of validity claims. I wish to consider artistic truth to be internal to art phenomena, as Adorno claims, yet differentiated into three dimensions, in a manner reminiscent of Habermas's theory of validity. These dimensions can be understood either as three relationships that art phenomena sustain or as three functions they fulfill. Moreover, the prevalence of one or another dimension correlates with the historically conditioned status of the phenomenon – that is, with whether or not it is institutionally constituted as a work of art.[32]

I propose that all the art we know of, whether "high" or "low," whether "popular" or "esoteric," whether "mass art" or "folk art," has as one of its tasks to proffer and provoke imaginative insight. To call insight "imaginative" in this connection is to suggest that it arises within intersubjective processes of exploration, presentation, and creative interpretation. Imaginative insight depends on the discovery and deployment of aesthetic signs. In Western societies, art has become differentiated as a cultural domain where people continually invent and test media for such discovery and deployment. To be imaginative, the insight cannot be divorced from such media of imagination – images, stories, metaphors, musical compositions, dramatic enactments, and the like. To be insightful, the media of imagination cannot be deployed in either arbitrary or rigid ways. Perhaps, to avoid the static and visual metaphor of "insight," one should speak of imaginative inseeings, imaginative inhearings, imaginative intouchings, and the like. As a generic term I use the word "disclosure" rather than "insight."

In general, as the previous two chapters show, I regard truth as a process of life-giving disclosure marked by fidelity to the commonly holding-and-held. By "life-giving disclosure" I mean a historical process of opening up in which human beings and other creatures come to flourish. By "fidelity" I mean responsiveness to principles such as solidarity and justice that people hold in common and that hold them in common. These principles are historical horizons that are learned, achieved, contested, reformulated, and ignored. Imaginative disclosure, as it prevails in art, is no less crucial to this general process than is the assertoric or propositional disclosure that prevails in academic disciplines. Propositionally inflected theories of truth mistakenly reduce disclosure to whatever can be asserted, and they reduce the marks of fidelity to criteria for assertoric correctness, whether these be criteria of correspondence, coherence, consensus, or pragmatic consequences. The complementary mistake made by Heidegger's *Kunstwerk* essay is to turn all of disclosure into imaginative disclosure, of an ethically burdened sort, for which assertoric correctness has little purchase. Yet, compared with, say, Beardsley's propositionally inflected denial of artistic truth, Heidegger's approach has the advantage that art remains a site where truth occurs. The truth that occurs there can belong to a process of life-giving disclosure.

I take it that when people talk about truth in art, they refer to how art discloses something of vital importance that is hard to pin down. When philosophers disagree about how to theorize truth in art, their disputes usually concern what art does or can disclose, how this disclosure takes place, and whether this disclosure is important, legitimate, preferable, and the like. Philosophers also disagree as to whether this disclosure is simultaneously a concealment (Heidegger), and, if so, how the process of disclosure and concealment contributes to human knowledge. In general, art can be true in the sense that its imaginative disclosures can uncover what needs to be uncovered. Art can be false in the sense that its imaginative disclosures can cover up what needs to be uncovered. Once we realize what is at stake in artistic truth or falsehood, it will not do to say "This is merely imaginative, just playful or ironic or parodic exploration, the work of creative genius." Such special pleadings have the inadvertent effect of making art seem irrelevant or frivolous, as if imagination has little to do with life-giving disclosure. But it also will not suffice simply to attack disturbing art as "blatantly immoral" or "sacrilegious" or "repressive." Such hyperbolic accusations inadvertently make art seem more directly effective than the imaginative character of its truth or falsity permits, as if artistic disclosure is not tied to intersubjective exploration and interpretation.

Philosophers who reflect on contemporary art, and who engage in cultural and social criticism, must ask, What needs to be disclosed in an imaginative way? This is not so different from the question facing every truth-oriented artist. There is no way to answer the question once and for all, especially not when one is an artist, since that which needs disclosure is continually changing, as are the media of imaginative disclosure. In the broadest terms, a philosopher must appeal to a general understanding of good and evil. At various stages of social history one or another pathology may have priority. Hence, for example, Adorno may have been right to connect the truth of modern art with the memory of suffering and the exposure of antagonisms in a society that erases this memory and resists such exposure while suffering multiplies and antagonisms deepen. Nevertheless, where imaginative disclosure is genuinely needed, what needs to be disclosed cannot be limited to the truth content of autonomous artworks, nor can the identification of these needs be the sole prerogative of philosophy.

It is crucial, I think, that imaginative disclosure occurs in art itself, and not merely in people's lives when they experience artworks, talk about them, and engage in arts-related discourse. Yet I see little reason to restrict imaginative disclosure to the "import" of autonomous works of art. Art phenomena, whether or not they are institutionally constituted as works of art, occur in contexts of production and use. Accordingly, the idea of imaginative disclosure can be differentiated into concepts of mediated expression, interpretable presentation, and configured import. "Mediated expression" indicates a relationship to the context of production. It pertains to the phenomenon's status as an imaginative artifact. "Interpretable presentation" indicates a relationship to the context of use. It pertains to the phenomenon's status as an imaginative object of appreciation, commentary, and criticism. "Configured import," however, indicates the phenomenon's relationship to its own internal demands, and it may well be peculiar to artworks. In traditional terms, which Adorno also uses, import has to do with how, within phenomena that are institutionally constituted as works of art, the relationship between content and form makes the work a self-referential symbol of something else.

This implies that an art phenomenon can be true in three ways: true with respect to the artist's intentions, true with respect to the audience's interpretive needs, and true with respect to an artwork's internal demands. In each way, as I explain, the art phenomenon's "being true with respect to" amounts to "being imaginatively disclosive of." Moreover, an art phenomenon succeeding in one or two respects can nonetheless fail in another, just as a well-formed speech act asserting a proposition can be inappropriate, or a genuine act of promising can lend itself to misinterpretation. I designate these three dimensions of artistic truth with the terms authenticity (vis-à-vis the artist's intentions), significance (vis-à-vis the audience's interpretive needs), and integrity (vis-à-vis the work's internal demands). Perhaps "great works of art" display all three of these and continue to display them in new contexts of use.

6.2 AUTHENTICITY, SIGNIFICANCE, INTEGRITY

Each term – authenticity, significance, integrity – indicates a relationship within which or with respect to which an art phenomenon can be true. Because of these relationships, people in modern Western societies bring certain expectations concerning imaginative disclosure to their interactions with art and with each other within the domain of art. One such expectation is that of authenticity. Thanks to a complex sociocultural history that Charles Taylor and others have told,[33] both artists and their publics expect art to arise from art making that is authentic. To be authentic, writing or video making or choreographing must be true with respect to the artist's own experience or vision.[34] This does not mean that the art event or art product must be transparent in this regard. Sophisticated publics often prize a lack of transparency. Yet, no matter how obscure the artist's intentions may be, we unavoidably experience an art product as not only arising via art making from someone's experience but also imaginatively disclosing that experience to some degree. The expectation of authenticity is the expectation that art phenomena be true with respect to – imaginatively disclosive of – the experience or vision from which competent art making allows them to arise. Authenticity is a matter of mediated expression that is imaginatively disclosive.

Judgments concerning authenticity can occur instantaneously, but they are enormously complex. One complication arises because everyone who experiences an art phenomenon brings a socioculturally acquired and personal sensibility concerning which experiences or visions are worth disclosing, and which would be better left undisclosed. Together with variations in preparation and ability for interpreting art in different media, this complication partially explains why public disputes about artistic authenticity become difficult to resolve, quite apart from the political and legal struggles in which they commonly occur. Celebrated cases of "arresting images"[35] in the United States during the 1980s and 1990s had conflicts among sensibilities at their core. Many also raised the question whether authenticity is itself a legitimate expectation, or at least whether art-in-public[36] is appropriately produced or experienced under the expectation of authenticity. The expectation has not disappeared, however, and I doubt that it will, so long as the Western artworld remains relatively intact.

Within that artworld we also expect art phenomena to be significant. "Significance" is not the same as "relevance," with which it is often confused. An art event or art product may be found relevant, in the sense that it addresses a timely issue or makes a direct connection with an audience's interests or concerns. But in itself that does not tell us whether it is also significant. To be significant, an art phenomenon must be true with respect to a public's need for cultural presentations that are worthy of their engagement. Artistic significance is, if you will, a quasi-normative expectation. People expect art to be "worth their while," and they criticize art that does not live up to this expectation.

This does not mean that all the members of a public have the same personal needs for cultural presentations, or that they either share or come to share the same communal need. Yet they do all expect a concert or mural or an event of performance art to be a cultural presentation that, for various personal and public "reasons," offers something that merits their attention. What is offered could be the sheer quality of the playing or the visual highlighting of a neighborhood's story or the provocative reenactment of a traumatic event. Amid the variety of responses, we cannot avoid experiencing art events and art products as offering something more or less significant. The expectation of significance is the expectation that art phenomena be true with respect to – imaginatively disclosive of – a public's need for worthwhile cultural presentations. Significance is a matter of interpretable presentation that is imaginatively disclosive.

This formulation suggests that art serves to bring to our attention interpretive needs that might otherwise remain hidden. Accordingly, it would be a mistake to think that artists should simply provide what audiences want or demand. It would also be a mistake to think that audiences have such well-defined needs that they always know beforehand "what they will like." My formulation also suggests a reason why straightforward political or moral or religious readings of the supposed "message" of an artwork tend to backfire. What such approaches miss is the reflexivity built into art interpretation and demanded by the imaginative character of art itself. When we interpret art we simultaneously interpret our need for what the art in question may or may not offer. This reflexivity does not preclude political or moral or religious interpretations. Rather it encourages them, provided they remain open to having art challenge the self-interpretation that a community or social agent brings to the hermeneutic process. Art phenomena that deserve interpretation cannot shed the imaginative character of the cultural presentations they offer. That is why, as I suggested earlier, simpleminded attacks on disturbing art prove inadequate, quite apart from the rhetorical ineffectiveness of moral hyperbole in a pluralistic society.

When the art phenomenon is institutionally constituted as a work of art, the expectations of authenticity and significance usually accompany a third expectation, which I label "integrity." Integrity has to do with a peculiarity in how artworks function as aesthetic signs. In general, aesthetic signs function as presentations that make nuances of meaning available in ways that either exceed or precede both idiosyncratic expressions of intent and conventional communications of content. What aesthetic signs present is their purport. Their purport is about something other than the aesthetic signs themselves, something various interpreters can share and do share. Artworks, too, are aesthetic signs in all of these respects, but with a peculiar doubling that most other aesthetic signs lack. I mark the difference by reserving the term "import" for the meaning internal to artworks. Artworks usually present something else by presenting themselves, and they present themselves in presenting something else.

Adorno captures this doubling when he argues that truth in art requires both the successful mediation of content and form and the suspension of form for the sake of what exceeds this mediation. For an artwork's import to be true, the artwork must succeed in being fully about itself while also succeeding in not being only about itself. Or, in Heidegger's terms, the work's thrust (*Anstoss*) must be carried by a configuration (*Gestalt*) that allows the establishing not simply of tensions internal to the work but of a larger (indeed, world historical!) strife. I would put the matter like this: for an artwork's import to be true, the artwork must live up to its own internal demands, one of which usually is that it live up to more than its own internal demands. The expectation of integrity is an expectation that the artwork be true with respect to – imaginatively disclosive of – its own internal demands. Integrity is a matter of configured import that is imaginatively (self-)disclosive.

Much could be said about this third dimension of artistic truth, which artistic truth theorists from Hegel onward have emphasized. Let me simply note that my formulation of the notion of integrity attempts to close a gap in Wellmer's conception between the artwork's "aesthetic validity" (*Stimmigkeit*) and the work's "truth potential" (*Wahrheitspotential*). I aim to close this gap without either letting aesthetic validity replace artistic truth, à la Seel, or falling into the "esoteric" conception of artistic truth that Wellmer criticizes in Adorno's writings.[37] The expectation of integrity does not restrict us to exploring a work's "potential" for disclosing something in our world on the occasion of our experiencing the work. The expectation is stronger than that. It requires us to interpret the work as itself "standing for" or "representing" or "symboling" something, and to find clues to what the work is about not simply in our own experience or in conversations with others but *in the work itself* – in the specific way it configures whatever it makes perceptible. At the same time, the expectation of integrity requires us to interpret this configuration as the work's way of telling us about itself. Moreover, the expectation requires us to take both interpretive paths simultaneously, and repeatedly, with respect to the same artwork, since the work's self-disclosing world disclosure is itself imaginative, enveloped in processes of exploration and creative interpretation.

My distinguishing three dimensions of artistic truth raises a question about how they intersect. Let me give two responses to this question, first with regard to the internal workings of art, and then with regard to art's "world relations." I discuss the first topic by returning to the notion of aesthetic validity, and the second topic by returning to the notion of cultural orientation.

Internal Intersections

I have described "aesthetic validity" as a horizon of "imaginative cogency" within which people employ aesthetic standards such as complexity, depth, and intensity. Aesthetic validity pertains to the cogency of exploration, creative interpretation, and presentation and, within these processes, to the imaginative cogency of aesthetic signs. Although I resist the tendency to restrict aesthetic validity to art, I do not deny that aesthetic validity is an especially prominent concern in art as an expert culture. Now I wish to show how imaginative cogency provides a horizon within which authenticity, significance, and integrity intersect.

I have indicated that all three are dimensions of "truth with respect to" in the sense of "being imaginatively disclosive of." While the idea of imaginative disclosure recalls Heidegger's anti-aesthetics, my three-dimensional account opposes his tendency to reduce validity to disclosure, both in his account of artistic truth and in his general conception of truth. I have proposed instead that any disclosive "creating and preserving" in art, and any judgments about artistic disclosure, must appeal to imaginative cogency as a principle of aesthetic validity. Hence, what unifies authenticity, significance, and integrity, beyond their all being modes of imaginative disclosure, is the requirement that they measure up to a principle of aesthetic validity – that they all occur within the horizon of imaginative cogency.

This suggests that the purported authenticity of a particular art product or art event is not self-contained. Along with the expectation that the art phenomenon imaginatively disclose the art maker's experience or vision comes the expectation that this disclosure be "original." Other things being equal, we properly prefer an art product that gives surprising and compelling expression to the artist's experience or vision, rather than one that fails to do this. Similarly, the perceived significance of a particular art phenomenon is not sufficient. The expectation that it imaginatively disclose the audience's need for worthwhile cultural presentations brings with it an expectation that this disclosure be "gripping" or "inspiring" or "illuminating." Other things being equal, we properly prize an art product whose cultural presentation is provocative and telling, not one whose cultural presentation is insipid or trite. Again, the integrity of an artwork is open-ended. We normally expect more than the artwork's having configured import that is imaginatively (self-)disclosive. We also expect this doubled disclosure to be "unique" and "challenging." Other things being equal, we properly give sustained attention to an artwork whose internal demands are high, also with respect to living up to more than its internal demands. And we properly give less attention to an artwork that "makes life easy for itself."

Further, in the case of artworks, as distinct from other art phenomena, questions about authenticity and significance necessarily lead to questions of integrity. For in the final analysis, our emerging interpretation of the artwork's import necessarily guides our interpretation of the artist's vision and of our own interpretive needs. The work uncovers facets of the artist's experience and the interpreter's situation by disclosing a world in disclosing itself. An artwork lacking integrity or having little integrity might also be less disclosive of personal and intersubjective worlds.

Matters stand somewhat differently with art products and art events that are not institutionally constituted as artworks, however. Such art phenomena need not have the doubling that characterizes import in artworks. Often, in fact, they lack this doubling. They do have aesthetic meaning, however, as does any nonartistic aesthetic sign. Sometimes this fact, plus a close proximity to artworks proper, may raise the expectation that they be imaginatively self-disclosive. But we also often "read" their nuances of meaning in less demanding ways, recognizing their disclosive character to be little more than an amalgam of authenticity and significance for which the question of integrity scarcely arises. This is how many people experience so-called popular music and mainstream movies. Yet the boundaries between artworks "proper" and other art phenomena, being dependent on institutional constituting, are fluid. And the fact that all aesthetic signs have purport provides a basis for more demanding interpretations of even the most occasional of art phenomena. The risk, of course, is that one looks for more in the product or event than its institutional constitution and internal configuration warrant. As some forays into cultural studies have inadvertently demonstrated, interpreting ephemeral art phenomena as if they were artworks occasionally manufactures silk purses from sows' ears.

World Relations

The three dimensions of artistic truth also intersect in supporting pursuits of cultural orientation. I have described cultural orientation as how individuals, communities, and organizations find their direction both within and by way of culture. Aesthetic processes of exploration, creative interpretation, and presentation lend nuance and vigor to this pursuit. Because the artworld has developed as an institutionalized setting for promoting aesthetic processes and adjudicating aesthetic validity claims, art has become a crucial site for aesthetically laden pursuits of cultural orientation. Art serves simultaneously to help people find their way in art and to find their way in aesthetic matters outside art. Beyond this, however, my critical interpretation of Heidegger's anti-aesthetics suggests that such art-supported pursuits lend themselves to larger processes of disorientation and reorientation. Although I am loathe to portray these as a world-earth striving in which the tension between sociocultural orientation and transhistorical preorientation gets disclosed, something like this must enter an account that aims to link artistic truth with truth as life-giving disclosure marked by fidelity to the commonly holding/held. How should this intuition be articulated?

Earlier I sought to reclaim Heidegger's insight that there is more to validity than intersubjective principles and validity claims. I described this "more" as a calling that comes to us from beyond ourselves and beyond the entities and people with which we have dealings. The calling, which occurs in the very holding of principles, urges upon us an orientation toward that which sustains validity and gives life. It reorients our worlds, by spanning them, by connecting them with worlds we do not inhabit, and by continually placing them in question.

The worlds in question, both with respect to art and with respect to ordinary language, are of three sorts: personal, social, and postsubjective.[38] First there is a personal world, to which each individual has unique access. Mediated expression in art opens a window on personal worlds as they are inhabited by the makers of art, whether or not these are professional artists. An underlying assumption within our expectation of artistic authenticity is that art makers' worlds are, in some relevant sense, sufficiently like our own personal worlds that we can learn from the expression of their experience and vision. We turn to mediated expression to gain cultural orientation, even when we recognize that, no matter how authentic the expression, it will never relieve us from finding our own way.

In fact, the more authentic the art product or art event, the more it will push us to come to terms with a second world, the intersubjective or social world, which Habermas describes as "the sum total of legitimately ordered interpersonal relations."[39] More specifically, the art phenomenon will challenge us to come to terms with interpretive needs that go beyond personal desires and preferences. Such needs belong to the fabric of a world we share with other people. Deep within our expectation of artistic significance lies the assumption that art can illuminate our shared interpretive needs and even transform them. We turn to interpretable presentations to find new ways or rediscover old ways of recognizing and meeting interpretive needs for cultural presentations. This, too, is a way to gain cultural orientation.

The import of artworks, however, has the capacity to wrench us free from both the personal and social worlds we already inhabit. It directs us toward yet another world, if you will, perhaps not an "objective world (as the sum total of what is or could be the case),"[40] but a postsubjective world of what neither is nor is not the case. This is another world, not in the sense that it excludes personal or social worlds, but in the sense that, though it may include them, it cannot be equated with them. It is what Wolterstorff, under different ontological commitments from my own, might call "the world of the work," to which Adorno would immediately add that it is not simply the world of the work. It is not an entirely different world from that which discloses itself in ordinary language and to which speakers employing propositions refer. But it is a world whose disclosure via artworks is sufficiently different from what such language discloses that one hesitates to call it the same world.[41]

Because artworks present themselves in presenting something else, they elicit from us interpretations that are not simply about personal or social worlds. Artworks elicit interpretations of themselves, of their configured import, and, in this, interpretations of that to which they point, which is more than the world of the artist or the world of the interpreter. In expecting artistic integrity, we also open ourselves to a world that is not completely our own but that also cannot exist on its own. Although any art phenomenon can lend itself to larger processes of disorientation and reorientation, the doubling of import in artworks gives them special "truth potential" in this regard. That, I take it, is why artistic truth theorists from Hegel and Nietzsche through Heidegger and Adorno have singled out artworks as sites of more-than-artistic-truth. For the configured import of an integral artwork unavoidably puts personal and social worlds in question. In that sense every such artwork can provide favorable conditions under which a world-crossing call can be heard. Yet this call does not require any artwork, no matter how import-ant, nor does any artwork itself lie beyond the question whether it also contributes to a process of life-giving disclosure. Both Heidegger and Adorno were misdirected to suggest otherwise.

6.3 ART TALK AND ARTISTIC TRUTH

My connecting artistic truth with world relations allows one to regard the three dimensions of artist truth as marking different "universal pragmatic" functions. Thus, for example, authenticity pertains to the expression of personal experience, significance to the establishing of intersubjective re-lations, and integrity to the presenting of a world, all within a process of imaginative disclosure. If this is right, then one can postulate more precise links between artistic truth and the sorts of speech acts that commonly oc-cur when people engage in art appreciation, interpretation, and criticism – more precise than a diffuse entering into ordinary experience where three validity domains intermesh, as described by Wellmer and Habermas.

To indicate these links, let me return to the distinction within art talk between conversation and discourse. "Art talk" refers to all the various ways in which language is used in the experience of art. When it occurs in rela-tively straightforward attempts to reach an understanding, it can be called "art conversation." But when it becomes more reflective, and implicit valid-ity claims become explicit topics, it can be called "art discourse." I want to consider how art conversation makes the truth dimensions of art available for art discourse.

Conversations about art address, among other topics, the artist's inten-tions, the audience's interpretations, and the artwork's internal demands. These conversations shift readily across descriptive, explanatory, evaluative, and prescriptive registers. Frequently one discussion partner or another will find a particular art phenomenon lacking in authenticity or significance or integrity, saying this painting is not genuine or that piece of music doesn't do anything for me or that film is a piece of trash. If someone else disagrees, then the implicit expectations of authenticity, significance, and integrity can themselves become topics of discussion. Someone, for example, may ask why you do not find the painting genuine, or why you think it should be genuine, or what you mean by "genuine," and you might respond by appealing to some notion of authenticity. When, in response to a question or challenge, you give reasons for your judgment and explain your criteria, your conversation tends to turn into discourse.

Art discourse does more than thematize the dimensions of artistic truth, however. It also thematizes the validity dimensions of art conversation itself. Hence the topic for discursive consideration might very well be not simply the authenticity, significance, or integrity of the art phenomenon but the sincerity or appropriateness or correctness of a discussant's speech acts. Often, in fact, the topics of art discourse jump back and forth between artistic truth and conversational validity claims. I might assert that a painting by Norman Rockwell presents too rosy a picture of American family life. You might dispute my assertion and ask me to defend or explain it. I might reply by appealing to certain facts – the clean-scrubbed look of the children, or the sentimental happiness of the dog. You might grant these facts, but say they do not make up a rosy picture. Or you might grant that they make up a rosy picture, but deny that such a picture is too rosy. Very soon we would find ourselves discussing what Rockwell "was trying to depict" (intention) and how others have responded to this painting (interpretive needs). And so it would go.

At a minimum, this dispute would have two inseparable and simultaneous poles: the painting's import and the asserted proposition. To reach an understanding concerning the first pole, we would need to look at the painting together and try to see "what the painting is all about." To reach an understanding about the second pole, we would need to establish whether certain shared facts bear out the asserted proposition. If we had not both looked at the painting with an eye to its import, we would be hard pressed to find sufficient shared facts relevant to the disputed proposition. Facts are funded (not founded) by objects as experienced, even though, according to Habermas, facts play a role only in discourse.

Or, to use a different example, you might suggest that Marcel Duchamp's *Fountain* is an artistic fraud. How could a genuine artist exhibit an ordinary urinal and expect art lovers to enjoy it as a work of art? A defender of Duchamp might reply that you obviously have not understood his intention. Duchamp wasn't asking anyone to enjoy this mass-produced fixture as a work of art. Rather, he was challenging an artworld that arbitrarily installs certain products as artworks and just as arbitrarily rejects others. You might entertain this suggestion but reply that Duchamp himself was acting in no less an arbitrary way, unlike a genuine artist. In response, your interlocutor might ask what prompts you to say what artists should or should not do. Are you an artist yourself? Pursued at sufficient length, a discussion along these lines would also raise questions about what *Fountain* "tells us" about the artworld itself (import) and why anyone should find *Fountain* worth his or her while (interpretive needs).

As constructed here, the primary dispute would have two inseparable and simultaneous poles: the artist's intention, and the sources of a viewer's responses. To reach an understanding with regard to the first pole, the discussants must figure out, to the extent possible, what the artist "had in mind" and whether the displaying of *Fountain* achieved this intention. To reach an understanding about the second pole, they must establish "where they are coming from" and whether such autobiographical positioning authorizes their judgments. In considering the artist's intentions, they will also seek to establish the sincerity of their own responses.

Or, to take a third example, let's say Joyce and Rosa are talking about Käthe Kollwitz's *Saatfrüchte sollen nicht vermahlen werden* (*Seed Corn Must Not Be Ground*). Joyce might say she considers it a powerful twentieth-century protest against the human consequences of war. Rosa might respond that she finds the piece personally moving but ineffective as a protest. Joyce might wonder aloud how this piece can be personally moving but politically ineffective. Rosa might reply that it takes more than a print of a mother protecting her children to persuade power brokers to lay down their arms. Joyce might answer that such persuading is not art's task anyway. At least a gesture of protest can raise people's consciousness, and this piece certainly does that. "But," Rosa might object, "what evidence is there that this piece actually raised or raises people's consciousness?" At this point the discussion would quickly turn to what *Saatfrüchte* is about (import) and what Käthe Kollwitz was trying to accomplish when she made it (intention).

A discussion along these lines can be highly instructive. Its primary focus is the social functions of the piece in question. But it also raises questions about the social status of claims made in this regard. Again, the disagreement has two poles: the work's significance, and the normative legitimacy of speech acts in which such claims arise. To reach an understanding about the first pole, the conversation partners need to sort out the roles such a work plays in people's lives. To reach an understanding about the second pole, they must explore the merits of their own political and ethical stances. Considering a work's social functions gives people an occasion to sort out their political and ethical differences.

So I wish to postulate not simply a general connection between artistic truth and conversational validity claims, but more specific links between each of the three dimensions of artistic truth and each of the three validity claims: between artistic authenticity and expressive sincerity, between artistic significance and normative legitimacy, and between artistic integrity and propositional truth. Moreover, the links are dyadic. In the first place, art conversations about artistic authenticity often raise a conversational claim to sincerity; frequently they address artistic significance by raising a conversational claim to normative legitimacy; and, when considering an artwork's integrity, they usually raise a conversational claim to propositional truth. In the second place, our experience with issues of authenticity, significance, and integrity in art, and our art conversation about these issues, are part of the hermeneutical matrix from which the content of the correlative validity claims arises.

My examples do not fully bear out such dyadic links, however. This is because I have reconstructed instances of art talk primarily in the mode of argumentation, where assertoric, descriptive, and other constative speech acts tend to dominate. Hence in all three examples it seems as if "what's really going on" is a dispute over claims to propositional truth: not only, for example, whether it is correct to say that the Rockwell piece paints too rosy a picture but also whether it is correct to say that Duchamp's *Fountain* is an artistic fraud or that Kollwitz's *Saatfrüchte* is a powerful protest piece. My reconstructions do not effectively capture the expressive and regulative speech acts that ordinarily occur in conversations about art, raising claims to nonpropositional validity.[42] So let me fill in the conversational texture to the second and third examples, beginning with the discussion of Duchamp's *Fountain*.

Expressive speech acts typically occur as first-person avowals or confessions. The reconstructed dispute about Duchamp's *Fountain* might have started with two people in a gallery or museum, one of them visibly upset, the other ironically distanced. Being upset, you might say "I hate this piece" or "I just don't get it" or, more maliciously, "This really pisses me off." Taking the stance of a formalist critic, your partner might ignore your comment altogether or declare it irrelevant. Or, adopting a therapeutic role, he or she might ask "Do you want to tell me about your feelings?" But let's say the two of you are friends who are out for the day, and you respect one another's felt responses to art. Then a more likely reply to your comment might be your partner's own expressive speech act: "I don't hate it; actually, I find it rather funny." Or your partner might be so bold as to question your sincerity: "Do you really hate it? Aren't you exaggerating a bit?" Disputes about artists' intentions and the authenticity of art products arise most readily from expressive speech acts of this sort.

According to Habermas, the validity claim most prominently raised by expressive speech acts is a claim to truthfulness or sincerity (*Wahrhaftigkeit*) in the sharing of experiences to which the first-person speaker has privileged access. As he points out, the "warranty" (*Gewähr*) for expressive speech acts concerns the consistency of the speaker's actions with what the speaker says.[43] If, for example, you had been a big fan of dada prior to expressing your hatred of *Fountain*, your partner might well question the sincerity of your pronouncement. The same would occur if one hour later you bought the piece for display in your home's atrium. Overlooking or discounting the importance of such speech acts has been a fundamental flaw in anti-intentionalist accounts of art talk such as Monroe Beardsley's. Anti-intentionalism, while salutary in other respects, has reinforced the cultural insularity of professional art making and art criticism. In the past, the official artworld in Western countries has deliberately discouraged or disallowed art talk in which expressive speech acts prevail.[44]

Now let's turn to the example involving Kollwitz's *Saatfrüchte* and imagine that the disagreement began with a regulative speech act. Regulative speech acts typically occur as requests or promises "employed in the attitude of the second person."[45] One person asks another to do something, or ego promises alter that ego will do something. Suppose Joyce is a patron, Rosa a curator, and they are brainstorming about an upcoming exhibition of antiwar art. Joyce asks Rosa to include Kollwitz's *Saatfrüchte*, but Rosa refuses this request. They agree on Kollwitz's stature as an important twentieth-century artist and on the formal merits of this piece. But they disagree in other respects.

Structurally, this case is more elaborate than the previous example. One motivation for Rosa's refusal could be that she does not consider the patron entitled to make this request. This could become a reason why, at the level of discourse, she challenges Joyce's political interpretation. If so, then a dispute about the work's political merits would be somewhat "beside the point." Instead they should discuss the proper roles of patron and curator in the formation of an exhibition at this museum. Alternatively, however, the roles of patron and curator could be well established and each party be within her rights in either making or refusing the request. Then each party's political interpretation of the piece would indeed be on the table. Political interpretations, like moral and religious interpretations, have the propensity to put each discussant's own social involvements at issue. Joyce and Rosa cannot simply bracket how they participate in political processes and with whom they associate politically. In questioning one another's political interpretation of Kollwitz's *Saatfrüchte*, they would also question the normative legitimacy of their own speech acts of request and refusal, not at the level of organizational policy, but at the level of sociopolitical engagement. At this level, the very acts of requesting and refusing inclusion of the piece are a political interaction. Here art talk as political conversation gives rise to controvertible claims about the political significance of the artwork.

Habermas argues that the validity claim most prominently raised by regulative speech acts is a claim to rightness (*Richtigkeit*) with respect to normative expectations that both parties recognize. The warranty for regulative speech acts concerns a speaker's readiness to give reasons why the request or promise in question meets normative expectations that are themselves worthy of recognition. Two people trying to reach a decision about the appropriateness of an artwork or art event for a specific occasion already assume some standard according to which the artwork would be appropriate. That is why their art talk can easily shift from conversational uses of regulative speech acts to discursive thematizing of both their own entitlement to make or refuse requests and the societal importance of the product in question. If, in the case of Kollwitz's *Saatfrüchte*, Joyce backs up her request by appealing to her own political orientation in order to claim that the piece has great political significance, then a shift to discourse will already have begun. It is a fundamental flaw in existential accounts of art talk such as Albert Hofstadter's to ignore or dismiss the importance of regulative speech acts. This simply reinscribes the privatizing of art interpretation that emotivists such as I. A. Richards had already encouraged earlier in the twentieth century.

The dyadic links I have illustrated are neither necessary nor exclusive.[46] Being highly fluid, art talk rarely follows the linear paths I have mapped. Indeed, people do not have to engage in either constative, expressive, or regulative speech acts, respectively, in order for the "counterparts" of artistic integrity, authenticity, and significance to be discussed. You or your discussion partner need not make a personal avowal in order to talk about an art product's authenticity, nor must one of you engage in a regulative speech act in order to discuss the product's significance. Yet my examples do suggest that art products resemble speech acts in the types of world relations they allow people to sustain – namely, relations to a postsubjective world, to a personal world, and to a social world. It is because of parallels in world relations that the dyads are neither simply occasional nor completely contingent.

Like speech acts, artworks are ways in which people address one another about something. In principle each artwork makes available all dimensions of artistic truth, regardless of which dimension stands out. When an artwork is highly "expressive" of its maker's experience, for example, this does not render the work's import or significance inaccessible or nonexistent, any more than a spoken avowal immunizes itself from concerns about propositional truth or normative legitimacy. But in artistic intersubjectivity and reference, unlike "communicative action," imaginative disclosure prevails.

Thanks to parallels in world relations, and to loosely dyadic links between truth dimensions in art and validity dimensions in ordinary language, imaginative disclosure is neither esoteric (Adorno) nor peripheral (Habermas). Elaborated at greater length, my proposal could provide a way to build disclosure into the very fabric of communicative action, rather than relegating it to a preliminary stage within language usage. At least it would offer a different perspective on propositional validity, both by tying it more closely to imaginative disclosure than standard truth theories allow, and by indicating truth itself to be a multidimensional idea whose reduction to propositional truth leads to theoretical impoverishment and practical dead ends. Adorno's intuitions about artistic truth would not be blind, although to articulate them would require Habermasian concepts that are not empty. In this way the critical-utopian thrust of Adorno's social philosophy would be preserved. Subsequent chapters develop my proposal as a critical appropriation of debates about "artistic truth" among Anglo-American philosophers, most of whom restrict truth proper to propositional validity.

PART III

LINGUISTIC TURNS

7

Logical Positivist Dispute

It ought to be impossible to talk about poetry or religion as though they were capable of giving "knowledge".... A poem ... tells us, or should tell us, nothing.

C. K. Ogden and I. A. Richards[1]

A work of art [is] the artistic expression of ... descriptive and evaluative propositions with a discoverable referendum.

Theodore Meyer Greene[2]

Propositionally inflected correspondence theories of truth have governed the mainstream of Anglo-American aesthetics since the 1920s.[3] By "propositionally inflected" I mean any account in which propositions are the sole or the primary locus of truth. Although not all propositionally inflected accounts are correspondence theories, very few correspondence theories are not propositionally inflected. By "correspondence theories of truth" I mean theories that consider the correspondence of proposition to fact, or some equivalent correspondence, to be the sole or the primary criterion of truth. Even the alternatives offered by theorists such as I. A. Richards and Nelson Goodman, who explicitly challenge propositionally inflected correspondence theories, bear marks of the theories they reject. Together, the propositional view and correspondence theory are like banks within which mainstream discussions of "artistic truth" have flowed. Their erosion in recent decades has helped diversify Anglo-American aesthetics, but without significantly revitalizing the idea of artistic truth.

One can distinguish three historical stages in Anglo-American discussions of artistic truth. Stage 1 parallels the rise of logical positivism, and it lasts from the 1920s until the early 1950s. Appeals to a propositional view and a correspondence theory are relatively direct and uncomplicated in this stage. For convenience, I label this stage "logical positivist aesthetics," even though not all of the dominant figures were logical positivists and some adamantly opposed logical positivism. Stage 2 arises after World War II and extends into the 1980s. In this stage appeals to a propositional view and a correspondence theory are relatively sophisticated and indirect. I label this stage "analytic aesthetics," because of a dominant emphasis on linguistic analysis. Appearing in the early years of stage 2, Beardsley's *Aesthetics* transfigured the logical positivist dispute into a denial of "artistic truth" that has characterized much of analytic aesthetics. This helps explain why his book was a strategic place from which to open my own exploration in Chapter 1.

The 1989 publication of the anthology *Analytic Aesthetics*[4] provides a convenient point at which to mark a transition to stage 3, which I label "postanalytic aesthetics." During this stage – the contemporary stage – the propositional view and correspondence theory lose their grip, and greater interaction arises between analytic philosophy and currents of thought having other sources: American pragmatism, continental philosophy, cultural studies, ecology, feminism, and postcolonial theory, to name several. The transition also arises internally, however, as one can trace in the lifework of Richard Rorty. The contemporary weakening of propositionally inflected correspondence theories makes it imperative to ask whether some other conception of truth is needed to do justice to the arts, or whether the topic of truth in art has simply become uninteresting or unimportant.

This book argues that a different conception of artistic truth is needed. To complete my argument, and to test my own conception, the next three chapters reconstruct two debates in the history of Anglo-American aesthetics. The first debate occurs in logical positivist aesthetics, between emotivists and propositionists, concerning art's ability to carry truth. The present chapter selects I. A. Richards and Theodore Meyer Greene as representatives of these two positions, respectively. My notions of integrity and artistic import provide the primary lenses through which I read their logical positivist dispute. The next debate, discussed in the following two chapters, occurs during the stage of analytic aesthetics. It centers on the ontological status of the work of art and features nominalists such as Nelson Goodman and realists such as Nicholas Wolterstorff.[5] The notions of significance and authenticity figure prominently in my responses to their debate. In reconstructing these two debates, I aim to show how my own conception of artistic truth can incorporate insights from various sides while avoiding serious pitfalls. Showing this will confirm the philosophical potential of regarding artistic truth as a three-dimensional process of imaginative disclosure. It will also conclude my argument that a nonpropositional view and a noncorrespondence theory of truth are needed to do justice to the arts in their contemporary institutional settings.

7.1 EMOTIVISM VERSUS PROPOSITIONISM

I. A. Richards

In an original study of how language influences thought, first published in 1923, C. K. Ogden and I. A. Richards argue that ordinary language has two fundamentally distinct functions: the "symbolic" use of words to record, support, organize, and communicate references, and the "emotive" use of words "to express or excite feelings and attitudes."[6] Both functions are causal, they claim. A speaker who makes symbolic use of words causes, or seeks to cause, a reference in the hearer that is similar to the speaker's own reference. A speaker who makes emotive use of words causes, or seeks to cause, certain emotions, moods, or attitudes in the listener.[7] Even though the two functions often occur together, truth pertains only to the first: "So far as words are used emotively no question as to their truth in the strict sense can directly arise." The truth question can arise indirectly, in poetry, for example, where statements "capable of truth or falsity" occur. The purpose of poetry, however, is not to make statements but to evoke attitudes and feelings, and "any symbolic function that the words [in poetry] may have is instrumental only and subsidiary to the evocative function." What holds for poetry holds for all the arts: their purpose is emotive rather than symbolic, evocative rather than communicative, and works of art cannot be true or false in the strict sense – that is, "in the ordinary strict scientific sense" (p. 150).[8] Clearly, then, decisive contrasts lie between science and art, between reference and emotion, and between truth and whatever measures the "success" of art and of emotive language.

These contrasts presuppose the authors' notion of "reference." Ogden and Richards propose a triangular model of meaning involving words, things, and thoughts, or, in the more precise vocabulary they prefer, symbols, referents, and references. *Symbols* (such as words in their symbolic use) record, organize, and communicate references. *Referents* are entities about which people think or to which they refer. And, as acts of thought whereby people "grasp" the entities about which they are thinking,[9] *references* are mental links in the causal chain between things (referents) and words (symbols). References are caused by their referents, and a symbol has acts of referring "among its causes in the speaker, together no doubt with desires to record and to communicate, and with attitudes assumed towards hearers" (p. 205).

The fundamental point to this triangular model is that the relation between symbol and referent can only be indirect. Whereas a symbol can directly symbolize a reference (i.e., be caused by it), and a reference can directly refer to a referent (i.e., be caused by it), a symbol can only indirectly stand for a referent. Both symbolizing and referring are "causal relations," but "standing for" is not; it is an "imputed relation" (p. 11). A symbol can stand for a referent only to the extent that someone performing an act of reference uses the symbol for that purpose. There is no direct – that is, no natural and causal – link between a symbol such as the word "cats" and the feline creatures to which one refers by talking about cats. Symbols are instruments of thought, nothing more, nothing less.

To apply this model of meaning to questions of truth, Ogden and Richards introduce a "contextual" theory of interpretation. As psychological behaviorists, they think all interpretations of signs (including the interpretation of those signs which are used as symbols) involve the linking of external (physical) contexts with internal (mental or psychological) contexts that have established themselves in prior experience: "Interpretation . . . is only possible thanks to these recurrent contexts . . ." (p. 55). To use the authors' favorite example, we "interpret" the striking of a match as the "sign" of an imminent flame because an expectation to that effect has formed in previous contexts when matches were struck.[10] When the expected flame occurs, our expectation is true. Otherwise the expectation is false. And this, for the authors, is the primary sense in which references can be true or false, as well as the primary way in which truth or falsity, in "the ordinary strict scientific sense," can properly be attributed to anything.[11] General references, such as the belief "All match-scrapes are followed by flames" (p. 64), are compounds of simple references, even when the structure of their symbols does not reflect the compound structure of the references.

This approach enables the authors to deny the existence of propositions as such and to make references, not propositions, the locus of truth. They redefine propositions as "relational characters of acts of referring" or, more simply, as "references." When we say two people think of the same "proposition," or one person thinks of the same "proposition" on two different occasions, this merely means that two "thinkings" are "contextually linked in the same way with the same referent" (p. 74).[12] Whether such references are true or false depends entirely on whether the physical referent turns out as expected. Hence Ogden and Richards replace a propositional view of truth with a referential view, although their "references" fulfill roughly the same role as propositions do in propositionally inflected accounts of truth. Although the authors acknowledge that symbols, as distinct from references, can also be "true" or "false," they distinguish the "truth" of symbols, as correctness, from the "truth" of references, as adequacy. Whereas a "true" *symbol* "correctly records an adequate reference" (p. 102), a "true" *reference* adequately refers to a real referent. In both cases, however, causality is the key to truth: "A symbol is correct when it causes a[n] [adequate] reference similar to that which it symbolizes in any suitable interpreter" (p. 206; cf. p. 102), and an adequate reference is one that is borne out by its referent.

At the same time as they shift the locus of truth from propositions to references, Ogden and Richards revise the criterion of truth from a correspondence between proposition and fact to the probability of causal links between psychological references and physical referents. The degree of probability becomes an index of truth: "Whether an interpretation is true or false . . . does not depend only upon psychological contexts. . . . We may have had every reason to expect a flame when we struck our match, but this, alas! will not have made the flame certain to occur. That depends upon a physical not a psychological context" (p. 76). Indeed, no correspondence theory of truth is needed once one recognizes that "an adequate reference has as its referent not something which *corresponds* to the fact or event which is the meaning of a sign . . . but something which is identical with [the fact or event]" (p. 205).[13]

Accordingly, the primary difference between science and art does not lie in a contrast, say, between causality and intentionality: the authors propose a causal account of both science and art. Rather, the difference stems from a contrast between the types of causal links prevalent in each field. In science the dominant causal link lies between referents, references, and symbols. In art, it occurs between situations, emotions (or attitudes or moods or interests), and whatever expresses these emotions – whether this be an utterance in ordinary language or a work of sublime art. The arts, especially poetry, are "the supreme form of emotive language," just as the sciences are the pinnacle of cognitive language:

It ought to be impossible to pretend that any scientific statement can give a more inspiring or more profound "vision of reality" than another. It can be more general or more useful, and that is all. On the other hand it ought to be impossible to talk about poetry or religion as though they were capable of giving "knowledge." . . . A poem – or a religion . . . – has no concern with limited and directed reference. It tells us, or should tell us, nothing. It has a different, though an equally important and a far more vital function . . . to induce a fitting attitude to experience. . . .

. . . As science frees itself from the emotional outlook . . . , so poetry seems about to return to the conditions of its greatness, by abandoning the obsession of knowledge and symbolic truth. It is not necessary to know what things are in order to take up fitting attitudes towards them, and the peculiarity of the greatest attitudes which art can evoke is their extraordinary width. (pp. 158–9)

We shall return to this emotivist conception of art later.

T. M. Greene

Nothing seems more diametrically opposed to I. A. Richards's emotivism than the propositionist account of artistic truth given by Theodore Meyer Greene. In *The Arts and the Art of Criticism*, a richly illustrated tome first published in 1940, Greene proposes a modern Aristotelian aesthetic in which perfection, truth, and greatness are the supreme "criteria" for judgments about artistic value.[14] Before explaining these criteria, he elaborates the categories central to his philosophy of the arts: matter (both raw material and artistic medium), form, and content. Artistic content – what "finds expression *via* artistic form in an artistic medium" (p. 229) – is what makes artworks capable of truth and falsity. Whether true or false, an artwork's content is its distinctive expression of an interpretation of a specific subject matter.[15] Art, then, is a cognitive enterprise, more similar to science than an emotivist such as Richards would allow: "Just as the true scientist . . . seeks to use his reason and his logic for the attainment of scientific truth, so the true artist . . . strives to express, in terms of beauty, his interpretation of a wider reality and a richer experience. And just as scientific truth involves not merely logical consistency but also correspondence to the real world of spatio-temporal events, so too does artistic truth demand not only the presence of formal beauty but the expression of a true understanding of certain aspects of human experience and reality" (pp. 233–4). Whereas Richards contrasts scientific (referential) cognition with artistic (emotive) expression, Greene compares science and art as two types of cognition, both of which are expressive, in the sense that they reflect and interpret conscious human experience (pp. 256–9).[16]

The differences between science and art lie in their approach, goal, and manner.[17] Science, says Greene, arises from an attitude of "temporary detachment from utilitarian and spiritual concerns" (p. 237); it aims at "conceptual apprehension" of the universal structures and processes of nature (p. 248); and it involves abstract, precise expression that lacks "emotive, affective, and conative overtones" (p. 259). Art, in contrast, arises from an attitude of imaginatively contemplating "the significance of things for human life" (p. 238); it aims at insightful revelation of both the "complex individuality" and the "significant universality" of natural and human phenomena (pp. 252–5); and it involves concrete, imagistic expression that exploits emotive, affective, and conative overtones (pp. 262–5).

With the exception of portraiture, whose content is individual, the "chief content of a work of art consists of the artist's interpretation of certain universals." This content and its "re-creation" among listeners, viewers, or readers are not explicitly conceptual. Yet the content is universal, consisting of either "perceptual universals" such as perceptual objects and qualities or "spiritual universals" that arise in religious, social, and introspective experience (pp. 269–73). To express such content, artistic specificity is required – the specific formal organization of this or that artwork. But once a work's specific subject matter is "selected and organized" to express "*any* given kind of universal content," it becomes "an artistic propositional function which refers us to *all* actual or possible occurrents . . . embodying the universal quality or relation in question" (p. 315). Such referring is indeterminate, to be sure, yet it is a reference, and it is propositional as well. Greene's account of artistic truth will need to negotiate a tricky terrain between specificity and universality, between expression and reference, and between the nonconceptual and the propositional. This need is all the greater because he insists that artistic and scientific truth are "species of a common genus" (p. 425).

Greene's account of artistic truth begins with the generic locus and criteria of truth (pp. 425–38). The locus lies in propositions. Truth and falsity are properties of propositions, he says, and only of propositions. Propositions are true or false insofar as they purport to describe the objects to which they refer. Acts of judgment can affirm or deny propositions, but propositions are not judgments. Propositions are always expressed in certain media, but the media need not be conceptual; in fact, artistic media usually are not conceptual.[18] Postulating that human beings can achieve knowledge of "a complex and diversified objective reality" through the "rational interpretation" of "immediate empirical data," Greene identifies two criteria of truth: consistency and correspondence. Both are necessary, he says, and they are jointly sufficient for determining the truth of propositions. *Consistency* is what "the clear expression of ideas in any medium" requires. It pertains to both the medium used and the ideas expressed (pp. 427–9).[19] *Correspondence* has to do with the degree to which a proposition matches the "facts" or describes its "referendum" (what Richards would call "referent"): "It must set forth in its own way whatever characteristics of its referendum it purports to exhibit." Negatively, the proposition must avoid "empirical discrepancy." To be true, a proposition cannot be "*discrepant* with *any* reliable available evidence." Positively, the proposition must be empirically adequate. For a proposition to be true, "*all* available empirical evidence which is both relevant and reliable [must] be taken fully into account" (pp. 432–3). This, in turn, requires tests for the accuracy of empirical observation, ways to delimit the contexts of relevance, and recognition for the finitude of human knowledge.

These two general criteria – consistency and correspondence – apply to all truth, whether scientific or not. Yet both language and reality justify our distinguishing between scientific and artistic truth:

[T]he various media of inter-subjective communication differ radically in expressive power. . . . Each of these languages has its own expressive potentialities *and* limitations. And since reality itself is infinitely various and complex . . . , certain aspects of it lend themselves far better to apprehension and interpretation in and through a given medium than any other. Thus the artist, apprehending human experience and its objects in and through an artistic medium, can grasp their individuality and human significance as the scientist cannot, whereas the scientist can apprehend and express the skeletal structure of the phenomenal world with a precision which art cannot rival. (pp. 437–8)

Hence the master of one language such as art expresses a truth that "cannot be translated without vital loss" into another language such as science (p. 438).

Since propositions are the generic locus of truth, artistic content, as the locus of artist truth, must be propositional. Greene explicitly defines artistic content as a proposition or a set of propositions that both describes and evaluates something objective: "I can therefore re-define a work of art as the artistic expression of one or more descriptive and evaluative propositions with a discoverable referendum. These artistically expressed propositions are what I have previously entitled artistic content.... [A]rtistic truth is necessarily a function not of the artistic medium as such, or of the artistic form as such, but of the content of a work of art. The *locus* of artistic truth is artistic content" (p. 444). What distinguishes such artistic propositions from, say, scientific propositions, are the artist's cognitive approach and goal, for which significant originality and expressive individuality are crucial, and the distinctive character of artistic media.

Greene tries to make this differentiation of propositions plausible by specifying the criteria of truth in artistic terms: artistic consistency as "perfection" and "integrity," and artistic correspondence as the satisfaction of "artistically relevant evidence." Drastically trimming his rather bloated account of artistic consistency, we can say that it involves stylistic "correctness" and "felicity" in the way an artwork organizes a chosen medium to express "the ideas which the artist wishes to express" (p. 449). Artworks measuring up in this regard display artistic "perfection." Artistic "integrity," in turn, measures how successfully the ideas have been expressed. Unlike my own notion of integrity, Greene's notion refers not to the artwork's meeting its own internal demands but rather to the coherence of the artwork's propositional content. An artwork manifesting artistic integrity will express "in an artistically felicitous manner a genuinely coherent interpretation of a given subject-matter" (p. 450).

As we know from Greene's generic criteria of truth, however, consistency by itself is not enough. To be true, "a stylistic interpretation of reality," an artistic content, "must satisfy the criterion of correspondence as well." In his explanation of this second criterion for artistic truth, everything turns on his notion of "artistic," summarized earlier in the contrast between art and science as types of cognition. Like scientists, artists must base the interpretation of their subject matter on "empirical observation" and "empirical evidence." In the case of art, however, interpretation must yield "*artistic* insight," observation must take the form of "*artistic* intuitions," and the empirical evidence must be "artistically relevant." Negatively, then, Greene's criterion of correspondence, applied to art, requires that an artwork's (propositional) content avoid "*discrepancy with artistically relevant evidence.*" Positively, it requires that the content satisfy "*all artistically available empirical evidence which is artistically relevant and artistically reliable*" (pp. 452–3).[20] So Greenian evaluations of the purported truth of any artwork's content would consider the accuracy and acuity of the artist's empirical observations and the synoptic and universal reach of the artist's interpretations.[21]

To summarize: Greene regards art as a cognitive enterprise complementary to science. What makes art cognitive is its capacity for expressing artistic interpretations of specific subject matters in specific media. These interpretations make up the propositional content of artworks, which is either true or false. The truth of the artwork has two types of criteria: first, the quality and success with which the artwork expresses the artist's interpretation (i.e., the artwork's "perfection" and "integrity"), and, second, the empirical acuity and interpretative scope of that interpretation (i.e., the degree of "correspondence" with empirical reality). For Greene, the artwork's truth is a propositional truth subject to criteria of consistency and correspondence. Whereas I. A. Richards considers art to be a nonpropositional language of emotions, T. M. Greene regards art as an expressive language of propositions.

Despite this remarkable difference, with Richards denying art precisely the propositional truth that Greene considers crucial, the two agree on three fundamental points. First, they agree on the locus of truth, though Richards prefers to speak of "references" rather than "propositions." Second, both Richards and Greene consider science to be the paradigmatic field of knowledge, although Greene allows more fields onto the map of cognition, such as art, morality, and religion, than Richards does. Third, both of them link the arts with feeling and desire and see the sciences as highly distanced from feeling and desire. What they share, in other words, is a general scientism with respect to knowledge, combined with nearly stereotypical divisions between emotion and reason and between the arts and sciences.

Within this shared framework, however, they disagree in two respects: whether artworks contain and convey propositions (or references), and whether the correspondence of propositions to facts (or of references to referents) is a relevant and legitimate standard for evaluating art. Richards gives a negative response to both questions and hence, within the context of a propositional (referential) view, denies truth to art. Greene gives a positive response to both questions, thus, within the same context, affirming truth as a leading goal of art and a crucial standard for art criticism. It is possible, of course, to ascribe or deny truth to art without subscribing to a propositional view, as I have already tried to show. But that possibility does not emerge on either the emotivist or the propositionist side of the debate. Rather, each side suffers from tunnel vision imposed by a propositionally inflected theory of truth. Let me explore limitations on each side, beginning with the emotivism of I. A. Richards.

7.2 PROPOSITIONAL ACTS

Many problems in both Richards's account of truth and his emotivist account of art stem from his causal theory of reference. He is mistaken, not in thinking that the relation between symbols and referents is indirect, but in thinking that relations between symbols and references, and between references and referents, are direct – that is, natural and causal. Consider, for example, the situation of someone expecting a flame when a match is struck. There may be loosely causal connections between the match striking and the person's expectation, and between this expectation and the expected flame, but it is odd to regard the expectation as a "reference," the match striking as a "sign" or "symbol," and the expected flame as the referent that, when it occurs, makes the "reference" true. A successful act of reference, properly so called, must both identify something and be about what it identifies. If I were to say "This match is hot" in such a way that you can identify the match in question, then a reference might have occurred. But my simply expecting a flame when you or I strike a match is not in itself an act of referring: my expectation neither identifies something nor is it about something identified.[22] It follows from this that even on a correspondence theory of truth, Richards's favorite examples of reference (expectation) and symbol (match striking) can be neither true nor false, because they lack the necessary ingredients of identification and "aboutness." The expectation can be fulfilled or disappointed, but that is not the same as its being true or false. Equating propositions with references and treating references as causal are equally problematic. Let me discuss each problem in turn.

Predicating and Referring

Setting out a complete theory of propositions and reference exceeds the scope of my purpose here. Let me simply adapt some of John Searle's account, even though I do not agree with all of his premises and conclusions. Searle suggests that we regard referring and predicating as acts of a certain sort – what he calls "propositional acts." Referring and predicating usually occur in connection with (other) speech acts, such as asserting, promising, and the like. Propositions, however, are not speech acts. Rather, speakers express propositions when they refer and predicate, in the context of performing (other) speech acts. Propositions are what get asserted and stated, for example, in the speech acts of asserting and stating, and their being expressed always involves the propositional acts of referring and predicating.[23] Searle's suggestion does not entail the independent, "third-world" existence of propositions à la Frege, an entailment Richards would oppose. But it does require that one not only distinguish propositions from references but also acknowledge the propositional character of both referring and predicating.

The distinction and connections go like this. In the act of *predication*, the speaker predicates expressions of objects. These expressions are true or false of objects. Asserting is only one of the types of speech acts in which, or in connection with which, predication occurs. *Reference* is also an act. In the act of reference, the speaker uses expressions to identify something. Although such expressions may be called "referring expressions," it is crucial that the referring is done by the speaker, who uses the expression to accomplish this.[24] Speakers express *propositions* when they refer and predicate, in the context of performing various speech acts. Searle describes propositions as the *content* of speech acts, in distinction from the *function* of speech acts. Speech acts having different functions – asserting, promising, requesting, and the like – can nevertheless have the same content. Equivalently, one can say that speech acts of different types allow a speaker to express the same proposition.[25] For example, "The fire has been lit," "I promise to light the fire," and "Please light the fire" – a statement, a promise, and a request – have the same (propositional) content, which one could indicate, perhaps, as "The fire 'is' lit." Regardless of their type, speech acts that employ a referring expression as their grammatical subject (such as "the fire") typically also employ predicate expressions (such as "is lit"). Whereas referring expressions identify (i.e., refer to) objects, predicate expressions do not identify or refer. To predicate is not the same as to refer, even though predications involve referring expressions as grammatical subjects.[26] Predicate expressions are used in the "act" of predication[27] to raise the question of the predicate expression's truth "of the object" to which the referring expression refers.[28]

Searle's account of "propositional acts" suggests that the locus of truth resides primarily in predicate expressions as applied to objects and secondarily in propositions that can be abstracted, via predications, from speech acts of diverse types. But propositions do not "exist" in the same sense that, say, material objects exist.[29] In that regard it would be problematic to consider propositions the primary locus of truth. At the same time, however, Searle clearly appeals to an implicit criterion of correspondence between empirical objects and linguistic expressions – both referring expressions and predicate expressions – to ground his account of reference and predication. It is not accidental that his book opens with the question "How do words relate to the world?" or that he describes language as "our mode of representing the world."[30]

My sketch of Searle's account indicates that Richards's equation of propositions with references is misguided, both as a theory of propositions and as a theory of reference. There are three reasons for rejecting that equation. In the first place, Richards makes "reference" so broad that it cannot serve as a notion of linguistic reference. His "references" include all nonemotive but mental "acts" both prompted by the objects of thought and (potentially) prompting symbols, which indirectly stand for those objects. Hence "to refer" is simply "to think," and all symbols, whether linguistic or not, and regardless of their syntactic functions and pragmatic contexts, are instruments of reference. Richards has no way to distinguish referring expressions from other expressions, nor any reason to link reference to language as such.

A second reason is that his notion of reference lacks ingredients that are necessary to both references and predications. As the example of the match and flame indicates, Richards fails to explain why, when language users refer, they refer *to something*, and they use referring expressions to identify that to which they refer. The point of their doing this is not to cause their interlocutors to have thoughts like their own, but to come to an understanding with them of whatever the referring expressions help identify. In this respect there is no appreciable difference between poetry and ordinary language. To suggest, as Richards does, that the one stirs up emotions while the other stirs up thoughts is simply to ignore that linguistic referring is not mental stirring. Similarly, Richards's notion of reference forgets that in ordinary language referring expressions rarely occur in disconnection from predicate expressions, even though predicate expressions serve a different function. Simply "having a thought" and conveying it to (i.e., causing it to occur in) someone else need not require any predication. If "mind readers" are to be believed, mental telepathy would suffice. Conversely, predicating something in ordinary conversation need not require anyone's having a thought or being caused to have a thought. Verbal communication is much more sophisticated and publicly constituted than the causal theory of reference suggests. Specifically, language users employ a predicate expression to say something about whatever the referring expression identifies. It is irrelevant to the predicative function whether the predicate expression (or its alleged mental counterpart) was "caused" by the "referent" (i.e., by whatever the referring expression identifies). It is also irrelevant whether the predicate expression "causes" some thought to arise about the "referent." Language users are concerned, instead, with whether the predicate expression, as used, says something about the referent that is meaningful, important, accurate, appropriate, or interesting. Whether their "thoughts" about "the object" are similar is incidental to linguistic predication.

Because Richards includes both too much and too little in his notion of reference, a third issue arises: he ignores altogether some important ways in which references are not the same as propositions. This lack of identity obtains, first of all, for his own equating of reference with either thought or an act of thinking. If propositions were simply "references" or "relational characters of acts of referring"[31] in his sense, then neither referring expressions nor predicate expressions in Searle's sense would be required. We could simply strike matches and watch what happens. But surely this would both trivialize and mystify ordinary language usage. Richards also misses an important sense in which references, as Searle discusses them, are not the same as propositions: by itself, the use of referring expressions does not give rise to propositions; it does so only in connection with predicate expressions. Of course, an old chestnut of logic and linguistic theory holds that propositions link up with the grammar of subject and predicate. And there are many reasons not to think such linkage adequately explains propositions. But there are also many reasons not to think that propositions can be explained in complete abstraction from that grammar or, better, in complete abstraction from the pragmatics of referring and predicating in ordinary language. Specifically, by equating propositions with thoughts, Richards makes it entirely mysterious how people hearing ordinary assertions could tell whether the speaker's expectations concerning the physical "referent" turned out "true" or "false" – not to mention, how they could talk about it. Richards's underlying assumption of a one-to-one causal "correspondence" between reference (thought) and referent (object) confuses propositions with beliefs and reduces both to mental "facts."

Reference and Interpretation

A closely related limitation arises from the treatment of reference as causal. Because of this, Richards fails to distinguish between the intentional and the causal aspects of ordinary language usage. This failure either forces or sustains too neat a juxtaposition between reference and science, on the one hand, and emotion and art, on the other. Let me explain, using Searle's theory of speech acts once again.

Searle approaches ordinary language usage as "engaging in a rule-governed form of behavior" in which speech acts "such as making statements, giving commands, asking questions, making promises, and so on" are "the basic or minimal units of linguistic communication."[32] Richards, by contrast, approaches ordinary language usage as engaging in causal (stimulus-response) behavior, as the instrumental use of words for "referential" and "emotional" ends. This is not to suggest that Searle denies the "causal" or "instrumental" ends to which speech acts are put. He accommodates this feature by distinguishing the "perlocutionary" from the "illocutionary effect" of various speech acts. The perlocutionary effect is the effect a speech act has, or is intended to have, upon a hearer's action or thought or belief by virtue of the meaning of the utterance: "For example, by arguing I may *persuade*... someone, by warning him I may *scare* or *alarm* him, by making a request I may *get him to do something*, by informing him I may *convince him*. . . . The italicized expressions above denote perlocutionary acts."[33] The hearer's being persuaded or frightened or convinced would be the perlocutionary effect of the speech act in question. The illocutionary effect, however, is the hearer's understanding of the meaning of the utterance. Criticizing Paul Grice's account of meaning, Searle makes two crucial points in this connection. First, the understanding of meaning is fundamental to the intentions and conventions that govern all speech acts. Second, when utterances are made, the accomplishment of any effect beyond understanding, such as persuading or scaring or convincing, depends on the speaker and hearer successfully communicating linguistic meaning. In other words, the perlocutionary effect depends upon the illocutionary effect, and the two cannot be equated without losing track of what distinguishes speech acts from other types of action.[34] According to Searle, Grice confuses illocutionary with perlocutionary effects.

Richards surpasses Grice's confusion by failing to recognize any distinction at all. For Richards, all language usage, whether referential or emotional in effect, is perlocutionary. None of it is illocutionary. Whether words are used "symbolically" to record and communicate references, or whether they are used "emotively" to express and excite feelings, language usage is simply a matter of causing certain mental states (references and emotions) in the hearer, according to Richards. From a speech act perspective, however, none of these effects could be brought about if the speaker did not intend to communicate meaning according to certain constitutive rules of linguistic behavior, and if the hearer did not recognize this intention and follow the same constitutive rules.[35] Richards fails to distinguish between the intentional and the causal aspects of ordinary language usage.

The consequences for his theory of art are devastating. Richards postulates that a poem (and, by extension, all art) tells us nothing, but it has a "far more vital function," namely, "to induce a fitting attitude to experience." Cognitive considerations are irrelevant to art's performing this function and to our evaluating art: "It is not necessary to know what things are in order to take up fitting attitudes towards them, and the peculiarity of the greatest attitudes which art can evoke is their extraordinary width."[36] When people bring cognitive terms such as "true" or "false" into their interpretations of art, what they really mean to discuss is either (1) how convincing or acceptable some element is relative to their experience of the work as a whole or (2) how sincere the artist was, in the sense of not trying to bring about effects on the audience that do not work for the artist. Either that, or art interpreters are using "true" and "false" in an emotive fashion to excite attitudes of admiration or disapproval.[37] On this emotivist theory, art becomes a blunt instrument of attitudinal adjustment. It offers no internal resources for sorting out which attitudes are more "fitting" or "great" or "extraordinary."[38] Moreover, Richards gives little thought to why art interpreters would settle on cognitive terms to excite certain attitudes if they did not intend their discussion partners to understand these terms in their ordinary usage. Otherwise, would it not be more effective to scream and shout? He reduces the various dimensions of art to emotive causes and effects, and he denies art's cognitive dimension altogether.[39]

Yet Richards has noticed something crucial that many artistic truth theorists have missed. He has noticed, but emotivistically misconstrued, the role of intentions and interpretive needs in the recognition of artistic truth. So he is not entirely wrong to claim that people use truth talk to discuss either the artist's "sincerity" or the art phenomenon's "acceptability." If my own account is right, however, then such art interpreters are actually discussing either the art phenomenon's authenticity or its significance: authenticity relative to art making that lends a voice to the artist's own experience or vision, and significance relative to a public's need for worthwhile cultural presentations. But recognizing either authenticity or significance is not a simple emotive response, nor is using truth talk in these ways simply an attempt to stir up emotive responses in others. Rather, such recognition and usage are hermeneutic efforts employing ordinary language to do what ordinary language does – namely, to help people reach an understanding. In seeking to understand an art phenomenon's authenticity and significance, art interpreters make claims about the imaginative disclosiveness and cogency of the art phenomenon under discussion. They thereby also either implicitly or explicitly raise claims about the sincerity, normative legitimacy, and propositional truth of their own language usage. Further, if the art product or event under discussion is indeed an artwork, then recognizing its authenticity and significance will unavoidably involve our considering the artwork's integrity. The only way to accomplish this is to go beyond the artist's intentions and interpreters' needs to the import of the work of art. Concerning this third and crucial dimension of artistic truth, however, Richards has nothing to offer.

7.3 MEANING AND INTEGRITY

In contrast, Theodore Greene, who would reject Richards's emotivist theory out of hand, does have a detailed account of artistic import. But he subscribes to a propositionally inflected correspondence theory of truth. So Greene bites the bullet, arguing that propositions and their correspondence to facts are as central to artistic truth as he supposes they are to scientific truth. Unfortunately, his laudable attempt to credit art's cognitive capacities suffers from (1) a failure to distinguish propositions from meaning and (2) a tendency to equate the artwork's import ("content," in Greene's terms) with the artist's cognitive intention (the artist's "interpretation" of his or her "subject matter," in Greene's terms).

Propositions and Meaning

When Greene distinguishes propositions from the judgments that affirm or deny propositions, he equates propositions with meanings that can be expressed in various media.[40] There are three reasons why I find his equating propositions with expressible meanings problematic. In the first place, meaning is not a set of preexistent content that simply awaits expression in various media. Rather, meaning is what occurs when human beings engage successfully in interpretation and communication, for which Searlian speech acts are emblematic. When I tell you "The fire is lit" and you understand what I am saying, no preexistent meaning is getting expressed. Instead, we are reaching an understanding about a shared situation by engaging in a linguistic process in which both of us are competent.

In the second place, propositions are not the primary units of linguistic meaning. Neither, for that matter, are words, sentences, or, more broadly, symbols or signs. Rather, if we follow Searle, the primary units of linguistic meaning are speech acts of various sorts. If one wishes to extend the notion of meaning beyond that of linguistic meaning, or to acknowledge that "linguistic meaning" itself derives in part from a broader idea of meaning, then one should look for parallels to speech acts in nonlinguistic fields, rather than try to pin meaning to propositions.[41] Doing this would introduce greater flex between meaning and propositional truth than Greene and many Anglo-American philosophers of his generation could acknowledge. It would also remove the worry that art cannot be capable of truth unless artworks function like sentences, or like the statements and assertions that such philosophers regard as primary functions of sentences.

Insofar as this worry drives the debate between emotivists and propositionists, removing it would help reposition that debate.[42] Instead of asking whether artworks can contain propositions or function like propositions, one would look for parallels in art to how various speech acts are performed and understood in language. To coin a phrase, "art acts," not supposedly propositional "artistic content," would be the locus of meaning in art. To put it more precisely, the locus of meaning in art would be the hermeneutic interactions people sustain when they "employ" art phenomena to address one another about a rich diversity of "topics." The locus would be interactive art practices, where "art practices" include all the ways in which art products and events get created, shared, and interpreted. Even if, strictly speaking, there are no referring expressions and predicate expressions in nonliterary arts, there might be parallel means by which, in the context of "art acts," agents make identifications and articulate something about what they identify. It would not be peculiar to art if such identification and articulation were not primary goals in the field, being mostly assumed in artistic creation and interpretation rather than singled out. In ordinary language, too, most speech acts do not aim at reference and predication. They refer and predicate – or, rather, language users refer and predicate – in the service of promising, warning, requesting, and the like.

Moreover, and in the third place, it is doubtful how often propositions get expressed per se. It is unfortunate that Greene does not define propositions, since his account of artistic truth hinges on this notion. At a minimum, however, he must regard them as discrete units of predicable insight into reality. He thinks these units must be expressed in order to be affirmed or denied. Once expressed, whether in art or in science, they exist somewhat independently from the medium in which they are expressed. That is why Greene thinks the "truths" expressed in art can be translated into scientific terminology, although not without "vital loss."[43] I doubt, however, that propositions regularly get expressed in ordinary language, not to mention art or much of normal science.[44] Instead, while people engage in asserting, questioning, warning, and the like, they make references and predicate something about that to which they refer. Studying the inscribed results of such interactions, linguists and logicians abstract referring expressions and predicate expressions from their conversational context and fit them into patterns of "content" that philosophers stylize as "propositions." In the pretheoretical context of ordinary language usage, however, propositions do not exist independently of linguistic interactions, and they do not get expressed as if they were ready-made units waiting to be packaged. Rather, propositions emerge from ordinary language usage to the extent that theorists abstract them from the way certain expressions function. "The cat is on the mat," a favorite example in logic and epistemology, is itself an abstraction from ordinary language and carries no indication of the speech acts in which it occurs. To identify the "proposition" this example supposedly "expresses" simply takes the abstraction one step further. Such abstraction serves important theoretical purposes, of course. Yet it is a mistake to transfer it to ordinary language and view ordinary language as normally or even primarily "expressing propositions." It is equally mistaken, if not more so, to regard art as expressing propositions. In that very specific sense, and despite my earlier criticisms, Beardsley was right to deny artistic truth.

Artistic Import

By criticizing Greene's emphasis on propositions, I am not claiming that artworks or, more broadly, "art acts" lack cognitive import. Unfortunately, Greene's account of import is just as problematic as his emphasis on propositions. As we have seen, Greene tends to equate artistic content with the artist's "interpretation" of his or her "subject matter." Correlatively, when Greene specifies the general truth criteria for art (i.e., consistency and correspondence), what the artist wishes to express becomes the litmus test for artistic "perfection," "integrity," and "empirical adequacy." Anyone attempting to judge the truth of "artistic content" along these lines would quickly fall prey to the "intentional fallacy" so effectively demonstrated and demolished by Monroe Beardsley.[45]

There are two problems here. One is epistemological. Often the most important clues to "what the artist wishes to express" come from the import of the artwork itself. Hence evaluating the work's perfection, integrity, and adequacy in a Greenian fashion would presuppose the conclusion one is trying to reach. The other problem is ontological. Greene's theory supposes that the artwork is primarily a material artifact on which the artificer imposes form and into which the artificer permanently injects his or her ideas.[46] But if one pays attention to how art works, rather than merely the artwork, the appropriate ontology will be one of dialogical dissemination, not artificial insemination. On a disseminatory model, no one agent-position, whether artist or interpreter or critic, has paternity or maternity rights to the artwork's import. Nor can the import's truth or falsity be decided simply by asking how well the artwork expresses the artist's ideas (Green's "perfection"), how coherent these ideas are ("integrity"), and how reliable and relevant are the artist's observations or intuitions ("empirical adequacy").

If, contra Greene, artistic import is neither propositional nor straightfor-wardly expressive of the artist's ideas, how should it be characterized? And if, contra Richards, art's nonpropositional character ("nonreferential," in his terms) is not a reason to deny art's cognitive capacities, in what sense can artistic import be true or false? I have suggested that, along with explo-ration and creative interpretation, presentation is central to aesthetic pro-cesses and to art, in which aesthetic processes stand out. By "presentation" I mean an intersubjective process in which creatures, events, and products become "aesthetic signs" and make nuances of meaning available beyond the strictures of either idiosyncratic expression or conventional communi-cation. In their aesthetic dimension, artworks are reflexive aesthetic signs: they make multiple nuances of meaning available; "reading" them requires acknowledging their having arisen from prior processes of presentation; and all of this occurs by their calling attention, through their structure, to a peculiar doubling in their presentation – namely, that usually only in pre-senting themselves do they present something else. I have also suggested that presentation has a crucial role to play in the pursuit of cultural orien-tation and reorientation. So does art talk that raises validity claims pertain-ing to the complexity, depth, and intensity of aesthetic signs and aesthetic processes.

Understood along these lines, artistic import will be the complex mean-ing an artwork makes available by calling attention to the peculiar doubling of its own presentation. The truth or falsity of such import will involve (1) the artwork's peculiarly doubled (self-)disclosure, (2) the imaginative cogency of the artwork's structure and (self-)reference, and (3) the potential contri-bution of this presentation to the pursuit of cultural orientation. Eliminating any one of these three factors would result in a truncated conception of the truth of artistic import.[47] Artistic integrity, as I have described it, is a matter of configured import that is imaginatively (self-)disclosive.

Artistic import has an "aboutness" that emotivist theories ignore and propositionist theories misconstrue. It is not the aboutness of propositions and predicate expressions, but of artistic structures and aesthetic signs. The expectation of artistic integrity requires us to interpret the artwork as "stand-ing for" something, and to find clues to this meaning in the specific way the work configures whatever it makes perceptible. What an artwork is about will seldom be a single "referent" or "predicable." But this does not mean that the artwork is not about anything.

The either-or central to the emotivist-propositionist debate needs to be resisted, for two reasons. On the one hand, in the context of ordinary lan-guage a "propositional act" is seldom so univocal as philosophers suggest. Its being about what the referring expression identifies does not require that the referring expression always and only identify one and the same referent or that only a single quality be predicated. Lack of permanence and univocality is no more a reason to doubt the aboutness of artworks than it is a reason to dismiss aboutness in ordinary language. On the other hand, the suggestiveness of artistic import does not entail that there is no limit to what it is about. It is not the case that the artwork is about everything and therefore about nothing. The imaginative structures in any one artwork rule out many more possibilities of meaning than they make available. Consequently the artwork lends itself to a definite array of interpretations and cultural orientations.

Although Richards recognizes the culture-orientational role of artistic import, he misdescribes it as an attitudinal adjustment that the artwork emotively induces. So too, Greene recognizes the meaning-constitutive role of imaginative structures, but he misleadingly construes these as the rules of the medium and genre in which an artist works. Both authors overlook how the cogency and disclosiveness of an artwork's import are a direct function of the artwork's own imaginative structure and (self-)reference. What an artwork suggests, and the import-ance of its suggestions, derive to a significant degree from the artwork's internal configuration and how the artwork calls attention to this internal configuration. Moreover, both authors overlook, or at least they insufficiently emphasize, how the configured import of an integral artwork puts personal and social worlds in question, thereby disclosing a postsubjective world and providing favorable conditions under which a world-crossing call can be heard. An artwork achieves integrity when it is an imaginatively cogent and self-disclosing world disclosure. So artistic integrity is not stylistically correct and felicitous coherence among the ideas or propositions an artwork supposedly expresses, à la Greene. Nor is it simply a function of emotive responses to the work, à la Richards. Rather integrity is the imaginatively cogent self-disclosiveness of the artwork's nonpropositional import. To ask about the truth of artistic import is to ask whether an artwork has integrity in this regard and to what degree.

8

Goodman's Nominalism

Truth and its aesthetic counterpart amount to appropriateness under different names.

Nelson Goodman[1]

The debate between Richards and Greene assumes a general agreement that science is the paradigmatic field of knowledge. They disagree on whether artworks convey propositions and whether correspondence is a legitimate criterion for evaluating art. With the Goodman-Wolterstorff debate, the areas of agreement and disagreement shift. Their debate does not assume that science is the paradigmatic field of knowledge or that art is somehow more emotive than science. Perhaps the most unexpected area of agreement is that art has important cognitive functions – unexpected, given the emotivism of logical positivists such as Richards and the anticognitivism of other analytic aestheticians such as Beardsley. Both Goodman and Wolterstorff set out to explain these cognitive functions, Goodman in terms of symbolization, and Wolterstorff in terms of world projection. Both of them wish to locate the arts in a larger ontology within which the arts make important contributions to understanding and knowledge. They share a type of antiempiricism with respect to knowledge, combined with cognitive functionalism with respect to cultural areas such as art and science. They differ, however, in three crucial respects. Whereas Wolterstorff's ontology is realist, Goodman's is nominalist. Whereas Wolterstorff regards art as a field of action, Goodman regards art as a symbol system. And whereas Wolterstorff has an intentionalist account of art's cognitive contributions, Goodman's account is a version of conventionalism.

Two disagreements in particular are crucial for the topic of truth in art: whether propositions are the locus of truth, and whether correspondence governs the cognitive functions of the arts. Goodman has a negative response to both questions, such that he attributes truth to art, but only in quotation marks. Wolterstorff has a positive response to both questions, such that he denies truth to art, although primarily as an explicit label. Their debate is especially instructive for an account of artistic truth that rejects propositionally inflected correspondence theories. Once propositions lose their privilege as carriers of truth, as occurs in Goodman's work, correspondence theories of truth begin to unravel – and, with them, previously shared assumptions about what it would mean for art to carry truth. Alternatively, by anchoring propositions in a realist ontology, Wolterstorff not only resists their Goodmanian demotion but also inadvertently demonstrates the limits to a correspondence theory of artistic truth. Although much of this remains implicit in the Goodman-Wolterstorff debate, Chapters 8 and 9 draw out such implications, using my own notions of "significance" and "authenticity" as points of orientation.

Few analytic philosophers have more effectively freed Anglo-American aesthetics from propositionally inflected correspondence theories of truth than Nelson Goodman. The dominance of such theories before 1968 is hard to miss. The primary reason given in Monroe Beardsley's *Aesthetics* (1958) to dismiss theories of "artistic truth," for example, is that nonverbal artworks lack propositional content corresponding to empirical data. Unlike Beardsley, Goodman rejects propositions as truth bearers and doubts that correspondence governs art's cognitive functions. This allows him to wrest "representation" and "expression" from the grip of correspondence theories and to give these concepts an insightful new account. After summarizing Goodman's account (section 8.1)[2] and examining the alternative theory of truth it implies (section 8.2), I argue that Goodman ignores artistic import and misconstrues artistic significance, thereby missing the intersubjective character of artistic truth (section 8.3).

8.1 ART AS SYMBOL SYSTEM

Goodman's *Languages of Art* works toward a general theory of symbols. Such a theory would provide a "comprehensive grasp of the modes and means of reference and of their varied and pervasive use in the operations of the understanding" (p. xi). The relevant "modes and means" include both linguistic and nonlinguistic "symbol systems."[3] Symbols come in many formats, Goodman says: "letters, words, texts, pictures, diagrams, maps, models, and more" (p. xi). A "symbol system consists of a symbol scheme correlated with a field of reference" (p. 143).[4] A "symbol scheme" consists of characters (i.e., classes of inscriptions), "usually with modes of combining them to form others" (p. 131). For example, a standard alphabet with its different characters and its rules of usage, is a symbol scheme. As Figure 8.1 illustrates, the two main patterns of symbolic reference[5] are denotation and exemplification. These, in turn, display at least two varieties each: representation and description, in cases of denotation, and expression and literal exemplification, in cases of exemplification. Within this general framework concerning symbols

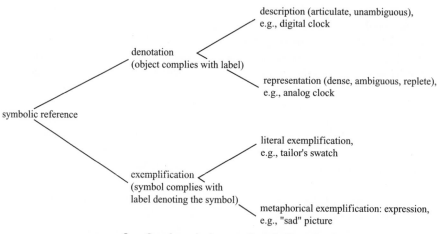

FIGURE 8.1. Goodman's theory of symbolic reference.

and their usage Goodman proposes an ingenious approach to representation, expression, and aesthetic cognition.

Representation

Goodman's account of representation is a good place to begin.[6] He argues that representation involves nondescriptive and denotative reference, and it does not involve exemplificational reference, whether expressive or literal.[7] Contrary to traditional aesthetic expectations, however, he does not hard-link either representation to art or description to language. Just as representations can run the gamut from artistic pictures to scientific diagrams, so descriptions can range from sentences in ordinary language to artistic notations such as musical scores. Indeed, a symbol is not hard-linked to any one symbolic function: "Nothing is intrinsically a representation; status as representation is relative to symbol system. A picture in one system may be a description in another; and whether a denoting symbol is representational depends not upon whether it resembles what it denotes but upon its own relationships to other symbols in a given scheme" (p. 226).

But what does it mean to say of either a representation or a description that it "denotes"? According to Goodman, symbols that denote what they refer to belong to symbol systems in which inscriptions have compliants. To comply with an inscription is equivalent to being denoted by that inscription.[8] All denotation, whether representational or descriptive, involves reference to an object. Whether pictures representing objects or predicates applying to objects, denotative symbols or labels stand for objects. More specifically, they denote objects (p. 5): they refer in such a way that an object complies with the label assigned to it, whether that label be a picture or a predicate. Such compliance occurs, not because the "right" label has been found for a nonlabeled and supposedly independent object, but because the symbol occurs appropriately within a successful symbol system for classifying and characterizing objects.

The emphasis on denotation, so described, is what separates Goodman's account of representation from all mimetic accounts, whether Plato's, Aristotle's, T. M. Greene's, or Wolterstorff's. Goodman says standard criteria such as resemblance, imitation, and perspectival accuracy are irrelevant to understanding representation: "Denotation is the core of representation and is independent of resemblance" (p. 5). And that is why appropriateness, not accuracy or verisimilitude, is just as crucial to representations as it is to descriptions:

Both depiction and description participate in the formation and characterization of the world; and they interact with each other and with perception and knowledge. They are ways of classifying by means of labels having singular or multiple or null reference. . . . Application and classification of a label are relative to a system; and there are countless alternative systems of representation and description. Such systems are the products of stipulation and habituation in varying proportions. The choice among systems is free; but given a system, the question whether a newly encountered object is a desk or a unicorn-picture or is represented by a certain painting is a question of the propriety, under that system, of projecting the predicate "desk" or the predicate "unicorn-picture" or the painting over the thing in question. (p. 40)

Although pictorial representation (e.g., as in painting) brings with it additional constraints – namely, that the picture must "function in a system such that what is denoted depends solely upon the pictorial properties of the symbol" (pp. 41–2) – such constraints have nothing to do with traditional notions of resemblance or imitation. Through the link to denotation, Goodman claims to have freed representation "from perverted ideas of it as an idiosyncratic physical process like mirroring" and to have recognized it "as a symbolic relationship that is relative and variable" (p. 43). This allows him to emphasize what I have called the hermeneutical character of art phenomena and aesthetic signs.

What about the differences, then, between representation and description as modes of denotation?[9] According to Goodman, representation differs from description "primarily through lack of differentiation – indeed through density (and consequent total absence of articulation) – in the symbol scheme" (p. 226). Representational systems require syntactic density, semantic density, and semantic ambiguity. This distinguishes them both from notational systems, which require syntactic articulation, semantic articulation, and semantic unambiguity,[10] and from ordinary languages, which have syntactic articulation but lack semantic articulation and unambiguity (pp. 179, 226). A symbol scheme is syntactically dense "if it provides for infinitely many characters so ordered that between each two there is a third" and no inscription can be determined to belong to just one character (p. 136). A symbol system is semantically dense if it "provides for an infinite number of characters with compliance-classes so ordered that between each two there is a third" (p. 153). And a symbol system is ambiguous when more than one compliance class can share the same character (pp. 147–8).

Digital and analog clocks illustrate the difference, say, between an unambiguous and articulate notational system, on the one hand, and an ambiguous and dense system, on the other. A digital watch that numerically registers the exact second, minute, hour, and date permits neither ambiguity nor lack of differentiation. It will record unequivocally, for example, whether it is 9:50 or 9:51 P.M., leaving no other options. By contrast, an analog watch with rotating hour and minute hands and only four equidistant dots on its circumference permits neither unambiguity nor differentiation. It will be equivocal as to whether the time is, say, 9:50.55 or 9:51 or 9:51.25 or 9:51.30, leaving open many other options.[11] Representations, in their syntactic density, semantic density, and semantic ambiguity, are like analog watches.

Beyond this, however, a representational scheme differs from a diagrammatic scheme, which is also dense and ambiguous, in being relatively more "replete." By repleteness Goodman means the multiplicity of features that have syntactic weight. Whereas only certain lines and coordinates are relevant to the syntax of "a momentary electrocardiogram," the thickness, color, intensity, contrast, size, and placement of lines are all relevant to the syntax of "a Hokusai drawing of Mt. Fujiyama" (p. 229). A change in any one of many features would have syntactical significance. Syntactic repleteness, together with syntactic and semantic density, tends to characterize aesthetic experience.

Expression

Unlike representation, which is a mode of denotation, expression is a mode of exemplification. In Goodman's account, exemplification reverses the relationship between symbol and object that characterizes denotation. For a symbol (picture, predicate, or some other label) to denote an object, *the object* must comply with that symbol or label. For a symbol to exemplify something, however, *the symbol* must "comply" with a label denoting that symbol. In either case, the symbol refers to (stands for) that which it denotes or exemplifies. Goodman's well-known example of literal exemplification is swatches of cloth in a tailor's booklet. These "function as samples, as symbols exemplifying certain properties" such as "color, weave, texture, and pattern" (p. 53). What makes the swatches symbols is their referring to such properties. What makes them exemplifications is their possessing the very properties to which they refer: "Exemplification is possession plus reference.... The swatch exemplifies only those properties that it both has and refers to." Just which properties it exemplifies "depends upon what particular system of symbolization is in effect" (p. 53).

At this point Goodman makes a crucial move. He switches from the vocabulary of "properties" to the vocabulary of "predicates" and other "labels."[12] Rather than talk about the tailor's swatch as exemplifying the cloth's redness, he prefers to say that the swatch "exemplifies some label coextensive with 'red'" (p. 55). So samples exemplify – "comply with" – the predicates and other labels that apply to them, that denote them, in the relevant context. Whereas "anything may be denoted, only labels may be exemplified" (p. 57). This does not mean that exemplification can only occur when a linguistic label (a predicate) denotes the sample: the sample can be denoted by nonverbal symbols "for which we have no corresponding word or description" (p. 57).[13] Although this does not make exemplification more "intrinsic" or less "arbitrary" than denotation, it does restrict exemplification to those symbols which relevant labels denote. A swatch cannot exemplify redness (i.e., exemplify some label coextensive with "red") if the swatch is not denoted by some label coextensive with "red."

Goodman's account becomes especially relevant for the arts when he distinguishes between literal and metaphorical exemplification. Expression, he says, is a matter of metaphorical exemplification. To get at the precise features of expression as a mode of exemplification, he first explains the difference between literal and metaphorical denotation.

Literal and metaphorical denotation differ in the way predicates (and other labels) are applied to objects. To call a room "cold" whose temperature is below freezing is to make a "routine projection" based on "habit," Goodman suggests (p. 69). To call a room "cold" that is sparsely furnished and painted gray is to take a word whose extension is "established by habit" and apply it "elsewhere under the influence of that habit" (p. 71). The first is a literal, the second a metaphorical application of the label "cold" to an object. More precisely, metaphorical application involves detaching a label (e.g., "cold") from its "home realm" (e.g., the ranges of extension of terms for temperature perception) and applying it "for the sorting and organizing of an alien realm" (p. 72; e.g., the ranges of extension of terms for color and space perception). The organization that such a "calculated category mistake" (p. 73) effects in the alien realm "is guided by [the label's] habitual use in the home realm" (p. 74). Both literal and metaphorical applications of "cold" are actual applications, however, and either one can be true or false. Falsity in either case involves what Goodman calls "misassignment of a label" (p. 70). The standards of truth for both literal and metaphorical applications of labels are "much the same," even though truth guarantees the effectiveness of neither literal nor metaphorical applications. An effective metaphor combines "novelty with fitness" and it "satisfies while it startles" (p. 79).[14]

Just as the difference between literal and metaphorical denotation hinges on how labels are applied to objects, so the difference between literal and metaphorical exemplification revolves around how labels are applied to the symbols that refer to these labels. For example, a picture "metaphorically exemplifies sadness if some label coextensive with 'sad' is referred to by and metaphorically denotes the picture." Such a picture expresses sadness, is "metaphorically sad," and is "actually but not literally sad" (p. 85). The crux to this account is that the symbol itself possesses the property it expresses (i.e., the symbol itself refers to the label that metaphorically denotes the symbol), "regardless of cause or effect or intent or subject-matter" (p. 85). So the sadness of the picture is not determined by the artist's emotions, by the feelings stirred up in the spectator, by the ideas the artist wanted to convey, or by the emotional state or outward demeanor of the person depicted in the painting.

Once one translates the vocabulary of "properties" into one of "predicates" and other "labels," it may appear that Goodman is "making what a symbol expresses depend upon what is said about it" (p. 87).[15] This appearance arises because the labels expressed are often verbal labels. Goodman has two responses to this, but he only exploits the second. First, many labels are nonverbal, so that their expression cannot simply depend on what is said about the symbols expressing them.[16] Second, on Goodman's account of labels, simply calling something "sad," whether literally or metaphorically, does not make it sad. The label must apply, whether literally or metaphorically, and its applicability depends upon either "practice" or "precept." The fact that practice and precept vary and change does not make the applicability of labels arbitrary. At the same time, because nonverbal expression (like all other metaphorical exemplification) has an impact on which verbal labels get used and how they apply to objects (including symbols), the relation between symbolic expressing and verbal labeling is a two-way street: "Pictures are no more immune than the rest of the world to the formative force of language even though they themselves, as symbols, also exert such a force upon the world, including language. Talking does not make the world or even pictures, but talking and pictures participate in making each other and the world as we know them" (pp. 88–9).

In Goodman's account, then, the structure of expression piggybacks on the structure of denotation, in the following two ways. For a symbol to *exemplify* a label, there must be a suitably applicable label to denote that symbol. In the absence of such a denotative label, no exemplification could take place. Moreover, for a symbol to *express* (i.e., metaphorically exemplify) a label, this label must be capable of metaphorically denoting that symbol: the label must be both detachable from its "home realm" of habitually established extensions and newly but suitably applicable to an "alien realm" of other extensions. This piggybacking on (1) literal denotation and (2) metaphorical denotation leads Goodman to describe expression as "doubly constrained": "Expression, since limited to what is possessed and moreover to what has been acquired at second-hand, is doubly constrained as compared with denotation. Whereas almost anything can denote . . . almost anything else, a thing can express only what belongs but did not originally belong to it" (p. 89). What I have described as "piggy-backing" also supports Goodman's claim, in the following summation, that exemplification and denotation are "intimately related":

Yet though exemplification and expression are distinct from . . . representation and description, all are intimately related modes of symbolization. In these varied ways, a symbol may select from and organize its universe and be itself in turn informed or transformed. Representation and description relate a symbol to things it applies to. Exemplification relates the symbol to a label that denotes it, and hence indirectly to the things . . . in the range of that label. Expression relates the symbol to a label that metaphorically denotes it, and hence indirectly not only to the given metaphorical but also to the literal range of that label. (p. 92)

Aesthetic Cognition

Goodman uses his contrasts between representation and description and between denotation and exemplification to identify several "symptoms of the aesthetic": syntactic density, semantic density, relative repleteness, and exemplificationality (pp. 252–5).[17] "Exemplificationality" indicates a tendency to show rather than to say. Experiences are exemplificational insofar as they are "concerned with properties exemplified or expressed – i.e., properties possessed and shown forth – by a symbol, not merely things the symbol denotes" (p. 253). Or, in Goodman's preferred language of labels, an exemplificational experience is concerned with the labels that a symbol simultaneously "satisfies" (i.e., complies with) and denotes. These four "symptoms" or "earmarks" of the aesthetic are all cognitive and "call for maximum sensitivity of discrimination" (p. 252).

Hence the contrast between art and science should not be drawn between the noncognitively aesthetic and the cognitively nonaesthetic: "Phases of a decidedly aesthetic compound may be utterly nonaesthetic; for example, a [musical] score and its mere reading are devoid of all aesthetic aspects. On the other hand, aesthetic features may predominate in the delicate . . . discrimination required in testing some scientific hypotheses. Art and science are not altogether alien" (p. 255). Nor should we distinguish "aesthetic experience" from "scientific experience" in terms of a "deeply entrenched" and "domineering" dichotomy between "the emotive" and "the cognitive." Unlike I. A. Richards, Goodman thinks the dichotomy makes no sense here, since "aesthetic and scientific experience alike are . . . fundamentally cognitive in character" (p. 245).[18] The way to dismantle the dichotomy is to recognize that "in aesthetic experience the *emotions function cognitively*": we discriminate among them and relate them "in order to gauge and grasp the [artwork] and integrate it with the rest of our experience and the world" (p. 248). At the same time, however, some aesthetic experience lacks cognitive employment of the emotions, while much nonaesthetic experience includes it. Even scientific experience permits the "use of feeling in exploration and discovery, the impetus of inspiration and curiosity, or the cues given by excitement over intriguing problems and promising hypotheses" (p. 251). Hence not even the cognitive use of emotion serves to distinguish aesthetic from nonaesthetic experience. For that distinction, we need the four "symptoms of the aesthetic," all of which, being tied to symbol and reference, are cognitive in an extended sense.

Goodman concludes *Languages of Art* with reflections on the cognitive purpose of "symbolization," including aesthetic symbolization, and on the relative importance of truth for both art and science. The primary purpose for using symbols is cognitive, he says: to understand, to know, to discover, and to apprehend and formulate what is to be communicated. Hence all symbolization "is to be judged fundamentally by how well it serves the cognitive purpose: by the delicacy of its discriminations and the aptness of its allusions; by the way it works in grasping, exploring, and informing the world; by how it analyzes, sorts, orders, and organizes; by how it participates in the making, manipulation, retention, and transformation of knowledge" (p. 258). Because aesthetic experience, like scientific experience, is primarily a matter of symbolization, aesthetic excellence is simply such cognitive excellence "in any symbolic functioning that... qualifies as aesthetic" (p. 259).

Goodman's emphasis on cognitive purpose raises the question whether truth is as important to art as it is to science. He has a twofold response. First he questions whether truth matters all that much in science (pp. 262–3). Here he seems to equate truth with mathematical correctness and empirical accuracy. Neither correctness nor accuracy suffices to generate worthwhile scientific hypotheses, he says, nor do they help us decide which alternative hypotheses to choose. Then he redefines truth as a matter of fitness or appropriateness, and claims that this is "equally relevant for the aesthetic symbol." Both science and art aim to achieve truth as a fit between symbol and object: "Truth of a hypothesis... is a matter of fit – fit with a body of theory, and fit of hypothesis and theory to the data at hand and the facts to be encountered. And... goodness of fit takes a two-way adjustment – of theory to facts and of facts to theory – with the double aim of comfort and a new look. But such fitness, such aptness in conforming to and reforming our knowledge and our world, is equally relevant for the aesthetic symbol. Truth and its aesthetic counterpart amount to appropriateness under different names" (p. 264). When it comes to truth in this preferred sense of appropriateness, the main difference between art and science lies in the "domination of certain specific characteristics of symbols" (p. 264). Goodman goes along with the convention of reserving the terms "true" and "false" for "symbols in sentential form," but nothing in principle prevents him from assigning truth as much weight in art as it has in science. How much weight remains undecided in his all-too-brief discussion.

His subsequent reflections on knowledge and truth take a slightly different tack, however. In *Ways of Worldmaking* Goodman subsumes the specific distinction between true and false under a "general distinction between right and wrong versions" of the worlds that different symbol systems make and present.[19] "True" and "false" pertain specifically to the rightness and wrongness of world versions that consist of verbal statements.[20] But even there truth is not the only standard for choosing among statements.[21] Moreover, truth is "irrelevant" for "nonverbal versions and even for verbal versions without statements." It is confusing, he says, to "speak of pictures or predicates as 'true of' what they depict or apply to."[22] The standard of rightness for a representation is not how much "it resembles what it depicts" or whether "it makes a true statement" but a certain "rightness of fit" for the world it renders.[23] So too the standard of rightness for nonrepresentational artworks "that present worlds by exemplification or expression"[24] is not truth but either the "fairness" of the sample or the "accord" among samples: "Briefly, then, truth of statements and rightness of descriptions, representations, exemplifications, expressions – of design, drawing, diction, rhythm – is primarily a matter of fit: fit to what is referred to . . ., or to other renderings, or to modes and manners of organization. . . . And knowing or understanding is seen as ranging beyond the acquiring of true beliefs to the discovering and devising of fit of all sorts."[25] Because rightness of fit, not the truth of verbal statements, governs all symbol systems, "the arts must be taken no less seriously than the sciences as modes of discovery, creation, and enlargement of knowledge in the broad sense of advancement of the understanding."[26] A crucial corollary to this emphasis on rightness of fit is Goodman's effort to conceive truth "otherwise . . . than as correspondence with a ready-made world."[27]

In describing "truth and its aesthetic counterpart" as "appropriateness under different names," Goodman dispenses with propositions and correspondences as hallmarks of truth. This is what enables him to accord legitimacy and worth to aesthetic cognition, and what makes his accounts of representation and expression so provocative for a theory of artistic truth. At the same time, Goodman's approach raises two obstacles to such a theory, namely, a lack of truth bearers and an absence of what I label "appropriation." The next two sections discuss each obstacle in turn.

8.2 TRUTH WITHOUT TRUTH BEARERS

As I suggested at the outset, Goodman denies, in effect, that propositions are the locus of truth. Let me explain. In the few places where *Languages of Art* thematizes the notion of truth, Goodman links it to the way in which predicates apply to objects. Such passages display remnants of a correspondence theory according to which truth consists of the correspondence between proposition and fact. But Goodman complicates this picture in two directions. First, he allows for both literal and metaphorical application of predicates to objects, such that either application can be true or false. Second, he also says that nonpredicate labels apply to objects. In an extended sense, these nonpredicative applications also can be true or false. Both complications inform his concluding discussion of truth in science and art. On the one hand, he wants to acknowledge that scientific predicates (hypotheses and theories) can apply to objects (data and facts) and be literally true. On the other hand, he does not want to restrict science to such "literal" pursuit of truth, nor does he want to require of art that it imitate science in this pursuit. In principle, the ways of pursuing "truth" are as diverse as the ways in which symbol systems get created and used, whether literally or metaphorically and whether linguistically or nonlinguistically. The main reason why Goodman hesitates to attribute truth to art and speaks instead of truth's "aesthetic counterpart," it seems to me, is that Anglo-American philosophy customarily restricts truth to carriers that are literal and linguistic. If propositions are quintessentially literal and linguistic (or semantic in a linguistically accessible way), then, despite the caution of his formulations, Goodman has in effect demoted propositions as bearers of truth. He has made them no more privileged than other ways of labeling objects.

Someone who wishes to free truth from its propositional cage will applaud Goodman's efforts, as I do. Yet a problem sets in exactly here. For in depriviljeging propositions, Goodman cuts truth loose from any truth bearers and lowers its importance as a cognitive standard or goal.[28] Much turns on his notion of denotation (as reference plus compliance) and the correlative notion of "propriety" (p. 40), "appropriateness" (p. 264), or "fit," which *Languages of Art* does not define. In fact, everything in his accounts of representation and expression hinges on these two notions: representation involves dense and ambiguous denotation, expression involves metaphorical compliance with that which denotes, and their success depends on the fit either between symbols and what they denote or between symbols and what denotes them.

Goodman is right to insist that compliance and propriety cannot simply obtain between single symbols and their objects but must involve the placement and operations of symbols within symbol systems. He is also correct in claiming that there are no nonlabeled objects to which symbols can refer. Rather there is a host of objects, each one multiply labeled. Whether a particular symbol denotes a certain object depends on that symbol's placement and operations within a relevant symbol system. Against Goodman, however, this need not entail that "given a [symbol] system, the question whether a newly encountered object is a desk or a unicorn-picture ... is a question of the propriety, under that system, of projecting the predicate 'desk' or the predicate 'unicorn–picture' ... over the thing in question" (p. 40). Unless there were some distinction or play between these two questions, there would be little possibility of the discovery and creativity that Goodman prizes: the answer to the first question would be prescribed by whatever symbol system is "in effect." The question whether something is a desk is not simply a question about the propriety of projecting a "desk" predicate or some other "desk" label. Normally, in most contexts other than illustrating a philosophical theory, it is also a question about how the object itself functions relative to other objects as well as to the builders and users of furniture. Does it function in a desklike way, or does it not? Could it? Should it? Obviously one cannot raise such questions without asking about propriety in labeling. But one also cannot answer them simply by addressing questions about labeling. One needs to address questions of *existence*. Yet one need not postulate metaphysical kinds in order to recognize the importance of distinguishing questions of existence from questions of symbolization. Asking how the object itself functions does not require it to have an essence or to be grasped "in itself" apart from all other objects and subjects.

Goodman avoids questions of existence (e.g., Does this function in desklike ways?) by proposing circular descriptions of compliance and propriety. For an object to comply with the label assigned to it, he says, the appropriate label must be applied to that object. But for an appropriate label to apply to an object, that object must comply with the label in question. Whether the object complies and whether the label applies both depend on which symbol system is in effect. It is because of this circularity that Goodman thinks some labels – unicorn-pictures and unicorn-descriptions, for example – have "null denotation." Goodman says that pictures of fictional entities such as unicorns "are representations with null denotation" (p. 21). We can sort out such pictures in terms of what kind of pictures they are (e.g., a unicorn-picture) without claiming that they represent something. This is similar, he says, to the way we sort out descriptions, some of which (e.g., "unicorn") denote nothing but nevertheless are distinct labels (a unicorn-description rather than, say, a Pegasus-description). Moreover, pictorial "representation" differs from pictorial "representation-as": whereas representation requires only the picture's denoting its object, representation-as requires both the picture's denoting its object and the picture's being classified as the right sort of picture: "A picture that represents a man denotes him; a picture that represents a fictional man is a man-picture; and a picture that represents a man as a man is a man-picture denoting him. Thus while the first case concerns only what the picture denotes, and the second only what kind of picture it is, the third concerns both the denotation and the classification" (pp. 27–8).[29]

Goodman's point is that one cannot conclude from the fact that some label applies an object that the object exists. Nor can one conclude from some object's seeming not to exist that some label does not apply to it. So he postulates labels that denote, but in this denoting they denote nothing: they have null denotation. His clearest example is the picture "of" a unicorn: it is a unicorn-label but does not denote a unicorn. One of the problems with this account, however, is its equivocation.[30] Insofar as for Goodman denotation simply means the application of a label to an object that complies with the label, it is doubtful that "null denotation" is denotation at all. For if there is no object – no unicorn to be pictured or predicated – then it becomes doubtful that an object complies with the label. And if it is doubtful that an object complies with the label, then it is also doubtful that the label applies to the object. "Null denotation" means that a label denotes nothing, or that it does not denote anything. In other words, "null denotation" is equivalent to "no denotation" and "not a denotation." The counterpart to a realist's populating possible worlds with countless nonoccurrent objects is the nominalist's filling symbol systems with a vast array of empty labels.

The systematic source to Goodman's equivocation about "denotation" lies in his failure to give an account of the "aboutness" of symbols. This failure, which has far-reaching implications, is ironic, since Goodman makes "reference" the most general mode of symbolization, common both to all symbol systems and to more discrete symbolic functions such as representation, description, expression, and (literal) exemplification. On most other accounts of reference,[31] the symbol or speech act or sentence must go beyond identifying something. It is not enough for a label to apply to an object and the object to comply with the label. In addition, and necessarily, the symbol or speech act or sentence must be about what it identifies. The label must be about the object to which it applies, and the object must be encompassed by the label with which it complies. Presumably nominalism does not preclude giving an account of "aboutness."[32] Yet anything close to such an account is difficult to find in *Languages of Art.*

Goodman's neglect of "aboutness" releases the acids that cut truth loose not only from propositions but also from any other truth bearers, and diminish its importance as a cognitive goal. Here the first problem in his account of truth becomes evident. For if a symbol does not need to be about something in order to refer to it, then the fact that a picture or predicate or pronoun refers to x, y, or z tells us nothing about its tendency or capacity to be true or false with respect to x, y, or z. It only tells us that, in whatever symbol system is in effect, this picture or predicate or pronoun "has been assigned" to x, y, or z. For Goodman, whether a label is true or false with respect to x, y, or z is simply a matter of whether the label has been properly assigned or misassigned according to the established practices or precepts that govern labeling when the relevant symbol system is in effect. The symbol or label's truth (with respect to that to which it refers) is neither its being "true to" that object nor its being "true of" that object, but simply its being appropriate within the relevant symbol system.

Appropriateness is not equivalent, however, to what I have described as the integrity of artistic import. In fact, Goodman has no notion of artistic import. The absence of such a notion stems directly from his neglect of "aboutness." His account of such "symptoms of the aesthetic" as semantic density and ambiguity and exemplificationality is completely structural and conventional: what matters is whether a particular symbol functions within a symbol system where characters and compliance classes are thickly cross-linked and where the relation between symbol and label is a two-way street. Since no symbol is "by nature" of a certain sort, and since the practices and precepts governing symbol systems change, Goodman would find it inappropriate to attribute import to any symbol as such. What a word or text or picture or sketch "means," and how it means it, depends entirely on which symbol system is "in effect" – which itself can vary from one occasion to the next, depending on how the symbol is being deployed. In other words, Goodman destroys outdated conceptions of representation and expression by virtually eliminating the intrinsic meaning of artworks as such, thereby dismissing the question of how such intrinsic meaning relates to other social and cultural phenomena that provide occasions, reasons, and purposes for deploying artworks. Consequently, traditional concerns about the importance and relative stature of artworks also melt away. Whereas T. M. Greene, for example, thinks that perfection, integrity, and greatness are supreme criteria for evaluating works of art, Goodman thinks judgments along these lines are "minor aids to insight" and "not the best way of understanding" works of art (p. 262).

In fact, Goodman's conception of truth is fundamentally ethical rather than epistemic.[33] He liberates truth from its propositional cage by eliminating the very notion that something can carry truth. Although this allows him to ascribe truth (or its "aesthetic counterpart") to art phenomena, what he ascribes is not what philosophers who speak of "artistic truth" have recognized as the truth of artistic import. Instead he ascribes ethical or instrumental capacities: fit, propriety, appropriateness, and the like. The notion of appropriateness allows him to attribute "truth" to art, but only in quotation marks.

8.3 APPROPRIATENESS AND SIGNIFICANCE

Nevertheless, Goodman's notion of appropriateness does carry elements of what I have called significance. I have described significance as the quasi-normative expectation that art phenomena should be true with respect to a public's need for cultural presentations that are worthy of the public's engagement. In Goodmanian language, perhaps we could say that participants in the symbol systems of art (in modern Western societies) have developed the convention of finding various art symbols to be more or less fitting to their needs or to their labels for needs. But this way of putting the matter misses something crucial. It misses the fact that finding art phenomena to be significant includes finding them to be imaginatively disclosive of a public's need for worthwhile cultural presentations. As I shall show, Goodman's "appropriateness" lacks "appropriation."

This second area of concern arises from Goodman's manner of questioning whether correspondence governs art's cognitive functions. One strength of his questioning is that it demolishes both traditional mimetic and post-Kantian expressivist accounts. With respect to outdated conceptions of representation and expression, he is a skilled equal-opportunity destroyer. A weakness stems, however, from the way this destruction works. Goodman does not explain the distinctiveness of the arts and their cognitive functions. This lack of explanation stems from his conception of symbol systems. Unlike Ernst Cassirer and Susanne K. Langer, whom he mentions in passing (pp. xii, 77),[34] Goodman does not provide a theory of "symbolic forms" that can describe the distinctive cognitive contributions of, say, myth, religion, language, art, and science. In fact, his understanding of what would count as a "general theory of symbols" is incompatible with efforts to distinguish and interrelate various branches of culture. Just as he regards any attempt to trace his agreements and disagreements with such writers "a purely historical matter" that should not receive "disproportionate and distracting prominence" (p. xiii), so the historical differentiation and reconfiguration of cultural realms has little relevance for his general theory of symbols.

Like much of analytic philosophy after World War II, Goodman's theory is ahistorical in both topics and method. The historical differentiations, say, among art, science, and morality, and among the theories of these areas, especially since the European Enlightenment, do not matter for his general theory. What does matter are systematic distinctions between such functions as denotation and exemplification, distinctions that supervene, as it were, on historically differentiated branches of culture. The question never seems to arise as to why a general theory should account for these functions and only these functions. Historically, of course, Goodman's theory helps address conundrums that had arisen in logical positivism, partly as a result of its scientism, and it helps expand the reach of structural linguistics toward a semiotics of "nonverbal symbol systems" (p. xi). But he never tells us why, given the social history and current state of Western culture, one should explicate denotation and exemplification rather than, say, communication and mediation.

Goodman does not ignore altogether the question of historical differentiation. As we have seen, he identifies four symptoms of the aesthetic: syntactic repleteness, syntactic density, semantic density, and exemplificationality. These "may be *conjunctively* sufficient and *disjunctively* necessary" for aesthetic experience, he says (p. 254). Together they tend to distinguish art from science. Yet this manner of differentiation says nothing about art's distinction from, say, myth or language. Nor does it tell us how art's "aesthetic symptoms" cohere with its nonaesthetic aspects.[35]

Perhaps further reflection on Goodman's notion of "exemplification-ality" can illustrate how to describe art's historically differentiated character. Let me propose "allusivity" as another term for "exemplificationality." Calvin G. Seerveld uses "allusivity" to summarize what distinguishes the aesthetic dimension of experience, culture, and society from nonaesthetic dimensions.[36] The term derives from "allusion," meaning "an implied or indirect reference." To the extent that Goodman thinks exemplification piggybacks on denotation, exemplification can be described as a less direct form of reference. Goodman's "exemplificationality" and Seerveld's "allusivity" have in common a refusal to divorce the supposed "ineffability" of "aesthetic ideas" (Kant) from pedestrian reference and ordinary language. Their terms suggest that this phenomenon, symptomatic of "the aesthetic," is inescapably widespread in modern Western societies.

Looked at with Goodmanian eyes, perhaps allusivity has to do with the way in which cultural products and practices (symbols) can not only point beyond themselves (reference) but also make it a point to be the point of their own pointing (exemplification). As Goodman suggests, this cultural doubling back can be relatively direct (literal exemplification) or indirect (expression), a distinction one could mark within allusivity with the terms "iterability" and "expressivity," respectively. Together with other suitably described tendencies or "symptoms," allusivity (as both iterability and expressivity) would help distinguish aesthetic from nonaesthetic aspects of culture, whether, for example, in art or in science. If one adds, as Seerveld does, that allusivity tends to pervade the arts in ways that it does not pervade the sciences or myths or languages, then art's distinctive cognitive contributions would be tied in part to the allusivity of its import.

Unlike Seerveld or Langer or Cassirer, however, or Adorno, Gadamer, Heidegger, Marx, and Hegel, for that matter, Goodman has no notion of an import that could be more or less allusive. Hence he cannot have any notion of how such import might bear upon anything external to art. One will find no equivalent to either Greene's "empirical adequacy" or Heidegger's "unconcealedness" in Goodman's account of art's cognitive functioning. The "fit" or "appropriateness" of an "aesthetic symbol" – Goodman's "aesthetic counterpart" to truth in science – has little to do with connections between a truth-bearing symbol and something external to the symbol system in effect. Instead, aesthetic appropriateness has to do with the fit between characters and compliance classes, and between symbols and labels, *within* the relevant symbol systems. Similarly, the "aesthetic symptoms" that tend to characterize art have to do with the multiplicity of plausible matches for any given symbol. Any truth-making relation between truth-bearing symbol and other phenomena seems to be ruled out.

Goodman's drastic revision of the correspondence theory need not destroy the idea of artistic truth. In fact, more often than not, the correspondence theory itself has generated resistance to this idea. Yet his discussion of aesthetic appropriateness does raise questions about the potential and limits of art's cognitive functioning. Goodman's "aesthetic counterpart" to truth amounts to appropriateness without appropriation. By "appropriation" I mean the processes through which (1) art interacts with its nonartistic contexts and (2) people interact via art. The absence of appropriation, in both senses, becomes clear from his descriptions of art's cognitive functioning, which emphasize exploration and invention rather than adjudication and confirmation. He describes aesthetic experience, for example, as a "dynamic" process of "making delicate discriminations," "discerning subtle relationships," and "reorganizing the world in terms of [art] works and works in terms of the world." It involves restless "creation and re-creation" (pp. 241–2). The cognitive role of emotions in aesthetic experience, he says, is to serve as "a means of discerning what properties a work has and expresses" and to help us "gauge and grasp the work and integrate it with the rest of our experience and the world" (p. 248).[37] Later he says that aesthetic symptoms such as density and repleteness "call for maximum sensitivity of discrimination" (p. 252). In the passage quoted earlier, Goodman describes the cognitive purpose of symbolization using terms such as "discriminations" and "allusions"; "grasping, exploring, and informing the world"; analyzing, sorting, ordering, and organizing; and "the making, manipulation, retention, and transformation of knowledge" (p. 258). On this basis he then describes aesthetic excellence as the cognitive excellence of those artworks which help us make discoveries, provide a basis for further exploration, "disclose significant new subtleties" within their symbol systems, and inform our perception of the world. And this, he suggests, is a reciprocal process: "Not only do we discover the world through our symbols but we understand and reappraise our symbols progressively in the light of our growing experience" (p. 260).

Two things stand out from these descriptions. First, they employ the very subject-object paradigm of cognition that Goodman's account of aesthetic symbols tries to neutralize. He contrasts "work" and "world" and relates them, and he does the same with "our experience" and "the world." Yet it remains a mystery how movement occurs from aesthetic symbols within symbol systems to "the world" and "our experience." Without some such movement, art would seem to have few cognitive functions. In the second place, Goodman describes cognition primarily in nondialogical terms, despite his emphasis on understanding and symbol systems. He focuses on *intra*subjective functions of perception, formation, and conceptualization rather than on *inter*subjective processes of formulation, discussion, and debate.

As a result of these two peculiarities, he limits the cognitive functions of art to creating, refining, and re-creating the subject's perceptual and conceptual capacities and potential – not that different, in the end, from Kant's notion of aesthetic ideas, except that Kant had a more restricted view of what counts as cognition. Mostly absent from art's cognitive functions, on Goodman's account, are not only the ability to disclose something about matters outside art but also art's tendency to address a public's needs and aspirations and art's roles in establishing interpersonal relations. Correlatively, Goodman does not really account for that aspect of artistic truth which I have identified as significance.

If my theory of artistic truth is on the right track, then the significance of artworks cannot be divorced from the integrity of their import. Nor can integrity be divorced from significance, even though a particular artwork lacking in significance may not lack integrity, or vice versa. Accordingly, it makes sense that, despite Goodman's emphasis on "appropriateness," a theory not accounting for import would also give insufficient attention to the topic of significance. On my own theory, by contrast, questions about the significance of artworks necessarily lead to questions of integrity, just as interpretations of an artwork's import necessarily guide interpretations of a public's interpretive needs in relationship to the artwork. By disclosing a world in disclosing itself, an artwork uncovers facets of the interpreters' situation. The significance of an artwork lies partly in how, specifically, it challenges interpreters to come to terms with interpretive needs in the social world they inhabit. In expecting significance, interpreters also expect the work to illuminate and perhaps even to transform shared needs for cultural presentations. Such illumination and transformation stem in part from how an artwork's import disturbs a social world and points interpreters toward what I have called a postsubjective world. The configured import of an integral artwork both guides interpretations of a public's interpretive needs and suspends the social world to which the needs belong.

In this sense – a sense different from Goodman's use of the phrase – artworks are "ways of worldmaking." Among the worlds they help make or remake is the social world inhabited by those who interpret artworks. The significance expected of artworks cannot be equated with Goodman's "appropriateness" or "rightness of fit." Significance is neither simply a "standard of acceptability"[38] nor a measure of congruence between symbols and that to which symbols refer. Significance involves a crossing of worlds rather than the mere making or rendering of a world.[39] In expecting significance of an artwork we open ourselves to having the artwork's import conflict with our own interpretive needs. We open ourselves to having the work's postsubjective world and our own social world disagree, and to having this disagreement call for changes in the social world. Such changes might not be mere readjustments or redescriptions of a public's interpretive needs. The changes may involve a larger transformation in the social fabric within which these needs occur.

At this point a defender of Goodman might plausibly object that his nominalism allows for a great plurality of worlds that one's experience of any particular work of art could enter repeatedly in surprising ways. Hence his notion of appropriateness does not preclude the crossing of worlds that I have emphasized.⁴⁰ What I find lacking in Goodman's work, however, is any notion of a cohesive social world, one where normative expectations are widely shared and are not simply conventional results of habituation. Normative expectations concerning justice and solidarity are examples of what I have in mind. I also find missing a recognition that these normative expectations are themselves open to challenge and transformation, and that the arts can play a crucial role in this regard. Such recognition is a correct intuition in the debates about artistic truth spawned by Plato and Aristotle, even though their correspondence theories of truth give normative expectations a metaphysical grounding that, like Rapaport, I find problematic.

If, by contrast, one regards truth in general as a process of life-giving disclosure marked by fidelity to the commonly holding-and-held, then one can link the pursuit of artistic truth with the orienting and reorienting of human life in a societal context. Such (re)orientations are fundamentally at stake when art publics find artworks significant. For when publics interpret artworks with respect to shared interpretive needs, they also open themselves to having their interpretive needs be challenged, along with the normative expectations surrounding those needs. In this way questions can also arise whether a social world contributes to life-giving disclosure, and to what extent. Such potential for disruption and redirection at a prediscursive but intersubjective level is what gives the arts critical and utopian roles in society.

These roles would dissipate into countless individual experiences of novelty and discovery if one's ontology allowed for an infinite plurality of worlds and did not acknowledge the cohesiveness of the social world that art publics inhabit. Alternatively, the critical and utopian roles of the arts would harden into mere endorsements of a societal status quo if one's ontology did not allow for both a limited plurality of worlds (personal, social, and postsubjective) and a process of disclosure that occurs across these worlds and in the conflict among them. Similarly, artistic transformations in orientation would become little more than interesting changes of perspective if one's ontology allowed for an infinite array of interpretive needs. Or, alternatively, such transformations would become unimportant or nonexistent if one's ontology linked such needs directly to an unchanging set of human interests.

By emphasizing that the needs addressed through art are themselves both interpretive needs and subject to artistically motivated interpretation, I have suggested a path past either nominalist pluralism or rigid realism in social ontology. Although I posit a limited array of "human interests" such as the pursuit of solidarity and justice, I consider the principles at stake in these interests to be both historically achieved and historically openended. To the extent that people within a societal formation hold such principles in common and are held by them, the question whether such principles deserve fidelity is always already at issue. At bottom this question is whether the holding of the principles is one in which human beings and other creatures come to flourish. Due in part to the prevalence of imaginative processes in the arts within modern societies, art provides an important avenue through which such truth occurs, also with regard to the social world that interpreters of art inhabit. So my notion of "world crossing" is not one of individual connoisseurs moving at will across an infinite plurality of worlds. Rather it points to a limited plurality of worlds that come into conflict and, within this conflict, allow the question of life-giving disclosure to arise.

To account for such aspects of artistic truth, it does not suffice to demote propositions and reject a correspondence theory of truth. One also needs to explain how the import of artworks can be true and how artworks can facilitate intersubjective understanding and contestation. In failing to provide this explanation – indeed, in not seeing a need to provide it – Goodman's approach remains within the analytic aesthetic mainstream it has done so much to redirect.

9

Wolterstorff's Realism

We cannot evaluate the action of fictional projection by reference to the truth
and falsehood of what was claimed. For nothing was claimed.

Nicholas Wolterstorff[1]

Nicholas Wolterstorff's *Works and Worlds of Art* challenges modern aesthetic
emphases on expressive artistic creation (genius) and disinterested aesthetic
experience (taste). His alternative is to construe works of art as instruments
and objects of action, and to portray representation (mimesis) as an action
that is "pervasive and fundamental in the arts" (p. xv). This alternative implies a propositionally inflected and realist correspondence theory of truth.
Unlike Goodman, Wolterstorff retains propositions as the locus of truth, and
he endorses correspondence as the primary criterion of truth. But unlike
the propositionist T. M. Greene, he denies that the propositional content
of artworks can be substantially true or false. Central to Wolterstorff's account of art's cognitive functions is the "action" of fictive world projection:
presenting "states of affairs" for people "to reflect on, to ponder over, to explore the implications of, to conduct strandwise extrapolation on" (p. 233).
This presenting can be either direct ("introducing") or indirect ("posing
of"), and it can be true to actuality or true to a person's or community's
beliefs, including the artist's own vision. It does not appear as if the presenting, or the work itself, can be true *about* something, however. Hence for
Wolterstorff artworks cannot be substantially true or false: fictive world projection involves correspondence without truth. That, at least, is the interpretation I propose. I shall suggest that, because of an unduly restrictive theory
of truth in general, Wolterstorff's account gives cognitive status to art at the
expense of art's cognitive substance.

Let me first reconstruct Wolterstorff's account of fictive world projection, before I examine his implicit theory of truth. Wolterstorff's account of
fictive world projection includes an ontology of worlds, a theory of action,

and a distinction between fictive and assertive stances. I summarize enough of each component to elicit the general theory of truth they jointly imply (section 9.1). Then I show why this theory gives rise to an internally problematic account of artistic truth (section 9.2) that overlooks the dimension of authenticity (section 9.3).

9.1 FICTIVE WORLD PROJECTION

Worlds

Wolterstorff regards worlds as complex states of affairs. On his ontology, all states of affairs exist, but only actual states of affairs occur – that is, only states of affairs "true in our actual world" (p. 110). Possible and impossible states of affairs exist but do not occur; they differ in that possible ones can occur and impossible ones cannot (p. 127). Because Wolterstorff thinks the worlds that artists project usually consist of possible or impossible states of affairs, not actual ones, he says the artist projects a state of affairs that is "already existent but normally non-occurrent" (p. 130).[2]

What are states of affairs? Wolterstorff tells us they are identical with propositions. Propositions are entities that exist, are "capable of being asserted and of being believed to be true," and are "distinct from sentences" (p. 126). His identifying states of affairs with propositions sheds light on passages such as the following: "The artist's activity consists in projecting an already existent but normally non-occurrent state of affairs by way of indicating certain states of affairs" (p. 130). Wolterstorff could just as easily claim that the artist projects *propositions* by indicating certain *propositions*.

A world, then, is an actual, possible, or impossible state of affairs, and it usually consists of multiple states of affairs. If the world is actual or possible, then the states of affairs included within it are either true or false in the world to which they belong. Typically, the world of an artwork includes those states of affairs which the artist either mentions or suggests, plus some others that interpreters extrapolate.[3] But a work's world is not as comprehensive as either a possible world or the actual world. Strictly speaking, it is not a world, but only a segment of a (possible or impossible) world, and the states of affairs included within it are neither true nor false (pp. 131–4).[4]

Wolterstorff's ontology of worlds also distinguishes between states of affairs and events (pp. 191–7). Events are occurrences of states of affairs (which, as we have seen, always already exist). But instances of predicables (i.e., of attributes or properties) are also events. So the fundamental distinction in Wolterstorff's ontology is between kinds (which include states of affairs, attributes, and relations) and events (which include occurrences and instances). Wolterstorff understands a situation such as John's running a race to involve three "components" (my word, not his): (1) a state of affairs: John running; (2) an action attribute: running; and (3) an act event: John's (actually) running. The act event is an *occurrence* of (1) the state of affairs, and an *instance* of (2) the action attribute. Moreover, (1) the state of affairs – John running – is a *completion* of (2) the action attribute – running.[5] Applied to art, this suggests that a situation such as Rembrandt's projecting a world by painting a canvas involves (1) the state of affairs: Rembrandt projecting a world; (2) the action attribute: world projection; and (3) Rembrandt's (actually) projecting a world. The latter is an occurrence of (1) and an instance of (2), and (1) Rembrandt projecting a world is a completion of (2) the action attribute world projection.[6]

World Projection

Fundamental to Wolterstorff's account of world projection is his conception of doing one thing by doing another. Although reminiscent of Searle's theory of speech acts, Wolterstorff's conception extends to all human actions. Human actions characteristically generate other actions, he says.[7] Sometimes a person's action generates a different action by counting as that second action. Wolterstorff calls this "count-generation." For example, "my uttering the sentence, 'Would you close the door?' *counts as* my issuing the request to close the door" (p. 7). At other times a person's action generates a different action by causing that second action. Wolterstorff calls this "causal generation," and gives the example of John's playing a Brahms sonata and thereby delighting his piano teacher. Count-generation is the more important of these two concepts for explaining artistic world projection, for world projection is a count-generated action.[8]

   Wolterstorff sees a clear choice between considering either the art work or the artist as the "agent" of world projection. The first characterizes theories of symbol such as Goodman's or Susanne K. Langer's. The second characterizes theories of speech action such as Searle's or J. L. Austin's. Wolterstorff pursues the second option. He does not consider a third option, namely, that the audience or interpreter is the primary agent of world projection.[9] His focus on the artist as agent guides his attempt to differentiate among types of language-related actions. Yet the nature of artworks is crucial to his account of world projection.

   Art works, he says, are "norm-kinds" that have various "occurrences" (e.g., musical performances) or "objects" (e.g., print impressions, sculptural castings), or both (e.g., literary texts, films).[10] These occurrences and objects are "examples" of the art works with which they are associated. By perceiving the examples (such as a specific performance of Bartok's Fifth String Quartet), we perceive the art works they exemplify.[11] And because art works are not simply kinds but *norm* kinds, they can have both correct and incorrect examples.[12] According to Wolterstorff, world projection is one of the prominent actions people use art works to perform. Since world projection also occurs outside art, he needs to specify acts of projection that are plainly arts-related – hence the importance of distinguishing "fictional projection" from "assertive projection" (p. 107).

Before looking more closely at his account of fictive world projection, however, we must get clear about his concept of "the world of a work." Discussing literature, Wolterstorff writes: "[The world of a work] is not something that the artist brings into existence. Neither is it something that the artist makes occur.... The artist's activity consists in projecting an already existent but normally non-occurrent state of affairs by way of indicating certain states of affairs. ... The text is made and associated with the world [of the work] rather than the world [of the work] made and associated with the text. World-projection is a mode of selection, not a mode of creation" (p. 130). Although Wolterstorff prefers to talk about "states of affairs," this passage could just as easily have claimed that the artist projects (normally nonoccurrent) propositions by indicating certain propositions. And no artist, indeed, no one creates propositions: they always already exist. As he says about states of affairs, if one "exists at all, it exists necessarily and everlastingly" (p. 192).

Wolterstorff defines world projection by delimiting three categories of action. The relevant categories, in order of increasing specificity, are illocutionary actions, statal actions, and mood actions. He begins with "language actions," as distinct from other actions (presumably nonlanguage actions). Language actions consist of uttering (i.e., inscribing or speaking) sentences in certain manners and circumstances. "Illocutionary actions" are those which "can be purely count-generated by performing some language action." This category includes standard Searlian illocutionary acts such as asserting and promising, but also others such as "christening" and "making a parliamentary motion" (p. 219). In fact, Wolterstorff departs altogether from Searle by claiming that illocutionary actions do not require language actions: "[T]hey can be generated by actions of other sorts as well" (p. 220). This immediately raises a question of definition. If illocutionary actions do not need to be count-generated by way of language actions, although they can be, then what criterion do we have for including or excluding specific count-generated actions from the list of illocutionary actions? Illocutionary actions are, as he says, "a highly diversified lot" (p. 221).[13]

Next Wolterstorff discusses those illocutionary actions which he calls "statal actions" such as someone's asserting that, commanding that, asking whether, expressing the wish that, and promising that "my study door will be closed." Each "is a 1-degree action which takes a person as agent" and "is a *completion of* a 2-degree action which takes a person as agent and a state of affairs . . . as object" (pp. 221–2). For example, my asserting that the door will be closed completes the action of asserting that *x*. By including "that" or "whether" in his examples, Wolterstorff emphasizes the state of affairs or proposition serving as the "object" of such actions. This can be seen by considering his example of "promising." Strictly speaking, the "illocutionary action" performed by uttering the sentence "I promise that my study door will be closed" need not be the making of a promise. The speaker could simply be telling someone something. The speaker need not be promising to do something. It appears that the hearer plays no constitutive role in such actions. It is not even clear whether the speaker plays a constitutive role. For, despite Wolterstorff's emphasis on there being an agent of the action, he doesn't say anything in this context about who is doing the asserting or promising, and under what circumstances – a rather curious fact, given the personal pronoun "my" in his examples. In any case, he wants to say that world projection, even when it does not involve language actions, is statal action along these lines (p. 222). Projecting a specific world through creating the art work *Bathsheba* is a 1-degree statal action (parallel to, say, asserting that my study door will be closed). World projection "as such" is a 2-degree statal action (parallel to asserting as such).[14]

Wolterstorff's final move is to single out those statal actions which he calls "mood-actions": asserting, commanding, asking, expressing a wish, and the like. English usage suggests these by the grammatical "mood" (indicative, imperative, interrogative, or optative) of the sentence uttered. Because the sentence uttered is not the same as the illocutionary action performed by uttering it, however, and because not all languages have these features, Wolterstorff does not pin his specimens to a grammatical display board. Instead he says such mood actions "involve taking up a special sort of stance toward some state of affairs" (p. 224). Countering this formulation's intentionalist overtones, he argues that "stance-indicators" are built into the "system for mood-action" (pp. 224–30). More exactly, in the case of mood actions, each generating act (e.g., uttering a sentence) has a stance indicator. The stance indicator is that property by virtue of which, when a competent speaker asserts, for example, "I hereby command that the door (will) be closed," he or she must have done what was asserted (i.e., commanded something, in this case).[15] In Wolterstorff's vocabulary, to perform a mood action, such as commanding, on some state of affairs, such as the door's being closed, is to "introduce" that state of affairs. He claims that all cases of world projection (whether or not they involve language actions) are mood actions; they serve to introduce states of affairs (p. 231). It remains to be seen how nonlinguistic acts that generate world projection can have stance indicators, since the latter seem necessarily tied to features of language.

Now we have a general framework for understanding world projection that is fictive (as most artistic world projection is, according to Wolterstorff) rather than assertive (as most artistic world projection is not, according to Wolterstorff). World projection is a count-generated, 2-degree statal action that, like certain (other) illocutionary actions, introduces some state of affairs. The difference between the liar and the fictioneer, both of whom "take up a mood-stance toward certain states of affairs," is that the liar takes up an assertive stance and the fictioneer takes up a fictive stance (p. 231). This fictive stance consists not of pretending, and certainly not of deceiving, but of "*presenting*, of *offering for consideration*, certain states of affairs – for us to reflect on, to ponder over, to explore the implications of, to conduct strand-wise extrapolation on. And [the fictioneer] does this for our edification, for our delight, for our illumination, for our cathartic cleansing, and more besides" (p. 233). Thus what distinguishes fiction (or, more generally, art) from, say, history (or, more generally, nonartistic modes of discourse or culture) is neither "the nature of the states of affairs indicated" nor their "truth or falsity." Rather, the essence of fiction "lies in the mood-stance taken up" (p. 234). Given Wolterstorff's description, this could also be called the "presentational" rather than the "fictive" stance.

Whether presentational (fictive) or not, world projection can involve more than a 2-degree action introducing some state of affairs, Wolterstorff points out. World projection can also involve a "3-degree counterpart" of the mood action in question. He uses the phrase "pose of" to "cover all such mood-action counterparts" (p. 246). For example, my asserting that the door is closed has as its counterpart the distinct action of my assert-ing *of* (i.e., assertively posing of) the door that it is closed.[16] Similarly, an author's presenting (fictively introducing) that Bathsheba is melancholy has a counterpart: the author's "fictively posing of Bathsheba that she is melancholy" (p. 247). If such posing had occurred assertively rather than presentationally (fictively), then we could say that the author *predicated* (i.e., posed assertively) of Bathsheba that she is melancholy. Wolterstorff restricts the term "predication" to that "posing of" which is assertive (p. 246), even though his more encompassing account concerning "posing of" seems to take predication as its model.

Representation

The relevance of all this for his disagreements with Nelson Goodman emerges when Wolterstorff analyzes "the working of pictorial representa-tion as a medium of world-projection" (p. 262) in part 6 (pp. 262–355). Although I shall only skim the surface of this lengthy and fascinating dis-cussion, perhaps that will suffice for grasping the decisive issues. Adapt-ing terminology from Kendall Walton to rearticulate observations made by Goodman, Wolterstorff draws a distinction between "q-representation" and "p-representation." "Q-representation" is shorthand for pictorial rep-resentation that permits existential quantification over the things repre-sented. "P-representation" is shorthand for pictorial representation that does not permit such quantification. Unlike "rendering," both types of rep-resentation are means of world projection. When we apply the concept of q-representation, we make claims "to the effect that some existent en-tity was represented" (p. 266) – for example, when someone says that by means of the painting *Charles V* "Titian has represented a man on a horse" (p. 265). When we apply the concept of p-representation, we make no such claim – for example, when someone says "that the people who created the Unicorn Tapestry . . . represented a unicorn thereby" (p. 266).[17]

Against Goodman, who thinks that p-representation of something (such as the depiction of a unicorn, or of a horse, for that matter) simply "consists in the instantiation of a visual design of a certain sort" (p. 267), Wolterstorff argues that p-representation necessarily involves the performance of "a mood-action on certain states of affairs" (p. 282). In other words, p-representation is not simply a matter of visual design; it is also a matter of intentional action and propositional content. Since Wolterstorff assumes "that states of affairs and propositions are identical" (p. 282), p-representation is always world projective and *de dicto*. Hence, for example, "in picturing a unicorn one introduces the state of affairs of *there being a unicorn*. Unicorns have never existed. None the less there is the state of affairs, or proposition, that there is a unicorn – this proposition being false" (pp. 282–3). Wolterstorff finds a distinct advantage to claiming that in p-representing one introduces states of affairs or propositions, rather than claiming, as John G. Bennett does, that (p-representational) pictures are predicates. Whereas the extension of the predicate "is a man on a horse" is distinct from the extension of the predicate "is a horse being ridden by a man," a painting whereby someone represents a man on a horse is simultaneously and equally a painting whereby someone represents a horse being ridden by a man – the two matters being represented are the very same state of affairs. "Pictures lack extension" (p. 283). Their fundamental role "is to pick out states of affairs, not properties or extensions. In their fundamental role they are to be compared to sentences, not to predicates" (p. 279).[18]

There are more ways to introduce a state of affairs or proposition, however, than simply to use pictures. So Wolterstorff adds that, to be a case of picturing, one's introducing a proposition, say, "that there is a unicorn," must be generated by instantiating, in a certain context, a visual design that can be seen as a unicorn. This ties the representational visual artist to a stock of visual designs that can be seen representationally: "[O]nly with a visual design that can be seen as a unicorn can one p-represent a unicorn" (p. 295). And for the picturing actually to take place, the visual artist "must *intend* that his indication of the state of affairs of *there being a unicorn* shall be performed by the instantiation of a design that looks like a unicorn" (p. 297).

What remains is for Wolterstorff to give an account of q-representation that both distinguishes it from and relates it to p-representation.[19] Returning to the painting *Bathsheba*, Wolterstorff analyzes Rembrandt's q-representing Bathsheba as being "a woman sitting on a couch bathing" (my shorthand will be "woman-S"). On the one hand, if Rembrandt had not affixed the title "Bathsheba" to the painting, he might have only p-represented there being a woman-S. On the other hand, Rembrandt could not have used his painting to q-represent Bathsheba as a woman-S if he did not also use it to p-represent there being a woman-S. The fundamental difference between p-representation and q-representation parallels the difference, noted earlier, between asserting that p (assertion *de dicto*) and asserting of x that it is ø (assertion *de re*). P-representation is like asserting that p: it is representation *de dicto*. Q-representation is like asserting of x that it is ø: it is representation *de re*. "Q-representing Bathsheba as a woman sitting on a couch bathing is not like asserting (the proposition) that Bathsheba is a woman sitting on a couch bathing. Rather, it is like asserting *of* Bathsheba that she is a woman sitting on a couch bathing" (p. 330).

Hence q-representing along such lines is a pictorial species of "posing of." Unlike "predicating of," which can only be assertive, however, it is "stance neutral" (p. 330): it can function fictively or assertively or be linked to some other mood stance.[20] P-representing, by contrast, merely *introduces* a state of affairs or proposition and does not *pose* something *of* that which is represented. The link between q-representation and p-representation is such that one can pictorially *pose* "something" *of* that which is represented (e.g., pose of Bathsheba that she is a woman sitting on a couch bathing) only if one also pictorially *introduces* that there is this "something" (e.g., introduces that there is a woman sitting on a couch bathing).[21] Moreover, to q-represent Bathsheba (as distinct from q-representing her *as* a woman-S) is simply to denote Bathsheba in the context of such "posing of": "[T]o q-represent x is to denote x in the context of q-representing something of x" (p. 333).[22]

Hence, as Wolterstorff makes clear in an extended "appendix" (pp. 337–55), his theory of pictorial representation retains precisely those elements of resemblance between picture and pictured that Goodman dismisses. On Wolterstorff's account, to p-represent a unicorn is not simply to employ a unicorn-picture within the constraints of the "symbol system" that is "in effect." And to q-represent Bathsheba as "a woman sitting on a couch bathing" is not simply to employ a Bathsheba-picture "denoting" Bathsheba. Rather, in both cases, to represent pictorially is to "introduce" the relevant "state of affairs," and to do so by virtue of a visual design whose features are relevant to this task. The features of the visual design must be such that they can be "seen as" or they can "look like" what the picture depicts. According to Wolterstorff, Goodman's theory of representation does not explain what it would mean for a representational system to be "in effect." Nor does it explain how a picture can represent something either correctly or incorrectly.

Truth to Actuality

Not surprisingly, then, Wolterstorff has concerns about the relation between fictively projected worlds and the "actual world" that Goodman does not share. Part 7 ("Projected and Actual") mentions three "ways in which the worlds of works of art . . . are related to the actual world" (p. 356). First, these projected worlds "*actually* exist," and the claims people make regarding the states of affairs included in such worlds "are either true or false . . . in the actual world" (p. 356). Second, these projected worlds are anchored to entities that exist in the actual world, both "to such necessarily existing entities as states of affairs and kinds" and "to such contingently existing entities as cities, countries, events, and persons" (p. 356). Third, the world of a work can be true to actuality to the extent that some states of affairs included in it "occur in the actual world," and it can be true to some person's belief that some included state of affairs "does actually occur" (p. 357).[23] Wolterstorff adds, "In the fact that invariably the world of a work of art is true to reality [i.e., to actuality] in an indefinitely large number of respects lies the potential of works of art for illuminating us, and for confirming us in the knowledge we already have" (p. 357).

Then he sketches six ways in which the action of world projection "is related to human life as a whole" (p. 356). First, by projecting a world, the artist is actually count-generating various actions: for example, asserting, condemning, or expressing a wish. Second, the artist often is projecting "a world true in significant respects to what his community believes to be real and important" (p. 358), whether that community be one of religion or nationality or social class. Third, especially in "the modern contemporary West," artists often seek to alter or challenge prevalent convictions in their society or simply to express their own vision – "to give it concrete embodiment by composing a world true in significant respects to that vision" (p. 362).[24] Fourth, an artist can project a world that is false to actuality or to what someone believes, in the sense that the world projected is significantly different from or even apparently better than the actual world and thereby satisfies a desire "to escape the drudgery and pain, the boredom, perplexity, and disorder of real life" (p. 363). Fifth, in a manner that Wolterstorff notes but does not explain, the artist, by projecting worlds, "affects our emotional life" (p. 365). Finally, artistic world projection can model certain actions in ways that develop abilities and tendencies to perform the same actions in the actual world. Summarizing much of this in the language of action-generation, Wolterstorff concludes: "[T]he artist by his projection of worlds count-generates such actions as asserting and warning. Likewise he *causally*-generates . . . such actions as evoking emotions and altering our tendencies to action. In turn, his projection of a world is itself generated by such actions as rendering or 'capturing' one and another facet of the world around him. And through it all he reveals and expresses himself – his emotions, his beliefs, his commitments" (p. 367).

Now we can see that Wolterstorff's account of artistic world projection provides a mirror opposite to Goodman's antipropositional and conventionalist account of art's cognitive functions. If Kant's account of aesthetic ideas drove the first modern nails into the coffin of mimesis, then Goodman's nominalist contructivism seals the lid. Wolterstorff, however, deploys a sophisticated post-Kantian ontology to resuscitate a pre-Kantian concept of mimesis, which sustained art theories from Plato and Aristotle onward. Yet, unlike Plato and Aristotle, who would debate the truth of an artistic representation, Wolterstorff holds that the action of artistic world projection need not be substantially true or false. Here he agrees with Goodman. In good post-Kantian fashion, Wolterstorff ties truth to nonfictive assertions concerning actual states of affairs. In the words of Sir Philip Sydney, which he likes to quote, the poet "nothing affirms, and therefore never lieth."[25] Poets, like other world-projecting artists, "fictionally project a world distinct from our actual world" (p. 106). To that extent, they do not raise truth claims. Yet Wolterstorff locates the larger significance of artistic world projection in how the "world of a work" can be "true to" actuality and "true to" what various people take actuality to be. Here a tension arises between two notions of truth in Wolterstorff's account of art's cognitive functions: between being "true of" and being "true to," or, in the terminology proposed by John Hospers, between "truth-about" and "truth-to."[26] This tension surfaces as two problems in Wolterstorff's theory, which the following sections explore: a divorce between artistic import and truth-about (section 9.2), and inattention to authenticity as a dimension of artistic truth (section 9.3).

9.2 PROPOSITIONS WITHOUT IMPORT

The first problem has two sides. On the one hand, Wolterstorff limits truth-about to asserted propositions. On the other hand, he reduces artistic import to propositions that are not asserted. He thinks that whether something can be "true of" or "true about" something else depends on whether a proposition is asserted.[27] If the proposition is fictively projected rather than asserted, then it can be neither true nor false about something. The artist who presents certain states of affairs for our consideration does not thereby claim that these states of affairs are true as such, or true in the actual world, or true about something that occurs. At most, he or she is presenting states of affairs that happen to be true to the actual world or to someone's beliefs about the actual world.

What, then, does Wolterstorff think is the crucial difference between an assertive and a fictive mood stance? Initially, it seems to come down to extensionality. The agent who takes up an assertive mood stance introduces states of affairs as predicables, such that their extension is unavoidably at issue. When I assert "This (x) is a unicorn," I take up a stance such that it must matter whether x falls within the range of what "unicorn" denotes. The agent who takes up a fictive mood stance, by contrast, introduces states of affairs as ponderables, as worth considering without concern for their extension. When I pictorially represent a unicorn, I take up a stance such that it must matter whether the visual design can be seen as a unicorn, not whether, because of extensionality, it must be (seen as) a unicorn.[28]

Yet this contrast by itself does not warrant Wolterstorff's reticence to assign "truth-of" or "truth-about" to fictive world projection. Whether a visual
design can be seen as a unicorn would seem just as truth-related as whether a
referent falls within the range of what "unicorn" denotes. To detach artistic
import from truth-about, Wolterstorff must link extensionality with actuality. He must assume that, for the most part, the assertive mood stance points
one toward the "actual world," with its complex of necessarily and contingently existing entities. On this assumption, assertions can be true-about if
they introduce states of affairs that occur (or can occur) in the actual world,
if they introduce states of affairs that are "true in our actual world" (p. 110)
or true in possible worlds (p. 134). By contrast, he thinks that, for the most
part, the fictive mood stance points one away from the actual world, or at
least toward possible and impossible states of affairs. Fictive projections can
be neither true nor false, then, because the states of affairs they introduce
do not or cannot occur in the actual world.[29]

Unfortunately, this approach turns artworks into Platonic vehicles of
propositional content that can never measure up to the truth achieved
by theoretical and empirical disciplines. Although not as harshly as Plato's
Republic, Wolterstorff's *Works and Worlds of Art* relegates the arts to a low rung
on the cognitive ladder. On his account, artistic world projection could not
successfully challenge asserted "truth-about," nor could it disclose whether
and to what extent the projected content is "true to" the actual world or
actual beliefs. For him these accomplishments would require *asserted* propositional content *about actuality* of a sort that Wolterstorff makes a rare exception to art's fictive mode of projection.

This cognitive positioning of art presupposes his account of art works as
norm kinds. For Wolterstorff, an art work is not an occurrent phenomenon
but an immutable noumenon, to use Kantian language he would reject. Art
works govern what artists, performers, and audiences (properly) do, rather
than the other way around. The action of world projection is one such
activity. Fictive world projection is made possible by the fact that the preexistent work's preexistent world includes certain preexistent propositions
or states of affairs. Thus does artistic import get reduced to nonasserted
propositions. To Wolterstorff's credit, he does not deny the differentiation
of artworks from other cultural products, despite their allegedly being vehicles of nonasserted propositional content, nor does he turn artworks into
privileged vehicles of truth, despite their supposed immutability. But he
does decontextualize their import and dehistoricize their existence. This is
unavoidable, I think, if one regards artworks as norm kinds and their import
as fictively projected propositions or states of affairs.

The flip side to this reduction of artistic import to inactual, nonasserted
content is an all-too-expansive treatment of propositions. I find it altogether
implausible to make states of affairs identical with propositions and to detach
propositions from predication, à la Wolterstorff. States of affairs are simply

theoretical abstractions from the multitude of phenomena, practices, and institutions with which people are familiar. Propositions are logical reductions of what gets predicated in connection with various speech acts. Accordingly, states of affairs are not identical with propositions, nor are propositions simply about states of affairs. As logical reductions of predicated content, propositions are about the phenomena, practices, and institutions from which states of affairs can be abstracted. And artistic import, which on my view is mostly nonpropositional, is about the same "things." One does not need to deny that there are states of affairs and propositions to give them a more modest role in our cognitive adventures, but one does need to deny their ontological priority if one wants to provide a textured account of artistic truth. If artworks can be "true to" lived experience, then they must also have the capacity to be "true of" or "true about" that which is experienced, not by carrying abstract content ("states of affairs") that could be more reliably conveyed by the asserting of propositions, but by disclosing intricate import that usually suggests more than it says. In this regard, Goodman's demotion of propositions as truth bearers and his account of exemplification provide valuable correctives to Wolterstorff's theory of fictive world projection.

Another source to Wolterstorff's reduction of artistic import to non-asserted propositions lies in an undertheorized notion of intentionality. To get at this, let me explore some differences between his explanation of count-generation and Searlian speech-act theory. Wolterstorff's explanation, which anchors his account of artistic world projection, deviates from Searlian speech-act theory in two important respects. First, Wolterstorff assigns no structural role for responses to action, and, second, he rejects Searle's emphasis on linguistic conventions and constitutive rules.

The first departure becomes obvious from Wolterstorff's informal sketch of his theory of world projection: "Suppose I assert that the door is closed, and that I do so by uttering, in appropriate manner and circumstance, the English sentence 'The door is closed.' I would then have performed two distinct actions, the action of asserting that the door is closed and the action of uttering the English sentence 'The door is closed'" (pp. 200–1). From a Searlian perspective, however, it is unclear why one should think the action of asserting would have occurred in this scenario. Wolterstorff claims that the speaker asserts something, but he gives no indication, beyond a vague reference to "appropriate manner and circumstance," why uttering this sentence would count as an action of asserting rather than, say, an action of warning. A few paragraphs later, after saying that one could instead ask whether the door is closed or command that it be closed, he explains: "In each case I would be dealing with the same state of affairs – the door's being closed. But I would be dealing with it in different ways. I would be taking up toward it various different stances" (p. 201). And, he says, one could just as well use nonlinguistic means to perform any of these actions.

This informal sketch suggests that for Wolterstorff differences among types of (illocutionary) action hinge on the stance or attitude of the actor (speaker). Moreover, the actor need not engage in a linguistic transaction, nor do the action and stance of the person who hears the utterance (or experiences the nonlinguistic means of performing the action) make any difference to the type of action carried out or to the conditions for an action's succeeding. Thus the role of the hearer, which is constitutive for speech acts on a Searlian analysis, drops out altogether. Searle, for example, would say that asserting something requires (among other things) that it not be obvious to both speaker and hearer that the hearer already knows what is (to be) asserted. This hearer-related "preparatory condition" plays no role in Wolterstorff's analysis of asserting.

A second departure links closely to the first: Wolterstorff ignores Searle's analysis of the constitutive rules governing different types of illocutionary acts. The reason for this is clear. Wolterstorff rejects the emphasis on conventions or social practices or institutions in Alvin Goldman's *A Theory of Human Action* and in John Searle's *Speech Acts* (pp. 203–5). His alternative is to analyze count-generation as a matter of acquiring certain rights and responsibilities. This, he says, will yield a *normative* rather than a *conventional* analysis of count-generation. For someone to count-generate action Y by engaging in action X, he writes, is for that person to acquire the rights and responsibilities connected with doing Y. Two comments are in order before we proceed to his analysis, however. First, Wolterstorff's describing his analysis as normative rather than conventional is a red herring. Searle's account of speech acts is also normative. It explains various types of illocutionary acts as essentially rule-governed, such that to engage in them is for both speaker and hearer to acquire certain obligations. The real difference between Wolterstorff and Searle lies in how or whether they give these obligations ontological grounding. The second comment, in keeping with the previous paragraph, is that the person acquiring rights and responsibilities, on Wolterstorff's description, is what we might call the lead actor or speaker, rather than, say, the respondent or hearer.

To set the path for his analysis, Wolterstorff uses four examples, none of them involving speech acts in the strict sense.[30] His discussion introduces two central notions: that of "prima facie" rights and responsibilities, and that of someone's intentionally "inducing beliefs" in someone else. A summary of his analysis goes as follows.[31] For someone's doing X at time t to count as his or her doing Y, this person P must (1) generate Y by doing X at time t and (2) perform X freely. Moreover, (3) the prima facie rights and responsibilities of someone who does Y must have accrued to P at t by virtue of his or her doing X, (4) either because (a) person P has intentionally induced (or tried to induce) in interested parties the belief B that P would do X only in the relevant circumstance C where P has a prima facie responsibility to do Y or because (b) person P believes that the interested parties already have belief B. Hence, to return to the earlier example, for my uttering the English sentence "The door is closed" at 4:00 P.M. today to count as my asserting that the door is closed, I must (1 and 2) generate this asserting by freely uttering that sentence then; (3) by virtue of my uttering this sentence, I must accrue at that time both the responsibility of believing that the door is closed and the right to be believed (see pp. 206 and 214); and (4) I must accrue that responsibility and right either because (a) I have intentionally induced (or tried to induce) in my hearer the belief that I would utter this sentence only when or where I have a prima facie responsibility to assert that the door is closed or because (b) I believe that my hearer already believes this about me.

A moment's reflection shows that this account sheds little light specifically on either the uttering of sentences or the making of assertions. Wolterstorff's "normative analysis of count-generation" purportedly obtains for all count-generation, not just the making of assertions. As he himself acknowledges, it renders the generating acts (such as uttering a sentence) rather "innocuous" (p. 214). The problem, as I see it, is that it pitches normativity at such an abstract and general level that the specificity and typicality of linguistic rules disappear altogether. A similar lack of specificity and typicality also characterizes his account of artistic world projection. This has become apparent at various points in my reconstructing his account: there is no criterion for excluding specific count-generated actions from the list of illocutionary actions; differences among mood actions, and between mood actions and other statal actions, depend on stance indicators that are difficult to specify without reference to linguistic properties; and the difference between fictive and assertive world projection comes down to differences in the mood stances that world-projecting agents take up toward the states of affairs they introduce.

Hence, in Wolterstorff's discussion of pictorial representation, the difference between p-representing a unicorn and asserting (falsely, in his view) that there is a unicorn comes down to two factors: (a) the action of representing employs a visual design rather than a sentence, and (b) the agent p-representing the unicorn takes up the mood stance of fictive rather than assertive world projection. Otherwise the structure of the two actions – p-representing and asserting – is pretty much the same: they are count-generated, 2-degree statal actions that introduce the same proposition or state of affairs of there being a unicorn. Furthermore, since in principle the agent engaged in picturing could be taking up an assertive rather than a fictive mood stance,[32] the effect of the first factor (employing a visual design) is itself dependent on the second (taking up the fictive stance). Whether the picturing agent is representing seems, in the end, to depend on what mood stance the agent adopts. It is so, of course, that an agent cannot use just any visual design to represent a unicorn, no more than an agent can use just any combination of words to assert that something is a unicorn. On this score, however, Wolterstorff is just as much a conventionalist as Goodman is: which visual design to use depends on the available stock of visual designs. And the same would apply to using visual designs to make assertions: one can assert that something is a unicorn by using a certain visual design only if one selects the appropriate visual design from the available stock. To employ the logo of Apple computers would probably result in the failure of either p-representing or asserting there being a unicorn.

So Wolterstorff's reduction of artistic import to nonasserted propositions stems in part from a notion of intentionality that is undertheorized in two respects. First, he gives no account of the roles played by audiences or publics in framing situations where something like fictive world projection can occur. Second, he does not consider the art-institutional rules according to which artworks and art acts get constituted. Given his theory of art works as norm kinds and his theory of world projection as a statal mood action, it is hard to see how either of these accounts could be given within the framework of his realist ontology.

9.3 ACTUALITY AND AUTHENTICITY

The preceding discussion indicates that a propositionally inflected and realist correspondence theory of truth sustains Wolterstorff's book. This theory would claim, for example, that a world projection can be true *iff* it is assertive and introduces states of affairs that obtain (where all states of affairs exist necessarily, but only actual and possible ones can obtain). The primary relata are the action of assertive world projection and the obtaining of certain states of affairs. So artworks or their import are not "true of" or "true about" anything, for two reasons: they primarily function within nonassertive world projection, and they primarily serve to introduce states of affairs that do not obtain. Yet Wolterstorff says they can be "true to" actuality, and this claim introduces some new puzzles. To see why, let's review the relationships between projected and actual worlds that I noted earlier.

Wolterstorff mentions three relationships between the projected worlds of artworks and the actual world: artistically projected worlds "*actually* exist," they are "anchored to" actual-world entities, and they can be "*true to* reality (actuality)" (pp. 356–7). The first of these involves an obfuscation, it seems to me. To claim that a projected world "actually exists" is equivocal within Wolterstorff's ontology. It could mean that this world does indeed exist, although perhaps as a possible or impossible world rather than as the actual world. But then the adverb "actually" adds nothing, and the claim establishes no relationship between the projected world and the actual world, other than their both existing – which worlds do necessarily, according to Wolterstorff. Alternatively, to claim that a projected world "actually exists" could mean that this world exists within the actual world. But this would conflict with everything Wolterstorff has said about artistically projected worlds, and it would render pointless the question of how such projected worlds "are related to the actual world" (p. 356). Wolterstorff's elaboration of the claim does not help. First he says "there are those states of affairs that constitute these worlds." That, in itself, says nothing about whether such states of affairs and their worlds are *actual*, rather than possible or impossible. Then he says that the world-projecting artist "is dealing with what does actually exist" (p. 356). Unfortunately, however, the fact that the artist (who, presumably, exists in the actual world) "deals with" projected states of affairs does not tell us whether and how these states of affairs and their world "relate to" the actual world.

The second relationship – that artistically projected worlds are "anchored to" actual-world entities – is more precise. It has to do with the fact that certain states of affairs could not be included in an artistically projected world if they did not exist in the actual world. For example, the artistically projected "world of *David Copperfield* could not occur without London existing – *actually* existing" (p. 356). Since many states of affairs in artistically projected worlds are not so anchored, however, this second relationship must always be partial and incomplete.

The third relationship is the most important, it seems to me, and also the one where Wolterstorff's distinctions break down. He notes that usually an artistically projected world, although it exists, "does not, *as a whole*, occur. . . . Invariably, though, *some* of the states of affairs *included within* the work's world do actually occur." Hence the world of a work of art can be "true to actuality" in the sense that some states of affairs included within that world "actually occur" – they "occur in the actual world." And even if those states of affairs do not actually occur, some person in the actual world might actually believe that they actually occur. In this case the artistically projected world would, with respect to those states of affairs, be "true . . . to some person's *view* concerning actuality" (p. 357). So the relationship here is between certain states of affairs within the projected world and their occurring in the actual world, either as actual entities or as actual beliefs about entities.

There are two problems with Wolterstorff's account of this relationship. On the one hand, it says nothing about the quality and quantity of states of affairs that must occur in the actual world if the artistically projected world that includes them is to be "true to actuality." Does it suffice if just one state of affairs actually occurs, for example, that London has more than a million inhabitants? Does it matter whether the states of affairs are trivial or insignificant? Similarly, does it suffice for just one person to believe that the relevant state of affairs actually occurs, and does it matter whether that belief is plausible or warranted?

On the other hand, Wolterstorff's account of "truth to actuality" undermines his previous distinction between assertive and fictive world projection. Every artistically projected world would include at least one state of affairs that actually occurs or is actually believed by someone to occur. And if at least one, then why not many, and why wouldn't the artist be introducing them as actually occurrent states of affairs that are actually believable? If artistically projected worlds can be true to actuality in the manner described, then introducing states of affairs as predicables would seem to be one of the actions normally count-generated when the painter paints or the novelist writes. The artist would not simply introduce states of affairs as ponderables, without regard to their extension. The artist would also introduce states of affairs as having or not having extension among entities in the actual world.

Accordingly, a main reason for previously denying "truth-of" or "truth-about" to fictive projections disappears. It no longer makes sense to argue that, because the states of affairs they introduce do not or cannot occur in the actual world, fictive projections are neither true nor false. For an artistically projected world to be "true to actuality," an artist must introduce states of affairs that can and do occur in the actual world. So Wolterstorff's careful distinctions between assertive projection and fictive projection, and between assertive truth and fictive presentation, begin to unravel. Although he could avoid this by denying art's "truth-to actuality" or discounting its importance, neither of these does he seem ready to do, nor do I think he should. This is why I said earlier that he denies truth to art, but only as an explicit label.

Once one surrenders his scrupulous attempt to distinguish fictive from assertive projection, Wolterstorff's entire account of art's cognitive functions can be seen to revolve around an implicit correspondence between propositions (as possible and impossible states of affairs) and facts (as actual states of affairs). Indeed, the four noncausal ways in which the action of artistic world projection relates to human life all hinge on such correspondence: the artist's using such action (1) to "*say* something" (p. 358) or to make claims "about our actual world,"[33] (2) to express and confirm his or her community's convictions about what's "real and important" (p. 358), (3) to challenge prevalent convictions or to express the artist's own vision concerning what's "real and important" (p. 362), and (4) to project an alternative reality. All of these require that the artist's fictive projection be such that states of affairs in the projected world correspond to actual states of affairs that someone (whether artist, community, or society at large) asserts or can assert.

Not very prominent on Wolterstorff's list of art's cognitive functions are the elements of exploration, invention, and discovery that Goodman considers central. More prominent are the elements of adjudication and confirmation that Goodman tends to ignore. Like Goodman, however, Wolterstorff employs a subject-object paradigm of cognition and describes art's cognitive functions in nondialogical terms, despite his emphasis on community. He too focuses on intrasubjective functions – projection, expression, and single-agent action – rather than intersubjective processes such as communication and interaction. Where he differs from Goodman is in his readiness to consider art's ability to disclose something about matters outside art. He does not ignore the aspect of artistic truth that I identify as integrity, although I think he misconstrues it. Also, unlike Goodman, Wolterstorff acknowledges the importance of art's addressing a community's convictions. So he does not ignore the aspect of artistic truth that I identify as significance.[34] Yet the account he gives of art's cognitive functions, being tied to propositions and correspondence, cannot do justice to the creativity that characterizes imaginative disclosure at its best.

Let me elaborate this last point by returning to my notion of authenticity. The closest Wolterstorff comes to this topic is in his carefully dissecting the concepts of self-expression and self-revelation (pp. 21–9).[35] Using the example of Rebecca's expressing her gratitude by giving something to Mary, he analyzes "self-expression" as the disclosure (my term) of a "state of consciousness" that the self-expressing agent actually has at a certain time. This disclosure occurs by way of a contemporaneous action that the agent cannot "knowingly and sincerely perform" unless she or he has the feeling or attitude or belief in question.[36] Either that, or the agent wants to generate something congruent to the agent's state of consciousness, believes the action in question will accomplish this, and the action is successful in this regard. "Self-revelation," by contrast, is not restricted to states of consciousness, nor need it be done intentionally. It can involve other "states of self" (such as "one's origins" or "one's having a sore knee," p. 29), and it can occur nonintentionally (such as "writhing in pain and grimacing," p. 28). Moreover, self-revelation, unlike self-expression, requires that the disclosive act be "perceptible" and be "good evidence" for the state of self in question (p. 28). On Wolterstorff's analysis, "self-revelation" is the disclosure of a state that the self-revealing agent actually has at a certain time. This disclosure occurs by way of a contemporaneous and perceptible act[37] that the agent performs because the agent has that state or wants someone else to know that the agent feels or thinks as she or he does. To be a case of self-revelation, the act must constitute "good evidence" of the agent's state, and to be a case where self-revelation is transmitted, someone other than the agent must infer from the act that the agent has the state in question.

What these two concepts have in common, on Wolterstorff's analysis, is that the agent undertakes an action at a certain time and, in this, the agent's state is disclosed. Self-expression and self-revelation are "generated" by appropriate actions, he says, but in ways that are "more complex" than "either causal generation or count-generation" (p. 29). But such complexity raises a question that Wolterstorff does not address, namely, whether his bipartite theory of action-generation is adequate. If self-expression and self-revelation are as common and important in ordinary experience as they seem to be, then not building their structure into the theory of action-generation might signal a significant gap in Wolterstorff's theory and in its application to art. This gap might help explain why his theory of fictive world projection emphasizes the mood stance the artist takes up but not the experience or vision the artist brings to the artistic process. The role of the artist's experience or vision comes almost as an afterthought, discussed all too briefly in connection with the notion of the artwork's world being "true to" actuality.

My own account of authenticity differs from Wolterstorff's analysis of self-expression and self-revelation in several respects. I do not think that artists are primarily agents of action, that they have "states of self" or "states of consciousness," or that they create artworks as means of expressing or revealing such states. Nor do I regard the "truth" of artists' self-disclosure to consist in a correspondence between the world they project and the states they possess, whether those states be personal and group characteristics ("states of self") or feelings, attitudes, and beliefs ("states of consciousness"). I find Wolterstorff's philosophical anthropology too static and atomistic to do justice to what I have described as a hermeneutic process.[38]

I have said that, in relationship to their production, art products, including artworks, are mediated expressions that can be more or less authentic with respect to the artist's experience or vision. In modern Western societies, at least, authenticity is a dimension of artistic truth. We expect art products to be imaginatively disclosive of the experience or vision from which competent art making allows them to arise. Wolterstorff's analysis of "self-expression" and "self-revelation" notes this expectation but misses its connection to artistic truth. My account of authenticity implies that artists do not simply have certain states that they then use artworks to disclose. Nor do audiences or publics properly interpret an artwork when they use it as a window to the artist's supposed states of self or states of consciousness. Rather, both art making and art appreciation are processes of discovery, interpretation, and presentation. In these processes the "agents" themselves undergo important changes. They learn, they have new experiences, they revise their previous self-understandings, and the like. Recognizing this is one of the worthwhile insights in R. G. Collingwood's claim, when applied to art, that in expressing "an emotion" one clarifies that emotion. Whereas Wolterstorff takes from Collingwood's claim the point that self-expression need not involve a perceptible act (p. 28), I find the more interesting point to be that the artist's self-disclosure is a hermeneutic process changing both the art-making "agent" and the very "state" that might have helped trigger the "agent's" art making. The artist's self-disclosure is simultaneously a self-discovery, self-interpretation, and self-presentation.

That is one reason why it would be inadequate to analyze authenticity – an art product's "truth with respect to" the artist's experience or vision – as a "correspondence between" the artwork's "world" and the artist's "state." A realist correspondence theory of truth such as Wolterstorff's typically assumes a fixed correlation between two unchanging entities, even when it temporally indexes the correlation as holding at time "*t*." By understanding authenticity instead as an expectation that the art phenomenon be "imaginatively disclosive of" the artist's experience or vision, I emphasize that art products, including artworks, arise from and function within a dynamic hermeneutic process.

The other reason to avoid a correspondence theory of authenticity has to do with characteristics of art making. I suggested earlier, partly in line with Wolterstorff's account, that art making is a type of action. Now I wish to add that is not simply a type of action. Art making has a mediated character that aligns it more closely with production than with straightforward action, and a mediating character that aligns it most importantly with poeisis. Wolterstorff's otherwise laudable rejection of romantic myths of genius leads him to blur some important distinctions in this regard. To put my point as succinctly as possible: a bipartite model of "causal generation" and "count-generation" does not suffice to account for the hermeneutic process of art making. Nor can the conception of artworks as "norm-kinds" do justice to the creativity that characterizes art making in modern Western societies. Wolterstorff's theory of action omits precisely those hermeneutically generative activities that are central to art making and that inform the expectation of authenticity. *Pace* Wolterstorff, an artist such as Rembrandt does not primarily apply paint to canvas and thereby generate a chain of other actions such as "producing a rendering," "creating a painting," "representing," "projecting a world," "revealing his fondness for strong chiaroscuro," and "expressing his aversion to the Renaissance cult of the ideal body" (p. 17). Rather the artist primarily and from the outset undertakes a process of exploratory presentation that is interpretive through and through. Making a visual art product is not like painting a house, even when both involve applying paint to a surface. Nor is it like grimacing or like giving a gift to show one's gratitude, even when art making bears traces of genuine pain or gives evidence of generosity or some other attitude or disposition.

In making an artwork, an artist does not simply reveal or express some state of self, whether conscious or not. Nor does the artist "fetch about" for "some strategies" that would "inherently fit" certain of the artist's convictions, and then "hit on" certain "techniques" for doing this (pp. 26–7). The techniques an artist "employs" are themselves part of the art-making process. They are interpretive and presentational through and through. Often, in fact, they only come about in the making of the artwork itself and only make sense in that context. Even John Cage's aleatory techniques, which Wolterstorff mentions in this context, were not adopted as means of "expression" in Wolterstorff's sense. Cage did not simply *adopt* them as a means of expressing his preexisting convictions. He *fashioned* them as part of the presentational process of composing music, and in fashioning them he fashioned and interpreted his own convictions.

A critical hermeneutic account of authenticity requires a different ontology from one in which actual states of a self, which do not change during the time they are states of that self, get expressed or revealed by an agent's engaging in suitable actions, which themselves exist prior to the agent's engaging in them. More broadly, my account questions the art-theoretical fruitfulness of an ontology that distinguishes actual, possible, and impossible worlds and regards artistic import (the "world of the work") as a segment of one or another of these worlds. While I agree with Wolterstorff that art allows for the crossing of worlds, I regard all the worlds being crossed – personal, social, and postsubjective – as actual. Or, to modify Goodman's terminology, they are all versions of the actual world, and they are all of them dynamic rather than static. Like the Kristevan subject, they are world-versions-in-process rather than complex and unchanging "states of affairs."[39] So my theory of artistic truth presupposes an ontology that is neither nominalist nor realist with respect to what exists, and an epistemology that is neither conventionalist nor intentionalist with respect to what makes something true.

The ontology and epistemology required, which this book partially indicates, would not reduce truth to either conventional appropriateness à la Goodman or causal probability à la Richards. Nor would it deny the legitimate but limited role of assertions and propositional validity in the discovery and articulation of truth à la certain Heideggerians. But it would also neither limit "truth-about" to asserted propositions à la Wolterstorff nor reduce artistic import to propositional content à la both Wolterstorff and Greene. If one neither limits "truth-about" to asserted propositions nor reduces artistic import to propositional content, then the motivation for distinguishing between "truth-about" and "truth-to" vanishes. That distinction is necessitated by the hard links many philosophers have forged between "truth-about" and asserted propositions (or similar truth bearers). The notion of "truth-to" gives such philosophers a way to preserve art's cognitive status while denying its cognitive substance. It would be better to preserve the substance. For this, however, a different theory of truth would be required, one in which asserted propositions are not privileged truth bearers and the relation between propositions and facts or states of affairs is not the primary measure of truth. The theory required would do justice to the creativity and intersubjectivity that characterize artistic truth. By describing imaginative disclosure as an intersubjective process of exploring, interpreting, and presenting aesthetic signs under the triple expectation of authenticity, significance, and integrity, and by linking this process to societal flourishing, I have tried to introduce such a theory.

10

Aesthetic Transformations

> In their movement toward truth artworks need the very concept that they keep
> at a distance for the sake of their truth.
>
> Theodor W. Adorno[1]

In the Introduction I said that both the subject matter and my method-ological assumptions require philosophical border crossings. Having nearly completed our journey, we can review what was learned by crossing divides both between continental and analytic philosophy and within each tradition (section 10.1). Then I discuss the societal point of this journey (section 10.2), keeping in mind Adorno's suggestion that a philosophical idea of artistic truth might be both what contemporary art most needs and what it most resists.

Propositionally inflected correspondence theories of truth are promi-nent in the terrain we have traversed. Because of that, let me map in Table 10.1 various theories with respect to two questions, to which I have indicated my own negative responses: (1) Are propositions (or their equiv-alents) the primary bearers of truth? (2) Is correspondence the primary criterion of truth? Answers to these two questions govern the general dis-position of twentieth-century philosophies with respect to artistic truth. Yet philosophers who agree on the propositional character of truth or on a cor-respondence criterion can disagree about whether art has truth capacities. So Table 10.1 indicates whether each philosopher ascribes truth capacities to art.[2] Also, whereas some philosophers who allow for nonpropositional truth bearers or noncorrespondence criteria do not completely reject the role of propositions and correspondence in the pursuit of truth, others re-ject one or the other of these altogether. Hence I distinguish "non" from "anti" in both the dimensions of truth theory that I have depicted.

As one sees at a glance, most of the philosophers discussed ascribe truth capacities to art in some respect. In that sense a critical hermeneutic theory such as mine does not contradict what many previous philosophers have

TABLE 10.1. *General Theories of Truth, Sustaining Positions on Artistic Truth*

	Truth Bearers		
Criterion	Propositional	Nonpropositional	Antipropositional
Correspondence	Greene (+)	Hofstadter (+)	
	Beardsley (−)		
	Wolterstorff (*)		
Noncorrespondence	Habermas (*)	Adorno (+)	Heidegger (+)
Anticorrespondence	Richards (−)	Goodman (*)	Rapaport (*)

Notes: A plus sign (+) indicates that a philosopher ascribes truth capacities to art, a minus sign (−) that the philosopher denies truth capacities to art, and an asterisk (*) that the philosopher ascribes it either with significant qualifications or only indirectly.

said. Our disagreements concern the nature of truth in general and the character of artistic truth in particular, not the question whether "artistic truth" is a meaningful or legitimate idea to begin with. But there are two important exceptions to this pattern: the emotivist attack launched by I. A. Richards in the 1920s, and the subsequent metacritical denial of artistic truth provided by Monroe Beardsley in the 1950s. Their prominence in earlier stages of Anglo-American aesthetics warranted the careful scrutiny I attempted to give these exceptions. With map in hand, let's review the dialectical twists and turns through which my own account of artistic truth has unfolded.

10.1 TRACES OF TRUTH

I began with a discussion of Beardsley, not only because of his prominence but also because his position is so provocative. His denial that artworks can be true or false aims to remove art from competition with empirical science and thereby to secure art's autonomous status on the noncognitive grounds of "aesthetic value." His general argument, which he modifies to accommodate literary works, goes like this: to be true or false, an artwork must either contain propositions or directly contribute to knowledge about reality. Since knowledge is inferential, and since artworks are neither propositional nor inferential, no artwork can be true or false: no artwork can have propositional content that either corresponds or fails to correspond to reality.

Supporting this argument is a logical empiricist epistemology according to which truth is governed by the rules of first-order logic and the principles of empirical science. On this theory, truth proper consists in the correspondence between linguistically formulated beliefs and empirically perceived facts. Words are the basic units through which such correspondence occurs, and declarative sentences that are asserted are the main vehicles of truth. Declarative sentences that are not asserted, as these occur in literary texts, can be true or false only in a derivative and incomplete sense. Truth proper attaches to linguistically stated and asserted, logically consistent, and empirically confirmed (or confirmable) beliefs or predications about features of the real world. On the basis of this propositionally inflected correspondence theory, Beardsley denies that artworks can be true or false.

Despite my reservations about Beardsley's approach, I have credited him with attempting to find a legitimate place and role for the arts in modern culture, even though he retains empirical science as the paradigm of knowledge. A contemporary and alternative theory of artistic truth would need to show how the cognitive functions of the arts are constitutive to their aesthetic worth and societal importance. It would also need to provide a different account of either truth bearers or truth criteria or both.

The alternatives considered in Chapter 2 are of two different sorts. Whereas Albert Hofstadter's existential affirmation of artistic truth employs a nonpropositional correspondence theory, Herman Rapaport's postmetaphysical deconstruction adopts an antipropositional and anticorrespondence stance. Hofstadter does not deny that propositions play a role in the pursuit of theoretical truth. But he insists that the higher bearers of truth, including artworks, are "spiritual" and not propositional. Artistic truth is "spiritual," rather than "theoretical" or "practical," in the sense that it involves a mutual conformity between intellect and thing. More specifically, the artwork manifests the truth of being by being true in its very own being. The advantage to Hofstadter's account is that it acknowledges hermeneutic continuity between propositions and artworks: like all other results of cultural endeavor, both propositions and artworks articulate human existence. The disadvantage, however, is that Hofstadter provides no art-internal ways to distinguish between truth and falsity.

With his antipropositional and anticorrespondence approach, Herman Rapaport opposes both metacritical and existential accounts of artistic truth. He dismisses any effort to restrict truth in general to empirically based assertions. He also refuses to tie artistic truth to distinctively human existence. The Western metaphysical tradition expects art to align human existence with cosmic order, he says. Since Friedrich Nietzsche, however, that expectation concerning truth in art has shattered, giving rise to the postmetaphysical perspectives of Heidegger, Levinas, and Derrida. Rapaport's deconstructive story uncovers an important metalevel in philosophical efforts to identify specific truth bearers and to articulate universal criteria of truth. At this metalevel it matters little whether a philosophy identifies the truth bearers as assertible predications (Beardsley) or existential artworks (Hofstadter), whether it restricts the criteria to logical consistency and empirical accuracy (Beardsley) or expands them to encompass all theoretical, practical, and spiritual adequation (Hofstadter). Both Beardsley and Hofstadter assume that truth is the aligning of human existence with cosmic order, even though neither one uses this terminology.

Both Beardsley and Hofstadter also regard language as the primary link in this alignment. That helps explain why their theories of language do not emphasize its role in reaching intersubjective understanding. Neither one has made the turn from a metaphysically framed and epistemic model of subject and object to a postmetaphysical and communicative model of subject and subject. Yet, by making the question of truth in art depend on particular works of art, Rapaport himself remains locked into the same epistemic model. He simply gives a very peculiar object – the artwork – the initiative that "posthumans" forfeit. Under such postmetaphysical expectations, modernist autonomism à la Beardsley and Hofstadter collapses, taking Rapaport's deconstructive efforts with it. Accordingly, my own critical hermeneutic reconstruction of artistic truth abandons the fixation on autonomous artworks and seeks to recognize the sociohistorical situatedness of both art and aesthetics.

To these ends, Chapter 3 revisits Kant's aesthetics. Kant subscribes to a propositional and correspondence theory of truth, although not of the empiricist variety embraced by Beardsley. This theory affects Kant's account of aesthetic validity, which he considers noncognitive. Whereas philosophers who share Kant's emphasis on aesthetic validity discount art's capacity for truth, philosophers who share Hegel's critique of Kant render artistic truth esoteric. Chapter 3 proposes a critical hermeneutic account of aesthetic validity that supports a nonesoteric notion of artistic truth. Reading Kant through Hegelian lenses, I reconstruct the aesthetic dimension from modern societal polarities between play and work, between entertainment and instruction, and between expression and communication. This reconstruction generates a notion of the aesthetic as the intersubjective exploration, interpretation, and presentation of aesthetic signs. Labeling such intersubjective processes "imagination," I describe aesthetic validity as a horizon of imaginative cogency. This horizon is crucial to cultural pathfinding, I argue, and so are the aesthetic validity claims raised in art talk. Implicit in my description of aesthetic validity, cultural orientation, and art talk is a nonpropositional and noncorrespondence theory of truth that takes Kant's aesthetics in a critical hermeneutic direction. Chapters 4–6 give the outlines of this theory and fill in the details to my account of artistic truth.

Chapter 4 derives a sketch of my general theory from a critical interpretation of *Being and Time*. Heidegger's book develops a nonpropositional and noncorrespondence theory of truth as disclosure. I arrive at my own alternative by testing two of Heidegger's claims: (1) that assertion (*Aussage*) is a derivative mode of interpretation, and (2) that Dasein's disclosedness (and not propositions or assertions) is the primary locus of truth. While agreeing with Heidegger that asserting is a mode of interpreting, I take issue with his description of the supposedly derivative character of assertions. Not only do already available predications shape the hermeneutic "fore-structure" on which asserting draws, but also the movement from pre-predicative interpretation to assertions is not a "leveling" but a leap. Similarly, while endorsing Heidegger's claim that the agreement between assertion and object (what I call "correctness") derives from a more comprehensive process of disclosure, I criticize how he traces this derivation. By making Dasein's disclosedness the primary locus of truth, Heidegger seems to preclude asking how Dasein's disclosedness can be either truly disclosive or false.

In response, I propose to conceive of truth as a process of life-giving disclosure, marked by human fidelity, to which a differentiated array of cultural practices and products, including art phenomena, can contribute in distinct and indispensable ways. What helps distinguish true disclosure from false is life-promoting and life-sustaining fidelity to principles that people hold in common and that hold them in common. Such fidelity must always correlate with an opening of society to let human beings and other creatures come to flourish. The pursuit of "propositional truth" is one important but limited way in which fidelity occurs. That pursuit goes astray when it disconnects from the pursuit of solidarity, justice, and other principles.

Whereas propositional truth anchors validity for many correspondence theories, it does not anchor aesthetic validity in my own account. Yet I consider aesthetic validity an important principle in modern societies and in contemporary art. This, plus my relativizing of propositional truth, raises questions about the relationship between aesthetic validity and artistic truth. Chapter 5 pursues such questions by discussing Heidegger's essay "The Origin of the Work of Art." Unlike *Being and Time*, this essay tends toward an antipropositional view of truth bearers. My discussion seeks to retrieve a conception of artistic truth for which questions of aesthetic validity remain crucial. On the one hand, I endorse Heidegger's claims that artistic truth is nonpropositional, that it occurs by way of appropriate art practices, and that in artworks it requires a unique mediatory structure. I also share his view that, by helping to disclose something other than the artwork itself, artistic truth serves to place in question the intersubjective principles and validity claims that prevail in nonartistic domains. But I criticize Heidegger for privileging art's disclosive capacities and for absorbing the question of art's validity into the question of a community's historical destiny. I take these tendencies to indicate problems in Heidegger's general conception of truth, namely its ignoring questions of validity and its absolving human beings of responsibility for pursuing validity, whether in cognition, conduct, or imagination. On my own account, truth as disclosure within art must always be related to imaginative cogency. Although not identical with disclosure in art, imaginative cogency is a principle of aesthetic validity to which any disclosive art practices must appeal. Imaginative cogency is important in nonartistic cognition and conduct as well.

Chapter 6 elaborates this account of artistic truth as imaginative disclosure. The chapter begins with Habermasian responses to Adorno's aesthetics, most of which employ a propositional view of truth bearers. By contrast,

Adorno's idea of artistic truth content (*Wahrheitsgehalt*) implies a nonpropositional view. Adorno regards truth in art as carried by sociohistorical import (*Gehalt*) that emerges from artistic production, depends on the mediation of content and form, resides in particular works, transcends them, and invites critical interpretation. Although I agree with Habermasians such as Albrecht Wellmer and Martin Seel that Adorno tends to make artistic truth esoteric, I resist their own tendency to surrender Adorno's idea of an artwork's having nonpropositional import that can be true or false.

Instead I combine Adorno's insight into artistic truth content with Habermas's insight into the differentiated character of validity claims. On this alternative, artistic truth is internal to art phenomena, as Adorno claims, but differentiated into three dimensions, in a manner reminiscent of Habermas's theory of validity. The three dimensions of artistic truth are authenticity, significance, and integrity. Whereas authenticity and significance pertain to all art phenomena in modern Western societies, integrity pertains primarily to those art products which are institutionally constituted as artworks. "Authenticity" indicates the expectation that art phenomena be true with respect to the experience or vision from which competent art making allows them to arise. Here I use "true with respect to" as equivalent to "imaginatively disclosive of." Authenticity is a matter of mediated expression that is imaginatively disclosive. "Significance" indicates the expectation that art phenomena be true with respect to a public's need for worthwhile cultural presentations. It is a matter of interpretable presentation that is imaginatively disclosive. When an art phenomenon is institutionally constituted as an artwork, however, the expectations of authenticity and significance usually accompany one about the integrity of the artwork's import. For such import to be true, the artwork must live up to its own internal demands, one of which is to live up to more than its own internal demands. "Integrity" indicates the expectation that the artwork be true with respect to its own internal demands. It is a matter of configured import that is imaginatively (self-)disclosive.

These dimensions all occur within the horizon of imaginative cogency as a principle of aesthetic validity. They also support pursuits of cultural orientation, opening our personal and social worlds to ones we do not currently inhabit. This, in turn, allows art conversation to make art's truth dimensions available for art discourse. The final section of Chapter 6 explores loosely dyadic links between artistic truth and conversational validity claims: between artistic authenticity and expressive sincerity, between artistic significance and normative legitimacy, and between artistic integrity and propositional truth. Thanks to these links, imaginative disclosure is neither esoteric (Adorno) nor peripheral (Habermas). Elaborated at greater length, my account of artistic truth would offer a different perspective on propositional truth, both by tying it more closely to imaginative disclosure than standard truth theories allow and by indicating truth itself to be a multidimensional idea whose reduction to propositional truth bearers and correspondence criteria leads to theoretical impoverishment and practical dead ends. The result of such an elaboration would be a nonpropositional and noncorrespondence theory of truth in general that, while indebted to Heidegger, Adorno, and Habermas, addresses the concerns and objections of propositionally inflected correspondence theories.

Chapters 7–9 test my account by using it to sort out Anglo-American debates about the idea of artistic truth. The "logical positivist dispute" discussed in Chapter 7 occurs between an emotivist, who has a more or less propositional view of truth bearers but strongly opposes a correspondence criterion, and a propositionist, who employs a propositionally inflected correspondence theory. I. A. Richards thinks the arts epitomize an "emotive language" that has no cognitive function. Theodore Meyer Greene, by contrast, presents art as a cognitive enterprise whose propositional content can be either true or false. Problems and potentials occur on each side of this debate.

Richards's denial of artistic truth requires two problematic moves: his equating propositions with references, and his treating references as causal. The first is problematic because the concept of "reference" he employs is too broad to serve as a notion of linguistic reference. The second move is problematic because it equates linguistic referring with mental stirring. Richards fails to distinguish between the illocutionary force and perlocutionary effects of ordinary language usage. Only because of these problematic moves in his philosophy of language can Richards reduce art to a noncognitive instrument of attitudinal adjustment. Yet he has noticed the role of artistic intentions and interpretive needs in the recognition of artistic truth. My own accounts of "authenticity" and "significance" highlight these factors, which Richards emotivistically misconstrues.

Greene's affirmation of artistic truth also requires two problematic moves, namely, a failure to distinguish propositions from meaning, and a tendency to equate an artwork's import with the artist's cognitive intention. Greene's failure to distinguish propositions from meaning stems from a mistaken view of both propositions and meaning as discrete units of predicable insight that, once expressed, exist independently of the medium in which they are expressed. The tendency to equate import with intention stems from Greene's view of art making as permanently injecting such units of predicable insight into a material artifact by formal means. What Greene recognizes is the "aboutness" of artistic import and the legitimate expectation of integrity. These factors his propositionism misconstrues.

On my own account, artistic import is the complex meaning an artwork makes available by calling attention to the peculiar doubling of its own presentation. The truth or falsity of such import will involve (1) the artwork's peculiarly doubled (self-)disclosure, (2) the imaginative cogency of the artwork's structure and (self-)reference, and (3) a potential contribution to pursuing cultural orientation. Eliminating any one factor would result in a truncated notion of integrity. Hence the aboutness of artistic import, which propositionists emphasize and emotivists ignore, is not the aboutness of propositions and predicate expressions. Rather it is the aboutness of artistic structures and aesthetic signs. The fact that an artwork seldom has a single "referent" does not mean that the artwork is not about anything. But neither does the fact that artworks are about something mean that they express propositions. Both emotivism and propositionism are inadequate positions concerning artistic truth. It appears that both correspondence and anticorrespondence theories of truth fail in this regard, so long as they maintain a propositional view of truth bearers.

The next debate tests this assessment. Although primarily ontological rather than epistemological, the debate between Nelson Goodman and Nicholas Wolterstorff pits a nonpropositional anticorrespondence theory of truth against a propositionally inflected correspondence theory. Whereas Goodman's nominalist ontology of art as a symbol system rejects emotivism à la I. A. Richards, Wolterstorff's realist ontology of art as a field of action rejects propositionism à la T. M. Greene, but without embracing Beardsley's denial of artistic truth. Chapters 8 and 9 demonstrate that Goodman and Wolterstorff disagree on whether propositions are the locus of truth and whether correspondence governs art's cognitive functions.

Unlike Wolterstorff, Goodman has a negative response to both questions. As Chapter 8 shows, Goodman's *Languages of Art* demotes propositions as truth bearers and doubts that correspondence governs art's cognitive functions. This allows him to wrest "representation" and "expression" from the grip of correspondence theories and to give these concepts an insightful new account. In fact, Goodman argues that the primary purpose for using aesthetic symbols is cognitive. This implies, he says, that scientific truth and its "aesthetic counterpart" should be regarded as "appropriateness under different names."

In thus according legitimacy and worth to aesthetic cognition, however, Goodman raises two obstacles to a theory of artistic truth, namely, his ignoring artistic integrity and his misconstruing artistic significance. The first obstacle stems from Goodman's not accounting for the aboutness of symbols, whether these be propositional or not. Liberating truth from its propositional cage allows him to ascribe truth to art phenomena. But what he ascribes is not the truth of artistic import. Instead he ascribes ethical or instrumental capacities: rightness of fit, propriety, and the like. The second obstacle stems from Goodman's manner of questioning whether correspondence governs art's cognitive functions. Although his notion of "appropriateness" suggests that significance is important to artistic truth, Goodman limits art's cognitive functions to creating, refining, and recreating the subject's perceptual and conceptual capacities. They do not include art's ability to address a public's needs and aspirations. So he does not really account for significance. Nor is this surprising, given his inattention to import.

If my own account of artistic truth is correct, then questions about the significance of artworks necessarily lead to questions of integrity, just as interpretations of an artwork's import necessarily guide interpretations of a public's interpretive needs in relationship to the artwork. By disclosing a postsubjective world in disclosing itself, an artwork uncovers facets of its interpreters' situation. An artwork challenges interpreters to come to terms with interpretive needs in the social world they inhabit. Hence, to appropriate Goodman's phrase, artworks are "ways of worldmaking." But the significance expected of artworks cannot be equated with Goodman's "appropriateness." It involves a crossing of worlds rather than the mere making or rendering of a world. In expecting significance we open ourselves to having the artwork's import conflict with our own interpretive needs, to having the work's postsubjective world and our own social world disagree, and to having this call for changes in the social world.

Nicholas Wolterstorff, by contrast, does pay attention to this crossing of worlds, but within a realist ontology that renders the artwork's import an inactual "world of the work." His *Works and Worlds of Art* construes mimesis as an action of fictive world projection that pervades the arts. Chapter 9 argues that this construal, so much at odds with Goodman's account of "aesthetic cognition," implies a propositionally inflected and realist correspondence theory of truth. On Wolterstorff's theory, a world projection can be true *iff* it is assertive and it introduces states of affairs that obtain. The primary relata in this correspondence are the action of assertive world projection and the obtaining of certain states of affairs. He claims that artworks primarily function within nonassertive world projection, however, and they primarily introduce states of affairs that do not obtain. In that sense, artworks or their import cannot be true (or false) about anything: fictive world projection involves correspondence without truth. Yet Wolterstorff says that what the artist presents can be true to actuality. This claim introduces puzzles concerning the relationship between "truth-to" and "truth-about."

Chapter 9 explores two problems in this connection, namely, a divorce between artistic import and "truth-about," and inattention to authenticity as a dimension of artistic truth. The first problem stems, I argue, from Wolterstorff's treating artworks as "norm-kinds," from his proposing an all-too-expansive account of propositions, and from his having an undertheorized notion of intentionality. The second problem arises from his bipartite theory of "action-generation," coupled with a correspondence theory of the relation between artistic import (the "world of the work") and the artist's experience or vision (the artist's "states of self" or "states of consciousness"). These problems lead me to question the art-theoretical fruitfulness of a realist ontology that distinguishes actual, possible, and impossible worlds and regards artistic import as a segment of one or another of these worlds. While

I agree with Wolterstorff that art allows for the crossing of worlds, I regard all the worlds being crossed – personal, social, and postsubjective – as actual. Or, to modify Goodman's terminology, they are all versions of the actual world, and they are all of them dynamic rather than static.

I conclude that a realist and propositionally inflected correspondence theory of truth has difficulty with the hermeneutic character of art making and art experience. With regard specifically to art making, I consider art products, including artworks, to be mediated expressions that can be more or less authentic. People in modern Western societies expect art products to be imaginatively disclosive of the experience or vision from which competent art making allows them to arise. This implies that artists do not simply have certain states that they then use artworks to disclose. Nor do audiences or publics properly interpret an artwork when they use it as a window to the artist's supposed states of self or states of consciousness. Rather, both art making and art appreciation are hermeneutic processes of discovery, interpretation, and presentation. In these processes the "agents" themselves have new experiences and revise their previous self-understandings. Wolterstorff's theory of action neglects precisely those hermeneutically generative activities which are central to art making and which inform the expectation of authenticity.

Hence my assessment of Anglo-American debates shows that emotivists, propositionists, nominalists, and realists all draw attention to various aspects of artistic truth. None of them, however, proposes a sufficiently comprehensive and critically hermeneutic approach. Emotivists and nominalists do not account for the integrity of artistic import. Propositionists and realists provide such an account, but at the expense of art's nonpropositional character. Of the theories considered, Wolterstorff's realist theory of fictive world projection comes closest to giving an adequate account of significance as a dimension of artistic truth. But it neglects authenticity.

As an alternative, I regard authenticity, significance, and integrity as intersecting dimensions of artistic truth. The expectation of integrity is more prominent for artworks than it is for other art phenomena. Yet all three dimensions involve "truth with respect to" rather than either "truth-about" or "truth-to." In modern Western societies we expect art phenomena to be true with respect to the artist's experience or vision, with respect to a public's need for worthwhile cultural presentations, and with respect to an artwork's own internal demands. In other words, we expect art phenomena to be imaginatively disclosive in all three dimensions, and especially in the dimensions of authenticity and significance when the phenomena are not institutionally constituted as artworks.

This account of artistic truth requires an ontology that is neither nominalist nor realist with respect to what exists. It also requires an epistemology that is neither conventionalist nor intentionalist with respect to what makes something true. My account refuses to reduce truth to appropriateness or to deny the legitimate but limited role of assertions in discovering and articulating truth. But it also refuses to limit "truth-about" to asserted propositions or to reduce artistic import to propositional content. A critical hermeneutic approach employs a different general theory of truth, one in which asserted propositions are not privileged truth bearers and the relation between propositions and facts or states of affairs is not the supreme measure of truth. Being, like Adorno's, a nonpropositional and noncorrespondence theory, but not an antipropositional or anticorrespondence theory, this general theory can do justice to the creativity and intersubjectivity that characterize artistic truth. To arrive at such a theory, one cannot remain bound by continental divides. One must transform the maps of philosophical aesthetics.

10.2 FOOTPRINTS IN THE SAND

Upon crossing the divides within philosophy proper, one can see more clearly the societal landscape beyond. My discussion of artistic truth, although focused on technical debates about language, truth, and validity, has had a larger purpose. I have tried to articulate and test an idea of artistic truth that helps illuminate the contemporary cultural scene. In philosophical terms, my account attempts to shed light on art's aesthetic worth and societal importance in Western countries today. If the two cultural orientations most obfuscating in this regard during the 1950s were what Monroe Beardsley calls "aestheticism" and "moralism," then their counterparts a half century later might well be anti-aestheticism with respect to the arts and nihilism with respect to society in general. Describing these newer positions, and arguing against them, would require a full-fledged social theory of the arts, which I plan to provide in a companion volume. But let me conclude the current discussion by outlining some implications of my idea of artistic truth for what Beardsley calls "The Arts in the Life of Man [*sic*]."[3]

Despite my objections to Beardsley's metacritical denial of "artistic truth," I share his intuition that the arts, as they have developed in the West, have both aesthetic worth and societal importance. I also agree with Beardsley, and with Adorno, that the societal importance of the arts depends to a notable degree on their aesthetic worth. Our disagreements stem from differing accounts about what art is like and how its aesthetic worth arises. Those differences, combined with fundamental disagreements in epistemology and philosophy of language, result in diametrically opposed positions on the question of artistic truth. Whereas I insist that imaginative disclosure, in the dimensions of authenticity, significance, and integrity, is constitutive for art's aesthetic worth and societal importance, Beardsley denies artistic truth in order to preserve art's aesthetic worth and societal importance. His argument goes like this. Because the primary value of artworks lies in the aesthetic experiences they afford, and because their capacity to generate aesthetic experiences is independent of whatever minimal cognitive capacity they might possess, a capacity for artistic truth is not essential to their aesthetic worth. Indeed, nonliterary artworks are not even capable of artistic truth. Further, art's societal importance resides in "the capacity of aesthetic objects to produce good inherent effects – that is, to produce desirable effects by means of the aesthetic experience they evoke."[4] Because this capacity is neither cognitive nor dependent on cognition, a capacity for artistic truth is not essential to art's societal importance.

In line with this argument, Beardsley mentions seven good "inherent effects" that "we might say" artworks produce by means of aesthetic experience:[5] (1) relieving psychic tensions and quieting destructive impulses, (2) resolving conflicts within the self and creating harmony there, (3) refining perception and discrimination of aesthetic qualities,[6] (4) developing imagination and empathy, (5) helping prevent common neuroses and psychoses, (6) fostering mutual sympathy and understanding by drawing people together in their aesthetic experiences, and (7) offering an "ideal for human life," namely, one of "richness and joy."[7] Two features strike me in this list. First, with the possible exceptions of the sixth and seventh "effects," all pertain to the inner life of individual subjects. Second, again with the same possible exceptions, it is not readily apparent how these effects would give the arts an important role in society. For one can easily imagine a society in which many individuals regularly experience such intrasubjective effects, and yet ecological violence, economic injustice, and racism prevail. Not even aesthetically fostering mutual sympathy and offering an ideal of richness and joy would counter such life-destroying tendencies, so long as these effects remain within the province of individual psychology. Beardsley's account of art's societal importance cannot bridge the gap between individual psychology and societal structures. His account of aesthetic experience lacks sufficient underpinnings in social theory, and the philosophical anthropology behind his account minimizes the social, historical, and hermeneutical character of life and experience. His underlying assumption that certain experiences have causal "effects" on the individual psyche, while consistent with behaviorist elements in his theory of language, simply ignores the societal constitution of human existence.

Such limitations to philosophical accounts of aesthetic experience have helped prompt an anti-aesthetic stance among contemporary artists and cultural theorists who wish art to help transform society, and not simply to enrich individual experience. I see little prospect for resisting anti-aestheticism if one conceives aesthetic experience as primarily individual and perceptual and locates art's societal importance primarily in psychic "effects." My alternative is to conceive the aesthetic as societally framed and intersubjective processes in which people together create, explore, and present aesthetic signs. While such processes require individual agents and perceptual capacities, the processes themselves are intrinsically hermeneutical and historical.

They involve the interpretation of signs within a specific context. Moreover, when these processes occur within art, they normally involve the conversation and discourse I label "art talk." In that sense there is no linguistically and conceptually unmediated aesthetic experience of artworks that could then have some direct "effect" on an individual's prelinguistic and preconceptual emotions, dispositions, and character. Yet this does not imply that our imaginative engagements with art phenomena are simply linguistic and conceptual, nor that they are simply relative to a historical situation. For our imaginative engagements appeal to a distinct principle of validity, which I have labeled "imaginative cogency," and they contribute to a search for orientation that always pushes the boundaries of the specific situation in which they occur. This appeal and this pushing of boundaries enable the arts to be sites of imaginative disclosure.

Accordingly my objections to Beardsley's denial of artistic truth are not simply a semantic dispute. His defenders might think this. They might say my idea of artistic truth simply incorporates the "good effects" that Beardsley attributes to aesthetic experience, but otherwise our stances do not differ substantively concerning the aesthetic worth and the societal importance of the arts. Hence in the end his denial and my affirmation of artistic truth come down to the same position.[8] Although such a convergence would be remarkable, given the differences in our general conceptions of language and truth, the Beardsleyan reply merits consideration. For I do agree with him that the societal importance of the arts depends to a notable degree on their aesthetic worth. But he would not agree with me that their aesthetic worth is itself societally constituted, and that the aesthetic dimension to which such worth attaches is historical and hermeneutical through and through.

On my own account, the aesthetic worth of the arts, as these have taken shape in modern Western societies, resides in their providing dedicated societal sites for imaginatively pursuing cultural orientation and for raising and testing aesthetic validity claims. This is quite a different way to describe aesthetic worth from saying that the value of the arts lies in their affording aesthetic experiences of a noncognitive sort. My description emphasizes hermeneutic and interactive projects rather than individual perceptions. And intersubjective expectations concerning the authenticity, significance, and integrity of art phenomena – the dimensions of artistic truth – are intrinsic to the way people carry out such projects. Moreover, such aesthetic worth contributes to art's societal importance, not because individual aesthetic experiences produce good psychological effects, but because intersubjective imaginative processes within the arts both complement and disrupt other societally constituted sites in which cultural orientation occurs and validity claims arise and get tested. The modern sciences are one such site. Beardsley aims to separate the arts and sciences, assigning aesthetic worth to one site and truth to the other, in air-tight compartments. By contrast, I have attempted, like Goodman, to indicate a deeper continuity between the two; like Wolterstorff, to preserve their discontinuity; and, like Adorno and Heidegger, to see their conflicts as part of a larger sociohistorical struggle.

At the heart of this struggle is a striving for truth, to which both art and science can contribute. This striving is not simply the scientific endeavor to pursue empirical accuracy, logical consistency, and propositional correctness. Rather it is a striving for that fidelity to principles and that creaturely flourishing to which science can contribute and from which it receives its societal purpose. As John Dewey saw, the arts have a similar societal purpose, even though their modern trajectory makes their contribution primarily nonpropositional. The arts and sciences are contemporary societal sites for the ongoing process of life-giving disclosure. One site is more imaginative, and the other more propositional, but both are clearings in which a sociohistorical struggle for truth can occur.

But this does not imply that whatever occurs in these sites is true, or that no other sites are needed. Within the site called art we regularly find products and events that lack authenticity and significance. We find artworks that lack integrity. We find art phenomena that fall short of the principle of imaginative cogency. In these art-internal ways, a site for imaginative disclosure can also be a site of closure, and the process of life-giving disclosure can be blocked. So too, in their many interlinkages and overlappings with other sites, the arts can support untruth: by providing ideological support for imperialist regimes, for example, or by furthering patterns of economic injustice. And these other sites can block imaginative disclosure in the arts: by reducing art phenomena to mere propaganda, for example, or by turning artworks into hypercommodities. Their being a site for imaginative disclosure does not exempt the arts from hard questions about their actual role in the pursuit of solidarity and justice. Nor can such questions receive answers in the abstract and for all time. For the questions themselves arise within a specific societal formation that could change.

In the end, such questions provide the societal point to a theory of artistic truth. At a strictly disciplinary level the debate about artistic truth is a philosophers' dispute over characterizing and explaining aesthetics, discourse, and imaginative disclosure. At a metadisciplinary level, however, where philosophy remains part of a society-wide conversation, the issues are ones of life and death. At this metalevel philosophers need to do more than change the topic of conversation among their professional peers.[9] They also need to enter ongoing public conversations about societal change. They need to enter conversations about shifts in societal patterns, about the direction these shifts take, and about the degree to which the shifts can engender life-giving disclosure. The divisions of labor within philosophy itself, and between philosophy and other societal sites of disclosure, including the arts, are not least among the continental divides this book points across, from within the terrain of philosophy itself.

Contemporary artists sense keenly the need for such border crossings. Near the end of her dystopian novel *Oryx and Crake*, Margaret Atwood describes a new day for Snowman, possibly the last human survivor of a globe-encircling ecological catastrophe. On this day he will see new human footprints in the sand:

Snowman wakes before dawn. He lies unmoving, listening to the tide coming in, wish-wash, wish-wash, the rhythm of heartbeat. He would so like to believe he is still asleep.

On the eastern horizon there's a greyish haze, lit now with a rosy, deadly glow. Strange how that colour still seems tender. He gazes at it with rapture; there is no other word for it. *Rapture.* The heart seized, carried away, as if by some large bird of prey. After everything that's happened, how can the world still be so beautiful? Because it is. From the offshore towers come the avian shrieks and cries that sound like nothing human.[10]

In three words within a tightly knit passage, the novel voices the conundrum of why suffering gives rise to hope, why survivors refuse to let destruction have the final word, why the struggle for a better future is meaningful when all empirical evidence suggests otherwise: "Because it is." The conundrum redoubles with the ambiguity of bird cries that "sound like nothing human" – nothing so destructive as human beings? Nothing so enraptured as Snowman's heart? Without moralistic gestures, and without anti-aesthetic sleight-of-hand, the novel addresses this conundrum to the reader and invites an imaginative response. Coming where it does, this passage suggests why a new theory of artistic truth is needed to do justice to the arts in their contemporary institutional settings. We need a theory that recognizes how a novel like Margaret Atwood's, which ranges across topics of science, commerce, and genetic engineering that would have been inconceivable in nineteenth-century novels, helps its readers raise questions that contemporary politicians and economists would rather have us forget.

A brilliantly illuminated sculpture stands on nine blocks of wood in the center of an artist-run gallery in Toronto. It is opening night for a three-woman show on loss and retrieval titled *Speak on Memory*. People crowd around the sculpture but keep their distance, struck by its stark complexity. A young corkscrew willow has been cut off before it could flourish, its dead leaves removed, its bare branches disassembled. Now it stands forcibly reconstructed, twisting within and through a skeletal cage of whittled maple translucently twined. The willow's branches, their ends carved into spears, have been rejoined with sharp wooden rivets into the simulacrum of a tree. Snakelike, they writhe through each other as their trunk stands rootless in a nest made from tiny interlaced twigs. The nest lies on a bed of pointed lateral branches arranged in two crosswise layers. Cemented sand fills the nest, blasted soil where something once grew. Graying rocks, circling the tree trunk like petrified eggs, are all that remains. The gnarled but youthful branches of this caged and nested and refabricated tree spiral upward toward an elevation they will never reach. The piece, by Joyce Recker, is titled *Earth's Lament.*

Why does the sculpture so visibly move its public on this occasion, calling its attention and prompting conversation? It makes no direct statement and asserts no propositions. Yet it offers more than an innovative treatment of nontraditional materials that, under proper lighting and in the right space, creates wonderful juxtapositions of angles and curves, of light and shadow, of the found and the fabricated. It is simultaneously an open-ended metaphor for hope amid loss, for renewal amid destruction. And the import it offers comes through the sculpture's own imaginative and self-referential structure, even as it testifies to the artist's vision of art and life and interacts with a public's need for echoes of earth's lament. The piece is a work of imaginative disclosure, one that can meet the multidimensional expectation of artistic truth.

To these examples, one from literature and the other from visual art, one could add many of the collaborative and interventionist projects that make up "new genre public art."[11] Such contemporary artists may not use the technical vocabulary I have proposed. They may not talk about their efforts as imaginative attempts to foster life-giving disclosure. They may not even speak of the authenticity, significance, and integrity for which their projects strive. Yet they clearly seek ways in which their publics can pursue cultural orientation through interactively creating, exploring, and presenting aesthetic signs. Nor would they find it odd for their publics to ask the question they ask themselves: how can art products and events disrupt destructive patterns and promote worthwhile transformation in society? For them, as for philosophers who care about the future, the link between art and truth remains an urgent and protean question. It is the question why aesthetic worth is societally important. It is the question whether authenticity, significance, and integrity are necessary for the pursuit of solidarity and justice. It is the question how imagination can contribute to the historical opening of societal blockades. Indeed, it is a question of artistic truth.

Notes

Introduction: Critical Hermeneutics

1. Immanuel Kant, *Critique of Pure Reason*, trans. Norman Kemp Smith, unabridged ed. (New York: St. Martin's Press; Toronto: Macmillan, 1929), p. 97, A 57–8/B 82.

2. My use of the label "postmetaphysical" stems from recent Critical Theory. See, for example, Jürgen Habermas's *The Philosophical Discourse of Modernity: Twelve Lectures* (1985), trans. Frederick Lawrence (Cambridge, Mass.: MIT Press, 1987), and *Postmetaphysical Thinking: Philosophical Essays* (1988), trans. William Mark Hohengarten (Cambridge, Mass.: MIT Press, 1992); also Albrecht Wellmer's *The Persistence of Modernity: Essays on Aesthetics, Ethics, and Postmodernism*, trans. David Midgley (Cambridge, Mass.: MIT Press, 1991), and *Endgames: The Irreconcilable Nature of Modernity; Essays and Lectures*, trans. David Midgley (Cambridge, Mass.: MIT Press, 1998). Philosophers oriented to American neopragmatism or French poststructuralism might label the current paradigm differently, or they might dispute the assumption that there is a paradigm in which the various strands of contemporary philosophy converge.

3. Lambert Zuidervaart, "Postmodern Arts and the Birth of a Democratic Culture," in *The Arts, Community and Cultural Democracy*, ed. Lambert Zuidervaart and Henry Luttikhuizen (London: Macmillan Press; New York: St. Martin's Press, 2000), pp. 15–39.

4. The assumption that one must recast philosophical theories to address recent developments in the arts seems not to be shared by James Young, whose book on closely related topics arrived too late for me to discuss it here. Although Young and I both argue that the arts have cognitive functions, and we both take issue with propositional theories (e.g., T. M. Greene's) and exemplificational theories (e.g., Nelson Goodman's) of these functions, our background theories of both knowledge and art differ in significant ways. This can be seen from the fact that Young provides no account of truth in art, and he regards avant-garde art as cognitively deficient and therefore as either bad art or not art at all. See James O. Young, *Art and Knowledge* (London: Routledge, 2001).

5. Here I use "linguistic turn" in an expansive sense to include the later Heidegger, the later Wittgenstein, Gadamer, and Adorno (whom I consider half-turned) as

well as structuralism, poststructuralism, analytic philosophy after World War II, postanalytic philosophy, and most versions of feminist philosophy. I do not mean to suggest that topics such as mimesis or expression have fallen out of fashion – see, for example, Kendall L. Walton, *Mimesis as Make-Believe: On the Foundations of the Representational Arts* (Cambridge, Mass.: Harvard University Press, 1990), and Stephen Davies, *Musical Meaning and Expression* (Ithaca: Cornell University Press, 1994). Rather, these chestnuts of philosophical aesthetics now get roasted over a fire that feeds upon the linguistic mediation of art and aesthetic experience.

6. Posing the question in this second way allows one to connect Anglo-American philosophers such as Susanne K. Langer and Nelson Goodman with the German philosophers Hans-Georg Gadamer and Theodor W. Adorno, despite discontinuities between their intellectual traditions and strong contrasts in how each figure relates art and language. Adrienne Dengerink Chaplin makes astute comparisons between Langer and Goodman on this topic in her doctoral dissertation "Mind, Body and Art: The Problem of Meaning in the Cognitive Aesthetics of Susanne K. Langer" (Vrije Universiteit, Amsterdam, 1999).

7. Stephen Kinzer, "Merely 91 Years after Dying, Mahler Finally Hits His Stride," *New York Times*, January 17, 2002, pp. B1–2.

8. Ibid.

9. An excellent introduction to such theories in Anglo-American philosophy is by Richard L. Kirkham, *Theories of Truth: A Critical Introduction* (Cambridge, Mass.: MIT Press, 1992). Kirkham claims that "a failure to grasp the big picture about truth is the root cause of many philosophical mistakes" (p. ix). For an introductory treatment that gives greater attention to continental philosophy, see Barry Allen, *Truth in Philosophy* (Cambridge, Mass.: Harvard University Press, 1993).

10. See Kirkham, *Theories of Truth*, pp. 54–72; the quotations are from pp. 54 and 59. Kirkham does explore possible worlds in which teddy bears and flowers can be bearers of truth, but the teddy bears in his thought experiment function as linguistic objects, and the flowers seem to function as propositions; see pp. 61–3.

11. Kirkham points out that there is considerable confusion in the literature concerning the "nature" and "existence" of propositions. His own stipulated definition of a proposition is "the informational content of a complete sentence in the declarative mood" and "the thing named by the noun clause of statements predicating mental attitudes" (ibid., p. 57).

12. I owe this version of the approach to suggestions from Del Ratzsch, my former colleague in philosophy at Calvin College.

13. Kirkham, *Theories of Truth*, p. 70, describing a thesis that he rejects on pp. 69–72 and 329–39.

14. I summarize Adorno's idea in Chapter 6. For details, see Lambert Zuidervaart, *Adorno's Aesthetic Theory: The Redemption of Illusion* (Cambridge, Mass.: MIT Press, 1991).

15. I say "roughly" because truth theorists disagree about what they are trying to accomplish and have differing views concerning what can count as a theory of truth.

16. Kirkham, *Theories of Truth,* pp. 119–73.

17. "Opponents" appears in quotation marks because the differences between the two sides do not receive straightforward articulation in formal debates. In fact, Richards and Goodman both proposed their alternative accounts prior to the formulations by Greene and Wolterstorff. I have reconstructed the differences as "debates" in Chapters 1, 2, and 7–9.

18. Art's thoroughly hermeneutic character is the correct conclusion of Margolis's argument that artworks are "cultural entities" having an "Intentional structure." I do not agree with every consequence he would draw from this characterization, however. See Joseph Margolis, *What, after All, Is a Work of Art? Lectures in the Philosophy of Art* (University Park: Pennsylvania State University Press, 1999).

19. My reasons for thus distinguishing artworks from other art products are explained in Lambert Zuidervaart, "Fantastic Things: Critical Notes toward a Social Ontology of the Arts," *Philosophia Reformata* 60 (1995): 37–54. For an analysis of the institutional constitution of musical products as works of art, see Lydia Goehr, *The Imaginary Museum of Musical Works: An Essay in the Philosophy of Music* (Oxford: Clarendon Press, 1992).

20. For a complementary account of the same historical complex, see Anthony J. Cascardi, *Consequences of Enlightenment* (Cambridge: Cambridge University Press, 1999). Unlike Cascardi, I do not equate aesthetic validity with the intensity of feeling or affect.

21. I plan to develop a general theory of truth in a subsequent volume.

22. Lambert Zuidervaart, "Creative Border Crossing in New Public Culture," in *Literature and the Renewal of the Public Sphere,* ed. Susan VanZanten Gallagher and Mark D. Walhout (London: Macmillan Press; New York: St. Martin's Press, 2000), pp. 206–24.

23. Here "philosophy of discourse" encompasses theories of language, theories of interpretation, and theories of information and communication.

24. My implied social theory of art will be elaborated in a companion volume tentatively titled *Art Matters: Politics, Economics, and New Public Culture.* That volume will seek to counter recent anti-aesthetic rhetoric but without surrendering democratic aims. Its concerns resemble those expressed by Isobel Armstrong, *The Radical Aesthetic* (Oxford: Blackwell, 2000). Armstrong's leading question is: "What would be a radical reading of the aesthetic appropriate to a democratic politics and responsive to questions of gender?" (p. 56).

25. I borrow here from Habermas's excellent diagnosis of this shift, which appears in the best tradition-crossing collection of reflections by contemporary Western philosophers on the state of their discipline. See Jürgen Habermas, "Philosophy as Stand-In and Interpreter," in *After Philosophy: End or Transformation?,* ed. Kenneth Baynes, James Bohman, and Thomas McCarthy (Cambridge, Mass.: MIT Press, 1987), pp. 296–315. The same essay introduces Habermas's *Moral Consciousness and Communicative Action,* trans. Christian Lenhardt and Shierry Weber Nicholsen (Cambridge, Mass.: MIT Press, 1990), pp. 1–20. Habermas's essay opens with words I echo at the outset: "Master thinkers have fallen on hard times."

26. See my essay "The Great Turning Point: Religion and Rationality in Dooyeweerd's Transcendental Critique," *Faith and Philosophy* (January 2004), in press.

27. Both methodologically and theoretically this approach has much in common with the reformulation of Critical Theory in the book from which I borrow the phrase "critical hermeneutics." See Hans Herbert Kögler, *The Power of Dialogue: Critical Hermeneutics after Gadamer and Foucault*, trans. Paul Hendrickson (Cambridge, Mass.: MIT Press, 1996).

Chapter 1: Beardsley's Denial

1. Monroe Beardsley, *Aesthetics: Problems in the Philosophy of Criticism* (New York: Harcourt, Brace & World, 1958), p. 391; hereafter cited internally by page number. Occasionally I note the refinements Beardsley gives in "Postscript 1980 – Some Old Problems in New Perspectives," in the book's second edition (Indianapolis: Hackett, 1981), pp. xvii–lxiv. This postscript does not change his argument about artistic truth.

2. Joseph Margolis, "The Eclipse and Recovery of Analytic Aesthetics," in *Analytic Aesthetics*, ed. Richard Shusterman (Oxford: Basil Blackwell, 1989), pp. 161–89.

3. Beardsley qualifies this denial with reference to literary works, as we shall see.

4. This is the title to section 4 in Beardsley's "Postscript 1980." Section 4 indicates a new appreciation for speech-act theories of language, but it retains the account of meaning and metaphor given in the 1958 edition, with two exceptions: (1) Beardsley now acknowledges that "the meaning of a metaphorical word cannot be limited to its pre-existing connotations" (p. xxxiv), and (2) he admits that "logical incompatibility" cannot explain all metaphors, especially not metaphors that are denials of metaphors, such as "Marriage is no bed of roses" (p. xxxv).

5. The semantic aspect of meaning must be read into Beardsley's one-sentence summary of his conception: "The meaning of a linguistic expression, then, is its capacity to formulate, to give evidence of, beliefs" (p. 118). Taken out of context, this summary would immediately raise questions about the apparent equation of *formulating* beliefs with *evidencing* beliefs and the apparent collapse of semantic into syntactic or pragmatic considerations.

6. In a subsequent chapter on "Form in Literature" (chap. 5), Beardsley describes discourse more expansively as "a connected utterance in which something is being said by somebody about something" (pp. 237–8).

7. Beardsley (pp. 116n2, 147) acknowledges his debt to the causal account of meaning in chapter 3 of Charles L. Stevenson's *Ethics and Language* (New Haven: Yale University Press, 1944), and Stevenson's preface thanks Beardsley for "many profitable discussions" (p. viii).

8. "Sign" is an undefined term Stevenson seems to borrow from Charles W. Morris. See Stevenson, *Ethics and Language*, p. 42n3.

9. Ibid., p. 61.

10. Ibid., p. 70.

11. According to Stevenson, signs can have emotive meaning that is not a function of their descriptive meaning "but either persists without the latter or survives changes in it" (ibid., p. 72). Beardsley also rejects Stevenson's account of metaphor (and, by extension, of poetry) as involving an unusual relation between emotive and descriptive meaning. Compare Stevenson, ibid., pp. 73–6 and Beardsley, pp. 119–22, 147–8. In Chapter 7 I discuss the linguistic

theory of I. A. Richards, whose distinction between "emotive" and "symbolic" uses of words Stevenson and Beardsley assume and criticize, each in his own way.

12. Beardsley distinguishes within literary criticism among "explication" (determining the contextual meaning of a group of words), "elucidation" (filling out the characters, actions, and settings in the world of the work), and "interpretation" (determining the theme [general idea] and the thesis [ideological content] of a literary work). Interpretation presupposes explication and elucidation. It seeks "to determine the themes and theses of a literary work, given the contextual meanings of the words and a complete description of the world of the work" (p. 403).

13. Beardsley's first argument against literary-critical relativism – namely, that connotations of words are "objective parts" of their meanings and "a function" of the words' designations – is tantalizingly brief. It raises more questions than it answers. Most of these questions go back to his underlying ambivalence as to whether meaning is primarily sentence- or word-dependent and whether (behavioral) belief conveyance or (semantic) reference is the core of linguistic meaning.

14. Actually, chapter 8 is not clear about which question it addresses. Among the most likely candidates would be (1) whether paintings and musical compositions can *be* true or false, (2) whether they can be *considered* true or false, and (3) whether they can *properly be called* true or false. I interpret the chapter as addressing the first of these questions.

15. Here is Beardsley's formulation of the third rule: "Let us agree that truth involves a correspondence of something to reality, but let us not smuggle any assumptions about the *nature* of that reality into our definition of 'truth.' A person who believes that 'The soul is immortal' is true, and 'Grass is green' is true, is at liberty to say that souls and grass are different sorts of being, but not that the word 'true' is used in different senses" (p. 368).

16. "Postscript 1980" refines Beardsley's account of visual depiction, in response to Nelson Goodman's argument that similarity is not necessary for pictorial representation. Now Beardsley says that depicting "involves selective similarity:... the depicting surface has some visual features that match distinguishing, characteristic, telling features of objects of a certain kind – a car-shape, however distorted, for example" (pp. xxxvii–xxxviii).

17. Contrast this with the synonyms "discover," "disclose," "divulge," "tell," and "betray" and the three meanings suggested by *Webster's Ninth New Collegiate Dictionary* (1988): (1) "to make known through divine inspiration," (2) "to make (something secret or hidden) publicly or generally known," and (3) "to open up to view: display." What Beardsley's idiosyncratic stipulation reveals, in his sense, is the empiricistic and scientistic paradigm of knowledge that he begins to spell out many pages later.

18. The universals Beardsley discusses include sense qualities, "human regional qualities," essential qualities, and recurrent qualities.

19. Here Beardsley follows John Hospers, who himself cites Moritz Schlick and C. I. Lewis. Compare Beardsley, pp. 382–3, 396, with John Hospers, *Meaning and Truth in the Arts* (Chapel Hill: University of North Carolina Press, 1946; reprint, Hamden, Conn.: Archon Books, 1964), pp. 233–8.

20. A similar scientism, even more baldly stated, informs Hospers's Schlickian rejection of "knowledge by acquaintance": "The one is knowledge about things, the other is immediate acquaintance with them; the one is given *par excellence* by science, the other by art. When we hear music, we have deeper, richer acquaintance, not knowledge – it is not the function of music to give us that. When the arts give us knowledge, they do so only incidentally.... [T]he enrichment of our perceptions, the deepening of our affective life, this is by no means incidental. But *Erkenntnis* is the task of the special sciences." Hospers, *Meaning and Truth in the Arts*, p. 235.

21. I return to the hypothesis of a reciprocation between art and theory when I discuss "art talk" in Chapters 3 and 6. Beardsley comes close to this hypothesis when he writes that painting and music are "great and irreplaceable" because "they bring into existence new universals, never exemplified in any particulars before those particular paintings and musical compositions" (p. 386). We find in them qualities that "they alone afford" (p. 387). Yet he barely considers whether those qualities can be used "as data in future empirical inquiries" (p. 387), perhaps because his empiricism not only limits the range of relevant data but also includes no logic of discovery, only a logic of confirmation.

22. I do not hold these apparent imprecisions against Beardsley's account here, since he is mostly assuming rather than elaborating an empiricist epistemology. The requisite emphasis on truth and belief occurs later in his book, in chapter 9. Beardsley never clearly defines his conception of "belief," however. He seems to regard it as intellectual assent to a predication, on which assent the person having the belief is disposed to act. Cf. pp. 425, 450.

23. This argument simply ignores the intuitionists' claim that, of all the modes of human mediation, nonverbal artworks are uniquely qualified to convey intuitive insight. Since Beardsley himself grants that nonverbal artworks uniquely create "new universals" (p. 386), his final flourish comes across as a cheap shot.

24. Once I have proposed my own alternative theory of artistic truth, which does not fall neatly into one of the types Beardsley considers (i.e., Proposition Theory, Revelation Theory, and Intuitionist Theory), I shall consider one of the "proposition theories" he tries to refute, namely that of T. M. Greene. See Chapter 7.

25. Self-referential incoherence lurks just beneath Beardsley's discussion of fictional sentences, it seems to me. Since he resists postulating the existence of predications themselves, one wonders whether all his sentences about predications are also fictional and nonpredicative. Although the "Postscript 1980" does not address the problem of self-referential incoherence, it inadvertently removes it by applying a speech-act perspective to fiction. On Beardsley's new account, the composing of a fictional text is nonassertive because it is "the representation (i.e., depiction) of an illocutionary action, or series of them, in basically the same sense in which a painter depicts a cow, or an actor on the stage depicts an act of punching" (p. xliv).

26. In the "Postscript 1980" Beardsley acknowledges the need for a more satisfactory account of aesthetic value, including literary value, but he does not soften his claim that the primary point of literary criticism is to assess the *aesthetic* merits of the literary work: "A complication that arises very sharply in the case of

literature – and other artworks that have meaning or external reference – is that they can also be judged from a cognitive, as well as an aesthetic, point of view. . . . But the two forms of value are distinct, and only one applies to art as art and across the board; moreover, a high degree of aesthetic value by itself (but not a high degree of cognitive value in the absence of aesthetic value) suffices to make an artwork a very good one – so . . . aesthetic value is prior and basic in the critic's judgment . . ." (p. lv).

27. I ignore potential problems surrounding introspective, metaphysical, and metalogical beliefs, since Beardsley's book gives little indication how he would handle these challenges to logical empiricism. Based on his denying the independent existence of abstract propositions and of fictitious objects, I assume that he would deny the existence of metaphysical objects. Hence metaphysical claims, no matter how logically consistent, could not be about features of the real world and would be neither true nor false. Perhaps Beardsley considers them meaningless as well.

28. In terms of the two models of correspondence theory sketched by Kirkham, Beardsley's conception seems closer to Bertrand Russell's congruence model, with its isomorphic correspondence between belief and fact, than to J. L. Austin's correlation model, with its conventional correspondence between two correlations, the correlation of statement and particular state of affairs, on the one hand, and that of sentence and type of states of affairs, on the other. See Kirkham, *Theories of Truth*, pp. 119–40.

Chapter 2: Reciprocations

1. Albert Hofstadter, *Truth and Art* (New York: Columbia University Press, 1965), p. 209; hereafter cited internally by page number.

2. Herman Rapaport, *Is There Truth in Art?* (Ithaca: Cornell University Press, 1997), p. 24.

3. Note that I say "anti*scientistic*" not "anti*scientific*." To a philosopher who regards science as the paradigm of knowledge, a challenge to scientism can sound like a rejection of science as such.

4. "Referring" and "predicating" are my terms for the semantical functions that Hofstadter labels "exhibition" and "predication," respectively. See Hofstadter, pp. 73–5.

5. Although he derives this description of propositional truth from Husserl and especially from Heidegger, Hofstadter says it parallels "Rudolf Carnap's logistical formulation of the semantic concept of truth, on the basis of the earlier work of Alfred Tarski" (p. 97). Hofstadter refuses to abandon the ideal of propositional truth in favor of John Dewey's "warranted assertibility" or the logical empiricists' emphasis on "probability" (p. 102), even though Hofstadter's account of statements and propositions is hermeneutical and existential.

6. "Performatives, imperatives, and valuations" are my terms for the "three kinds of language" Hofstadter connects with practical truth (see pp. 115–20). An example of the first is a religious official ceremonially pronouncing two people spouses (p. 115). An example of the second is someone's commanding or requesting that the door be closed (p. 117). An example of the third is someone's calling an action or an artifact "good" (pp. 118–20).

7. Hofstadter adds to these "the lawful in law, and the sacred in religion" (p. 162) as also having authoritative weight and binding power.

8. Cogency and seizure also characterize the experience of sublimity, says Hofstadter, but here cogency is a matter of greatness rather than rightness, and seizure occurs as admiration, awe, or terror rather than as self-giving love (see pp. 165–70).

9. My summary omits Hofstadter's discussion of artistic style (pp. 199–209).

10. The process through which this occurs has four elements: the "particular material occasion" that triggers the artist's efforts; the artist's largely unconscious "substantive will" that churns up multiple images; the artist's largely conscious "formal understanding" that brings skill and critique to the process; and, governing and inspiring both will and understanding, the artist's spiritual concern or love that "looks longingly forward to true being that is connatural with it." The idea of the artwork is "the unity of all four . . . under the persuasion of the fourth" (p. 194).

11. Hofstadter does not stipulate whether this "other" must be human or divine, or, if human, whether it must be an individual, a community, or the whole human race.

12. I return to the notion of cogency in later chapters.

13. Beardsley describes aesthetic experience primarily in perceptual terms. It is attentive to "components of a phenomenally objective field," and it is intense, focused, internally coherent, and self-contained. Correlatively he describes aesthetic objects primarily as fictive. They are all "object *manqués*," he says, able "to call forth . . . the kind of admiring contemplation, without any necessary commitment to practical action, that is characteristic of aesthetic experience." (Quotations are from Beardsley, *Aesthetics*, pp. 527–9.)

14. Ibid., pp. 9–10. In fact, Beardsley organizes his entire metacritical project along these lines: chapters 2–5 deal with problems raised by descriptive statements, chapters 6–9 with those raised by interpretative statements, and chapters 10–12 with those posed by critical evaluations. Only the latter are "normative," in his terminology. Descriptive and interpretative statements are "nonnormative."

15. Rapaport, *Is There Truth in Art?*, p. 35; hereafter cited internally by page number. His is a reprise of Derrida's, Rapaport says, in the sense that the two books "have everything and nothing in common" (p. 36).

16. Rapaport claims that Nietzsche differs from Heidegger and Derrida in thinking that art "is fated to be metaphysical" because, in their "weakness and fallibility," human beings are not able "to live under the unbearable weight of a truth that shames and humiliates us" (p. 14). (Perhaps we can say that for Nietzsche art is fated to save us from the fatal weight of shame.)

17. According to Rapaport, Derrida and Levinas follow Heidegger in opposing the metaphysics of art. Rapaport reads Heidegger from the perspective of his later writings, especially the posthumous *Beiträge zur Philosophie* (Frankfurt am Main: Vittorio Klostermann, 1989), translated by Parvis Emad and Kenneth Maly as *Contributions to Philosophy (From Enowning)* (Bloomington: Indiana University Press, 1999). This introduces questionable elements into Rapaport's readings of *Being and Time* and "The Origin of the Work of Art." Since subsequent chapters

provide my own interpretation of these two texts, I do not belabor my disagreements with his readings here.

18. Rapaport regards this text as openly hostile to "politically correct" social realist imperatives of either the Nazi or Soviet sort (see pp. 20–1). He then reads this purported hostility to Nazi cultural policy back into Heidegger's essay "The Origin of the Work of Art." A remarkably innovative rescue operation results, whereby all "blood and soil" overtones in Heidegger's essay become traces of anarchic freedom. (If this political *Verharmlosung* [sanitizing] is the price for "restituting" Heidegger's "restitution," I think scholars would do better without either restitution.)

19. Primarily the lecture course *Vom Wesen der menschlichen Freiheit* and the essay "On the Essence of Truth" ("Vom Wesen der Wahrheit").

20. Rapaport's summary avoids such crucial questions as why human beings err and whether or how this tendency is peculiar to human beings. The refusal or inability to address such questions would be decisive for evaluating an Heideggerian moral or political philosophy. I take up this topic in Chapters 4 and 5.

21. To borrow the title of the collection of essays in which Heidegger's "The Origin of the Work of Art" was first published. The first English translation of this essay was by Albert Hofstadter in Martin Heidegger, *Poetry, Language, Thought* (New York: Harper Colophon Books, 1975), pp. 17–87. As the translator's preface to the first English translation of the entire collection explains, a *Holzweg* is both "a timber track that leads to a clearing in the forest where timber is cut" and "a track that used to lead to such a place but is now overgrown and leads nowhere." Hence, in a popular German idiom, to be 'on a *Holzweg*' is to be on the wrong track." Martin Heidegger, *Off the Beaten Track*, ed. and trans. Julian Young and Kenneth Haynes (Cambridge: Cambridge University Press, 2002), p. ix.

22. For Derrida, Rapaport says, the work of art interlaces an attachment to nonbeing and an attachment to beings (p. 43). For Lévinas the work of art performs a double flight from primordial non/Being (the "*il y a*" or "there is" or "existence") to beings ("existents") and from beings to non/Being: "Lévinas differs from Heidegger and Derrida in that he does not treat Being as a neutral ontological notion; for Lévinas, rather, Being is humanly unbearable and we are human insofar as we retreat from the fullness of Being.... The truth of the work of art, then, concerns the work's capacity, as representation, to reproduce and hence point to a condition of irremissible Being. But the truth of the work also concerns an allergy or resistance to that very Being to which it points, namely, the human need to retreat from such Being" (p. 55).

23. This transition is described in many works by Jürgen Habermas. See, for example, *The Philosophical Discourse of Modernity*, pp. 294–326, and *Postmetaphysical Thinking*, pp. 28–53.

24. Theodor W. Adorno, *Aesthetic Theory*, trans. Robert Hullot-Kentor (Minneapolis: University of Minnesota Press, 1997), p. 194; *Ästhetische Theorie*, ed. Gretel Adorno and Rolf Tiedemann, *Gesammelte Schriften* 7, 2d ed. (Frankfurt am Main: Suhrkamp, 1972), p. 289.

25. Zuidervaart, "Fantastic Things: Critical Notes toward a Social Ontology of the Arts."

Chapter 3: Kant Revisited

1. Immanuel Kant, *Critique of the Power of Judgment*, ed. Paul Guyer, trans. Paul Guyer and Eric Matthews (Cambridge: Cambridge University Press, 2000), §59, p. 227; V: 353. In-text citations are from this translation and use the abbreviation *CJ*, followed by the section number, translation pagination, and the pagination in volume 5 of *Kant's Gesammelte Schriften*, thus: *CJ* §§1–5, pp. 89–96; V: 203–11. I have also consulted the following edition and translations: *Kritik der Urteilskraft*, ed. Karl Vorländer (Hamburg: Felix Meiner, 1968); *Critique of Judgment*, trans. J. H. Bernard (New York: Hafner, 1972; originally published in 1892); *Critique of Judgment, Including the First Introduction*, trans. Werner S. Pluhar (Indianapolis: Hackett, 1987).

2. Hans-Georg Gadamer, *Truth and Method*, trans. Joel Weinsheimer and Donald G. Marshall, 2d, rev. ed. (New York: Crossroad, 1989); *Wahrheit und Methode: Grundzüge einer philosophischen Hermeneutik* (1960), 4th ed. (Tübingen: J. C. B. Mohr [Paul Siebeck], 1975); cited as *TM* and *WM*, respectively.

3. Theodor W. Adorno, *Aesthetic Theory*, trans. Robert Hullot-Kentor (Minneapolis: University of Minnesota Press, 1997); *Ästhetische Theorie*, ed. Gretel Adorno and Rolf Tiedemann, *Gesammelte Schriften* 7, 2d ed. (Frankfurt am Main: Suhrkamp, 1972); cited as *AT* and *ÄT*, respectively.

4. For a response to this challenge that complements my own, see Marcus Verhaegh, "The Truth of the Beautiful in the *Critique of Judgement*," *British Journal of Aesthetics* 41 (October 2001): 371–94. Verhaegh employs an "assertional spectrum principle" to argue that taste judgments provide "domain-specific enhancements of cognition" that themselves lead to "true propositions." Since I do not restrict truth to propositional truth, and seek a notion of artistic truth that is not so restricted, I find Verhaegh's illuminating and ingenious reading insufficient for connecting aesthetic validity with artistic truth.

5. A fountainhead for this reemergence is Johan Huizinga, *Homo Ludens: A Study of the Play-Element in Culture* (Boston: Beacon Press, 1972). The original Dutch version appeared in 1938.

6. See Habermas, *Moral Consciousness and Communicative Action*, especially pp. 116–94.

7. Kant's notion of "entertainment" or "amusement" contains more elements of bourgeois sociability than does the contemporary notion associated with the "entertainment industry." What he calls "agreeable arts" include "all those charms that can gratify the company at a table, such as telling entertaining stories, getting the company talking in an open and lively manner, creating by means of jokes and laughter a certain tone of merriment." He also includes setting the table, *Tafelmusik*, and "all games that involve no interest beyond that of making time pass unnoticed" (*CJ* §44, pp. 184–5; V: 305–6).

8. See especially Rudolf A. Makkreel, *Imagination and Interpretation in Kant: The Hermeneutical Import of the* Critique of Judgment (Chicago: University of Chicago Press, 1990). Makkreel argues that, by assigning imagination "the power of aesthetic comprehension, and also the capacity to create aesthetic ideas," Kant's *Critique of Judgment* gives it "the potential for . . . a 'reflective interpretation' of our world" (p. 1).

9. Implied here is a different account of metaphor from those given by Beardsley and Hofstadter – see Chapters 1 and 2. For an account of aesthetic signs that emphasizes deferral rather than referral, see Christoph Menke, *The Sovereignty of Art: Aesthetic Negativity in Adorno and Derrida*, trans. Neil Solomon (Cambridge, Mass.: MIT Press, 1998), a translation of *Die Souveränität der Kunst: Ästhetische Erfahrung nach Adorno und Derrida* (Frankfurt am Main: Suhrkamp, 1991). I discuss Menke's approach in "Autonomy, Negativity, and Illusory Transgression: Menke's Deconstruction of Adorno's Aesthetics," *Philosophy Today*, SPEP Supplement 1999, pp. 154–68.

10. This is not to deny that Kant regards both genius and taste as necessary for the production of fine art, however, or to deny that he would consider the lack of originality a deficiency in particular works of supposedly fine art. For a useful summary of the tensions in Kant's relating of genius to taste, see Henry Allison, *Kant's Theory of Taste: A Reading of the* Critique of Aesthetic Judgment (Cambridge: Cambridge University Press, 2001), pp. 298–301.

11. Gadamer sees presentation as central to the structure of both play and art. Unfortunately, the translation of *Truth and Method* obscures this by often rendering *Darstellung* as "representation," a term traditionally used to translate Kant's *Vorstellung*, which refers to all contents of consciousness and especially ones tied to ordinary perception. Adorno does not give the same prominence to the *term Darstellung*, but a Hegelian version of this *concept* is central to Adorno's conception of the artwork as an autonomous entity in whose inner tensions societal forces and relations of production "return" (*nachkehren*) in a formal way (cf. *AT* 236, *ÄT* 350–1). Tracing such terminological and conceptual connections becomes even more challenging when interpreters rely on different translations of Kant's Third Critique. Pluhar, for example, translates *Darstellung* as "exhibition" and *Vorstellung* as "presentation." I follow both Bernard and Guyer and Matthews in using "presentation" as an equivalent for *Darstellung* and "representation" as an equivalent for *Vorstellung*.

12. It is notoriously difficult to avoid confusion when talking about meaning. Witness, for example, Susanne K. Langer's struggle to distinguish "import" from "meaning" in *Feeling and Form: A Theory of Art Developed from "Philosophy in a New Key"* (New York: Charles Scribner's Sons, 1953), pp. 31–2 and elsewhere. In my own usage, "meaning" can be either linguistic or nonlinguistic. When it is nonlinguistic and attaches to aesthetic signs, I use the term "purport." When the aesthetic signs are in addition artworks, whose meaning typically involves self-referential doubling, I use the term "import." I explain the notion of artistic import in Chapter 6. My usage reverses the relation between "purport" and "import" in Beardsley's *Aesthetics*, where "import" has the wider extension. I also detach both terms from their specific function in his behaviorist theory of language.

13. A careful reading of Kant's account could distinguish three "presentational functions" fulfilled by the aesthetic idea expressed in an artwork: actualizing the artist's concept, symbolizing rational ideas, and communicating the feeling bound up with the aesthetic idea. I explain these functions and explore their significance in "'Aesthetic Ideas' and the Role of Art in Kant's Ethical Hermeneutics," in *Opuscula Aesthetica Nostra*, ed. Cécile Cloutier and Calvin Seerveld (Edmonton: Academic Printing and Publishing, 1984), pp. 63–72;

reprinted in *Kant's* Critique of the Power of Judgment: *Critical Essays*, ed. Paul Guyer (Lanham, Md.: Rowman & Littlefield, 2003), pp. 199–208.

14. This is a much–disputed point among Kant scholars. Here I follow the reading suggested by Allison, *Kant's Theory of Taste*, pp. 236–301.

15. Makkreel, *Imagination and Interpretation in Kant*, pp. 1, 5; cf. pp. 118–29.

16. Ibid., p. 129.

17. Here I am especially concerned to distinguish my approach from that of Adorno as well as from that of his successors Albrecht Wellmer and Jürgen Habermas, even though my approach otherwise resembles various aspects of theirs.

18. That is to say, in the sense of Kant's first two critiques. For an instructive attempt to derive a general and postmetaphysical account of validity from the Third Critique's account of reflective judgment, and thereby to reconcile universalism with the "fact of pluralism," see Alessandro Ferrara, *Reflective Authenticity: Rethinking the Project of Modernity* (New York: Routledge, 1998).

19. Even the common rejoinder "I know what I like; there's no point trying to change my mind" appeals to a shared expectation, namely, that everyone should be at liberty to follow private preferences in aesthetic matters. The rejoinder simply ignores just how widespread is the desire for private satisfaction in a consumer capitalist society, how peculiar this desire is relative to desires within other societal formations, and how much it depends on nonprivate patterns that make the pursuit of private passions somewhat viable.

20. See my summary of Hofstadter's notion in Chapter 2.

21. Nicholas Wolterstorff, *Art in Action: Toward a Christian Aesthetic* (Grand Rapids, Mich.: Eerdmans, 1980), pp. 158–68. Wolterstorff's list derives from Monroe Beardsley's account of "Objective Reasons" for finding artworks aesthetically good, in his *Aesthetics*, pp. 462–70.

22. For a brief summary of Adorno's account, see Zuidervaart, *Adorno's Aesthetic Theory*, pp. 199–201.

23. I use "horizon" in the historically inflected and phenomenological sense proposed by Gadamer. He describes a horizon as "the range of vision that includes everything that can be seen from a particular vantage point" (*TM* 302, *WM* 286) and as "something into which we move and that moves with us. Horizons change for a person who is moving" (*TM* 304, *WM* 288). From this passage and related ones (see *TM* 245–9, *WM* 231–5; *TM* 302–7, *WM* 286–9; *TM* 373–5, *WM* 355–7), it becomes apparent that Gadamer's "horizon" does some of the work Kant assigned to "taste" and, more broadly, to reflective judgment as a *sensus communis* (*CJ* §40, pp. 173–6, V: 293–6). Against Gadamer's explicit criticisms of Kant's "subjectivizing" of taste and common sense, Rudolf Makkreel reads Kant's *sensus communis* as making possible a critical appropriation of tradition: "The *sensus communis* provides a mode of orientation to the tradition that allows us to ascertain its relevance to ultimate questions of truth. It is transcendental... in the sense of opening up the reflective horizon of communal meaning in terms of which the truth can be determined" (*Imagination and Interpretation in Kant*, p. 158).

24. For a detailed account of the supportive role Kant gives aesthetic "cultivation" (*Kultur*) in the "formation" (*Bildung*) of character, and for an illuminating discussion of Kant's moral emphasis on "orientation," see G. Felicitas Munzel, *Kant's Conception of Moral Character: The "Critical" Link of Morality, Anthropology,*

and Reflective Judgment (Chicago: University of Chicago Press, 1999), especially chaps. 4 and 5.

25. This point has been explored by many philosophers, perhaps most prominently by Alasdair MacIntyre, *After Virtue: A Study in Moral Theory*, 2d ed. (Notre Dame, Ind.: University of Notre Dame Press, 1984). Jürgen Habermas gives an expansive social-theoretical account of the developments to which MacIntyre responds. See *The Theory of Communicative Action* (1981), trans. Thomas McCarthy, 2 vols. (Boston: Beacon Press, 1984, 1987).

26. For an elaboration of this implicit criticism that simultaneously defends Adorno against his postmetaphysical critics, see my essay "Metaphysics after Auschwitz: Suffering and Hope in Adorno's *Negative Dialectics*" (unpublished manuscript).

27. "Talk" is intended to include reading, writing, and listening. It is difficult to find one term for all of these, especially since, like Habermas, I reserve "discourse" as a more technical term, but I find "communicative action" problematic, for reasons similar to those given by Maeve Cooke in *Language and Reason: A Study of Habermas's Pragmatics* (Cambridge, Mass.: MIT Press, 1994), pp. 76–8. I use the terms "art conversation" and "art discourse" rather than "aesthetic" conversation and discourse for two reasons: to avoid a common tendency among philosophers to reduce art to its aesthetic dimension, and to avoid the equally common tendency to reduce the aesthetic dimension to art. My essay "Autonomy, Negativity, and Illusory Transgression" explains the importance of this antireductionism.

28. My drastically abbreviated account of Habermas's theory derives from many of his writings, including *The Theory of Communicative Action*. He gives a lucid summary in "Actions, Speech Acts, Linguistically Mediated Interactions and the Lifeworld," in *Philosophical Problems Today*, vol. 1, ed. G. Fløistad (Dordrecht: Kluwer, 1994), pp. 45–74. For a fuller version of this essay, see Jürgen Habermas, *On the Pragmatics of Communication*, ed. Maeve Cooke (Cambridge, Mass.: MIT Press, 1998), pp. 215–55. The same volume contains several other important essays on truth and meaning. The earliest comprehensive statement of his discursive theory of truth is "Wahrheitstheorien," in *Wirklichkeit und Reflexion. Walter Schulz zum 60. Geburtstag*, ed. Helmut Fahrenbach (Pfullingen: Neske, 1973), pp. 211–65; republished in Jürgen Habermas, *Vorstudien und Ergänzungen zur Theorie des kommunikativen Handelns*, 2d ed. (Frankfurt am Main: Suhrkamp, 1986), pp. 127–83. More recently, Habermas has extended and revised his theory of truth in a collection of essays titled *Wahrheit und Rechfertigung: Philosophische Aufsätze* (Frankfurt am Main: Suhrkamp, 1999).

29. For elaborations and criticisms, see especially the following three monographs, on Habermas's truth theory, ethics, and philosophy of language, respectively: James Swindall, *Reflection Revisited: Jürgen Habermas's Discursive Theory of Truth* (New York: Fordham University Press, 1999); William Rehg, *Insight and Solidarity: A Study in the Discourse Ethics of Jürgen Habermas* (Berkeley: University of California Press, 1994); and Cooke's *Language and Reason*.

30. "Primarily," because Habermas holds that every speech act implicitly raises all three types of validity claim. A specific speech act in a certain context will, however, raise one claim more directly and the other two claims more indirectly. A meteorologist's statement about weather conditions to a colleague, for example, would more likely be challenged for lack of truth than for lack of

appropriateness or lack of sincerity. Nevertheless, the colleague could always problematize the statement along regulative or expressive lines, if it were uttered loudly during a funeral, say, or simply dropped in the middle of a heart-to-heart sharing of their feelings toward one another.

31. See especially the following essays by Martin Seel: "The Two Meanings of 'Communicative' Rationality: Remarks on Habermas's Critique of a Plural Concept of Reason," in *Communicative Action: Essays on Jürgen Habermas's* The Theory of Communicative Action, ed. Axel Honneth and Hans Joas (Cambridge, Mass.: MIT Press, 1991), pp. 36–48; and "Kunst, Wahrheit, Welterschliessung," in *Perspektiven der Kunstphilosophie: Texte und Diskussionen*, ed. Franz Koppe (Frankfurt am Main: Suhrkamp, 1991), pp. 36–80. I discuss Seel's criticisms of Habermas at greater length in Chapter 6.

32. Moralizing critics tend to replace aesthetic considerations with nonaesthetic ones. Transgressive critics tend to dismiss both aesthetic and nonaesthetic considerations, preferring disorientation over any sort of orientation or reorientation.

33. See Zuidervaart, "Postmodern Arts and the Birth of a Democratic Culture," and "Creative Border Crossing in New Public Culture."

Chapter 4: Truth as Disclosure

1. *SZ* 226, translation modified. Passages in translation are taken from Martin Heidegger, *Being and Time*, trans. Joan Stambaugh (Albany: State University of New York Press, 1996). Page numbers refer to the pagination in *Sein und Zeit*, as found in the margins of English translations, and are indicated by the abbreviation *SZ*. The German edition I have used is *Sein und Zeit*, 15th ed. (Tübingen: Max Niemeyer, 1979). I have also consulted *Being and Time*, trans. John Macquarrie and Edward Robinson (New York: Harper & Row, 1962). I give preference to the Macquarrie and Robinson translation in retaining "Being" (capital "B") for "*Sein*" and in not hyphenating Dasein (which, for the most part, is not hyphenated in *Sein und Zeit* but is always hyphenated in Joan Stambaugh's translation). These modifications are made without comment in the citations and in my own text. Other relevant modifications to citations from the Stambaugh translation are marked by square brackets.

2. See Daniel O. Dahlstrom, *Heidegger's Concept of Truth* (Cambridge: Cambridge University Press, 2001). By "logical prejudice" Dahlstrom means a widespread assumption that assertions, propositions, sentences, and the like are the site of truth on which the truth of anything else depends. It is "the tendency to conceive truth in terms of a specific sort of discourse, namely, in terms of claims, assertions, and judgments, that are formed as indicative, declarative sentences.... For those who cling to this 'model of propositional truth,' 'the predicates "true," "false," are paradigmatically attributes of sentences, statements, claims, judgments, assertions, propositions, and the like'" (ibid., p. 17, citing an article by Carl Friedrich Gethmann). I should add that the logical prejudice need not be peculiar to correspondence theories of truth, although Heidegger's own conception is intended as an alternative to correspondence theories. It can also be found in coherence, consensus, and pragmatic theories of truth.

3. "Self-referential incoherence" is my cryptic formulation for the "paradox of thematization" so carefully described by Dahlstrom (ibid., pp. 202–10, 236–42, 252–5, 264–8, 433–56). I do not take up Heidegger's crucial notion of authenticity here, even though that would be required for a complete account of his conception of truth. Nor does this chapter trace permutations to his conception in Heidegger's subsequent lectures and writings. But I do try to do justice to the textual fabric within which Heidegger weaves his conception of truth. For an account that sticks closer to Heidegger's own vocabulary and raises additional issues of translation, see my essay "If I Had a Hammer: Truth in Heidegger's *Being and Time*," in *A Hermeneutics of Charity: Interpretation, Selfhood, and Postmodern Faith*, ed. James K. A. Smith and Henry Venema (Grand Rapids, Mich.: Brazos Press, 2004).

4. To avoid confusion with Habermas's notion of discourse (*Diskurs*), I use other terms than "discourse" to render Heidegger's "*Rede*" – usually "talk" or "conversation." Despite the originality and significance of Heidegger's discussion of attunement, especially with regard to fear (*Furcht*) and anxiety (*Angst*) in sections 30 and 40, I restrict my summary to understanding and talk, since these have a more direct bearing on Heidegger's critique of traditional theories of truth.

5. Here and elsewhere I ignore the distinction between *Zeitlichkeit* (temporality) and *Temporalität* (Temporality) in *Sein und Zeit*. Karin de Boer gives a detailed account of this distinction in *Thinking in the Light of Time: Heidegger's Encounter with Hegel* (Albany: State University of New York Press, 2000).

6. Stambaugh translates *die Aussage* as "statement." I follow Macquarrie and Robinson in translating it as "assertion."

7. My formulation here ignores Heidegger's careful distinctions among intelligibility (*Verständlichkeit*), meaning (*Sinn*), the totality of significations (*Bedeutungsganze*), and significations (*Bedeutungen*). "Meaning" refers to that which can be articulated (*das Artikulierbare*) in talk, just as "intelligibility" refers to that which can be understood and interpreted. The "totality of significations" refers to the entirety of what is articulated in talk. With this term, Heidegger draws attention to the claim that discrete articulations or "significations" belong to a larger totality. Similarly, although words accrue to discrete significations, this occurrence belongs to a larger process: "The totality of significations . . . *is put into words*" (*SZ* 161), and the totality of those words is language, in which talk gets expressed. (For more on the concept of "meaning," see *SZ* 150–3, 156, and 323–5.)

8. Contrary to my formulation, Heidegger would not say that falling prey is restricted to a mass society – idle talk, for example, "does not first originate through certain conditions which influence Dasein 'from the outside'" (*SZ* 177) – rather, falling prey "reveals an *essential*, ontological structure of Dasein itself" (*SZ* 179). Nevertheless, his characterization of falling prey is clearly indebted to and descriptive of a social condition in which the structure and principle of publicity (*Öffentlichkeit*) hold sway. In that sense, despite his disclaimer that the term "does not express any negative value judgment" (*SZ* 175), it is hard to read his account of "falling prey" or "entanglement" as anything other than a critique of mass society and of democratic tendencies within it.

9. My paraphrase from *SZ* 218 is closer to the Macquarrie and Robinson translation than to the Stambaugh translation. Heidegger writes that the discoveredness (*Entdecktheit*) of an entity "bewährt sich darin, dass sich das Ausgesagte, das ist

das Seiende selbst, *als dasselbe* zeigt." A few lines later he writes: "Die Aussage *ist wahr*, bedeutet: sie entdeckt das Seiende an ihm selbst."

10. In this context Heidegger says that his definition of truth provides "the *necessary* interpretation of what the oldest tradition of ancient philosophy primordially surmised and even understood in a pre-phenomenological way." That is to say, his definition recaptures the alethic sense in which apophantic reason and discourse (*logos*) can be true, namely, "to let beings be seen in their unconcealment [*Unverborgenheit*] (discoveredness [*Entdecktheit*]), taking them out of their concealment [*Verborgenheit*]" (*SZ* 219). (See also the discussion of the concepts of *logos* and *aletheia* in Heidegger's introduction, *SZ* 32–4.)

11. Note the three characterizations of truth on *SZ* 226: "disclosedness, discovering, and discoveredness."

12. I take the clue for this dialectical line of critical interpretation from Adorno's discussion of Heidegger in *Negative Dialectics*, even though I think Adorno misinterprets Heidegger's attempt to interrelate Dasein, truth, and Being. See Theodor W. Adorno, *Negative Dialectics*, trans. E. B. Ashton (New York: Seabury Press, 1973), pp. 59–131; *Negative Dialektik, Gesammelte Schriften* 6 (Frankfurt am Main: Suhrkamp, 1973), pp. 67–136. Here are some representative passages from Adorno: "The concept of 'existential' things [*des Existentiellen*] . . . is governed by the idea that the measure of truth is not its objectivity, of whichever kind, but the pure being-that-way and acting-that-way of the thinker. . . . But truth, the constellation of subject and object in which both penetrate each other, can no more be reduced to subjectivity than to that Being whose dialectical relation to subjectivity Heidegger tends to blur" [*zu verwischen trachtet*] (*ND* 127; *GS* 6: 133). "[Heidegger's notion of] historicality immobilizes history in the unhistorical realm, heedless of the historical conditions that govern the inner composition and constellation of subject and object" (*ND* 129; *GS* 6: 135).

13. Another way to put the point is to say that meaning does not determine reference. This formulation is central to the critique of Heidegger's relativistic reification of language in Cristina Lafont, *Heidegger, Language, and World-Disclosure*, trans. Graham Harman (Cambridge: Cambridge University Press, 2000).

14. This predicative manner of taking something is to be contrasted with the manner of taking entities as something-as-which in pre-predicative interpretation. Cf. *SZ* 148–9 and 157–8.

15. The translation of the first sentence in this quotation is somewhat misleading. The point of this particular sentence is not that some entity changes from being at hand into something else, but rather that a changeover (*Umschlag*) occurs in Dasein's fore-having, from a circumspect "with which" to an assertoric "about which": "Das *zuhandene womit* des Zutunhabens, der Verrichtung, wird zum '*Worüber*' der aufzeigenden Aussage" (*SZ* 158). It is correlatively to this changeover in Dasein's fore-having that the entity also undergoes a change: its handiness becomes veiled, its objective presence gets discovered, and it gets defined (*bestimmt*) as a "what" rather than being interpreted as a "with which."

16. A similar ambiguity returns in Heidegger's subsequent account of the truth of assertion. On the one hand, confirming the truth of an assertion depends on whether the asserted entity "shows itself *as [that] very same thing. Confirmation* [of

an assertion] means *the being's showing itself in its self-sameness.* Confirmation is accomplished on the basis of the being's showing itself" (*SZ* 218). On the other hand, the truth of an assertion simply is the assertion's capacity to discover the entity in its (specific) identity: "To say that [an assertion] is *true* means that it discovers the beings in themselves [*sie entdeckt das Seiende an ihm selbst*]. It asserts, it shows, it lets beings 'be seen' (*apophansis*) in their discoveredness. The *being true* (*truth*) of the [assertion] must be understood as *discovering* [*entdeckend-sein*]" (*SZ* 218). I take up this ambiguity concerning assertoric truth later.

17. In fact, Heidegger says that all talk, whether assertoric or not, is *about* something. "[Talk] is [talk] about.... That which [talk] is *about* does not necessarily have the character of the theme of a definite statement; in fact, mostly it does not have it. Even command is given about something; a wish is about something. And so is intercession.... In all [talk] there is *what is spoken* as such, what is said as such when one actually wishes, asks, talks things over about..." (*SZ* 161–2).

18. Readers familiar with the ontology developed by the Dutch philosophers Herman Dooyeweerd and D. H. Th. Vollenhoven will recognize the term "predicative availability" as a modification of their notion of a "logical" (or "analytic") "object function." I avoid their particular terminology for two reasons: it presupposes a subject-object paradigm, which both Heidegger and I want to challenge, and the terms "logical" and "analytic" are less precise than "predicative." I recognize, however, that the account of subject-object relations given by Dooyeweerd and Vollenhoven breaks with the epistemological emphasis of the modern subject-object paradigm. For a concise and updated version of this account, see Hendrik Hart, *Understanding Our World: An Integral Ontology* (Lanham, Md.: University Press of America, 1984), pp. 221–42. See also Herman Dooyeweerd, *A New Critique of Theoretical Thought* (1953–8), vol. 2, trans. David H. Freeman and H. De Jongste (Philadelphia: Presbyterian and Reformed Publishing, 1969), pp. 386–91.

19. Ernst Tugendhat, "Heideggers Idee von Wahrheit," in *Heidegger: Perspektiven zur Deutung seines Werks,* ed. Otto Pöggeler (Cologne and Berlin: Kiepenheuer & Witsch, 1970), pp. 286–97; translated by Richard Wolin as "Heidegger's Idea of Truth," in *The Heidegger Controversy: A Critical Reader,* ed. Richard Wolin (New York: Columbia University Press, 1991), pp. 245–63. My modifications to this translation (indicated by square brackets) are intended to maintain some consistency with the Stambaugh translation of *Being and Time.* A longer version of Tugendhat's critique occurs in a seminal study that has not been translated into English: Ernst Tugendhat, *Der Wahrheitsbegriff bei Husserl und Heidegger* (1967), 2d ed. (Berlin: Walter de Gruyter, 1970).

20. Tugendhat, "Heidegger's Idea," pp. 250–2; "Heideggers Idee," pp. 288–9. The three formulations, all of them on *SZ* 218, are: (1) The assertion is true if it discovers the entity *"just as* it is in itself." (The word "just" appears in the Macquarrie and Robinson translation, p. 261, but not in the Stambaugh translation, p. 201. Heidegger's formulation in German reads "Das gemeinte Seiende selbst zeigt sich *so, wie* es an ihm selbst ist....") (2) The assertion is true if it discovers the entity "in itself." (3) The assertion is true if it discovers the entity. Whereas Tugendhat accuses Heidegger of sliding through these three formulations, Dahlstrom argues that formulations (2) and (3) can be understood as synonyms or metonyms for (1), and he gives textual evidence for this

interpretation (pp. 405–7). I think that Tugendhat could easily concede this reading without giving up his main criticism, however.

21. "Heidegger's Idea," p. 254; "Heideggers Idee," pp. 290–1. Although Tugendhat applauds Heidegger's "dynamic" conception of assertion as a mode of disclosedness, I wonder how dynamic this conception can be, given Heidegger's emphasis on disclosed*ness* as a state of Being rather than on disclos*ure* as a process of mediation.

22. "Heidegger's Idea," p. 254; "Heideggers Idee," p. 291.

23. "Heidegger's Idea," p. 255; "Heideggers Idee," p. 291.

24. "Heidegger's Idea," p. 256; "Heideggers Idee," p. 292.

25. "Heidegger's Idea," p. 257; "Heideggers Idee," p. 293. The translation of Tugendhat's essay does not bring out the close terminological connection between the assertion's correctness (*Richtigkeit*) and the assertion's being directed (*gerichtet*) by the entity's self-givenness.

26. This is a general but not an exhaustive stipulation. Not included, for example, would be first-order statements about which one makes second-order statements (assuming for the sake of illustration that first-order statements can properly be called entities). In such cases, the relevant accord might be with other *predicative* aspects of the "entity's" availability.

27. The adjective "systatic" derives from Herman Dooyeweerd's discussion of the "intermodal systasis of meaning" that grounds any "theoretical synthesis." In Dooyeweerd's account, "systasis" refers to the wholeness or integrality with which the "modal aspects" of reality present themselves in ordinary or "pre-theoretical" experience. See *A New Critique of Theoretical Thought*, 2:427ff. My term systatic availability refers to the multidimensional "handiness," both predicative and nonpredicative, of the entities with which human beings have dealings.

28. My summary introduces the terms "practice of asserting" and "accomplished assertion" at points where these seem consistent with Heidegger's account.

29. Cf. Theodor W. Adorno, *Against Epistemology: A Metacritique; Studies in Husserl and the Phenomenological Antinomies*, trans. Willis Domingo (Cambridge, Mass.: MIT Press, 1982), pp. 186–234; *Zur Metakritik der Erkenntnistheorie: Studien über Husserl und die phänomenologischen Antinomien* (1956), *Gesammelte Schriften* 5 (Frankfurt am Main: Suhrkamp, 1970), pp. 190–235. In *The Philosophical Discourse of Modernity*, Jürgen Habermas argues that, in both earlier and later articulations, Heidegger "remains caught in the problems that the philosophy of the subject in the form of Husserlian phenomenology had presented to him" (p. 136).

30. "Heidegger's Idea," p. 261; "Heideggers Idee," p. 296. Tugendhat adds: "What must have appeared so liberating about this conception was that, without denying the relativity and lack of transparency of our historical world, it once again made possible an immediate and positive relation to truth: an alleged relation to truth that no longer stakes a claim to certainty, yet which also no longer poses a threat to uncertainty." It seems to me that Heidegger does not so much surrender the idea of critical consciousness, however, as transpose it into the demand for authenticity.

31. According to Dahlstrom, *Heidegger's Concept of Truth*, p. 392, Tugendhat tries to retain the "logical prejudice" that Heidegger's conception of truth aims to expose and dismantle.

32. For a detailed comparison between Deweyan and analytic aesthetics that also reflects on the reasons why Dewey's progressivism and holism fell out of favor, see the first chapter in Richard Shusterman, *Pragmatist Aesthetics: Living Beauty, Rethinking Art* (Oxford: Blackwell, 1992), pp. 3–33.

33. John Dewey, *Art as Experience*, in *The Later Works, 1925–1953*, vol. 10: *1934*, ed. Jo Ann Boydston (Carbondale: Southern Illinois University Press, 1987), pp. 346–7.

34. Ibid., p. 348.

35. Ibid., p. 349. Dewey takes this point even farther when the next page claims, too forcefully, in my opinion, that imagination "is the chief instrument of the good" (p. 350).

36. Quoted by Dewey, ibid., p. 352.

37. This approach to principles has some similarities to the "international feminism" of Martha Nussbaum, *Women and Human Development: The Capabilities Approach* (Cambridge: Cambridge University Press, 2000). While I support her call to articulate "universal norms of human capability" (p. 35), I have reservations about the Aristotelian elements of her theory and about her embrace of political liberalism. I would also propose a different list of "central human functional capabilities" (pp. 78–80), although my list would overlap hers and would share the underlying intuition of there being a limited plurality of central ways in which people in contemporary societies need to be active if they are to flourish as human beings.

38. In *The Genesis of Heidegger's Being and Time* (Berkeley: University of California Press, 1993), Theodore Kisiel introduces "troth" to translate Heidegger's use of *verwahren* (in the early 1920s) for a nontheoretical and practical or even religious sense of truth. The most prominent usages occur in Heidegger's courses on Aristotle's *Nicomachean Ethics* and in his October 1922 typescript titled "Phänomenologische Interpretationen zu Aristoteles (Anzeige der hermeneutischen Situation)." Kisiel suggests that Heidegger's concept of truth as "taking into troth and holding in troth" derives from his appropriation of Christian sources such as Paul, Augustine, and Luther, which "infiltrate Heidegger's understanding of the Aristotelian senses of practical truth" (p. 226). Heidegger, commenting on Aristotle, claims that holding being(s) in troth (*Seinsverwahrung*) is the fundamental experience of truth. Moreover, *nous, sophia, episteme, techne,* and *phronesis* are all modes of "true-ing." In a gloss to Heidegger's handwritten note to the October 1922 typescript, Kisiel connects troth to care as well: "To care is to take into troth and hold in troth, the kind of having . . . involved in the habits of truth" (pp. 537–8n17). See further Kisiel, ibid., pp. 227–5, 302–6, 491–2. Michael Bauer, by contrast, translates "verwahren" as "truthful safe-keeping," in Martin Heidegger, "Phenomenological Interpretations with Respect to Aristotle: Indication of the Hermeneutical Situation," *Man and World* 25 (1992): 355–93.

Chapter 5: Imaginative Disclosure

1. Martin Heidegger, "The Origin of the Work of Art," in *Off the Beaten Track*, ed. and trans. Julian Young and Kenneth Haynes (Cambridge: Cambridge University Press, 2002), pp. 1–56; "Der Ursprung des Kunstwerkes," in *Holzwege* (Frankfurt

am Main: Vittorio Klostermann, 1950), pp. 7–68. Citations use the abbreviations OW and UK, respectively. The epigraph for this chapter comes from OW 19, UK 28. I have also consulted Albert Hofstadter's translation in *Poetry, Language, Thought,* pp. 17–87.

2. I borrow this term from the title of a significant comparative study by Hermann Mörchen, *Adorno und Heidegger: Untersuchung einer philosophischen Kommunikationsverweigerung* (Stuttgart: Klett-Cotta, 1981). For a study in English that shares Mörchen's motivations but has greater systematic intent, see Fred Dallmayr, *Between Freiburg and Frankfurt: Toward a Critical Ontology* (Amherst: University of Massachusetts Press, 1991).

3. Except when I directly translate specific Heideggerian terms such as *Erschlossenheit* (disclosedness) and *Entdecktheit* (discoveredness), this chapter and subsequent chapters use "disclosure" for the topic in dispute. This usage reflects my own general conception of truth, as explained in the previous chapter, as well as standard terminology in recent debates "between Freiburg and Frankfurt," to quote Dallmayr's phrase. It also reflects Heidegger's own turn toward a more processual conception of truth after *Sein und Zeit* – as becomes apparent in the Kunstwerk essay discussed in this chapter.

4. Habermas, *Postmetaphysical Thinking*, p. 51.

5. I borrow this description from the illuminating discussion of Heidegger in J. M. Bernstein, *The Fate of Art: Aesthetic Alienation from Kant to Derrida and Adorno* (University Park: Pennsylvania State University Press, 1992).

6. See in particular Friedrich-Wilhelm von Herrmann, *Heideggers Philosophie der Kunst: Eine systematische Interpretation der Holzwege-Abhandlung "Der Ursprung des Kunstwerkes,"* 2d rev. and exp. ed. (Frankfurt am Main: Vittorio Klostermann, 1994).

7. A better term might be "nonassertoric," but I use the more familiar term "nonpropositional" to indicate the absence or relative unimportance of both propositions and assertions.

8. Besides truth's artistically setting itself to work, Heidegger mentions the following historical ways in which truth takes place: the political state-founding deed, the spiritual proximity of Being, the moral essential sacrifice, and the thinker's questioning of Being (OW 37, UK 50).

9. Heidegger has sound systematic grounds for finding his own terminology, since his philosophy of art attempts a fundamental break with the Kantian conceptual apparatus that informs the standard vocabulary, even in its more dialectical versions, for example, in Hegel and Nietzsche. Unfortunately I am not able to lay out his grounds in this context.

10. "World is that always-nonobjectual [*das immer Ungegenständliche*] to which we are subject as long as the paths of birth and death, blessing and curse, keep us transported into [B]eing. Wherever the essential decisions of our history are made, wherever we take them over or abandon them, wherever they go unrecognized or are brought once more into question, there the world worlds....As a work, the work holds open the open of a world" (OW 23, UK 33–4).

11. Young and Haynes do not capitalize "Being" when translating *Sein*, for reasons they explain in *Off the Beaten Track*, p. x. Because confusions easily occur when both *Sein* and *das Seiende* are rendered with the lower case as "being," I reinsert

the capitalization, and I indicate that with square brackets in direct quotations from their translation. Often I also render *das Seiende* as "entity."

12. For examples of the two directions in describing what art opens up, compare the following: "Das Kunstwerk eröffnet in seiner Weise das Sein des Seienden" (OW 19, UK 28). "Dadurch kam ... an den Tag, was im Werk am Werk ist: die Eröffnung des Seienden in seinem Sein ..." (OW 18, UK 27).

13. I do not attempt to lay out the continuities and changes between *Being and Time* and the Kunstwerk essay. My evaluation of Heidegger's conception of truth in *Being and Time* can be found in Chapter 4.

14. Using even stronger language, Heidegger writes: "The essence [*Wesen*] of truth, i.e., unconcealment, is ruled throughout by a denial.... *Denial, by way of the twofold concealing, belongs to the essence of truth as unconcealment.* Truth, in its essence, is un-truth" (OW 31, UK 43).

15. Cf. OW 30, UK 41, where Heidegger says that the lighted clearing or "illuminating center" "encircles all beings – like the nothing that we scarcely know."

16. Although I cannot elaborate the point here, this "hypermetaphysical" tendency seems to have become virulent in some of so-called postmodern thought. It also lies at the core of Heidegger's cultural politics, which cannot be adequately grasped in merely biographical and sociological terms.

17. On the concept of "horizon," see the discussion of imaginative cogency in Chapter 3.

18. Seel, "Kunst, Wahrheit, Welterschliessung."

19. In this context Heidegger formulates the world-earth strife in terms of decision making: "World ... is the clearing of the paths of the essential directives with which every decision complies. Every decision, however, is grounded in something that cannot be mastered, something concealed, something disconcerting. Otherwise it would never be a decision" (OW 31, UK 44).

20. In a parenthetical and revisionist reference to *Being and Time*, Heidegger adds that Being (*Sein*) itself ushers in truth as the place of openness (*der Spielraum der Offenheit*) or the lighted clearing of the There (*die Lichtung des Da*) where each being blooms (*jegliches Seiende ... aufgeht*) in its own way (OW 36, UK 49). The reference is revisionist insofar as Dasein occupies the privileged position in *Being and Time* that the artwork comes to occupy in the Kunstwerk essay – as that entity which truth requires in order to establish itself in the open center.

21. Heidegger's own formulation is worth quoting in full: "Weil es zum Wesen der Wahrheit gehört, sich in das Seiende einzurichten, um so erst Wahrheit zu werden, deshalb liegt im Wesen der Wahrheit der Zug zum Werk als einer ausgezeichneten Möglichkeit der Wahrheit, inmitten des Seienden selbst seiend zu sein" (UK 50; cf. OW 37).

22. It would be problematic for Heidegger to draw such conclusions, since his account of art's vocation employs categories (not always the terminology, however) such as autonomy, originality, and "the work of art" that come from eighteenth- and nineteenth-century art and philosophy. Heidegger's implicit antimodernism (implicit only insofar as he poses his apparent conclusions as questions) clashes with the unacknowledged modernity of his philosophy of art. The dissonance is particularly striking in his reliance on a painting by van Gogh to elicit the "work character" of the work of art.

23. I deliberately give Heidegger's descriptions less passive and less grandiose for-
    mulations, to avoid his mystification of the historical "destiny" of *das Volk*.

24. In this regard Heidegger seems to have abandoned the attempt in *Being and Time*
    to secure the correctness of assertions by anchoring both correctness and the
    "discoveredness" of entities in the "disclosedness" of Dasein. Another important
    shift, although more implicit, is his attaching "authenticity" primarily to the
    community rather than to the individual.

25. Although there is some overlap between "uniqueness, provocativeness, integrity,
    and originality" and the standards of "intensity, complexity, and depth" men-
    tioned in Chapter 3, the overlap is not complete. Nor is either list to be consid-
    ered exhaustive of the sorts of aesthetic standards to which people in Western
    societies appeal. Taken separately and in combination, however, the two lists are
    quite representative of such standards.

26. Bernstein, *The Fate of Art*, p. 131.

27. Bernstein tends in this second direction (see, e.g., ibid., pp. 134–5), although
    there is more to his account than I can adequately summarize here.

28. See Chapter 3.

Chapter 6: Artistic Truth

1. Adorno, *AT* 335, *ÄT* 498.

2. Jürgen Habermas, "Questions and Counterquestions," in *Habermas and Modernity*, ed. Richard Bernstein (Cambridge: Mass.: MIT Press, 1985), p. 203; republished in Habermas, *On the Pragmatics of Communication*, p. 415.

3. My genealogy regards Theodor W. Adorno and Max Horkheimer as first-
   generation and Albrecht Wellmer and Jürgen Habermas as second-generation
   critical theorists. Whereas the first generation entered university shortly after
   World War I and the second generation shortly after World War II, the third
   generation entered university in the 1960s and 1970s.

4. "Without sensibility no object would be given to us, without understanding no
   object would be thought. Thoughts without content are empty, intuitions without concepts are blind." Kant, *Critique of Pure Reason* (trans. Norman Kemp
   Smith), p. 93, A 51/B 75. For a reading of Adorno's response to Kantian epistemology that takes issue with Habermasian criticisms of Adorno, see Ståle Finke,
   "Concepts and Intuitions: Adorno after the Linguistic Turn," *Inquiry* 44 (2001):
   171–200.

5. See, for example, the weight given to "fugitive ethical events" in J. M. Bernstein,
   Adorno: Ethics and Disenchantment (Cambridge: Cambridge University Press,
   2001) and the notion of a "politics of the mimetic shudder" in Martin Morris,
   *Rethinking the Communicative Turn: Adorno, Habermas, and the Problem of Commu-
   nicative Freedom* (Albany: State University of New York Press, 2001). I address
   the social-philosophical potential of Adorno's metacritique of metaphysics, in
   response to Habermasian criticisms, in "Metaphysics after Auschwitz: Suffering
   and Hope in Adorno's *Negative Dialectics*."

6. I base my discussion on essays published in the *Deutsche Zeitschrift für Philosophie*
   in 1993 and republished in *Thesis Eleven*. The essays are cited from the versions in *Thesis Eleven*, no. 37 (1994): Nikolas Kompridis, "On World Disclosure:
   Heidegger, Habermas and Dewey" (pp. 29–45); Martin Seel, "On Rightness and

Truth: Reflections on the Concept of World Disclosure" (pp. 64–81); James Bohman, "World Disclosure and Radical Criticism" (pp. 82–97).

7. Seel, "On Rightness and Truth," p. 64.
8. Bohman, "World Disclosure," p. 91.
9. See especially pp. 11–15 in Albrecht Wellmer, "Truth, Semblance, Reconciliation: Adorno's Aesthetic Redemption of Modernity," in Wellmer, *The Persistence of Modernity*, pp. 1–35.
10. In fact, Seel is especially troubled by the source for Habermas's identification, namely, the retention by Seel's own mentor Albrecht Wellmer of utopian elements in Adorno's truth aesthetics. See "Kritik der ästhetischen Utopie," the concluding subsection in Martin Seel, *Die Kunst der Entzweiung: Zum Begriff der ästhetischen Rationalität* (Frankfurt am Main: Suhrkamp, 1985), pp. 325–33.
11. Kompridis distinguishes between "first-order disclosure," the discovery of previously hidden horizons of meaning in the "already interpreted, symbolically structured world" in which we find ourselves, and "second-order disclosure," the creative introduction of new horizons of meaning that "can produce either *decentring* or *unifying-repairing effects*" ("On World Disclosure," pp. 29–30). His essay concerns itself primarily with second-order disclosure.
12. Ibid., pp. 41–3.
13. "Kunst, Wahrheit, Welterschliessung," pp. 36–80.
14. Ibid., p. 39. Later the essay gives the following more differentiated description of the three dimensions of validity: theoretical validity concerns the truth of assertions, the existence of states of affairs, and the acceptability of assertoric systems; practical validity concerns the appropriateness of actions and norms, the acceptability of practical demands (*Aufforderungen*), and the legitimacy of social institutions; aesthetic validity concerns the beauty or success (*Gelungenheit*) of artifacts, the favorability of sensuous experiences (*Erfreulichkeit von Empfindungen*), and delight in a style of life.
15. Seel characterizes practical and aesthetic assertions as value assertions (*Wertaussagen*). Whereas a claim to validity (*Anspruch auf Geltung*) is raised and justified (*erhoben und gerechtfertigt wird*) by maintaining and confirming assertions, the validity of actions-maxims and taste-perception can be thematized and shown (*thematisiert und erwiesen* [or *aufgewiesen*] *werden kann*) by maintaining and confirming value assertions (ibid.).
16. "Cultural perception" is a weak rendering of what Seel refers to as *Weltweisenwahrnehmung*, which could be translated either as "ways of perceiving the world" or "perception of worldly modes." Occasionally I render this term as "modalities of cultural perception." I translate the closely related term *Weltweisenartikulation* (ways of articulating the world, or articulation of worldly modes) as "the articulation of cultural perception." *Welt* has the sense here of culture rather than nature. In addition to cultural perception, Seel's list of aesthetic functions includes aesthetic contemplation and the stylizing of human existence (ibid., pp. 42–4). For a more extensive account, see Seel's book *Die Kunst der Entzweiung*.
17. Seel, "Kunst, Wahrheit, Welterschliessung," pp. 44–6.
18. Ibid., pp. 58–62.
19. My attempt in Chapter 3 to link aesthetic validity with cultural orientation tries to avoid this consequence. Unlike Seel, I do not link aesthetic validity with cultural perception and its articulation, but with intersubjective processes of

imagination. Nor do I share his tendency to restrict art's validity to its supposed aesthetic validity. Yet, like Seel, and unlike Habermas, I neither link aesthetic validity with sincerity (*Wahrhaftigkeit*) nor postulate that aesthetic validity can only be borne out by way of special "world-disclosing productions."

20. Seel, "Kunst, Wahrheit, Welterschliessung," p. 41.

21. Ibid., p. 36.

22. Seel, "On Rightness and Truth," p. 78. Seel is emphatic on this score. Earlier in the same essay he writes: "The fact that not every kind of knowledge *aims* at propositional truth does not entail that knowledge is not always mediated through the possibility of validating propositions.... Precisely this is the point that I would like to make against Goodman (and Heidegger): that there can be no knowledge that does not involve at least the *medium* of propositional truth. Even in the extreme case of art, we cannot gain access to the non-propositional aesthetic knowledge *through* the work of art without the medium of propositional knowledge about the work of art" (pp. 72–3).

23. Here I simply summarize parts of my detailed account in *Adorno's Aesthetic Theory*. As one would expect from a critical follower of Hegel and Marx, Adorno's characterizations are neither merely descriptive nor purely normative. They are simultaneously descriptive and normative.

24. Adorno's conception of the artwork's autonomy is dialectical, complex, and not easily summarized. Autonomy has to do with the work's relative independence in society and its lack of obvious social functions, such that in enacting self-criticism it can expose hidden "contradictions" in society. For a reexamination of this conception, see my essay "Autonomy, Negativity, and Illusory Transgression."

25. I elaborate these observations and criticisms in *Adorno's Aesthetic Theory*. See especially chaps. 8 and 9.

26. One motivation for Martin Seel's account of aesthetic validity is to reject both Habermas's identification of expressive sincerity as a concept of validity and Habermas's tendency to link aesthetic validity with expressive sincerity. See Seel, "Kunst, Wahrheit, Walterrchliessung," pp. 55–60.

27. Later in this chapter I replace Habermas's term "objective" with the term "post-subjective," for reasons I shall explain. The notion of an "objective" world is particularly problematic when it comes to art, it seems to me, since much of what art is "about" is itself constituted within either personal or social horizons.

28. Habermas, "Questions and Counterquestions," p. 203. Habermas's revision of his earlier account of art comes in response to Martin Jay's essay "Habermas and Modernism" in the same volume, pp. 125–39.

29. See Charles Taylor, "Language and Society," in *Communicative Action: Essays on Jürgen Habermas's* The Theory of Communicative Action, ed. Axel Honneth and Hans Joas (Cambridge, Mass.: MIT Press, 1991), pp. 23–35. Despite granting Taylor the point that ordinary language can open up new perspectives on the world, interpersonal relations, and one's self, Habermas does not treat this as a central function of language. Note, for example, how little Habermas actually concedes to Taylor on pp. 221–2 in "A Reply," in *Communicative Action*, pp. 214–64.

30. Habermas's stance on disclosure has prompted sympathetic critics such as Maeve Cooke to ask him to admit additional types of validity claims beyond the three he identifies, and to include within his conception of communicative action

the sorts of interpretation and formulation that occur in both art and ordinary language. See Cooke, *Language and Reason*, pp. 62–3, 74–84.

31. "When experiences of inner nature . . . gain independence as aesthetic experiences, the ensuing works of autonomous art take on the role of objects that open our eyes, that provoke new modes of seeing things, new attitudes, and new modes of behavior. Aesthetic experiences are not forms of everyday practice; they do not refer to cognitive-instrumental skills and moral ideas, which develop in innerworldly learning processes, but rather are bound up with the world-constituting, world-disclosing function of language." Habermas, "Actions, Speech Acts, Linguistically Mediated Interactions and the Lifeworld (1988)," in *On the Pragmatics of Communication*, pp. 245–6.

32. I indicate the need to historicize the concept of "artwork" in "Fantastic Things: Critical Notes toward a Social Ontology of the Arts." My suggestions about artistic truth take up where the last page of that essay left off.

33. See especially Charles Taylor's *Sources of the Self: The Making of the Modern Identity* (Cambridge, Mass.: Harvard University Press, 1989) and *The Ethics of Authenticity* (Cambridge, Mass.: Harvard University Press, 1992).

34. This experience or vision need not be merely personal, nor does it have to be construed in an individualistic manner, for reasons I explain in the essay "Creative Border Crossing in New Public Culture."

35. The phrase comes from Steven C. Dubin, *Arresting Images: Impolitic Art and Uncivil Actions* (New York: Routledge, 1992), which gives illuminating sociological accounts of several culture-political outbreaks.

36. As I explain in a companion volume on the politics and economics of the arts, I have coined the term "art-in-public" to encompass "public art" (art that is government-sponsored or government-owned), "publicly funded art" (art supported directly or indirectly by government agencies), and "publicly accessible art" (art whose exhibition or performance occurs in public spaces or public media). Depending on how one defines "indirect support" and "public spaces or public media," much of the art produced in North America today could be considered art-in-public, contrary to a still prominent myth that art is something made and enjoyed by individuals in the so-called private domain. The term "art-in-public" implies a critique of the traditional public-private split that continues to inform many debates about the arts and their role in society.

37. See especially Wellmer's "Truth, Semblance, Reconciliation." I discuss Wellmer's "stereoscopic" reading of Adorno in chapter 11 of *Adorno's Aesthetic Theory* and will not rehash that discussion here.

38. Here I follow Habermas, although I replace his notion of an "objective world" with the notion of a "postsubjective world."

39. Habermas, *Moral Consciousness and Communicative Action*, p. 25.

40. Ibid.

41. I discuss the ontology of worlds at greater length in two subsequent chapters on Wolterstorff and Goodman. What I have stated here is a first sketch that requires greater elaboration.

42. A similar tendency undermines the important criticisms Maeve Cooke directs at Habermas's account of normative validity claims. She confuses speech acts with validity claims, and she tends to equate validity claims with assertions about validity. In other words, her own analysis moves too quickly from the level of

communicative action proper to the level of argumentation within discourse. See *Language and Reason*, pp. 63–72.

43. "In general, obligations result from the meaning of expressive speech acts only in that the speaker specifies what his past or future behavior may not contradict. That a speaker means what he says can be made credible only in the consistency of what he does and not through providing grounds. . . . [Expressive speech acts] contain an offer to the hearer to check against the consistency of the speaker's past or future sequence of actions whether he means what he says." Habermas, *The Theory of Communicative Action*, 1: 303.

44. Recently this has changed – with a vengeance, one is tempted to say – thanks in part to the impact of new social movements and in part to narcissistic patterns imported from (pseudo)confessional uses of mass media such as talk radio, celebrity testimonials, and "reality" television.

45. Habermas, *Postmetaphysical Thinking*, p. 76.

46. Here I revise an earlier essay's suggestion that the dyadic links are necessary. See "Artistic Truth, Linguistically Turned: Variations on a Theme from Adorno, Habermas, and Hart," in *Philosophy as Responsibility: A Celebration of Hendrik Hart's Contribution to the Discipline*, ed. Ronald A. Kuipers and Janet Catherina Wesselius (Lanham, Md.: University Press of America, 2002), pp. 129–49.

Chapter 7: Logical Positivist Dispute

1. C. K. Ogden and I. A. Richards, *The Meaning of Meaning: A Study of the Influence of Language upon Thought and of the Science of Symbolism* (1923), 8th ed. (New York: Harcourt, Brace & World, Harvest Book, 1946), p. 158.

2. Theodore Meyer Greene, *The Arts and the Art of Criticism* (1940), 2d ed. (Princeton: Princeton University Press, 1947), p. 444.

3. For the purposes of my account, the "mainstream" excludes such important works as John Dewey's *Art as Experience* (1934) and Susanne K. Langer's *Philosophy in a New Key* (1942) and *Feeling and Form* (1953). It also excludes other important works either translated into English or heavily indebted to works in French, German, or other languages.

4. Richard Shusterman, ed., *Analytic Aesthetics* (Oxford: Basil Blackwell, 1989).

5. A third debate, also from the stage of analytic aesthetics, concerns the truth of literary interpretations, and it pits objectivists such as Monroe Beardsley against relativists such as Joseph Margolis. It introduces additional issues, but most of them can be derived from those raised in the other two debates.

6. Ogden and Richards, *The Meaning of Meaning*, p. 149; hereafter in this section cited internally by page number.

7. This is one half of the causal picture, according to Ogden and Richards. Symbolic use is also caused by a reference in the speaker, and emotive use is also caused by (i.e., expresses) emotions and the like in the speaker.

8. In *Principles of Literary Criticism* (New York: Harcourt Brace Jovanovich, 1926), where I. A. Richards makes the contrast between art and science even starker, the link between reference and science becomes even stronger: "An immense extension of our powers of referring has recently been made. With amazing swiftness Science has opened out field after field of possible reference. Science is simply the organisation of references with a view solely to the convenience and

facilitation of reference. It has advanced mainly because other claims, typically the claims of our religious desires, have been set aside" (p. 265). See also his book *Science and Poetry*, 2d ed. (London: Kegan Paul, Trench, Trubner, 1935).

9. The pages (pp. 8–23) that introduce the triangular model of reference do remarkably little to characterize either "reference" or "thought." The use of "grasps" in scare quotes occurs on p. 15, where Ogden and Richards say the reference (rather than, as one might expect, the person referring) grasps its object: "The completeness of any reference varies; it is more or less close and clear, it 'grasps' its object in greater or less degree."

10. The authors' technical term for such an expectation is "engram": "This simple case is typical of all interpretation, the peculiarity of interpretation being that when a context has affected us in the past the recurrence of merely a part of the context will cause us to react in the way in which we reacted before. A sign is always a stimulus similar to some part of an original stimulus and sufficient to call up the engram formed by that stimulus. An engram is the residual trace of an adaptation made by the organism to a stimulus. The mental process due to the calling up of an engram is a similar adaptation: so far as it is cognitive, what it is adapted to is its referent, and is what the sign which excites it stands for or signifies" (p. 53).

11. It is telling that the authors speak about *reference* immediately after they discuss the truth and falsity of *expectations* with regard to match scraping and flames: "If now there be an event which completes the external context in question, the reference is *true* and the event is its referent. If there be no such event, the reference is *false*, and the expectation is disappointed" (p. 62). This indicates just how expansive their notion of reference is. Several pages later the authors propose to speak of beliefs, interpretations, and ideas as references (p. 73).

12. In fact, the authors deny the independent existence of any universals. Cf. pp. 45, 49–50, 62–4, 95–103.

13. The combination of a reference view of truth and a causal criterion supports the authors' rejection of Wittgenstein's account of propositions as pictures whose structure corresponds to "the configuration of objects in the state of affairs" (*Tractatus Logico–Philosophicus*, Prop. 3.21). Ogden and Richards do not think that propositions are pictures, they do not restrict the locus of truth to propositions (arguing, instead, that even references symbolized by single words can be true or false), and they do not believe sentences should have the privileged position these have occupied in post-Kantian logic and grammar. See their appendix A, pp. 251–62.

14. Greene distinguishes three aspects of art criticism: historical, re-creative, and judicial. Artistic perfection, truth, and greatness are the concerns of "judicial criticism," which assesses "the value of a work of art in relation to other works of art and to other human values" (*The Arts and the Art of Criticism*, p. 370; hereafter in this section cited internally by page number).

15. I deliberately phrase this in an impersonal manner, unlike Greene, who usually equates an artwork's expression and interpretation with the artist's expression and interpretation. Summarizing, he describes the work of art as "a distinctive expression, in a distinctive medium, and by means of a distinctive type of formal organization, of a distinctive type of interpretation of [human] experience and of the real world to which this experience is oriented" (p. 230).

16. Greene's fundamental distinction in this connection is between natural "manifestation" and human "expression." To treat either symbolic reference or emotive expression as causal processes, à la Richards, would blur this distinction and miss the senses of purpose and goal that are central to an Aristotelian philosophy of culture.

17. My summary omits morality, the third member of Greene's cognitive-expressive trio. Greene sees art as mediating between science and morality in a way that recalls both Kant's *Critique of Judgment* and Aristotle's *Nicomachean Ethics.*

18. Although he also suggests that the media in which propositions are expressed need not be intersubjective, Greene restricts his attention to propositions that can be expressed in (potential or actual) media of "inter-subjective communication," of which art and science are prime examples (pp. 426–7).

19. Within the criterion of "consistency" Greene distinguishes (1) medial correctness, (2) medial felicity, (3) ideational noncontradiction, and (4) ideational coherence, and he places these in a rising hierarchy of necessary conditions (see pp. 430–2). Later he specifies these subcriteria for art in terms of *stylistic* correctness, felicity, noncontradiction, and coherence (see pp. 446–52). I take them up in that connection.

20. These formulations call for an explanation of reliability, relevance, and availability in the artistic context, which Greene provides. See pp. 453–8.

21. Since art, like science, is "highly specialized," such evaluations require "a trained sensitivity to artistic expression in general" and "an understanding of the specific language used by the artist in the work in question" (pp. 455–9).

22. Perhaps it was to avoid this simple rebuttal that Ogden and Richards were so vague when they first characterized "reference" and "thought" – see note 9.

23. John Searle, *Speech Acts: An Essay in the Philosophy of Language* (Cambridge: Cambridge University Press, 1969), pp. 26–31.

24. Searle prefers to think of the thing identified as individual or particular, although he does allow for expressions that are used to refer to universals. He specifies that the term "referring expression" is short for "singular definite expression used for referring to particulars" (ibid., p. 28). Proper names, certain noun phrases, and pronouns are paradigmatic referring expressions in English.

25. Ibid., p. 29.

26. This is a crucial point for Searle: "[T]he tendency to construe predication as a kind of, or analogous to, reference is one of the most persistent mistakes in the history of Western philosophy. No effort to eradicate it is too great" (ibid., p. 122). Although the footnote in this passage cites a "striking example" from V. Lenin, perhaps betraying Searle's ideological leanings, he directs his argument against Frege's account of predication, Quine's criterion of ontological commitment, and Strawson's term theory of propositions. See pp. 97–119.

27. Strictly speaking, predication is not a speech act; rather, it is a dimension of various (types of) speech acts or an abstraction from them: "It is a slice from the total illocutionary act.... We need the notion [of predication] because different illocutionary acts can have a common content...and we need some way to separate our analysis of the illocutionary force aspect of the total illocutionary act from the propositional content aspect.... What we are speaking of, though, is that portion of the total illocutionary act which determines the content applied

to the object referred to by the subject expression, leaving aside the illocutionary mode in which that content is applied" (ibid., p. 123).

28. Ibid., p. 124. Note that Searle's formulation is cryptic, perhaps because it is difficult to speak about the truth of predicate expressions without suggesting an element of reference or "aboutness." Consider the following passage: "To predicate an expression '*P*' of an object *R* is to raise the question of the truth of the predicate expression of the object referred to. Thus, in utterances of each of the sentences, 'Socrates is wise,' 'Is Socrates wise?' 'Socrates, be wise!' the speaker raises the question of the truth of 'wise' of Socrates." A few sentences later Searle says such sentences "raise the question of his [Socrates'] being wise (of whether 'wise' is ... true of him)" (p. 124). Would it be equivalent to Searle's formulation to say that a predication raises the question of truth "about" the predicate expression or "with reference to" the object referred to? What is the force of "of" (used four times in the first sentence quoted!) in his formulation? At one point Searle says that when the speech act is one of describing or characterizing, the predicate expression "serves to describe or characterize" the object identified by the subject expression (p. 119). This suggests that there is no general way to characterize what predication "does," since this depends on the type of speech act in which the predication occurs.

29. Here I simply extend to propositions what I take to be an implication of Searle's account of universals: "Entities such as universals do not lie in the world, but in our mode of representing the world, in language. . . . [T]hey are linguistic in the way that meanings of words are, and hence linguistic in the way that words with meanings are" (ibid., p. 115). "Universals are ... identified not by appealing to facts in the world, but in the utterance of expressions having the relevant meanings" (p. 116). "[T]o understand *the name of a universal* it is necessary to understand the use of the corresponding general term. But the converse is not the case. 'Kindness' is parasitic on 'is kind': 'is kind' is prior to 'kindness'" (p. 119).

30. Ibid., pp. 3, 115.

31. Ogden and Richards, *The Meaning of Meaning*, p. 74.

32. Searle, *Speech Acts*, p. 16.

33. Ibid., p. 25.

34. Ibid., pp. 42–50. The crux to Searle's account of meaning is as follows: "Uttering a sentence and meaning it is a matter of (*a*) intending (*i*–I) to get the hearer to know (recognize, be aware of) that certain states of affairs specified by certain of the rules obtain, (*b*) intending to get the hearer to know (recognize, be aware of) these things by means of getting him to recognize *i*–*I* and (*c*) intending to get him to recognize *i*–I in virtue of his knowledge of the rules for the sentence uttered" (p. 49).

35. For an account of "constitutive rules," as distinct from "regulative rules," see ibid., pp. 33–42.

36. Richards, *Principles of Literary Criticism*, pp. 158–9.

37. Ogden and Richards make this suggestion in *The Meaning of Meaning*, p. 151. For a slight elaboration, see Richards, *Principles of Literary Criticism*, pp. 268–71.

38. Perhaps this is why Ogden and Richards take the elitist Humean position that the evaluation of attitudes evoked by art "must rest ultimately upon the opinions of those best qualified to be judges by the range and delicacy of their experience

and their freedom from irrelevant preoccupations" (*The Meaning of Meaning*, p. 159).

39. The account Richards gives of science is equally problematic, for different but related reasons, but to criticize that account would take me too far afield.

40. The following passage in *The Arts and the Art of Criticism*, p. 426, is telling: "This distinction between a judgment and a proposition is important because in appraising the truth or falsity of a work of art we are concerned only with the truth or falsity of the *meaning* it expresses, and not ... whether the creative artist himself has wished to affirm or deny what he has expressed in his art. It also rules out *a fortiori* all questions concerning the artist's sincerity." Here "meaning" is an equivalent for "proposition," and the artist's affirming or denying that meaning is an equivalent for judgment. Presumably, the artist's sincerity is tied to the artist's judgment, and not to the meaning the artwork expresses. In other passages, however, the artist's *interpretation* of his or her subject matter seems identical with the meaning or (propositional) *content* the artwork expresses. Perhaps for Greene the artist's interpreting a subject matter is not quite the same as the artist's judging the meaning expressed in that interpretation or by way of that interpretation. Or perhaps he is not entirely consistent in his claims about the relation between an artwork's truth content and the artist's intention.

41. Oddly enough, George Dickie's institutional theory of art takes speech acts as a clue to defining art but does not consider how meaning gets constituted in art. By implication, however, Dickie's definition of art places "meaning-constitution" in the hands of institutional authorities (e.g., directors of museums and galleries) rather than in the constitutive rules (if there are such) according to which "art acts" occur. This introduces an element of arbitrariness that is directly contrary to Searle's account of how language works. See George Dickie, *Art and the Aesthetic: An Institutional Analysis* (Ithaca, N.Y.: Cornell University Press, 1974).

42. Another alternative, suggested by the work of Donald Davidson, would be to retain an emphasis on sentences but give a holistic account of linguistic meaning: "The meaning (interpretation) of a sentence is given by assigning the sentence a semantic location in the pattern of sentences that comprise the language." Davidson, *Inquiries into Truth and Interpretation* (Oxford: Clarendon Press, 1984), p. 225. But I do not think this alternative holds much promise for a conception of artistic truth, despite suggestive critical interpretations of Davidson by authors such as Bjørn T. Ramberg, *Donald Davidson's Philosophy of Language: An Introduction* (Oxford: Basil Blackwell, 1989).

43. Greene seems to waffle on the importance of predicability. He denies "that propositions are identifiable with their formulation in a conceptual medium." He does not deny that artistic truth can be translated into a conceptual medium, however, but merely that it can be translated into a conceptual medium "without vital loss" (*The Arts and the Art of Criticism*, p. 427). So I do not think he denies that propositions must, in principle, be predicable. This would still allow for certain propositions to be expressed without predication actually occurring.

44. Here I not only take issue with Greene but also depart from Searle's tendency to say propositions are the content of speech acts and are expressed when people perform speech acts. My position on propositions stems in part from

Heidegger's account of the interpretive character of assertions, discussed in Chapter 4.

45. For criticisms of intentionalist descriptions and interpretations of artworks, see Beardsley, *Aesthetics*, pp. 17–29; on intentionalist evaluations, see pp. 457–61.

46. This loosely Aristotelian ontology generates the medial "purism" ridiculed by Beardsley (ibid., pp. 493–4).

47. I should note that my comments here are restricted to "integrity" – the truth of artistic import – which is only one dimension, albeit a crucial one, in what I call artistic truth. The other two dimensions I have labeled "authenticity" and "significance."

Chapter 8: Goodman's Nominalism

1. Nelson Goodman, *Languages of Art: An Approach to a Theory of Symbols* (New York: Bobbs-Merrill, 1968), p. 264; hereafter cited internally by page number.

2. Rather than simply follow the meandering path of Goodman's own exposition, section 8.1 lays out the deep structure to his accounts of representation and expression.

3. For this reason Goodman notes that "languages" in his book's title "should, strictly, be replaced by 'symbol systems'" (p. xii).

4. Goodman suggests in various passages that, depending on which symbol systems are "in effect," the relationships symbols sustain are either referential or not referential. Here is one such passage: "An element may come to serve as a symbol for an element related to it in almost any way. Sometimes the underlying relationship is not referential, as when the symbol is the cause or effect of . . . , or is just to the left of, or is similar to, what it denotes. In other cases reference runs along a chain of relationships, some or all of them referential" (p. 65). This point is not important for my exposition, so I set it aside in what follows.

5. "Symbolic reference" (my term) would be pleonastic for Goodman. So far as I can tell, he thinks all symbols are capable of reference, and all reference occurs by way of symbols. I use "patterns" as an ontologically neutral term in the context of the Wolterstorff-Goodman debate. One challenge in sorting out this debate is that the interlocutors have fundamentally opposed intuitions about "the nature" of types, classes, kinds, universals, and the like.

6. "Representation" is the topic on which Wolterstorff draws the sharpest contrasts between Goodman's book and his own. See Nicholas Wolterstorff, *Works and Worlds of Art* (Oxford: Clarendon Press, 1980), pp. 263–70 and 339–55. I ignore Wolterstorff's critique of what he calls "The Goodman Alternative" (pp. 98–105) to his own account of art works as norm kinds. Wolterstorff regards Goodman's book as providing a "theory of the nature of art works" (p. 98). Given Wolterstorff's technical definition of "art works," I think Goodman's book provides no such thing, nor does it try to.

7. Comparing the general terms of Goodman's account of representation with Wolterstorff's, one immediately notices two telling differences: (1) Goodman's usages of "reference" and "denotation" are nearly as broad as Wolterstorff's are narrow, and (2) Goodman's definitive contrast lies between representation and exemplification, while Wolterstorff's lies between two types of representation.

8. Here "inscription" is used in a sense broad enough to include utterances and marks (see *Languages of Art*, p. 131).

9. For ease of exposition, I leave aside Goodman's discussion of "fictions" and "representation-as" (see pp. 21–33), even though it provides a foil for Wolterstorff's account of representation. I introduce this discussion later in this chapter and return to it in the next chapter.

10. Goodman specifies two syntactic requirements upon a notational scheme and three semantic requirements upon a notational system: (1) the syntactic disjointness of characters – that no inscription within a notation "may belong to more than one character" and "the characters must thus be *disjoint*" (p. 133); (2) the syntactic "finite differentiation" or "articulateness" of characters – "*For every two characters K and K' and every mark m that does not actually belong to both, determination either that m does not belong to K or that m does not belong to K' is theoretically possible*" (pp. 135–6); (3) the semantic unambiguity of a notational system – that all the inscriptions of a character must have the same compliance class (p. 147); (4) the semantic disjointness of compliance classes in a notational system; and (5) the semantic finite differentiation of compliance classes in a notational system – "*for every two characters K and K' such that their compliance-classes are not identical, and every object h that does not comply with both, determination either that h does not comply with K or that h does not comply with K' must be theoretically possible*" (p. 152). Semantic requirements (4) and (5) parallel syntactic requirements (1) and (2). He summarizes: "A system is notational, then, if and only if all objects complying with inscriptions of a given character belong to the same compliance class and we can, theoretically, determine that each mark belongs to, and each object complies with inscriptions of, at most one particular character" (p. 156).

11. Cf. Goodman's discussion of clocks and of analog and digital instruments on pp. 157–64. He points out that a normal nondigital watch is not a purely analog instrument, since it "speaks notationally" in certain respects (p. 158).

12. Goodman's stated reason for switching is that, to sort out cases where S exemplifies property x but not coextensive property y or identical property z, "we seem to need a different property for every predicate" (p. 54). In general, of course, Goodman's nominalism makes him wary of positing properties that can be exemplified.

13. Goodman does not give an example of this here (wisely, perhaps, since providing an example in writing would require linguistic labeling of that which the nonverbal symbol denotes). He suggests, however, that "the orientation that distinguishes exemplification from denotation does seem to derive from the organization of language even where nonverbal symbols are involved" (p. 57). Be that as it may, one could imagine a linguistically nonlabeled hue of red that is denoted by a particular manipulation of a computerized color wheel and that is exemplified by a tailor's swatch. Upon seeing the swatch a customer might exclaim "That's the hue I want!" without the customer or tailor or anyone else having a precise vocabulary to denote the hue. For a realist, however, this would raise the question whether such a linguistically unlabeled and nonverbally denoted hue of red should not more simply be called a property. Goodman suggests a response to this on p. 67.

14. Goodman dismisses in passing the question of why *predicates* apply as they do (whether metaphorically or literally), suggesting that "there is no real question."

And the explanation of why things have the *properties* they do have he is "content to leave to the cosmologist" (p. 78).

15. It's puzzling why, when he discusses expression (pp. 85–95), Goodman reverts to the property talk he had so diligently avoided when explaining literal exemplification and metaphor (pp. 52–85). He claims to be deferring here "to a prissy prejudice" even though he thinks "such pussyfooting" removes "no difficulty or obscurity" (p. 87). So why doesn't he stick to his nominalist guns? My own exposition takes the liberty – indeed, takes "the bolder course" that "is surely to be recommended"! – of translating Goodman's property talk and "speaking forthrightly of expression of labels rather than properties" (p. 87n33).

16. Consider, for example, movements in modern dance that exemplify rhythms and dynamic shapes and "reorganize experience" by "enriching allusion or sharpening discrimination." Seldom can the "just wording be found" to describe such movements, Goodman says. "Rather, the label a movement exemplifies may be itself; such a movement, having no antecedent denotation, takes on the duties of a label denoting certain actions including itself" (p. 65).

17. Goodman adds "multiple and complex reference" to this list in *Ways of Worldmaking* (Indianapolis: Hackett, 1978), p. 68.

18. Insofar as the arts and sciences are social institutions in ways that aesthetic experience is not, Goodman's language is imprecise. Rather than comparing "aesthetic" and "scientific" experience, he should be comparing "artistic" and "scientific" experience. The tendency to conflate the aesthetic and the artistic is endemic to post-Kantian philosophy, and Goodman does not challenge that tendency.

19. Goodman, *Ways of Worldmaking*, p. 109.

20. Ibid., p. 17.

21. Ibid., pp. 120–1.

22. Ibid., p. 19.

23. Ibid., pp. 130–3.

24. Ibid., p. 109.

25. Ibid., p. 138.

26. Ibid., p. 102.

27. Ibid., p. 94.

28. Such detachment and deflation provide grist for Wolterstorff's realist mill. What really concerns him about Goodman's theory is that Goodman does not allow "that works of music can have incorrect performances" (Wolterstorff, *Works and Worlds of Art*, p. 101) and does not distinguish between a symbol's merely denoting something and its representing something "*either correctly or incorrectly*" (ibid., p. 353). To uphold standards of correctness, Wolterstorff's alternative posits metaphysical kinds and states of affairs that Goodman would find baffling. One does not need to be an ontological realist, however, to detect problems in how Goodman detaches truth from truth bearers.

29. Goodman does not consider mixed cases of representation-as, such as a picture that represents a historical man as a fictional man and one that represents a fictional man as a current male leader. Both cases would involve man-pictures, but would they have null denotations or not? (Later he says that fictive representations [e.g., a unicorn-picture], fictive descriptions [e.g., a unicorn-description],

and representations-as are actually "modes of exemplification rather than of denotation" [p. 66].)

30. Without accusing Goodman of equivocation, Wolterstorff teases out some of these problems in *Works and Worlds of Art*, pp. 340–5.

31. One exception is the account of reference given by I. A. Richards. As I have noted elsewhere, Richards expands "reference" to encompass all nonemotive uses of symbols, and he neglects the "aboutness" of reference. Whereas he makes all reference natural and causal, Goodman makes it entirely cultural and conventional.

32. Goodman is not unaware of the need for some account. He signals this on p. 22n19, for example, where he cites three of his papers, including one titled simply "About," *Mind* 70 (1961): 1–24.

33. In that sense Goodman is closer to pragmatism than is Wolterstorff, who nevertheless emphasizes the pragmatics of symbols. This fact is obscured by Wolterstorff's criticizing Goodman for sticking to symbol systems and semantics, as in the following summary of why Goodman's theory of representation is unsatisfactory: "[T]he root of the difficulty lies in the fact that Goodman's theory, being a purely semantic theory, is unable to cope with the many different ways in which pictures *are used*. Our scrutiny of Goodman's theory confirms us in the conviction that we must go beyond semantics into pragmatics if we wish to have anything near a satisfactory theory of picturing." Wolterstorff, *Works and Worlds of Art*, pp. 354–5. On my own reading, although Wolterstorff emphasizes action, his theory of action is *not* pragmatic; and although Goodman emphasizes symbol systems, his theory of symbolization *is* pragmatic.

34. *Ways of Worldmaking* begins, however, with themes articulated by Cassirer – appropriately so, since the first chapter "was read at the University of Hamburg on the one-hundredth anniversary of the birth of Ernst Cassirer" (p. ix).

35. Goodman readily acknowledges art's nonaesthetic aspects when he explains artistic notations as characteristically articulate, unambiguous, and denotative. Clearly one confronts a fine line here between so highlighting art's distinctiveness that it becomes noncognitive (à la I. A. Richards) and so downplaying its distinctiveness that art becomes cognitively superfluous (à la T. M. Greene).

36. Calvin G. Seerveld, *Rainbows for the Fallen World: Aesthetic Life and Artistic Task* (Toronto: Tuppence Press, 1980). I review Seerveld's approach in "Transforming Aesthetics: Reflections on the Work of Calvin G. Seerveld," the introduction to *Pledges of Jubilee: Essays on the Arts and Culture, in Honor of Calvin G. Seerveld*, ed. Lambert Zuidervaart and Henry Luttikhuizen (Grand Rapids, Mich.: Eerdmans, 1995), pp. 1–22.

37. To do this, the emotions must function "in combination with one another and with other means of knowing" such as perception and conception (p. 249). In general, feeling is a means of classifying things and discerning them, Goodman writes (p. 251).

38. *Ways of Worldmaking*, p. 110.

39. In general, I find myself agreeing with Goodman that all worlds are "actual worlds" (*Ways of Worldmaking*, pp. 94–7) but disagreeing about how many worlds are actual and how they interrelate. For Goodman, a world is a symbolically constructed world version. In principle he seems to allow as many worlds as there are intact symbol systems. Although he considers conflicts among world

versions, he does not propose an ontological principle for reducing the number of worlds, nor does he give a general account of how they interrelate. Goodman's underlying assumption seems to be that, for the most part, the worlds of science, art, and the like run parallel, neither interacting nor interfering with each other. My own background assumptions about personal, social, and postsubjective worlds do not concur with such a benignly pluralistic parallelism.

40. For an objection along these lines I am indebted to an anonymous reader for Cambridge University Press.

Chapter 9: Wolterstorff's Realism

1. Nicholas Wolterstorff, *Works and Worlds of Art* (Oxford: Clarendon Press, 1980), p. 109; hereafter cited internally by page number.

2. For Wolterstorff, states of affairs, like "art works" as "norm-kinds," cannot but exist, even if they do not occur. So it strikes me as odd to say of any state of affairs that it is "already existent." What is the significance of the temporal "already"?

3. Wolterstorff subsumes both "mention" and "suggest" under the author's indication of certain states of affairs, and he uses the term "elucidation" for readers' discovering what the author has indicated. Elucidation and extrapolation together make up the activity of interpretation. Wolterstorff gives two alternative formulations for what states of affairs, beyond those indicated by the author, are included in the work's world, but I leave those formulations aside (see pp. 115–26). I also leave aside his analysis of a state of affairs' being included in the world of a work (see pp. 128–9).

4. The contrast here is between a "noncomprehensive" state of affairs such as the world of a work and a "maximally comprehensive" state of affairs such as a possible world. The latter, unlike the former, either "prohibits or requires every state of affairs whatsoever" (p. 131). Wolterstorff restricts the locution "true in a world" to states of affairs that are either "true in our actual world" (p. 110) or true in possible worlds (p. 134). Whereas states of affairs "included within" actual or possible worlds are "true in" their worlds, typically the states of affairs included within an artwork's world (i.e., world segment) are neither true nor false.

5. Wolterstorff summarizes these distinctions and relationships in a useful diagram on p. 197.

6. As we shall see, this suggestion receives confirmation and elaboration from the general account of world projection given in part 4 (pp. 198–247).

7. I leave aside the technical distinction between actions and acts (see pp. 3–4). Being "ontologically profligate" like Wolterstorff in these matters would needlessly complicate my reconstruction.

8. The preliminary discussion of Rembrandt's painting *Bathsheba* on pp. 16–29 illustrates the priority of count-generation. Wolterstorff portrays Rembrandt's action of (1) applying paint to canvas as the first link in an intricate chain whereby Rembrandt causally generates the actions of (2) producing a rendering of his beloved Hendrickje and (3) creating the painting *Bathsheba*; thereby count-generates the actions of (4) representing Bathsheba as bathing and (5) projecting a world that includes a woman bathing; causally generates the actions of (6) giving people aesthetic delight, (7) embarrassing Hendrickje, and

(8) getting his smock dirty; and, in a manner that fits neither causal nor count-generation, (9) reveals his fondness for strong chiaroscuro and (10) expresses his aversion to the Renaissance cult of the ideal body. Actions like (4) and (5) – both of them count-generated – figure prominently in Wolterstorff's account of artistic world projection.

9. This approach is suggested by reader response theories (e.g., Hans Robert Jauss and Stanley Fish) and some hermeneutic theories (e.g., Hans-Georg Gadamer on a certain inaccurate reading).

10. Wolterstorff uses "art works" to indicate the norm kinds in question, and "works of art" to cover both the norm kinds and their occurrences or objects (see pp. 41, 57–8). My reconstruction employs "artworks" (one word) as a neutral term that does not imply Wolterstorff's ontological commitments.

11. I have drastically simplified Wolterstorff's discussion of artworks, which assumes the ontology in his book *On Universals: An Essay in Ontology* (Chicago: University of Chicago Press, 1970). Prior to discussing Nelson Goodman's alternative at the end of part 2 (see pp. 98–105), Wolterstorff portrays set theory as the main rival to his account of art works as kinds. He argues that art works cannot be sets because an art work "might always have had different and more or fewer occurrences or objects than it does have," whereas, according to Wolterstorff, "whatever members a set has, it has essentially" (p. 44).

12. This account leads Wolterstorff to make several claims about music that would be problematic on a different ontology. Let me mention three: (1) that to compose a musical work is to select "properties of sound for the purpose of their serving as criteria for judging correctness of occurrence" (p. 62); (2) that musical art works "exist everlastingly" and "are immutable" with respect to both their essential and their normative properties (pp. 88–90); (3) that the composer does not create a musical art work, but, (normally) by creating a copy of the work's score, simply brings it about "that a preexistent kind becomes *a work*" (p. 89). A controversial corollary to this view is that striving for aesthetic excellence is neither here nor there when it comes to the "correctness" of a work's musical occurrences – see pp. 64, 82. This suggests that striving for aesthetic excellence is not essential to the tasks of composing, performing, and listening.

13. Incidentally, it is uninformative for Wolterstorff to say that the action of communicating something to someone is not an illocutionary action. On the one hand, his reason for this – that communicating is "causally but not count-generated" (p. 220) – is odd, since his general definition of count-generation seems to require either the agent's communicating a belief to "interested parties" or causing ("intentionally inducing") a belief among interested parties. On the other hand, regardless of what his own definition of count-generation implies, it is not readily apparent why communication should be thought of along causal lines.

14. Presumably, Rembrandt's projecting that world in that way on a specific occasion and under specific circumstances is an occurrence of that 1-degree statal action and an instance of that 2-degree statal action (an occurrence and instance parallel to my asserting here and now that my study door will be closed). One can derive this analysis from Wolterstorff's discussion on pp. 193–7 of John running (state of affairs), running (action attribute), and John's running (act event).

15. This is an informal rendering of Wolterstorff's analysis. Since I do not find the analysis persuasive, and also do not find it crucial to the larger argument, let me leave matters informal and perhaps imprecise, and also ignore Wolterstorff's distinction between "statal indicators" and "stance-indicators." This distinction roughly parallels and implicitly rejects Searle's distinction between the "propositional indicator" and the "illocutionary force indicator" in the syntactical structure of (English) sentences. See Searle, *Speech Acts*, especially pp. 30–3.

16. In Wolterstorff's terminology, what gets *asserted* is a "proposition" (e.g., "that the door is closed"), and what gets *asserted-of* is a "propositional function" (e.g., "that it is closed," when this is asserted of, say, the door).

17. Wolterstorff's formulation is not quite precise, it seems to me. As he acknowledges in a long footnote on Robert Howell's theory of representation, Wolterstorff takes for granted "that there are no entities which do not exist" (p. 268n4). Yet his discussion of unicorns makes it seem as if unicorns do not *exist*, even though he makes no claim about this one way or the other. It would be more precise, in his own vocabulary, to say that (for all we know) unicorns do not *occur*. (Another option would be to claim that unicorns are not entities [and hence do not exist], but I don't know how the argument for that claim would go, nor what it could possibly mean.) Also, it would be more precise to say that the concept of q-representation is used to make claims to the effect that some *occurrent* entity was represented.

18. Wolterstorff directs this against John G. Bennett's essay "Depiction and Convention," discussed on pp. 270–9. Wolterstorff thinks pictures resemble sentences in that both can be used to generate mood actions.

19. I omit Wolterstorff's discussion of pictorial and perceptual conventions and his sympathetic criticisms of Kendall Walton's spectator-based theory of picturing; see pp. 295–325.

20. If, as Wolterstorff suggests, "one can use a pictorial design to assert of Bathsheba that she is [a woman] sitting on a couch bathing" (p. 330), wouldn't the picture in this case be a predicate or serve predication? For one would be "asserting of A that it is a k which is ø" (p. 330), that is, assertively posing of, that is, predicating. Perhaps not much hangs on this point, but it does raise questions about Wolterstorff's criticisms of Bennett's theory of pictures as predicates.

21. In Wolterstorff's more formal language, "to q-represent of A the property of being a *k* which is ø ... is to count-generate the action of posing of A that it has the property of being a *k* which is ø. And it is to do so (i), by using some design D to p-represent that there is a *k* which is ø, and (ii), by denoting A with design D or some part thereof ..." (p. 331).

22. For Wolterstorff's account of denotation, see pp. 242–4.

23. Similarly, Wolterstorff says that fictional characters can be "*accurate portrayals* of actual persons" in the sense that some person actually exemplifies certain "less determinate person-kinds within which a work's characters are included" (p. 357).

24. Wolterstorff suggests, further, that what is most characteristic of "modern high-art artists" is that they give expression to the vision of a "*sub*community," namely, "the culture élite, in opposition to that of the bourgeoisie" (pp. 362–3). He develops this characterization at greater length in *Art in Action: Toward a Christian Aesthetic*.

25. Quoted from Sydney's *Apology for Poetry* by Wolterstorff, p. 106.
26. Hospers, *Meaning and Truth in the Arts,* especially p. 162.
27. Recall that, on Wolterstorff's account, a proposition (or state of affairs) can be true in the actual world, or it can be true in a possible world, but it cannot be true in an impossible world.
28. The mode of presentation – visual depiction – does not matter to this example. As a contrast to the verbal assertion concerning a unicorn, one could just as easily substitute the verbal presentation of a unicorn in a piece of literary fiction, let's say "the Unicorn" in Timothy Findley's *Not Wanted on the Voyage* (New York: Penguin Books, 1984).
29. I recognize that Wolterstorff explicitly claims the essence of literary fiction (and, by extension, the essence of fictive world projection) "consists not in the nature of the states of affairs indicated, nor in the truth or falsity of those states of affairs. It lies in the mood-stance taken up" (p. 234). But I think his analysis of fiction and of fictive world projection only goes through if, for the most part, what the fictioneer projects are neither actual nor possible states of affairs.
30. One example comes from a legal setting, two from athletic competition, and one from car driving; see pp. 205–11. I have decided not to comment on his discussion of the examples, for frequently I find it puzzling, and detailed comments would take us too far afield.
31. My summary avoids some of Wolterstorff's qualifications and technical language. For a more detailed and precise version, see pp. 211–12.
32. I'm not sure Wolterstorff would grant this point, but I'm also not sure why he shouldn't. In his account of q-representation he suggests that, as a pictorial species of "posing of," q-representing Bathsheba as a woman sitting on a couch bathing is "stance neutral": it can function fictively or assertively or linked to some other mood stance. In fact, "one can use a pictorial design to assert of Bathsheba that she is [a woman] sitting on a couch bathing" (p. 330). Couldn't one also use a pictorial design to p-represent a unicorn in an assertive mode, so that in depicting the unicorn one would not fictively introduce "there being a unicorn" but (falsely) assert "there being a unicorn"?
33. Wolterstorff explains this elsewhere as the artist's fictionally projecting a world in such a way that the artist suggests various states of affairs toward which the artist "takes up an assertive stance" (p. 242).
34. Wolterstorff does not really consider the role of art in establishing interpersonal relations, however, preferring instead to talk about how artistically projected characters and incidents can help produce inclinations to act in similar ways (pp. 366–7). To give a fuller account of significance would require an intersubjective model of truth rather than a realist correspondence theory.
35. Wolterstorff's *Art in Action* repeats this discussion, sometimes verbatim, in an appendix titled "Expression and Revelation" (pp. 215–21). There he shows the relevance of his analysis for understanding the limits and legitimacy of ideological or "worldview" criticism.
36. Here I omit the complication that arises when the self-expressive act is itself count-generated – see *Works and Worlds of Art*, pp. 26–7.
37. Here, as in earlier reconstructions, I leave aside Wolterstorff's distinction between acts and actions.
38. I should note, however, that in subsequent writings Wolterstorff has developed a more holistic idea of "social practices" and has argued that we should think of the

arts in terms of ongoing composition-, reception-, and performance-practices. See, for example, his seminal essay "Philosophy of Art after Analysis and Romanticism," in *Analytic Aesthetics*, ed. Richard Shusterman (Oxford: Basil Blackwell, 1989), pp. 32–58. I briefly touch on the implications of this revision in my essay "A Tradition Transfigured: Art and Culture in Reformational Aesthetics," *Faith and Philosophy*, in press.

39. See Julia Kristeva, *Revolution in Poetic Language*, trans. Margaret Waller (New York: Columbia University Press, 1984). Writing about modern poetry, Kristeva argues: "In thus eroding the verisimilitude that inevitably underlaid classical mimesis and . . . the very position of enunciation (i.e., the positing of the subject as absent from the signifier), poetic language puts the subject in process/on trial. . . . But the moment it . . . becomes part of the linguistic order, poetry meets up with denotation and enunciation – verisimilitude and the subject – and, through them, the social" (p. 56).

Chapter 10: Aesthetic Transformations

1. Adorno, *AT* 133, *ÄT* 201, translation modified.
2. For convenience, I list Heidegger as having an "antipropositional" view of truth bearers, even though *Sein und Zeit* can be read as having a "nonpropositional" view. The later Heidegger has a more clearly antipropositional view, which shows up in "The Origin of the Work of Art."
3. Chapter 12 in Beardsley, *Aesthetics*, pp. 557–83. For his discussion of "aestheticism" and "moralism," see pp. 558–71.
4. This is one half of Beardsley's argument, the half that pertains "to the worth of art to the consumer, so to speak" (ibid., p. 573). The other half pertains to such worth for professional and amateur creators of aesthetic objects, which comes down to certain beneficial psychological effects (see pp. 572–3).
5. Ibid., pp. 573–6. I substitute the term "artworks" for Beardsley's "aesthetic objects." He is primarily interested here in aesthetic experience generated by artworks in their aesthetic dimension, not by other art phenomena, and also not by nonartistic aesthetic objects.
6. Beardsley uses the term "regional qualities" rather than "aesthetic qualities," for reasons he explains much earlier (ibid., pp. 78–107).
7. Ibid., pp. 575–6.
8. This sort of reply has been suggested by an anonymous reader for Cambridge University Press.
9. Here I am responding to Richard Rorty's frequent suggestion that philosophy should stop talking about "the nature of Truth and Goodness" and become edifying conversation. See, for example, his essay "Pragmatism and Philosophy," in Baynes et al., *After Philosophy*, pp. 26–66. My own response to the linguistic turn and its postmetaphysical aftermath is to say that philosophers need to find new ways of talking about truth and goodness, new ways within philosophy as a discipline and Western tradition, and new ways in relation to challenges in contemporary society. My theory of artistic truth offers one step in that direction.
10. Margaret Atwood, *Oryx and Crake* (Toronto: McClelland & Stewart, 2003), p. 371.
11. See Suzanne Lacy, ed., *Mapping the Terrain: New Genre Public Art* (Seattle: Bay Press, 1995).

Bibliography

Adorno, Theodor W. *Aesthetic Theory*. Trans., ed., and with a translator's introduction by Robert Hullot-Kentor. Minneapolis: University of Minnesota Press, 1997.

Against Epistemology: A Metacritique; Studies in Husserl and the Phenomenological Antinomies. Trans. Willis Domingo. Cambridge, Mass.: MIT Press, 1982.

Ästhetische Theorie (1970). *Gesammelte Schriften* 7. Ed. Gretel Adorno and Rolf Tiedemann. 2d ed. Frankfurt am Main: Suhrkamp, 1972.

Jargon der Eigentlichkeit: Zur deutschen Ideologie (1964). *Gesammelte Schriften* 6. Frankfurt am Main: Suhrkamp, 1973.

The Jargon of Authenticity. Trans. Knut Tarnowski and Frederic Will. London: Routledge & Kegan Paul, 1973.

Kierkegaard: Construction of the Aesthetic. Trans., ed., and with a foreword by Robert Hullot-Kentor. Minneapolis: University of Minnesota Press, 1989.

Kierkegaard: Konstruktion des Ästhetischen (1933). *Gesammelte Schriften* 2. Frankfurt am Main: Suhrkamp, 1979.

Zur Metakritik der Erkenntnistheorie: Studien über Husserl und die phänomenologischen Antinomien (1956). *Gesammelte Schriften* 5. Frankfurt am Main: Suhrkamp, 1970.

Negative Dialectics. Trans. E. B. Ashton. New York: Seabury Press, 1973.

Negative Dialektik (1966, 1967). *Gesammelte Schriften* 6. Frankfurt am Main: Suhrkamp, 1973.

Allen, Barry. *Truth in Philosophy*. Cambridge, Mass.: Harvard University Press, 1993.

Allison, Henry. *Kant's Theory of Taste: A Reading of the* Critique of Aesthetic Judgment. Cambridge: Cambridge University Press, 2001.

Anderson, Joel. "Review Essay: The Persistence of Authenticity." *Philosophy & Social Criticism* 21 (January 1995): 101–9.

Anker, Roy, ed. *Dancing in the Dark: Youth, Popular Culture, and the Electronic Media*. Grand Rapids, Mich.: Eerdmans, 1991.

Apel, Karl-Otto. *Towards a Transformation of Philosophy*. Trans. Glyn Adey and David Frisby. London: Routledge & Kegan Paul, 1980.

Transformation der Philosophie. 2 vols. Frankfurt am Main: Suhrkamp, 1973.

Armstrong, Isobel. *The Radical Aesthetic*. Oxford: Blackwell, 2000.

Atwood, Margaret. *Oryx and Crake*. Toronto: McClelland & Stewart, 2003.

Baynes, Kenneth, James Bohman, and Thomas McCarthy, eds. *After Philosophy: End or Transformation?* Cambridge, Mass.: MIT Press, 1987.

Beardsley, Monroe. *Aesthetics: Problems in the Philosophy of Criticism.* New York: Harcourt, Brace & World, 1958. 2d ed. Indianapolis: Hackett, 1981.

Beiner, Ronald. "Hermeneutical Generosity and Social Criticism." *Critical Review* 9 (Fall 1995): 447–64.

Benhabib, Seyla. *Situating the Self: Gender, Community and Postmodernism in Contemporary Ethics.* New York: Routledge, 1992.

Bernstein, J. M. *Adorno: Ethics and Disenchantment.* Cambridge: Cambridge University Press, 2001.

  The Fate of Art: Aesthetic Alienation from Kant to Derrida and Adorno. University Park: Pennsylvania State University Press, 1992.

Bernstein, Richard J. *Beyond Objectivism and Relativism: Science, Hermeneutics, and Praxis.* Philadelphia: University of Pennsylvania Press, 1983.

  ed. *Habermas and Modernity.* Cambridge: Mass.: MIT Press, 1985.

Bohman, James. "World Disclosure and Radical Criticism." *Thesis Eleven*, no. 37 (1994): 82–97.

Bowie, Andrew. *From Romanticism to Critical Theory: The Philosophy of German Literary Theory.* London: Routledge, 1997.

  "Revealing the Truth of Art." *Radical Philosophy* 58 (Summer 1991): 20–4.

Brandom, Robert B., ed. *Rorty and His Critics.* Oxford: Blackwell, 2000.

Brunkhorst, Hauke. "Adorno, Heidegger and Postmodernity." In *Universalism vs. Communitarianism: Contemporary Debates in Ethics*, ed. David Rasmussen, pp. 183–96. Cambridge, Mass.: MIT Press, 1990.

Bruns, Gerald L. *Heidegger's Estrangements: Language, Truth, and Poetry in the Later Writings.* New Haven: Yale University Press, 1989.

Bürger, Peter. *The Decline of Modernism.* Trans. Nicholas Walker. University Park: Pennsylvania State University Press, 1992.

Caputo, John. *Radical Hermeneutics: Repetition, Deconstruction, and the Hermeneutic Project.* Bloomington: Indiana University Press, 1987.

Cascardi, Anthony J. *Consequences of Enlightenment.* Cambridge: Cambridge University Press, 1999.

Casey, Edward S. "Truth in Art." *Man and World* 3 (November 1970): 351–69.

Chaplin, Adrienne Dengerink. "Mind, Body and Art: The Problem of Meaning in the Cognitive Aesthetics of Susanne K. Langer." Ph.D. dissertation, Vrije Universiteit, Amsterdam, 1999.

Collingwood, R. G. *The Principles of Art.* New York: Oxford University Press, 1958.

Cooke, Maeve. *Language and Reason: A Study of Habermas's Pragmatics.* Cambridge, Mass.: MIT Press, 1994.

  "Meaning and Truth in Habermas's Pragmatics." *European Journal of Philosophy* 9 (April 2001): 1–23.

Crowther, Paul. *Critical Aesthetics and Postmodernism.* Oxford: Clarendon Press, 1993.

Cumming, Robert Denoon. "The Odd Couple: Heidegger and Derrida." *Review of Metaphysics* 34 (1981): 487–521.

Dahlstrom, Daniel O. *Heidegger's Concept of Truth.* Cambridge: Cambridge University Press, 2001.

Dallmayr, Fred. *Between Freiburg and Frankfurt: Toward a Critical Ontology.* Amherst: University of Massachusetts Press, 1991.

Danto, Arthur C. *The Transfiguration of the Commonplace: A Philosophy of Art.* Cambridge, Mass.: Harvard University Press, 1981.

Davidson, Donald. *Inquiries into Truth and Interpretation.* Oxford: Clarendon Press, 1984. Reprinted with corrections 1985, 1986.

Davies, Stephen. *Musical Meaning and Expression.* Ithaca: Cornell University Press, 1994.

de Boer, Karin. *Thinking in the Light of Time: Heidegger's Encounter with Hegel.* Albany: State University of New York Press, 2000.

Derrida, Jacques. *Margins of Philosophy* (1972). Trans. Alan Bass. Chicago: University of Chicago Press, 1982.

    Of Spirit: Heidegger and the Question (1987). Trans. Geoffrey Bennington and Rachel Bowlby. Chicago: University of Chicago Press, 1989.

    The Truth in Painting (1978). Trans. Geoff Bennington and Ian McLeod. Chicago: University of Chicago Press, 1987.

Dewey, John. *Art as Experience.* In *The Later Works, 1925–1953*, vol. 10: *1934*, ed. Jo Ann Boydston. Carbondale: Southern Illinois University Press, 1987.

DiCenso, James J. *Hermeneutics and the Disclosure of Truth: A Study in the Work of Heidegger, Gadamer, and Ricoeur.* Charlottesville: University Press of Virginia, 1990.

Dickie, George. *Art and the Aesthetic: An Institutional Analysis.* Ithaca, N.Y.: Cornell University Press, 1974.

Dooyeweerd, Herman. *A New Critique of Theoretical Thought* (1953–8). 4 vols. Trans. David H. Freeman and H. De Jongste. Philadelphia: Presbyterian and Reformed Publishing, 1969.

Dorter, Kenneth. "Conceptual Truth and Aesthetic Truth." *Journal of Aesthetics and Art Criticism* 48 (Winter 1990): 37–51.

Dubin, Steven C. *Arresting Images: Impolitic Art and Uncivil Actions.* New York: Routledge, 1992.

Dufrenne, Mikel. "The Truth of the Aesthetic Object." In *The Phenomenology of Aesthetic Experience* (1953), trans. Edward S. Casey et al., pp. 501–38. Evanston, Ill.: Northwestern University Press, 1973.

Eagleton, Terry. *The Ideology of the Aesthetic.* Oxford: Basil Blackwell, 1990.

Ferrara, Alessandro. "Authenticity and the Project of Modernity." *European Journal of Philosophy* 2 (1994): 241–73.

    "A Critique of Habermas's Consensus Theory of Truth." *Philosophy & Social Criticism* 13 (Fall 1987): 39–67.

    Reflective Authenticity: Rethinking the Project of Modernity. New York: Routledge, 1998.

Findley, Timothy. *Not Wanted on the Voyage.* New York: Penguin Books, 1984.

Finke, Ståle. "Concepts and Intuitions: Adorno after the Linguistic Turn." *Inquiry* 44 (2001): 171–200.

Gablik, Suzi. *The Reenchantment of Art.* New York: Thames and Hudson, 1991.

Gadamer, Hans-Georg. *Philosophical Hermeneutics.* Trans. and ed. David E. Linge. Berkeley: University of California Press, 1976.

    The Relevance of the Beautiful and Other Essays. Trans. Nicholas Walker. Ed. Robert Bernasconi. Cambridge: Cambridge University Press, 1986.

    Truth and Method. 2d, rev. ed. Trans. and rev. Joel Weinsheimer and Donald G. Marshall. New York: Crossroad, 1989.

Wahrheit und Methode: Grundzüge einer philosophischen Hermeneutik (1960). 4th ed. (Reprint of the 3rd, expanded ed.) Tübingen: J. C. B. Mohr (Paul Siebeck), 1975.

"Zur Einführung." In Martin Heidegger, *Der Ursprung des Kunstwerkes*, pp. 102–25. Stuttgart: Reclam, 1960.

Gelven, Michael. *Truth and Existence: A Philosophical Inquiry.* University Park: Pennsylvania State University Press, 1990.

Gethmann, Carl Friedrich. "Zu Heideggers Wahrheitsbegriff." *Kant-Studien* 65 (1974): 186–200.

Goehr, Lydia. *The Imaginary Museum of Musical Works: An Essay in the Philosophy of Music.* Oxford: Clarendon Press, 1992.

Goodman, Nelson. "About." *Mind* 70 (1961): 1–24.

Languages of Art: An Approach to a Theory of Symbols. Indianapolis: Bobbs-Merrill, 1968.

Ways of Worldmaking. Indianapolis: Hackett, 1978.

Greene, Theodore Meyer. *The Arts and the Art of Criticism* (1940). 2d ed. Princeton: Princeton University Press, 1947.

Grondin, Jean. *Hermeneutische Wahrheit? Zum Wahrheitsbegriff Hans-Georg Gadamers.* Königstein: Forum Academicum, 1982.

Guignon, Charles B. *Heidegger and the Problem of Knowledge.* Indianapolis: Hackett, 1983.

"Truth as Disclosure – Art, Language, History." *Southern Journal of Philosophy* 28 (1989 Supplement): 105–20.

Habermas, Jürgen. "Actions, Speech Acts, Linguistically Mediated Interactions and the Lifeworld." In *Philosophical Problems Today*, vol. 1, ed. G. Fløistand, pp. 45–74. Dordrecht: Kluwer, 1994.

Knowledge and Human Interests (1968). Trans. J. J. Shapiro. Boston: Beacon Press, 1972.

Moral Consciousness and Communicative Action (1983). Trans. Christian Lenhardt and Shierry Weber Nicholsen. Introd. Thomas McCarthy. Cambridge, Mass.: MIT Press, 1990.

On the Pragmatics of Communication. Ed. Maeve Cooke. Cambridge, Mass.: MIT Press, 1998.

The Philosophical Discourse of Modernity: Twelve Lectures (1985). Trans. Frederick Lawrence. Cambridge, Mass.: MIT Press, 1987.

Postmetaphysical Thinking: Philosophical Essays (1988). Trans. William Mark Hohengarten. Cambridge, Mass.: MIT Press, 1992.

"Questions and Counterquestions." In *Habermas and Modernity*, ed. Richard Bernstein, pp. 192–216. Cambridge, Mass.: MIT Press, 1985.

The Theory of Communicative Action (1981). Trans. Thomas McCarthy. 2 vols. Boston: Beacon Press, 1984, 1987.

"Wahrheitstheorien." In *Wirklichkeit und Reflexion. Walter Schulz zum 60. Geburtstag*, ed. Helmut Fahrenbach, pp. 211–65. Pfullingen: Neske, 1973. Reprinted in Jürgen Habermas, *Vorstudien und Ergänzungen zur Theorie des kommunikativen Handelns*, 2d ed., pp. 127–83. Frankfurt am Main: Suhrkamp, 1986.

Wahrheit und Rechfertigung: Philosophische Aufsätze. Frankfurt am Main: Suhrkamp, 1999.

"Work and Weltanschauung: The Heidegger Controversy from a German Perspective" (1988). In *The New Conservatism: Cultural Criticism and the Historians' Debate*, ed. and trans. Shierry Weber Nicholsen, pp. 140–72. Cambridge, Mass.: MIT Press, 1989.

Hamburger, Käte. *Wahrheit und ästhetische Wahrheit*. Stuttgart: Klett-Cotta, 1979.

Hans, James S. *Contextual Authority and Aesthetic Truth*. Albany: State University of New York Press, 1992.

Hart, Hendrik. "The Impasse of Rationality Today: Revised Edition." In *Wetenschap, Wijsheid, Filosoferen*, ed. P. Blokhuis, pp. 174–200. Assen: Van Gorcum, 1981.

Understanding Our World: An Integral Ontology. Lanham, Md.: University Press of America, 1984.

Hegel, G. W. F. *Aesthetics: Lectures on Fine Art*. Trans T. M. Knox. 2 vols. Oxford: Clarendon Press, 1974, 1975.

Phenomenology of Spirit. Trans. A. V. Miller. Analysis and foreword by J. N. Findlay. Oxford: Oxford University Press, 1977.

Heidegger: A Critical Reader. Ed. Hubert L. Dreyfus and Harrison Hall. Cambridge, Mass.: Blackwell, 1992.

Heidegger, Martin. *Basic Writings from Being and Time (1927) to The Task of Thinking (1964)*. Ed. David Farrell Krell. New York: Harper & Row, 1977.

Being and Time. Trans. John Macquarrie and Edward Robinson. New York: Harper & Row, 1962.

Being and Time. Trans. Joan Stambaugh. Albany: State University of New York Press, 1996.

Beiträge zur Philosophie. Gesamtausgabe 65. Frankfurt: Vittorio Klostermann, 1989.

Contributions to Philosophy (From Enowning). Trans. Parvis Emad and Kenneth Maly. Bloomington: Indiana University Press, 1999.

"A Discussion between Ernst Cassirer and Martin Heidegger." Trans. Francis Slade. In *The Existentialist Tradition: Selected Writings*, ed. Nino Languilli, pp. 192–203. Garden City, N.Y.: Anchor Books, 1971.

Off the Beaten Track. Ed. and trans. Julian Young and Kenneth Haynes. Cambridge: Cambridge University Press, 2002.

"On the Essence of Truth." In *Basic Writings from Being and Time (1927) to The Task of Thinking (1964)*, ed. David Farrell Krell, pp. 117–41. New York: Harper & Row, 1977.

"The Origin of the Work of Art" (1935–6). In *Off the Beaten Track*, ed. and trans. Julian Young and Kenneth Haynes, pp. 1–56. Cambridge: Cambridge University Press, 2002.

"Phenomenological Interpretations with Respect to Aristotle: Indication of the Hermeneutical Situation." Trans. Michael Bauer. *Man and World* 25 (1992): 355–93.

Poetry, Language, Thought. Trans. Albert Hofstadter. New York: Harper Colophon Books, 1975.

Sein und Zeit (1927). 15th ed. Tübingen: Max Niemeyer, 1979.

"Der Ursprung des Kunstwerkes." In *Holzwege*, pp. 7–68. Frankfurt am Main: Vittorio Klostermann, 1950.

Henrich, Dieter. *Aesthetic Judgment and the Moral Image of the World: Studies in Kant*. Stanford, Calif.: Stanford University Press, 1992.

Hermann, Friedrich-Wilhelm von. *Heideggers Philosophie der Kunst: Eine systematische Interpretation der Holzwege-Abhandlung "Der Ursprung des Kunstwerkes."* 2d rev. and exp. ed. Frankfurt am Main: Vittorio Klostermann, 1994.

Hesse, Mary B. "Habermas' Consensus Theory of Truth." In *Revolutions and Reconstructions in the Philosophy of Science,* pp. 206–31. Bloomington: Indiana University Press, 1980.

Hofstadter, Albert. "On Artistic Knowledge: A Study in Hegel's Philosophy of Art." In *Beyond Epistemology: New Studies in the Philosophy of Hegel,* ed. Frederick Weiss, pp. 58–97. The Hague: Martinus Nijhoff, 1974.

——— *Truth and Art.* New York: Columbia University Press, 1965.

Honneth, Axel, and Hans Joas, eds. *Communicative Action: Essays on Jürgen Habermas's* The Theory of Communicative Action. Cambridge, Mass.: MIT Press, 1991.

Hook, Sidney, ed. *Art and Philosophy: A Symposium.* New York: New York University Press, 1966.

Horkheimer, Max. "On the Problem of Truth." In *The Essential Frankfurt School Reader,* ed. Andrew Arato and Eike Gebhardt, introd. Paul Piccone, pp. 407–43. New York: Urizen Books, 1978.

——— "Zum Problem der Wahrheit." *Zeitschrift für Sozialforschung* 4 (1935): 321–64.

Horkheimer, Max, and Theodor W. Adorno. *Dialectic of Enlightenment: Philosophical Fragments.* Ed. Gunzelin Schmid Noerr. Trans. Edmund Jephcott. Stanford, Calif.: Stanford University Press, 2002.

Hospers, John. *Meaning and Truth in the Arts.* Chapel Hill: University of North Carolina Press 1946. Reprint, Hamden, Conn.: Archon Books, 1964.

——— "Truth in the Arts." In *Understanding the Arts,* pp. 233–75. Englewood Cliffs, N.J.: Prentice-Hall, 1982.

Houlgate, Stephen. *Hegel, Nietzsche and the Criticism of Metaphysics.* Cambridge: Cambridge University Press, 1986.

Huhn, Tom. "The Movement of Mimesis: Heidegger's 'Origin of the Work of Art' in Relation to Adorno and Lyotard." *Philosophy & Social Criticism* 22, no. 4 (July 1996): 45–69.

Huhn, Tom, and Lambert Zuidervaart, eds. *The Semblance of Subjectivity: Essays in Adorno's Aesthetic Theory.* Cambridge, Mass.: MIT Press, 1997.

Huizinga, Johan. *Homo Ludens: A Study of the Play-Element in Culture.* Boston: Beacon Press, 1972.

Hungerland, Isabel. "Contextual Implication." *Inquiry* 4 (1960): 211–58.

Ingram, David. "Hermeneutics and Truth." In *Hermeneutics and Praxis,* ed. Robert Hollinger, pp. 32–53. Notre Dame: University of Notre Dame Press, 1985.

——— "Philosophy and the Aesthetic Mediation of Life: Weber and Habermas on the Paradox of Rationality." *Philosophical Forum* 18 (Summer 1987): 329–57.

Jaeger, Hans. "Heidegger and the Work of Art." In *Aesthetics Today,* ed. Morris Philipson, pp. 413–31. New York: New American Library, Meridian Books, 1961.

Jameson, Fredric. *Postmodernism, or, The Cultural Logic of Late Capitalism.* Durham, N.C.: Duke University Press, 1991.

Jauss, Hans Robert. *Aesthetic Experience and Literary Hermeneutics.* Trans. Michael Shaw. Introd. Wlad Godzich. Minneapolis: University of Minnesota Press, 1982.

——— *Toward an Aesthetics of Reception.* Trans. Timothy Bahti. Introd. Paul de Man. Minneapolis: University of Minnesota Press, 1982.

Jay, Martin. "Habermas and Modernism." In *Habermas and Modernity*, ed. Richard Bernstein, pp. 125–39. Cambridge, Mass.: MIT Press, 1985.

Kant, Immanuel. *Critique of Judgment*. Trans. J. H. Bernard. New York: Hafner, 1972.

Critique of Judgment, Including the First Introduction. Trans. Werner S. Pluhar. Introd. Werner S. Pluhar. Foreword by Mary J. Gregor. Indianapolis: Hackett, 1987.

Critique of Pure Reason. Trans. Norman Kemp Smith. Unabridged ed. New York: St. Martin's Press; Toronto: Macmillan, 1929.

Critique of the Power of Judgment. Ed. Paul Guyer. Trans. Paul Guyer and Eric Matthews. Cambridge: Cambridge University Press, 2000.

Kritik der Urteilskraft. Ed. Karl Vorländer. Hamburg: Felix Meiner, 1968.

Kearney, Richard. *Poetics of Imagining: Modern to Post-Modern*. 2d ed. New York: Fordham University Press, 1998.

The Wake of Imagination: Toward a Postmodern Culture. Minneapolis: University of Minnesota Press, 1989.

Kegley, Jacquelyn Ann. "Truth and Art: An Analysis of the Propositional and the Revelational Theories." *General Education Journal* 15 (1968–9): 56–102.

Keyes, C. D. "Truth as Art: An Interpretation of Heidegger's *Sein und Zeit* (sec. 44) and *Der Ursprung des Kunstwerkes*." In *Heidegger and the Path of Thinking*, ed. John Sallis, pp. 65–84. Pittsburgh: Duquesne University Press, 1970.

Kirkham, Richard L. *Theories of Truth: A Critical Introduction*. Cambridge, Mass.: MIT Press, 1992.

Kisiel, Theodore. *The Genesis of Heidegger's* Being and Time. Berkeley: University of California Press, 1993.

Kögler, Hans Herbert. *The Power of Dialogue: Critical Hermeneutics after Gadamer and Foucault*. Trans. Paul Hendrickson. Cambridge, Mass.: MIT Press, 1996.

Kompridis, Nikolas. "On World Disclosure: Heidegger, Habermas and Dewey." *Thesis Eleven*, no. 37 (1994): 29–45.

Korsmeyer, Carolyn. "The Eclipse of Truth in the Rise of Aesthetics." *British Journal of Aesthetics* 29 (1989): 293–302.

Kristeva, Julia. *Revolution in Poetic Language*. Trans. Margaret Waller. Introd. Leon S. Roudiez. New York: Columbia University Press, 1984.

Lacoue-Labarth, Philippe. *Heidegger, Art, and Politics: The Fiction of the Political*. Trans. Chris Turner. Oxford: Blackwell, 1990.

Lacy, Suzanne, ed. *Mapping the Terrain: New Genre Public Art*. Seattle: Bay Press, 1995.

Lafont, Cristina. *Heidegger, Language, and World-Disclosure*. Trans. Graham Harman. Cambridge: Cambridge University Press, 2000.

"World Disclosure and Reference." *Thesis Eleven*, no. 37 (1994): 46–63.

Lamarque, Peter, and Stein Haugom Olsen. "Truth." In *Encyclopedia of Aesthetics*, vol. 4, ed. Michael Kelly, pp. 406–15. New York: Oxford University Press, 1998.

Langer, Susanne K. *Feeling and Form: A Theory of Art Developed from "Philosophy in a New Key."* New York: Charles Scribner's Sons, 1953.

Philosophy in a New Key: A Study in the Symbolism of Reason, Rite, and Art (1942). Cambridge, Mass.: Harvard University Press, 1996.

Lawry, Edward G. "The Work-Being of the Work of Art in Heidegger." *Man and World* 11 (1978): 186–98.

Levinson, Jerrold. *Music, Art, and Metaphysics: Essays in Philosophical Aesthetics*. Ithaca: Cornell University Press, 1990.

MacIntyre, Alasdair. *After Virtue: A Study in Moral Theory.* 2d ed. Notre Dame, Ind.: University of Notre Dame Press, 1984.

Macomber, William Burns. *The Anatomy of Disillusion: Martin Heidegger's Notion of Truth.* Evanston, Ill.: Northwestern University Press, 1967.

Makkreel, Rudolf A. *Imagination and Interpretation in Kant: The Hermeneutical Import of the* Critique of Judgment. Chicago: University of Chicago Press, 1990.

Margolis, Joseph. "The Eclipse and Recovery of Analytic Aesthetics." In *Analytic Aesthetics,* ed. Richard Shusterman, pp. 161–89. Oxford: Basil Blackwell, 1989.

———. *What, after All, Is a Work of Art? Lectures in the Philosophy of Art.* University Park: Pennsylvania State University Press, 1999.

———. *Martin Heidegger: Innen- und Aussenansichten.* Ed. Forum für Philosophie, Bad Homburg. Frankfurt am Main: Suhrkamp, 1989.

Marx, Werner. *Heidegger and the Tradition.* Trans. Theodore Kisiel and Murray Greene. Evanston, Ill.: Northwestern University Press, 1971.

McCarthy, Thomas. *Ideals and Illusions: On Reconstruction and Deconstruction in Contemporary Critical Theory.* Cambridge, Mass.: MIT Press, 1991.

McCumber, John. *Poetic Interaction: Language, Freedom, Reason.* Chicago: University of Chicago Press, 1989.

Menke, Christoph. *Die Souveränität der Kunst: Ästhetische Erfahrung nach Adorno und Derrida.* Frankfurt am Main: Suhrkamp, 1991.

———. *The Sovereignty of Art: Aesthetic Negativity in Adorno and Derrida.* Trans. Neil Solomon. Cambridge, Mass.: MIT Press, 1998.

Mitscherling, Jeff. "The Aesthetic Experience and the 'Truth' of Art." *British Journal of Aesthetics* 28 (Winter 1988): 28–39.

Mörchen, Hermann. *Adorno und Heidegger: Untersuchung einer philosophischen Kommunikationsverweigerung.* Stuttgart: Klett-Cotta, 1981.

Morris, Martin. *Rethinking the Communicative Turn: Adorno, Habermas, and the Problem of Communicative Freedom.* Albany: State University of New York Press, 2001.

Munzel, G. Felicitas. *Kant's Conception of Moral Character: The "Critical" Link of Morality, Anthropology, and Reflective Judgment.* Chicago: University of Chicago Press, 1999.

Nietzsche, Friedrich. *The Birth of Tragedy* (1872) and *The Case of Wagner* (1888). Trans. Walter Kaufmann. New York: Vintage Books, 1967.

Nussbaum, Martha C. *Poetic Justice: The Literary Imagination and Public Life.* Boston: Beacon Press, 1995.

———. *Women and Human Development: The Capabilities Approach.* Cambridge: Cambridge University Press, 2000.

Ogden, C. K., and I. A. Richards. *The Meaning of Meaning: A Study of the Influence of Language upon Thought and of the Science of Symbolism* (1923). 8th ed. New York: Harcourt, Brace & World, Harvest Books, 1946.

Olthuis, James H., ed. *Knowing Other-wise: Philosophy at the Threshold of Spirituality.* New York: Fordham University Press, 1997.

Palmer, Richard E. *Hermeneutics: Interpretation Theory in Schleiermacher, Dilthey, Heidegger, and Gadamer.* Evanston, Ill.: Northwestern University Press, 1969.

Perpeet, Wilhelm. "Heideggers Kunstlehre." In *Heidegger: Perspektiven zur Deutung seines Werkes,* ed. Otto Pöggeler, pp. 217–41. Cologne and Berlin: Kiepenheuer & Witsch, 1970. Reprinted from *Jahrbuch für Ästhetik und Allgemeine Kunstwissenschaft* 8 (1963): 158–89.

Putnam, Hilary. *Reason, Truth and History.* Cambridge: Cambridge University Press, 1981.

Ramberg, Bjørn T. *Donald Davidson's Philosophy of Language: An Introduction.* Oxford: Basil Blackwell, 1989.

Rapaport, Herman. *Is There Truth in Art?* Ithaca: Cornell University Press, 1997.

Rehg, William. *Insight and Solidarity: A Study in the Discourse Ethics of Jürgen Habermas.* Berkeley: University of California Press, 1994.

Reid, Louis Arnaud. *Meaning in the Arts.* New York: Humanities Press, 1969.

Richards, Ivor A. *Principles of Literary Criticism.* 2d ed. New York: Harcourt Brace Jovanovich, 1926.

Science and Poetry (1926). 2d ed., rev. and enl. London: Kegan Paul, Trench, Trubner, 1935.

Ricoeur, Paul. *The Conflict of Interpretations: Essays in Hermeneutics.* Ed. Don Ihde. Evanston, Ill.: Northwestern University Press, 1974.

Hermeneutics and the Human Sciences: Essays on Language, Action and Interpretation. Ed. and trans. John B. Thompson. Cambridge: Cambridge University Press, 1981.

Roberts, Louise N. "Truth in Art." *Tulane Studies in Philosophy* 19 (1970): 79–87.

Rorty, Richard. *Essays on Heidegger and Others.* Philosophical Papers, vol. 2. Cambridge: Cambridge University Press, 1991.

"Is There a Problem about Fictional Discourse?" In *Consequences of Pragmatism (Essays: 1972–1980),* pp. 110–38. Minneapolis: University of Minnesota Press, 1982.

Objectivity, Relativism, and Truth. Philosophical Papers, vol. 1. Cambridge: Cambridge University Press, 1991.

Philosophy and the Mirror of Nature. Princeton: Princeton University Press, 1979.

Sallis, John, ed. *Reading Heidegger: Commemorations.* Bloomington: Indiana University Press, 1993.

Schönleben, Erich. *Wahrheit und Existenz: Zu Heideggers phänomenologischer Grundlegung des überlieferten Wahrheitsbegriffes als Übereinstimmung.* Würzburg: Königshausen & Neumann, 1987.

Schrag, Calvin O. "The Transvaluation of Aesthetics and the Work of Art." In *Thinking about Being: Aspects of Heidegger's Thought,* ed. Robert W. Shahan and J. N. Mohanty, pp. 109–24. Norman: University of Oklahoma Press, 1984.

Schufrieder, Gregory. "Art and the Problem of Truth." *Man and World* 13 (1980): 53–80.

Searle, John. *Speech Acts: An Essay in the Philosophy of Language.* Cambridge: Cambridge University Press, 1969.

Seel, Martin. *Die Kunst der Entzweiung: Zum Begriff der ästhetischen Rationalität.* Frankfurt am Main: Suhrkamp, 1985.

"Kunst, Wahrheit, Welterschliessung." In *Perspektiven der Kunstphilosophie: Texte und Diskussionen,* ed. Franz Koppe, pp. 36–80. Frankfurt am Main: Suhrkamp, 1991.

"On Rightness and Truth: Reflections on the Concept of World Disclosure." *Thesis Eleven,* no. 37 (1994): 64–81.

"The Two Meanings of 'Communicative' Rationality: Remarks on Habermas's Critique of a Plural Concept of Reason." In *Communicative Action: Essays on Jürgen*

Habermas's The Theory of Communicative Action, ed. Axel Honneth and Hans Joas, pp. 36–48. Cambridge, Mass.: MIT Press, 1991.

Seerveld, Calvin. "Imaginativity." *Faith and Philosophy* 4 (January 1987): 43–58.

Rainbows for the Fallen World: Aesthetic Life and Artistic Task. Toronto: Tuppence Press, 1980.

Sesonske, Alexander. "Truth in Art." *Journal of Philosophy* 53 (May 1956): 345–53.

Shusterman, Richard, ed. *Analytic Aesthetics.* Oxford: Basil Blackwell, 1989.

Pragmatic Aesthetics: Living Beauty, Rethinking Art. Oxford: Blackwell, 1992.

Silverman, Hugh J., and Don Ihde, eds. *Hermeneutics and Deconstruction.* Albany: State University of New York Press, 1985.

Smith, Barbara Herrnstein. *Contingencies of Value: Alternative Perspectives for Critical Theory.* Cambridge, Mass.: Harvard University Press, 1988.

Stevenson, Charles L. *Ethics and Language.* New Haven: Yale University Press, 1944.

Swindall, James. *Reflection Revisited: Jürgen Habermas's Discursive Theory of Truth.* New York: Fordham University Press, 1999.

Taminiaux, Jacques. *Heidegger and the Project of Fundamental Ontology.* Trans. and ed. Michael Gendre. Albany: State University of New York Press, 1991.

Taylor, Charles. *The Ethics of Authenticity.* Cambridge, Mass.: Harvard University Press, 1992.

Hegel and Modern Society. Cambridge: Cambridge University Press, 1979.

"Language and Society." In *Communicative Action: Essays on Jürgen Habermas's* The Theory of Communicative Action, ed. Axel Honneth and Hans Joas, pp. 23–35. Cambridge, Mass.: MIT Press, 1991.

Sources of the Self: The Making of the Modern Identity. Cambridge, Mass.: Harvard University Press, 1989.

Tugendhat, Ernst. "Heidegger's Idea of Truth." In *The Heidegger Controversy: A Critical Reader,* ed. Richard Wolin, pp. 245–63. New York: Columbia University Press, 1991.

"Heideggers Idee von Wahrheit." In *Heidegger: Perspektiven zur Deutung seines Werks,* ed. Otto Pöggeler, pp. 286–97. Cologne and Berlin: Kiepenheuer & Witsch, 1970.

Traditional and Analytical Philosophy: Lectures on the Philosophy of Language (1976). Trans. P. A. Gorner. Cambridge: Cambridge University Press, 1982.

Der Wahrheitsbegriff bei Husserl und Heidegger (1967). 2d ed. Berlin: Walter de Gruyter, 1970.

van der Hoeven, Johan. "Heidegger, Descartes, Luther. Wendingen in de vraag naar waarheid." In *Reflexies,* pp. 69–116. Amsterdam: Buijten & Schipperheijn, 1968.

"History and Truth in Nietzsche and Heidegger." In *Life Is Religion: Essays in Honor of H. Evan Runner,* ed. Henry Vander Goot, pp. 61–82. St. Catherines, Ont.: Paideia Press, 1981.

Verhaegh, Marcus. "The Truth of the Beautiful in the *Critique of Judgement.*" *British Journal of Aesthetics* 41 (October 2001): 371–94.

Walton, Kendall L. *Mimesis as Make-Believe: On the Foundations of the Representational Arts.* Cambridge, Mass.: Harvard University Press, 1990.

Weitz, Morris. "Art, Language and Truth." In *Philosophy of the Arts,* pp. 134–52. Cambridge, Mass.: Harvard University Press, 1950.

"Truth in Literature." *Revue Internationale de Philosophie* 9 (1955): 116–29.

Wellmer, Albrecht. *Endgames: The Irreconcilable Nature of Modernity; Essays and Lectures.* Trans. David Midgley. Cambridge, Mass.: MIT Press, 1998.

The Persistence of Modernity: Essays on Aesthetics, Ethics, and Postmodernism. Trans. David Midgley. Cambridge, Mass.: MIT Press, 1991.

Wolin, Richard, ed. *The Heidegger Controversy: A Critical Reader.* New York: Columbia University Press, 1991.

The Politics of Being: The Political Thought of Martin Heidegger. New York: Columbia University Press, 1990.

"Utopia, Mimesis, and Reconciliation: A Redemptive Critique of Adorno's *Aesthetic Theory.*" *Representations* 32 (Fall 1990): 33–49.

Wolterstorff, Nicholas. *Art in Action: Toward a Christian Aesthetic.* Grand Rapids, Mich.: Eerdmans, 1980.

"Philosophy of Art after Analysis and Romanticism." In *Analytic Aesthetics,* ed. Richard Shusterman, pp. 32–58. Oxford: Basil Blackwell, 1989.

On Universals: An Essay in Ontology. Chicago, University of Chicago Press, 1970.

Works and Worlds of Art. Oxford: Clarendon Press, 1980.

Young, James O. *Art and Knowledge.* London: Routledge, 2001.

Zemach, Eddy M. "Truth in Art." In *A Companion to Aesthetics,* ed. David Cooper, pp. 434–8. Oxford: Blackwell, 1992.

Zimmerman, Michael E. *Heidegger's Confrontation with Modernity: Technology, Politics, and Art.* Bloomington: Indiana University Press, 1990.

Zuidervaart, Lambert. *Adorno's Aesthetic Theory: The Redemption of Illusion.* Cambridge, Mass.: MIT Press, 1991.

"'Aesthetic Ideas' and the Role of Art in Kant's Ethical Hermeneutics." In *Opuscula Aesthetica Nostra,* ed. Cécile Cloutier and Calvin Seerveld, pp. 63–72. Edmonton: Academic Printing and Publishing, 1984. Reprinted in *Kant's* Critique of the Power of Judgment: Critical Essays, ed. Paul Guyer, pp. 199–208. Lanham, Md.: Rowman & Littlefield, 2003.

"Artistic Truth, Linguistically Turned: Variations on a Theme from Adorno, Habermas, and Hart." In *Philosophy as Responsibility: A Celebration of Hendrik Hart's Contribution to the Discipline,* ed. Ronald A. Kuipers and Janet Catherina Wesselius, pp. 129–49. Lanham, Md.: University Press of America, 2002.

"Art, Truth and Vocation: Validity and Disclosure in Heidegger's Anti-Aesthetics." *Philosophy & Social Criticism* 28 (2002): 153–72.

"Autonomy, Negativity, and Illusory Transgression: Menke's Deconstruction of Adorno's Aesthetics." *Philosophy Today,* SPEP Supplement 1999, pp. 154–68.

"Creative Border Crossing in New Public Culture." In *Literature and the Renewal of the Public Sphere,* ed. Susan VanZanten Gallagher and Mark D. Walhout, pp. 206–24. London: Macmillan Press; New York: St. Martin's Press, 2000.

"Cultural Paths and Aesthetic Signs: A Critical Hermeneutics of Aesthetic Validity." *Philosophy & Social Criticism* 29 (2003): 315–40.

"Fantastic Things: Critical Notes toward a Social Ontology of the Arts." *Philosophia Reformata* 60 (1995): 37–54.

"The Great Turning Point: Religion and Rationality in Dooyeweerd's Transcendental Critique." *Faith and Philosophy* (January 2004), in press.

"If I Had a Hammer: Truth in Heidegger's *Being and Time.*" In *A Hermeneutics of Charity: Interpretation, Selfhood, and Postmodern Faith,* ed. James K. A. Smith and Henry Venema. Grand Rapids, Mich.: Brazos Press, 2004.

"Metaphysics after Auschwitz: Suffering and Hope in Adorno's *Negative Dialectics.*" Unpublished manuscript.

"Postmodern Arts and the Birth of a Democratic Culture." In *The Arts, Community and Cultural Democracy,* ed. Lambert Zuidervaart and Henry Luttikhuizen, pp. 15–39. London: Macmillan Press; New York: St. Martin's Press, 2000.

"A Tradition Transfigured: Art and Culture in Reformational Aesthetics." *Faith and Philosophy,* in press.

"Transforming Aesthetics: Reflections on the Work of Calvin G. Seerveld." In *Pledges of Jubilee: Essays on the Arts and Culture, in Honor of Calvin G. Seerveld,* ed. Lambert Zuidervaart and Henry Luttikhuizen, pp. 1–22. Grand Rapids, Mich.: Eerdmans, 1995.

Index

aboutness, 89, 94, 160, 174, 175, 209, 210, 235
adequation, 37, 38
Adorno, Theodor W., 3, 5, 6, 8, 9–10, 11, 12, 13, 56, 57, 58, 60, 61, 65, 67, 78, 97, 101, 118–19, 121, 122, 125, 126, 127, 129, 133, 139, 177, 203, 207–8, 209, 213, 216, 229, 230, 234, 236
  Aesthetic Theory, 64
  on autonomy, 123, 124, 242
  on import (*Gehalt*), 123, 208
  on truth content (*Wahrheitsgehalt*), 8, 9, 119, 122–5, 208
aesthetic dimension, 11, 56–7, 58, 160, 177, 206, 214, 215
  experience, 39, 40–1, 58, 62, 63, 182, 215
  failure, 66
  merit, 65, 71
  practices, 58, 59, 60, 61
  presentation (*Darstellung*), 60, 229; *see also* presentation
  processes, 66–7, 160
  signs, 57–62, 129, 160, 210, 214, 218; *see also* purport of aesthetic signs
  validity, 9, 10, 39, 54, 56–65, 67, 71–2, 116–17, 120–2, 130–2, 206, 207; *see also* imaginative cogency
  worth of art, 213–18
aesthetics, 11
aletheia, 49, 50, 106
allusivity, 177
analytic aesthetics, 10, 13–14, 18, 143–4, 209, 212; *see also* philosophy, analytic
anti-aestheticism, 56, 213, 214, 217

Aristotle, 2, 6, 48, 107, 180, 191, 246
Armstrong, Isobel, 221
art, 7–8, 243
  acts, 158
  death of, 65; *see also* deaesthetization
  events, 7, 53, 128, 129, 131–2, 218
  as expert culture, 65, 101, 131
  hermeneutic character of, 6–7, 43, 54, 129, 133–4, 165, 200–2, 212, 214, 215
  and language, 2–3, 68
  making, 201–2, 212
  new genre public art, 218; *see also* art-in-public
  nominalist ontology of, 10, 180, 202, 210, 212
  phenomena, 7–8, 125, 127, 128, 175, 207, 208, 212
  postmodern arts, 1
  products, 7, 128, 129, 131–2, 139, 200, 201, 208, 212, 218
  realist ontology of, 10, 163, 180, 182, 196, 200, 202, 210, 211, 212, 256
  role of, 3, 121, 136, 176, 179, 198, 213, 256
  social ontology of, 54, 180, 213
  societal importance of, 213–18
art-in-public, 128, 243
art talk, 4, 9, 10, 43, 68–70, 73, 134–9, 156, 206, 231
  as conversation, 10, 68, 71, 134–5, 208
  and cultural orientation, 71, 257
  as discourse, 68, 72, 134, 135, 208
  examples, 70–1
  reflexivity, 72–3, 129

271

artistic import, 8, 127, 129–30, 133, 135, 157, 159–61, 174–5, 177, 179, 181, 191–6, 202, 208, 209–11, 212, 213, 249; *see also* import

artistic truth, 5, 11, 12, 28, 38–42, 45, 53–4, 77, 95, 96, 118–39, 143, 181, 200, 203–18

three-dimensional theory of, 127, 130–4, 136, 144, 208, 212
See also truth

artworks, 8, 45–6, 53, 131, 139, 160, 200, 201, 206, 212, 257

Atwood, Margaret, 217

Austin, J. L., 184, 225

authenticity, 10, 127, 128, 131, 133, 134, 157, 199–202, 208, 209, 212, 215, 218

autonomy, 9, 42, 45, 52–3, 112–13, 124, 127, 206

Beardsley, Monroe, 3, 6, 8–10, 14, 17–33, 51, 82, 87, 95, 97, 126, 137, 159, 162, 204, 205, 206, 210, 213, 215, 229, 244
on aesthetic experience, 18, 32
Aesthetics, 17–33, 144
on artistic truth, 18–19, 24–8, 29, 32–3, 42, 44, 49, 204–5, 215
on connotation, 19, 21, 22, 23, 33
on declarative sentences, 21
on designation, 21
on discourse, 20
and empiricism, 27, 28, 31, 32, 204–5
on fiction, 30, 226
and Hofstadter, 35–6, 38, 42–6, 205–6
on imperative sentences, 21
on import, 19, 20
on language, 19–20, 24, 42–3, 52
on literary predication, 29–33
on logic of explication, 22, 24, 223
on logical absurdity, 24
on meaning, 18, 19–20, 21, 22, 24, 33, 222
on metaphor, 22, 23, 24, 222
on purport, 19, 20
on reference, 20, 22, 24
on sentences, 20, 21, 22, 33
on societal importance of art, 213–15
on theory of literary work, 19, 21, 22–3
on truth-meaning distinction, 24–5
on universal-particular distinction, 26

Bennett, John G., 188

Bernstein, J. M., 116, 238, 240

Bohman, James, 6, 119–20

Brahms, Johannes, 13

Cage, John, 201

Cassirer, Ernst, 35, 176, 177

Collingwood, R. G., 14, 200

communicative action, 69, 70, 118, 124, 139, 231, 244

Cooke, Maeve, 242, 243

creative interpretation, 59, 61–2, 67, 68, 132, 206

critical dialogue, 12–14, 34–5, 203, 213

critical hermeneutics, 11–14, 35, 52, 54, 59, 123, 202, 203, 212, 213, 222

Critical Theory, 12, 118–19, 207–8, 240

Croce, Benedetto, 35

cultivation, 58–9, 65

cultural orientation, 9, 10, 65–8, 72, 132–4, 160, 206, 208, 210, 215, 218

culture, 66

Dahlstrom, Daniel, 232, 235, 236

Dallmayr, Fred, 238

Davidson, Donald, 248

deaesthetization, 65; *see also* art, death of

declarative statements, 33

Derrida, Jacques, 46, 47, 48, 51, 205, 227
Truth in Painting, 46

Dewey, John, 14, 97–8, 216, 244

Dickie, George, 248

disclosure, 47, 77, 101, 105, 108, 117, 120, 126, 133, 160, 199, 207, 209, 211, 238, 241; *see also* imaginative disclosure; truth

disclosure and validity, 102, 105, 107–17, 118, 119–22, 131

Dooyeweerd, Herman, 13, 235, 236

Duchamp, Marcel, 135–6, 137–8

dyadic links, 136–9

emotivism, 10, 139, 144, 151, 156, 158, 160, 204, 209, 210, 212

entertainment, 228

exploration, 57–8, 61–2, 68, 132, 206

expression, 2, 127, 220

Ferrara, Alessandro, 230

fidelity, 97, 98–9, 108, 125, 132, 207, 216, 218

formation, *see* cultivation

form-content dialectic, 103, 123, 127, 129

Frege, Gottlob, 152

Gadamer, Hans-Georg, 43, 56, 57, 58, 60, 61, 66, 101, 177, 229, 230
genius, 182
Goehr, Lydia, 221
Goldman, Alvin, *A Theory of Human Action*, 194
Goodman, Nelson, 6, 10, 13, 144, 162–81, 184, 202, 212, 215, 252
  on aesthetic cognition, 169–71, 176, 178
  on appropriateness, 165, 171, 174, 175–80, 210, 211
  on artistic truth, 162, 170–5, 210–11
  on cognitive purpose, 170–1
  on correspondence, 176, 177, 210
  on denotation, 164–6, 167, 172–4
  on exemplification, 166–9, 177
  on expression, 166–9, 172, 175, 210
  on inscription, 164
  on labels, 167, 168–9, 172, 173–4
  Languages of Art, 163, 174, 210
  on notational systems, 165–6, 250
  on propositions, 171–2, 210
  on reference, 164–6, 167, 172–4
  on representation, 164–6, 172, 175, 210, 251
  on symbols, 163–71, 172, 175, 176, 249
  on symptoms of the aesthetic, 169–70, 175, 176
  Ways of Worldmaking, 171, 252
  and Wolterstorff, 162–3, 187–9, 190–1, 196, 198–9, 210, 211, 249, 251, 252
Greene, Theodore Meyer, 6, 10, 14, 144, 147–51, 157–61, 162, 175, 177, 182, 209, 210, 246, 252
  on artistic content, 148
  on artistic perfection, 150
  on artistic truth, 149–51, 157–61, 209
  as Aristotelian, 147, 246
  The Arts and the Art of Criticism, 147
  on consistency, 149, 150, 246
  on correspondence, 149, 150
  on criteria of artistic value, 147
  on criteria for truth, 149–50
  on import, 159–60, 209
  on integrity, 150
  on propositions, 149–50, 157–9, 209, 246
  and Richards, 148, 151, 161
  on science and art, 148–9, 246
Grice, Paul, 243

Habermas, Jürgen, 7, 11, 65, 69–70, 72, 101–2, 118–19, 120, 124–5, 133, 134, 135, 139, 208, 209, 214, 221, 230
  on art, 101–2
  on propositional truth, 69
  on truth, 119, 231
  on validity claims, 69–70, 124–5, 137, 138
Hart, Hendrik, 235
Hegel, G. W. F., 2, 25, 38, 41, 56, 60, 61, 65, 97, 122, 177
  critique of Kant, 56, 206
Heidegger, Martin, 7, 9, 11, 12, 13, 36, 48–51, 77, 118, 121, 122, 131, 132, 177, 205, 209, 216, 220
  accused of subjectivism, 83–4
  on the aesthetic, 112
  on aesthetic validity, 112–13, 116–17
  on agreement (*Übereinstimmung*), 82, 83, 94–6, 99, 106
  and anti-aestheticism, 102, 117, 132
  on art as essential origin (*Ursprung*), 110
  on articulation (*Artikulation*), 81–2
  on artistic truth, 102, 105, 112
  on the asserted (*das Ausgesagte*), 88–90, 91
  on assertion (*Aussage*), 36, 81, 82, 83, 84–90, 91–6, 99, 100, 206, 233, 234
  on attunement (*Befindlichkeit*), 79, 113, 233
  on authenticity, 95, 233, 240
  on autonomy, 112–13
  on beginning (*Anfangen*), 110
  Being and Time, 9, 50, 78–100, 105, 106, 206, 207, 239, 240, 257
  Beiträge zur Philosophie, 50, 226
  on bestowing (*Schenken*), 109–10
  on care (*Sorge*), 80
  on clearing (*Lichtung*), 106, 107, 109, 114
  on communication (*Mitteilung*), 85
  on concealment (*Verbergung*), 106–7, 109, 111–12, 114–15, 126
  on configuration (*Gestalt*), 103–5, 130
  on correctness (*Richtigkeit*), 91–4, 100, 106, 108
  on correspondence theories of truth, 79, 80, 82, 83, 84–5, 95–6
  on creating (*Schaffen*), 103
  and Critical Theory, 101–2, 107–9
  on Dasein, 79–80, 82, 84, 87, 99, 106
  on disclosedness (*Erschlossenheit*), 7, 79–84, 90, 94–6, 97, 99, 206, 207, 238, 240

Heidegger, Martin (*cont.*)
  on discoveredness (*Entdeckheit*), 80, 82, 84,
    91, 92, 94–5, 96, 233, 238, 240
  on discovering (*Entdecken*), 91–4, 96
  on earth, 103–4
  on *Ereignis* (event), 53
  on fact (*Sache*), 106
  on forgetfulness of Being
    (*Seinsvergessenheit*), 49
  on freedom, 50
  on givenness, 91
  on grounding (*Gründen*), 110
  Holzwege, 227
  on human responsibility, 107, 114–15,
    207
  and hypermetaphysical tendency, 107, 239
  on idle talk (*Gerede*), 82, 233
  on intelligibility (*Verständlichkeit*), 233
  on interpretation (*Auslegung*), 80–1, 86, 87
  on meaning (*Sinn*), 81, 233
  on obstructing (*Verstellen*), 106–7
  "The Origin of the Work of Art," 9, 50,
    102–17, 126, 207, 257
  Parmenides, 49
  on poetry (*Dichtung*), 110
  on pointing out (*Aufzeigung*), 85, 86, 87
  and politics, 110, 227, 239, 240
  on predication (*Prädikation*), 85, 86, 87,
    89, 100
  on preserving (*Bewahren*), 103
  on proposition (*Satz*), 106
  on refusal (*Versagen*), 106–7
  on resoluteness (*Entschlossenheit*), 80
  on self-givenness, 92
  on significations (*Bedeutungen*), 233
  on strife, 103–5, 109, 239
  on talk (*Rede*), 79, 80, 81–2, 84, 94, 95,
    233, 235
  on *Temporalität*, 233
  on temporality (*Zeitlichkeit*), 79, 80,
    233
  on thrownness (*Geworfenheit*), 80
  on thrust (*Anstoss*), 103–5, 130
  on troth (*verwahren*), 99, 237; *see also*
    fidelity
  on truth, 49–51, 82–3, 99–100, 103–5, 107,
    109, 110, 206–7, 234, 239, 257
  on unconcealment (*Unverborgenheit*), 91,
    105–9, 111–12, 114, 177
  on understanding (*Verstehen*), 79, 80–1,
    82
  on untruth, 91

  on vocation of art, 109–13
  on world, 103–4
Hofstadter, Albert, 6, 8–9, 35, 49, 51, 82, 102,
    139, 205
  on aesthetic experience, 38, 39, 40–1
  on articulation, 36–7, 43
  on artistic creation, 40–1, 226
  on artistic import, 39, 40, 44–5
  on artistic truth, 35, 38–42, 49, 205
  on the artwork as aesthetic symbol, 39–40
  and Beardsley, 35–6, 38, 42–6
  on cogency, 38–9, 43, 226
  on correspondence theory, 35, 42, 43,
    44
  on imperatives, 37
  and internalism, 39–40
  on language, 35–8, 42–3, 52
  on love, 39, 41
  on natural beauty, 38, 41
  on performatives, 37
  on personhood, 38
  on practical truth, 35, 37
  on predication, 36
  on seizure, 38–9, 226
  on spiritual truth, 35, 37–8, 39, 41
  on statement, 36–7, 42
  on theoretical truth, 35, 37, 44
  Truth and Art, 35
  on truth of being, 38, 39–40
  on truth of recognition, 38
  on valuations, 37
horizon, 99, 108, 126, 131, 230
Hospers, John, 191, 223, 224
Huizinga, Johan, 228
Husserl, Edmund, 91, 92, 95

illocutionary acts, 21, 185, 194–5
illocutionary effect, 155, 209
imagination, 62, 98, 206, 218
imaginative cogency, 9, 10, 62–5, 108,
    116–17, 130–2, 160, 206, 207, 209, 215;
    see also aesthetic validity
imaginative disclosure, 9, 101–17, 125–7,
    134, 139, 144, 200, 201, 202, 207–9, 212,
    213, 215, 216; *see also* artistic truth;
    disclosure
imaginative insight, *see* imaginative
    disclosure
import, 127, 134, 208; *see also* artistic import
integrity, 10, 127, 129–30, 131, 134, 150, 157,
    159, 161, 174, 179, 208, 210, 211, 212,
    215, 218

Kant, Immanuel, 2, 5, 8, 9, 55–73, 107, 116,
119, 206, 246
on the aesthetic, 55, 58, 60–1, 68, 177, 178,
190, 229
on the antinomy of taste, 63, 64, 72
on beauty, 55
Critique of the Power of Judgment, 39, 57,
228
on fine art, 58
on genius, 59–60, 229
on imagination, 60, 61, 228
on nature-freedom dialectic, 57
on polarity of entertainment and
instruction, 58–9
on polarity of expression and
communication, 59–61
on polarity of play and work, 57–8
on rational ideas, 60, 61
on reflective judgment, 59, 60, 230
on schemata, 60
on *sensus communis*, 230
on taste, 59–60, 64, 229
Kirkham, Richard, 4–5, 225
Kisiel, Theodore, 237
knowledge, 3
knowledge by acquaintance, 26, 39,
224
knowledge by description, 26
Kögler, Hans Herbert, 222
Kollwitz, Käthe, 136, 137, 138–9
Kompridis, Nikolas, 120, 241
Kristeva, Julia, 155, 202, 257

Langer, Susanne K., 14, 176, 177, 184, 229,
244
Levinas, Emmanuel, 48, 51, 205, 227
linguistic turn, 2, 12, 219, 257
logical positivism, 10, 36, 122, 143–4, 176,
209

Mahler, Gustav, 3–4
Makkreel, Rudolf A., 60, 228, 230
Margolis, Joseph, 7, 18, 205, 221, 244
Maritain, Jacques, 35
Marx, Karl, 177
meaning, 120, 157–8, 209, 229, 234,
247
metaphysical objects, 225
mimesis, 190–1, 211, 220
Mörchen, Hermann, 238
Morris, Martin, 240
music, 3, 254

New Criticism, 18
Nietzsche, Friedrich, 48, 122, 205, 226
nominalism, 10, 144; *see also* art, nominalist
ontology of
Nussbaum, Martha, 237

Ogden, C. K., 145–7, 246; *see also*
Richards, I. A.
orientation, 3; *see also* cultural orientation

perlocutionary effect, 155, 209
philosophy, 13
analytic, 12, 13–14, 17, 36, 56, 176
of communication, 52; *see also* linguistic
turn
of consciousness, 52
continental, 12, 13, 17, 34, 46, 56
cross-disciplinary, 11–12, 203, 213, 216
postanalytic, 144
postmetaphysical, 52, 53, 206, 219, 257
reformational, 13
Plato, 2, 6, 180, 191, 192–202
play, 57, 229
Plotinus, 45, 48
pragmatics, 33
predication, 153–4, 246, 247
predicative availability, 89–90, 92, 100, 235
predicative self-disclosure, 92–4
presentation, 60–2, 127, 132, 160, 206,
229
propositional acts, 152–3, 160
propositional truth, 9, 120, 137, 207, 208;
see also theories of truth; truth
propositionism, 10, 144, 147, 151, 158, 160,
182, 209, 210, 212
propositions, 5, 25, 26, 28, 33, 120, 135, 146,
149–50, 152–3, 154–5, 157–9, 162,
171–2, 203, 205, 209, 210, 213, 220,
245, 247, 248
purport of aesthetic signs, 60, 61; *see also*
aesthetic signs

Rapaport, Herman, 8–9, 46–54, 102, 180,
205
on artistic truth, 46–7, 51, 53–4,
205–6
on artworks, 53–4
and Beardsley and Hofstadter, 51–3
on Derrida, 48, 51, 205, 226, 227
on Heidegger, 48–9, 50–1, 84, 205, 226,
227
Is There Truth in Art?, 46

Rapaport, Herman (*cont.*)
  on Levinas, 48, 205, 226, 227
  on Nietzsche, 48, 226
  on the existential difference, 47, 49–50, 52
  on the ontological difference, 47, 49, 52
realism, 10, 144; *see also* art, realist ontology of
Recker, Joyce, 217–18
reference, 152, 174, 234
Rembrandt, 188–9, 253
representation, 2, 55–73
Richards, I. A., 6, 10, 14, 139, 144, 145–7,
  151–7, 160, 162, 169, 202, 204, 209, 210,
  246, 252
  on artistic truth, 145, 146, 151–7, 209
  on contextual theory of interpretation,
    146
  on emotive use of language, 145, 156, 244
  and Greene, 148, 151, 161
  Principles of Literary Criticism, 244
  on propositions, 146, 154–5
  on reference, 145–6, 151–7, 209, 245, 252
  on referents, 145
  on symbolic use of language, 145, 244
  on symbols, 145, 146
Rockwell, Norman, 135, 137
Rorty, Richard, 144, 257
Russell, Bertrand, 26, 225

Schiller, Friedrich, 57
scientism, 34, 35, 225
Searle, John, 7, 11, 152–3, 154, 155, 157, 158,
  184, 185, 193, 194, 246, 247, 248
  Speech Acts, 194
Seel, Martin, 70, 72, 108, 119–22, 124, 125,
  130, 208, 241
Seerveld, Calvin, 177
Shusterman, Richard, 237
  Analytic Aesthetics, 144
significance, 10, 127, 128–9, 131, 134, 136,
  157, 175–81, 208, 209, 210, 211, 212,
  215, 218, 256
speech-act theory, 5, 7, 21, 152–3, 184, 193,
  194–5
speech acts, 24, 69, 136, 137, 139, 152, 153,
  155–6, 157, 158, 194–5, 231, 243, 246,
  248
  expressive, 137–8
  regulative, 138–9
Stevenson, Charles, 20–1, 22
  on descriptive meaning, 20, 21
  on emotive meaning, 20

Sydney, Sir Philip, 191
systatic availability, 92, 236

Taylor, Charles, 128, 242
theories of truth, 4–5, 6, 33, 53, 204, 209,
  213
  anticorrespondence, 203, 210, 213
  antipropositional, 5–6, 84, 203, 205, 207,
    213
  correspondence, 6–7, 42, 51, 85, 143, 144,
    162, 163, 171, 180, 182, 200, 203, 209,
    210
  deflationary, 5
  noncorrespondence, 144, 203, 206, 209,
    213
  nonpropositional, 5, 6, 84, 102–9, 120,
    123, 144, 203, 205, 206, 207, 208, 209,
    210, 212, 213, 238
  propositionally inflected, 5, 6–7, 14, 33,
    34, 40, 80, 83, 95, 126, 143, 144, 157,
    163, 182, 196, 203, 207–9, 210,
    212
  See also artistic truth; propositional truth;
    truth
truth, 12, 202, 204
  as life-giving disclosure, 9, 77, 78, 96–100,
    108, 125–6, 132, 180, 181, 207, 216,
    218
  criterion of, 6, 44–5, 47, 51–2, 143, 146,
    149–50, 203
  See also artistic truth; disclosure;
    propositional truth; theories of truth
truth-about, 25, 39, 182, 191–6, 202, 211, 213
truth potential, 124–5, 130, 134
truth-to, 10, 25, 39, 182, 191, 197–8, 202,
  211
truth-with-respect-to, 10, 127, 131, 208,
  212
Tugendhat, Ernst, 91–2, 93, 94, 96, 236

utopian impulse, 120, 121, 139

validity and disclosure, *see* disclosure and
  validity
validity claims, 7–8, 54, 65, 69, 120–1, 136,
  208, 231, 241, 243
Vollenhoven, D. H. Th., 13, 235

Walton, Kendall, 187
Wellmer, Albrecht, 124, 130, 134, 208,
  230
Wittgenstein, Ludwig, 5, 245

Wolterstorff, Nicholas, 6, 10, 13, 62–4, 133, 144, 182–202, 211–2, 216
  on action, 184–7, 193–4, 201, 211, 212
  Art in Action, 256
  on artist as agent, 184
  on artistic truth, 163, 182, 196, 198–200, 212, 256
  on count-generation, 184, 190, 194, 195, 253
  on events, 183–4
  on fictive and assertive projection, 185, 186–7, 191, 195, 197–8
  on fictive stance, 186–7
  and Goodman, 162–3, 187–9, 190–1, 196, 198–9, 210, 211, 249, 251, 252
  on illocutionary actions, 185, 186, 194–5, 254
  on import, 191–6, 211
  on intentionality, 193–6, 211
  on language actions, 185
  on mood actions, 186, 187, 191–6
  on nature of artworks, 184, 185, 254

  on norm kinds, 184, 196, 211
  on ontology of worlds, 183–4, 196–8
  on predication, 187
  on propositions, 191–6, 198, 211
  on representation, 187–9, 195–6, 255
  on self-expression, 199–200, 256
  on self-realization, 199–200, 256
  on statal actions, 185–6, 195
  on states of affairs, 183, 185, 192–3, 197, 198, 253
  on truth to actuality, 197–8
  Works and Worlds of Art, 182, 192, 211
  on world of the work, 185, 190, 211
  on world projection, 182, 183–91, 192, 195, 211
world
  personal, 133
  postsubjective, 133–4, 211
  social, 133, 211
world crossing, 179–81, 202, 211, 212
world relations, 10

Young, James, 219